Brougham

Crane-Neck Phaeton

Hansom Cab

Victoria

Private Omnibus

Concord Coach

Governess Cart

Landau

THE ENCYCLOPAEDIA OF
DRIVING

THE
ENCYCLOPAEDIA OF
DRIVING

SALLIE WALROND

COUNTRY LIFE BOOKS

Published by Country Life Books
an imprint of Newnes Books
84–88, The Centre, Feltham, Middlesex, England
and distributed for them by
The Hamlyn Publishing Group Limited
Rushden, Northants, England

The first edition of this *Encyclopaedia*, published
in 1974 by Horse Drawn Carriages Limited, was made
possible by the generosity of the Worshipful Company
of Saddlers.
This revised edition first published in 1979
Second impression 1984

ISBN 0 600 33182 2

Printed in England by
Hazell Watson & Viney Limited,
Member of the BPCC Group,
Aylesbury, Bucks

FOREWORD

The 19th century was undoubtedly the heyday of the driving horse, and although the coming of the railways in the middle of the century put paid to long-distance travel by coach or post-chaise, the increase in private and commercial vehicles in the second half of the century, kept driving very much alive until the advent of the motor-car in the early 1900s. Driving therefore, was so much a part of everyday life, and the terms applied to vehicles, harness, and horses, were so commonplace, that knowledge of the subject was taken for granted, and very little was recorded.

Consequently, when a revival in driving took place some fifty years later, and people became interested in the technique and history, there was a grave danger that much of the expertise – so widely known in the last century – had been forgotten, and with the passing of the years, would be lost to posterity.

In producing an *Encyclopaedia of Driving*, Sallie Walrond has filled a gap by providing us with a guide to driving in all its aspects – covering a very wide field, from the technicality of the art of driving; details of vehicles and harness; to the history of the subject.

How many of us would have known that the old coachman's phrase: 'Gentlemen, I leave you here', was in fact a reminder for a tip. Or, that a 'whirlicote' was a horse-drawn conveyance used by the nobility. *The Encyclopaedia of Driving* is much more than a glossary – containing as it does not only a wealth of technical information, but also a nostalgic glimpse into the past.

Mrs Walrond, besides being an indefatigable researcher, is a very experienced and accomplished whip, and it is this fact which makes the book so informative and readable. I am sure that it will appeal to anyone interested in history and research, as well as to the many people actively interested in the art of driving horses or ponies.

SANDERS WATNEY

LIST OF LINE DRAWINGS

ACKNOWLEDGEMENTS

The author would like to thank Mr and Mrs Sanders Watney for their invaluable suggestions and additions for both the first edition and this revised edition. She also thanks Major Tom Coombs for his help and advice, Janet Johnstone for her line drawings and Anne Grahame Johnstone for her lettering on the drawings and for completing the carriage illustrations on the endpapers.

Thanks are due to Mr John Richards and Mr Jack Watmough of *Heavy Horse and Driving* for permission to use pieces which the author had originally written for that magazine and to Mr A. Wyndham Brown, Mr Barry Dickinson, Mr David Dickson, Mr Bill Domoe, Miss Ann Fowler, Miss Frances Lee-Norman, Mr Tom Ryder, Mr Stan Ward, and many others who have helped to provide the author with additional text.

She also thanks Miss Cordelia Hislop, Mrs John Rigby and Mrs Derek Hatley for typing and correcting the manuscript, and Mrs Pam Greene who originally suggested that the book should be written and then helped with assembling additional material for this new and revised edition.

THE ENCYCLOPAEDIA OF
DRIVING

Abbot-Downing Company
A coachbuilding firm of Concord, New Hampshire, U.S.A., which was formed in the early 1800s. They built many different types of vehicles ranging from Stage Coaches to Mountain Wagons.

Accommodation
Also known as a two wheeled Pot Cart.

Accommodation
The first coach to be specially built in America for public service.

Adams & Hooper
A famous firm of coachbuilders who executed work for numerous noteworthy people.

Adam, William Bridges (1799–1872)
A London coachbuilder of great esteem who started as a partner in his father's business. He was also an engineer, inventor and the designer of Equi-rotal Carriages.

He was the author of *English Pleasure Carriages*, a manual on horse-drawn carriages, their design and building, their defects and improvements. This book was reprinted in 1971.

Advanced Dressage Test 1975 (F.E.I.)

		MOVEMENT	TO BE JUDGED
1.	A	Enter at collected trot	Driving in on straight line
	X	Halt, salute	Standing on the bit
2.	XCMBFAK	Collected trot	Impulsion, regularity
			Collection
3.	KXM	Extended trot	
	MCH	Collected trot	Extension, regularity
	HXF	Extended trot	transitions
	FAX	Collected trot	

		MOVEMENT	TO BE JUDGED
4.	XG G	Walk on the bit Halt, immobility 10 secs., Rein back 3 metres	Regularity Immobility, transitions straightness
5.	GCHXF	Walk on the bit	Regularity, impulsion
6.	FAKEHC C	Collected trot Circle 20 metres diameter	Position, accuracy of figure
7.	CM MF FAD	Collected trot 10 m deviation from side with reins in one hand Working trot, reins at discretion	Position, accuracy of figure
8.	D	Circle right, 20 m. diameter, followed by circle left, 20 m. diameter	Regularity, position, accuracy of figure
9.	DXG G	Extended trot Collected trot	Extension, regularity transitions
10.	C–A	Serpentine of five loops, commencing on the left rein	Position, accuracy of figure
11.	DXG G	Extended trot Halt, salute, leave arena at working trot	Extension, regularity transitions, immobility straightness
12.		Paces	Regularity and freedom (if team, maintenance of pace by all horses)
13.		Impulsion	Moving forward (if team all horses working)
14.		Obedience, lightness	Response to aids, willing and without resistance
15.		Driver	Use of aids, handling of reins and whip. Position on box. Accuracy of figures

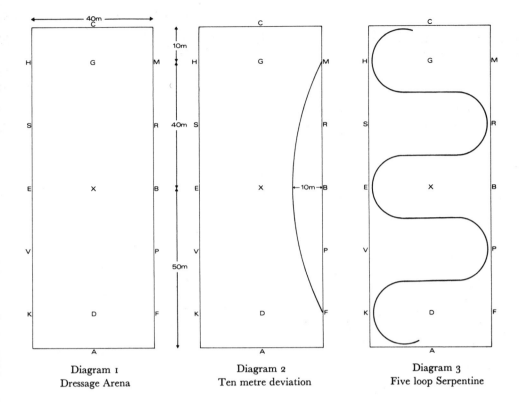

Diagram 1
Dressage Arena

Diagram 2
Ten metre deviation

Diagram 3
Five loop Serpentine

After-wale
That part of a collar which is behind the hames. *See* Collar.

'Age', The
A coach running between London and Brighton, put on the road in 1828 by Henry Stevenson, who was partnered by Sackville Gwynne in the venture. These two men were both of good families and they set a high standard of efficiency in the running of the 'Age'. It became recognized as the neatest public turnout seen at that time on the Brighton road. With this reputation, the coach flourished and its refinement was copied by other coach proprietors on the same road. After Stevenson's death in 1830, the 'Age' was driven by another gentleman professional, a Cambridge baronet, Sir St. Vincent Cotton, whose expertise in the art of driving was well known.

Ah
A heavy horse, working in plough gears, is frequently guided by word of mouth. In some parts of the country a turn to the left is commanded by saying 'Ah' or 'Ahve'.
   The words which are used vary considerably from one county to another.

Ahve. *See* Ah.

Albata
A name given to white brass. Used in the 1800s for ornamental work on carriages. *See* Brass.

3

Albert Cab
A type of hooded gig, of about 1860, with a cane body hung on side springs. It had a small platform at the back, reached by a rear step, to accommodate the tiger.

Albert Phaeton
An elegant hooded phaeton with a groom's seat at the rear. It was hung on four elliptic springs and had a full lock.

Aldin, Cecil (1870–1935)
An artist who specialized in sporting subjects, driving and hunting in particular. His driving pictures have a realistic vein and often show a great sense of humour. Also the author of *The Romance of the Road, Ratcatcher to Scarlet* and *Time I was Dead.*

Aldridges
A horse repository in St. Martin's Lane, London, where sales were mainly confined to carriage horses. Aldridges was closed in the 1920s.

Alexandra Dog Cart
A type of two-wheeled dog cart with an unusual curving profile which made it suitable for a lady Whip as the elegant lines showed off her dress to advantage and the sloping splashboards protected her clothes from dirt off the roads.

Alexandra Palace
For five years, from 1875 to 1879, some meets of the Coaching Club, which started at Hyde Park, terminated at Alexandra Palace.

Alken, Henry (1784–1851)
A famous and prolific artist, specializing in sporting events, driving, racing and hunting in particular. He illustrated books for such authors as Nimrod (C. J. Apperley), Surtees (creator of Jorrocks) and Pierce Egan. The Road was considered to be one of his best subjects. The accurate details depicted in his driving pictures, whether they be of single, tandem or team, prove that he had driven to some great extent. His pictures preserve for a future generation the atmosphere of the coaching era.

Alken, Henry Junior (1810–92)
Also an artist but one who never achieved such high regard as his father. He illustrated sporting events and had a leaning towards driving subjects. By signing his pictures with a similar signature to that of his father (H. Alken or H.A.), he caused a certain amount of confusion for posterity.

All Gears
A farm horse is known to work in all gears when he will go between shafts in a cart, in chain or sling gears in the lead of tandem to a cart, or plough gears for ploughing, cultivating or harrowing.

'All Ready, Outside and In'
The indication to passengers that their coach was soon to move off was this shout from the guard. This would be followed by a command from the driver to the ostlers and stable boys to 'let 'em go, then'.

'All Right Behind'
Before moving off, when driving a vehicle containing passengers, the warning should be given so that people are not caught unawares. A sudden jolt might otherwise result in them being thrown off the coach.

Alpha Air Collar
A type of pneumatic collar used at the turn of the century. *See* Collars.

Aluminium Bronze
In 1900 a strong yellow metal was made from the weight proportions of nine parts copper and one part aluminium. It was suitable for harness mountings as it did not tarnish quickly. Other aluminium bronzes are made at the present time but are not referred to in this entry as they have more importance in engineering than in driving.

Amble
A type of pace in which the legs are put down in lateral two-time. The near fore and near hind touch the ground together, making one beat, and the off fore and off hind go together making the second beat. From ambling is developed pacing which is used as an alternative pace to trotting for track racing in sulkies. A horse moving in this way is called an ambler in slow paces and a pacer at faster speeds.

Amempton
A small edition of the Dioropha, invented in the last half of the 19th century by Mr Kesterton.

American Birch
A wood which was claimed to be of great value for carriage building, as it could be procured in widths of up to 3 feet. It was pleasurable to plane and produced a satisfying surface, free from blemishes. Even the thinnest paint finish showed no grain marks. The end product was said to have the evenness of stretched canvas.

American Buggy
There are many varieties but basically it is a light four-wheeled vehicle hung on two elliptic, or semi-elliptic springs and a perch.

American Stage Driving
The four reins for a team of four horses, driven by an American Stage Driver, are held in two hands. The nearside reins lie in the left hand and the offside reins in the right hand. The near lead rein lies on top of the little finger and the near wheel rein below the same finger. The ends of both reins go upwards over the palm and out backwards over the top of the thumb. The offside lead rein lies on top of the middle finger and the offside wheel rein goes below the same finger. Both reins pass through the hand and fall down over the little finger. The whip is held in the right hand at the butt, with the stick resting against the left-hand reins. When all four reins are to be held in the left hand, which is known as to 'club' the reins, the offside reins are passed across so that the lead rein lies on top of the index finger of the left hand and the wheel rein below the index finger. The reins lie across the palm hanging downwards so that they cross the nearside reins, the ends of which are pointing upwards. This method enables the reins to be held securely and the crossing deters them from slipping. As stage drivers

frequently had to endure cold weather fur gloves were often worn and so a method with which reins could be held easily under difficult conditions was essential.

With a team of six horses, there are six reins. All of the nearside reins are held in the left hand and the offside reins in the right hand. The near lead rein lies under the middle finger, the near swing rein under the third finger and the near wheel rein under the little finger. The reins pass upwards and hang over the thumb. The off lead rein lies on top of the index finger, the off swing rein over the middle finger and the off wheel rein over the third finger.

Amish Buggy
An American buggy used by the people of the Amish order of Indiana, Ohio and Pennsylvania, whose creed does not permit them to employ motorized transport. It is of the conventional buggy design with a rectangular buck, resembling a shallow box, hung on two elliptic springs and a perch. The front wheels, which are slightly smaller than the rear wheels, can only achieve a quarter-lock before they touch the buck. The seat is set in the middle of the buck, leaving room for luggage behind. A rein rail surmounts the dash.

Anchor Pull
The single metal protrusion on the lower half of the hames with an eye through which the hame clip or hame tug ring passes, depending on the type of harness. For trade turnouts, ring draught is used. For modern private driving turnouts, an anchor pull and riveted hame clip is the most usual combination for securing the traces, shoulder-pieces or hame tugs.

Angle of Lock
This depends largely on the relationship between the front wheels and the body of the vehicle. If the body is low, the front wheels will contact the sides with a small angle of turn. If the body is cut under, but has a perch, the wheels will go under the body and a larger angle of turn can be made before the wheels touch the perch. A crane-neck perch is shaped so as to allow the wheels to turn underneath and therefore does not limit the lock. A large angle of lock can be achieved when there is no perch and the body is so designed to permit the wheels to turn under it.

Anglesey, Marquis of
Known for his well-appointed curricle which he drove up to the time of his death in 1854. This classic equipage was one of the few of its type to be artistically recorded and was done so by an amateur, The Hon. Henry Grave, who produced what is probably the finest illustration of a curricle of that period.

Appleby Fair
Held in June, for about seven hundred years, in the village of Appleby, North Westmorland. Gipsies from various parts of the country arrive to park their colourful wagons and picket their horses at Gallows Hill. Coloured and spotted horses dominate the scene. They are shown by being driven up and down the road, at a wild trot, between crowds of possible purchasers. There is no auctioneer and the price to be paid is agreed between buyer and seller. Some horses are

just tethered and a purchaser has to find the owner if he is interested. The animal will then be ridden or driven as required.

Appointments

A well-appointed turnout is one that creates a vision of overall harmony. Any display of gaudiness immediately detracts from what otherwise might have been a pleasing sight. That which is considered to be good form for one equipage may be totally inappropriate for another. Vehicles for country and sporting purposes are appointed very differently from those for State or town occasions. The harness must be suitable for the vehicle, and the horse for both. Apart from a general picture, appointments refer to such items as aprons, lamps, liveries, horn case, umbrella, whip, tool kit and watch, to name but a few. Details of appointments, deemed to be correct for various vehicles, are given as appropriate throughout this volume.

Apprentice

Various whips were used to get more work from coach horses. One resembling a cat o' nine tails was known as the apprentice.

Apron

The main purpose of an apron is to keep the wearer clean, dry and warm when sitting on a vehicle. Driving conditions vary and so, therefore, do the materials from which aprons are made. In warm weather, when the reasons for wearing an apron are purely to keep the grease from the reins and the dust from the road off the clothes, then a light apron of linen, such as the material used in summer sheets for horses, is adequate. A slightly heavier cloth, such as Bedford cord, may be favoured and this should be bound with a similar coloured material or hemmed. For use in cold weather, a heavy drab waterproofed cloth lined with a check material is best. This is sewn along the edge with three or four rows of stitching. In wet weather, an apron with a rubberized outside and woollen inside is the only real answer. In the early 1900s, an india rubber cloth was available. It could be purchased by the yard in either black or white, cut to the required size and used without binding. White was more fashionable than black but tended to leave a disagreeable light powder which showed up on dark cloths. An apron used on the box to protect both the Whip and passenger is preferable if it is made with a central gusset going between the two people. It is more effective and has a neater appearance. There should be a strap attached to the centre of the apron about 7 inches from the top edge which is then fastened to the rail behind the seat. This prevents the apron from sliding downwards. Some coaching aprons have a pigskin strip, of about 8 inches, lining the bottom edge along the width of the footboard to protect the apron from damage caused by the Whip's or passenger's feet. The ends are not bound with pigskin as this would make them too stiff to be tucked in. It is essential that aprons should be made large enough to allow for a generous tuck in to prevent them from continually slipping. A box apron for a Drag needs to be 6 feet 6 inches long and 4 feet 6 inches wide. One for the roof seat, 9 feet long and 4 feet wide, and that for the rumble seat 6 feet long and 4 feet wide.

The rumble seat apron should be made of cloth to match the liveries. It is frequent for aprons to have a monogram or crest embroidered on a bottom corner. For private driving an individual apron is usually worn. It is best made of a fawn-coloured cloth, bound discreetly or edged with rows of stitching. For summer weather a linen check bound with a matching braid is suitable. It is usually made to buckle round the waist and resembles a long skirt when the Whip is standing. It should be made wide enough to allow a good tuck in, in order to anchor it securely round the legs when driving.

Arcera
According to Beckman (*History of Inventors*), this was a covered carriage for use by the sick or infirm. Alleged to be the earliest Roman vehicle on record. It was superseded by the litter.

Arena
The size of the arena for a driven dressage test to be held under Federation Equestre Internationale rules must be 100 metres long by 40 metres wide and marked with the usual dressage letters.

Argand Lamp
A type of lamp used in the 1800s. The light was said to be far superior to that of candles and was produced by the combination of an oil-fed wick and a flow of air up a central tube through the wick. Difficulties were experienced in getting stable staff to acquire the skill required to trim this lamp. Further problems arose in that any violent movement executed by the carriage tended to cause a sudden rush of air or a flow of oil, either of which extinguished the flame.

Arlington Cab
A type of Hansom Cab invented by Mr Knight of Dorchester, in which the usual apron or half-door was replaced by tall curving doors with sliding glasses. These doors extended from the footboard to the roof, forming a half-circle. Curving grooves enabled the doors to slide round on each side of the body of the vehicle when they were opened and could be operated by either the passengers or the driver.

Arlington Club
The venue of a meeting which was held in 1870 or 1871 which resulted in the formation of the still-flourishing Coaching Club. It was decided that the entry fee to become a member should be £5, annual subscription £2, and that membership at that time should consist of 50 gentlemen. The Club was formed officially in 1871.

Army Harness
In 1911 service harness was introduced, reducing the number of parts to a minimum. There were no pads or cruppers. Saddles were worn by nearside horses when a pair or team were ridden postillion. The offside horses wore the same harness whether they were controlled by a postillion or driven from the box. Common to the double sets, whether lead, centre or wheel, were the bridles and breast collars. Wheel sets had breeching, double-hip straps, pole bar neck-pieces and adjustable wire traces. Lead and centre sets had long wire traces and loin straps.

The bridle was made up from a combination of a head collar and a strap called a bridle head which passed over the crown loop and cheek-pieces and buckled at each side to the bit. A head rope was attached to the bottom ring of the jowl-piece and then passed over the neck from the near side. It was made secure by the end being wound round the main rope in four complete coils and two half coils. The end of the coiling was about 4 inches from the jowl-piece ring.

The bit was a curb with elbow-shaped branches. The mouthpiece was either straight or with a low port and some were reversible, being rough on one side and smooth on the other. There were three positions for the buckling of the reins. The top ring, which was known as upper bar, the middle slot on the cheek, called centre bar, or the bottom slot, referred to as lower bar. The curb chain, made from nineteen links, was fixed to the eye of the bit on one side and hooked to the curb chain hook on the other side.

The collar used was sometimes a full one but frequently a breast collar. The latter differed from the usual breast collar in that there was a draught tug on each side to which the short wire traces of the lead or centre horses were fixed when a team was driven. This enabled both the central and lead horses to get a direct pull to the swingle tree. Wheel horses had an additional neck-piece in front of the usual neck-piece. A short chain running through the backing ring was then fastened with a link and strap to the pole bar or tug neck-piece. The latter was used with four-wheeled vehicles. The pole chains or straps were fastened through a ring on a sliding link on the neck-piece.

Traces were made from leather-covered galvanized steel wire rope and were attached by means of links, shackles and straps for quick release. Leaders had long traces which were held in position by a loin strap. A short wire trace went between the leaders' long wire traces and the wheelers' draught tug and, similarly, to the central horses' draught tugs if six horses were put to. Wheelers had a double hip-strap. One end supported the traces and the other kept the breeching in place.

Armytage, Lt Col Henry
He was the founder of the Coaching Club in 1871. An enthusiastic Whip who drove on a number of the southern 'Roads'. He was on the box seat at Coaching Club meets until 1878.

Arterxerxes
A fictional equine character featured in *Handley Cross*, by Surtees, as the second horse of John Jorrocks, m.f.h. A bay with white socks and so named because he was also the shaft horse in tandem behind 'Xerxes' and therefore came 'Arter' Xerxes.

Arter Xerxes
A horse owned by Mr Charles Enderby who, for two years, was driven by his owner without a collar, traces, bridle, crupper or breeching. The famous painting, by F. C. Turner, shows him to a Tilbury Gig, wearing only a pad and tugs to which the shafts are attached and by which the vehicle is drawn. The reins run through the pad terrets to his mouth, but there is no visible means of support to prevent the bit from dropping out of his mouth. He came to an untimely end in 1837 when he was bitten by a mad dog and had to be destroyed.

Artist
A coachman, deft in his handling of whip and reins, is known as an 'artist'.

Artist
He was employed by a coachbuilder for the production of carriage designs. Another job for an artist was that of painting heraldic bearings on the panels of carriages.

Ash
The chief timber used for framing, in carriage construction, owing to its favourable qualities of neither warping nor twisting. It can be shaped by a steaming process and is frequently used for making shafts.

Austrian Method of Driving
This is similar to the American method in that with a team the nearside horses' reins are held in the left hand and the offside reins in the right hand. The main difference is that the lead and wheel reins are buckled together. The leaders' reins are coupled in the usual way ending in one rein at the hand. The wheelers' reins are also coupled in the authentic way and the single rein passes through the hand. After these single reins have gone through the fingers the two reins are coupled together, at a point of about 10 inches beyond the wheelers' coupling buckle, with as much precision as is paid to the joining of draught and coupling reins. Therefore, the wheel rein ends in a buckle and the end of the lead rein drops down from the hand towards the footboard. The length of the team does not vary with this method of buckling. Once the reins are coupled to the desired length they are not moved. Traces are kept tight at all times, even going up or down hills and round corners. The wheelers are poled up more tightly than with the English or American methods. Gradual turns are made by chopping. For sharper turns a point is taken in the lead rein behind the fingers. The buckle causes a loop to be formed which is easily released when the turn is completed. A similar point is made to oppose the outside wheelers in a very sharp turn to prevent the corners from being cut.

Auto Seat Top Buggy
This is so named because the seat resembles that of an early motor car. The hood over the seat is collapsible but looks solid and has a small window at the back for rear observation. The rectangular box-shaped body is hung on two elliptic springs and a perch. The rear wheels are slightly larger than the front which only have a quarter-lock in turning before they touch the body of the vehicle.

Avondale
More commonly known as a Governess Cart.

Awning
A portable canopy, consisting of metal standards which were jointed for convenient storage, and a material awning, was sometimes carried in a Drag or similar vehicle which was to be used as a grandstand at a race meeting, cricket match and other sporting occasions. This awning gave protection from the sun to the spectators who would be sitting on the coach for some considerable time. The framework of wood and iron fitted into slots under the seats and the valance-edged awning, which was frequently made of a medium-weight striped material, was laid over the frame. The valance was so designed that it could be strung up out of the way with ribbons and braid if desired.

Axle

The axle is the metal axis on which the wheels of the vehicle turn. It consists of two axle arms and the strip of metal connecting the arms, known as the axle bed. The coachbuilder, William Bridges Adams, stated (in 1837) that to ensure that the axle would be strong enough (to withstand hard wear inflicted by unmade roads) a process known as faggoting was employed. Flat bars of metal were laid together and welded to form a solid strip. It appears that axle breakages were a fairly common occurrence during the 19th century. Early axles were made of wood. The axle arms were rounded, tapered and covered with a skein which was a conical tube made of thin iron. The wheel had a metal lining which ran against the skein. The tapered ends of the axle arms projected beyond the wheel hubs and the wheels were kept on by lynch pins. These were either made from hard wood or metal and driven through a hole in the end of the arm. This method of securing a wheel was used on some vehicles up to about 1840.

The simplest axle arm consists of that which has a shoulder between it and the axle bed, and has a threaded end for the wheel nut. The wheel is placed on to the arm and the nut holds the wheel in place. The nut screws against a shoulder to prevent it from being put on too tightly. The offside nut screws up in a clockwise manner, that is so that it tends to tighten as the wheel goes forward. The nearside nut screws up in an anti-clockwise direction for the same reason.

The most common type of axle to be found on existing vehicles is the Collinge's axle, first introduced in 1792 and named after its inventor. The axle arm is cylindrical with an oil groove running longitudinally. There is an enlargement at the bed end against which lies a leather washer, the purpose of which is to take up any inward play from the wheel and act as an oil seal. The axle box of the wheel fits accurately on to the arm and lies against the leather washer. The wheel is held in position by a collet, two nuts and a split pin. In assembling a wheel on to a Collinge's axle, firstly the leather washer is put on. Then the wheel is slid on to the oiled axle. Next the collet goes into place. This is a metal collar with a flat on one side to coincide with a corresponding flat on this part of the axle. The purpose of the collet is to prevent the nuts, which go on next, from being loosened by vibration and to take up any outward pressure which might otherwise be taken by a nut. The nuts go on next. One tightens with a left-handed thread and the other with a right-handed thread. This is to ensure that if one nut should loosen the other will tighten. Beyond the second nut, which is the smaller of the two, there is a small hole, going right through the axle, to accommodate a split pin. Should the nuts loosen, they are still held on the arm. Finally, the hub cap, into which some thick oil should be stored for lubrication, is put on. This screws into a threaded part of the axle box and turns with the wheel. The maker of the carriage frequently has his name written on the hub cap. Unfortunately, hub caps tend to get changed from one vehicle to another so this cannot be taken as being completely authentic.

The mail axle is so named because originally it was used on Mail Coaches. It consists of a cylindrical axle arm, to which a collar is welded. Beyond this, on the axle bed side, but still on the axle arm, is a moon plate (a mobile circular plate) into which three holes are drilled. The nave of the wheel has three corresponding holes drilled right through, from front to back. Bolts are driven through

11

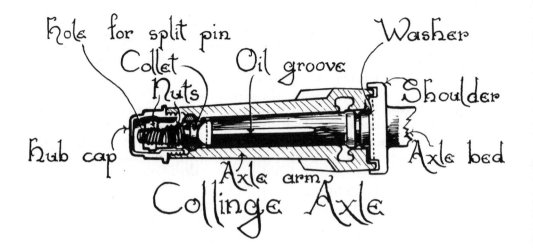

Hole for split pin

Collet

Nuts

Oil groove

Washer

Shoulder

Hub cap

Axle bed

Axle arm

Collinge Axle

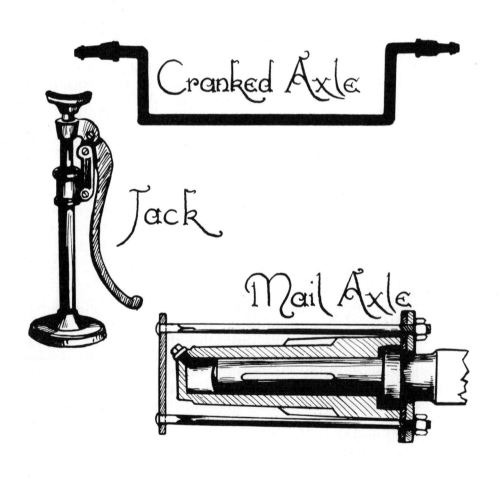

Cranked Axle

Jack

Mail Axle

these holes and those on the moon plate and three nuts are tightened sufficiently to hold the wheel on and to facilitate smooth running. The nave is completely covered at the front by a metal disc, with the three bolt heads visible. The disadvantage with a mail axle is that oiling cannot be done as easily as with a Collinge's axle. All three nuts have to be undone, causing threads to become worn and damaged. The amount of oil which can be placed along the axle soon becomes used, so lubricating has to be executed frequently. Some mail axles have a gap of about 1 inch between the end of the axle arm and the axle box, which acts as a container tank for the lubricant. The oil is put in through a small tube which goes through the nave. The hole is shut by a screw-type pin. The oil can circulate along the axle to another reservoir at the axle bed end. Two thick leather washers, one between the axle arm collar and the axle box, and a second between the axle arm collar and the moon plate, prevent the oil from escaping.

Axle Arm
That part of the axle on which the wheel of the vehicle rotates. *See* Axle.

Axle Bed
The centre transverse member of the bottom carriage of a four-wheeled vehicle. It is the counter part of the transom or top bed of the top carriage. It takes the perch bolt at its centre and will be bolted to the futchells and wheel iron stays if any.

Axle Bed
The centre part of the axle to which the axle arms are joined at either end. *See* Axle.

Axle Box
The centre of the hub of the wheel. *See* Axle.

Axle Oil
In the 1800s this commodity was available for purchase at inns by travellers to enable axles to be greased en route. *See* Axle.

Axle Plate
An iron strengthener for the axle or bottom bed.

Axle Tree
The original name for an axle because the early ones were made from hard timber with the ends shaped to a conical form to accommodate the wheels. Later, these wooden ends were plated with iron to prevent them from wearing so easily. From this there developed axles which were made up with wooden centres and iron ends bedded and bolted into the wood. Then came axles made of iron and steel. *See* Axle.

Axle-tree Maker
In the 1800s there were three skills involved in the making of axle-trees. These were executed by the vice man, the turner and the forger or fireman. The vice man was the lowest paid. His job entailed the filing of the axle. The turner's task was to produce an accurate axle arm and so he had an exceedingly skilful function to perform. The work of the forger was the highest paid and required both strength and expertise. His work consisted of uniting the masses of iron at

a very hot temperature and then reducing and shaping it to the required form. *See* Axle.

Azaline
A type of tub-bodied buggy, with panelled sides, to be found in Pennsylvania, U.S.A.

B.D.C. *See* Bensington Driving Club.

B.D.S.
British Driving Society.

B.H.S.
British Horse Society. *See* Combined Driving.

Back Band
On single harness the strap passing through the saddle over the top of the back, and to which the tugs are buckled, is known as the back band. For gig harness it is pointed at each end and the belly band is buckled on either side below the tugs. With working harness the belly band and back band are joined as one strap and buckle only on the near side.

Back Door Cab
A type of public cab. *See* Boulnois Cab.

Backing Ring
Found on Army harness. A steel, $2\frac{3}{8}$-inch, ring is attached to either side of the breast collar by a link sewn into the lay, about 7 inches from the centre. Steel links at the ends of the pole bar neck-piece pass through these backing rings before joining either the links on the pole bar, for a limbered or two-wheeled pole draught vehicle, or to the tug neck-piece when pole chains are used as in a GS wagon. The weight of the vehicle, in pulling up, is then distributed over breeching, hip straps and neck through the breast collar.

Back Stay
Part of an Army bridle. *See* Army Harness.

Back Strap
The dock-piece of the crupper is held in place by the back strap which goes round a dee on the back of the pad. Some back straps are buckled on to the crupper and others are sewn. The former are preferable for horses who resist, as the crupper can be unbuckled on one side and easily slipped into place. For leaders in a team or tandem it is safer to have the martingale type of back strap which goes straight from the crupper, round the pad dee and terminates in an unsewn buckle for adjustment, which is held in position by the leather going round it. This avoids the hazard created by a point of leather in which lead reins are inclined to get caught. For single, pair and wheelers it is usual to have

a back strap which passes round the pad dee and buckles in the orthodox manner. For working harness a back strap of single leather is used. Show harness has two layers of leather, joined by a row of stitching on each side. With cheap harness there may be seen dummy stitching holes on single leather which, at first glance, give the impression of double-stitched leather.

Badikins
The name given, in some parts of the country, to the whippletree used with a farm horse.

Badminton Book 'Driving'
An anthology first published in 1889 at the instigation of the Duke of Beaufort.

Badminton Club
A coaching club formed in 1875 by Mr Hurman. The premises, 100 Piccadilly, had, for years, been used by various horse dealers. They consisted of stabling for over fifty horses as well as all the usual out-buildings. Some of the stables and coach-houses were retained for the Club's two teams and vehicles. Surplus stabling and feed stores were converted into Club rooms and the yard into a garden. By 1883 membership had increased so much that it was necessary to secure the two adjacent houses in order to enlarge the Club.

Baggage Net
On a road coach there is, fixed to the rod connecting the side irons of the roof seats, a net made up from leather straps, the purpose of which is to carry wraps thrown on to the roof. Without the straps they would slide off.

Bagman's Gig
Commercial travellers (called bagmen in the 1800s) favoured gigs with spacious boots for transporting their samples. Such vehicles were light, only needed a single horse and were easy for the bagmen to drive.

Baited
In the days of coach travel a horse was said to be baited when he was stabled and fed.

Balance
To be sure of comfort for both the passengers and the horse it is important to see that the vehicle, in the case of a two-wheeler, is correctly balanced. It should ride with the shafts resting gently in the tugs, putting a light load on the back band and no load on the belly band. When in motion the tongues of the tug buckles should float. To achieve correct balance, the seat of some vehicles is made to slide on runners and can be altered and secured according to the number of passengers carried. Some dog carts were built with an arrangement whereby the whole body could be moved on the undercarriage. This is particularly useful for four-seat dog carts when it is extremely unpleasant for those on the rear, backward facing, seat if the vehicle is unbalanced. If the vehicle is balanced shafts heavy, the passengers will experience a disagreeable knee rock which will shake up even the toughest of travellers. It is also hard on the horse, who is having to carry a weight on his back as well as pull the load. A vehicle balanced shafts light is uncomfortable to ride in and puts pressure on to the belly band. If difficulty is experienced in getting a vehicle, without a movable

seat, to balance, a portable weight can be placed in the required position on the floor. One of the disadvantages of very small wheels on a two-wheeled vehicle is that the balance is sensitive to the gradient upon which it is being used. If the wheels are very small then a vehicle which is correctly balanced for a level road may be shaft heavy when going down hill and shaft light up hill.

Bald Face
The white marking which is often seen on the head of a Clydesdale. The blaze extends to cover the muzzle and part of the jaw and cheeks.

Bale
When working horses were kept in their hundreds they often stood in stalls separated by thick pieces of wood about 7 feet long and 1 foot 6 inches deep, which were suspended at trace height by two chains from the ceiling. These partitions were known as bales, or swinging bales. Some were made from two or three strips of wood of the same dimensions, bolted together. These gave more protection. During feeding times, if a horse became excited and kicked, the bale would just rattle and swing but the next-door horse would be protected from flying hooves. When a horse was turned round, in preference to being backed out of his stall, the bale could be easily held aside or hooked to the next bale, to give more turning space.

Ball *See* Lignum Vitae.

Bang up
A slang term, of the 1800s, used when referring to a showy private turnout kept purely for leisure driving. One such equipage, driven by Spicy Jack Everitt, consisted of a bright yellow phaeton drawn by a high-stepping pair wearing silver-mounted harness with red morocco collars.

Bar
Also known as Swingle-Tree.

Bar
With a Liverpool bit, when the reins are buckled on to the branches, they can be in upper, middle or lower bar. The lower the rein is buckled, and the longer the branch, the more severe the action.

Barbican, The
A horse repository in the City of London where commercial horses were sold. The Barbican specialized in horses for funerals, and was closed in about 1920.

Barclay, Captain
A gentleman who kept relays of horses, nearly all of which were piebald or skewbald, along the London to York road. They were stabled near to the changes of the York coach. His greatest delight was to set off, in his gig, at the same time as the Mail Coach, and cover the two-hundred-mile journey in less time than the coach. His pace would have averaged ten miles an hour including stops; he therefore spent about twenty hours on the box. Henry Alken Sen. painted a delightful picture called 'Something Slap' of Captain Barclay accompanied by a bonneted lady, driving a coloured horse to a Stanhope Gig.

16

Barge

An American vehicle used for conveying large numbers of people and quantities of luggage. The long covered body had open sides with bench seats facing inwards. Curtains could be let down to protect the passengers. It was entered from the rear and the four horses were driven from a low seat at the front.

Barge-horse

Canal Barges were all horse drawn, at one time, in England. The horse was led or ridden on the tow-path and sometimes walked free when he was fitted with a wicker or tin nosebag to prevent him from browsing en route. Barge horses became very expert at taking the strain on the heavy load to get the Barge started.

Barker & Company

Coachbuilders noted for the building of many fine carriages, and who were considered unrivalled for their Broughams. They built a Curricle for Count D'Orsay and also a Cabriolet which was superior to any previously built.

Barnet Fair

A famous fair held every September, since 1199, where harness horses and ponies, amongst others, change hands. Still a favourite venue for costers and similar people to buy or sell a horse.

Barouche

A luxurious open four-wheeled carriage, used extensively throughout the first half of the 19th century. It became an extremely fashionable summer vehicle which was considered unequalled for park driving. The canoe-shaped body was built on a perch and hung by leather braces on four cee-springs. The rear seat had a leather hood which could be erected to protect the passengers from rain. There was a knee flap which could also be drawn up at such times to give additional cover to those people and to the inner lining of the vehicle. Whilst this flap was in operation the front seat was rendered useless. The Barouche was either driven from a high box seat, resembling that of a Landau, or ridden postillion.

It was expensive to maintain as its dignity and size demanded that two, four or six large and high-class horses, superior to those required for other carriages, should be kept.

In 1808, a Four-Horse Club called The Barouche Club was formed for members driving Barouches instead of Drags.

Messrs Hooper, the coachbuilders, were famous for their Barouches.

The difficulty in obtaining good enough horses, and reduced incomes in the late 1800s, led to fewer being built. People turned to one-horse carriages such as Victorias.

There are two Barouches in the Royal Mews at the present time, which are used for official occasions.

Barouche Landau

A carriage built on the lines of a Barouche with some Landau characteristics. It had a high box seat and a rumble seat at the rear for two servants. The Prince Regent drove one at Brighton in the early 1800s when it became a fashionable carriage for amateur four-in-hand driving.

Barouche Sociable
A four-wheeled open carriage, driven from a box seat. The two *vis-à-vis* passenger seats both had folding heads so that the whole resembled two cabriolet bodies facing one another.

Barouchet
A smaller, lighter edition of the Barouche which was suitable to be drawn by a single horse.

Barrel Top Wagon
A type of Gypsy Wagon which is favoured owing to its lightness, unlikeliness to overturn and its inconspicuousness. The low side walls are surmounted by a bowed wooden roofing frame which supports a green canvas sheet to keep out the rain.

It is also known as a Bow Top, Leeds, Lincolnshire, Midland, Yorkshire and Bell Wagon.

Basil
A type of lining used for the collars of heavy transport horses.

Basket
On some early coaches there was an open-topped basket fixed over the rear axle for carrying passengers and parcels. If a large number of people were to be carried they stood, but if there was room they were able to sit. In cold weather, straw was put into the basket to give some warmth.

Another kind of basket is the type which is cylindrical and strapped to the rear of the near side of a vehicle for carrying such items as umbrellas, sticks and the horn.

Basket Phaeton
Little phaetons with basket-work bodies became popular in the 1860s for country driving. They were light, inexpensive, and required a minimum amount of maintenance on their bodies as there was little paint-work to get scratched. They were very suitable for conveying children and were also favoured by country clergy and those in the lower income brackets. Said to be the humble relation of the grander phaeton family, Basket Phaetons were driven with either a single pony or a pair of ponies.

Bastard Coaches
A slang name which was given to a Char-a-Banc with a dummy coach body. *See* Brake.

Basterna
A type of horse litter used in Roman times for conveying passengers. *See* Litter.

Bath Chair
Queen Victoria's Bath Chair, which was built in 1893 by Cheverton, is now in the possession of The Science Museum, London. The single, hooded, seat is placed low behind a tall curving dashboard. The body is hung on four small wheels by four elliptic springs. Curving splashboards protect the almost ground-level steps from mud. It was drawn by a small pony and built especially low to afford easy access to the Queen when she became old.

Numerous Bath Chairs were built to a similar design.

Bathing Machine Horse

These horses were ridden when they pulled the bathing machines (wooden huts on wheels) down to the water to a depth which permitted the occupant to step discreetly into the sea. After the bather had been let out, the horse was taken from the machine and ridden back to get another one. Although this was hard work, a summer which was spent working in salt water rendered many horses which had been unsound, fit for road work again throughout the winter.

Battenburg Phaeton

A four-wheeled vehicle resembling a type of four-wheeled Dog Cart or Ralli Car. The body is hung on four elliptic springs and there is accommodation for four people back-to-back. The sides of the body curve outwards with splashboards continuing the sweep over the wheels. It is suitable either for a single or pair, or if smaller animals are put to, it would take a unicorn or a team.

Battlesden Car

A two-wheeled general purpose vehicle, resembling a low-bodied Dog Cart, which was popular at the turn of the century. The spacious body, which accommodated four people sitting back-to-back, was similar in profile to a Moray Car, but was hung between two elliptic springs. The shafts ran inside the body. The splashboards formed a semi-circle over the wheels but did not extend to the front step as with the Moray Car. It was light and easily pulled by a cob or pony. In 1880, a convertible Battlesden Car was produced by Messrs Kerridge of Suffolk. The shafts were removed and in their place was fixed a fore-carriage by fitting a pair of cranes into sockets. The vehicle was then turned into a useful four-wheeled conveyance.

Beach Wagon

A square box top wagon, usually without a roof, which used to be found at the fashionable watering places along the Atlantic coast of U.S.A.

Beading

Joints or seams, unavoidable in carriage construction, were covered by narrow strips of brass, copper or silver-plated copper. Brass was polished, and copper painted. A number of vehicles, now in existence, Ralli Cars in particular, have wood or brass beading going along the body to cover what would otherwise be an unsightly seam.

Bealson's Road Protector

In 1796, Mr Robert Bealson devised a system to prevent ruts from being made by the wheels of a carriage and to keep them from sinking into existing ones. A heavy and broad roller was fixed to the bottom of a carriage in such a way that it was $1\frac{1}{2}$ inches above the ground when the vehicle was proceeding along a flat surface. When the wheels sunk into muddy ruts, the roller came into contact with the middle of the road and supported the carriage. The inventor claimed that it would be easier for the horses to pull the vehicle along on its roller than drag the wheels through muddy ruts, but the idea never caught on. The main objection was that the horses would have a constant additional weight of several hundredweights to haul at all times and that it was therefore not a practical proposition.

Bearing Rein
There are two types of bearing rein, the pulley and the plain. Both use a bridoon (also known as bradoon) snaffle which goes in the horse's mouth a little above the curb bit. For the pulley-bearing rein a snaffle with a special roller attached to the ring is used. The ends of the bearing rein are buckled to points on either side of the headpiece. The rolled leather straps go down through the rollers on the snaffle and then up either through rings which are fixed to small straps buckled to dees on the outsides of the headpiece, called bradoon hangers, or through swivels near the buckles on the throat latch. From beyond there, the rolled leather terminates in rings. A flat bearing rein is attached to these rings on either side, adjustable by means of buckles. It is this flat part which goes over the centre hook on the pad forcing the horse's head into the desired position. The plain bearing rein is simpler. The ends are clipped or buckled to the rings of the snaffle. The rolled leather then passes through the bradoon hangers or throat latch swivels before joining the flat adjustable part of the bearing rein which is hooked on to the pad. Some bearing reins are made from strong cord instead of rolled leather. The driving reins are usually fixed to the curb bit. They are attached to the bradoon in exceptional circumstances when dealing with hard pullers.

Bearing Rein Drop
Also known as a bradoon hanger.

Bearing Strap
Also known as trace bearer and trace carrier. It is a strap which goes over the loins and passes through a slot in the back strap of the crupper. At each end there is a loop through which the traces go so that they are held level. Bearing straps are sometimes found on team and pair harness and are nearly always employed for a tandem leader when long lead traces are used instead of tandem bars.

Bearskin Cape
A coachman's cape which was worn for town driving, on smart coaches, when the weather was cold.

Beaufort, His Grace the 8th Duke of
Elected President of the Coaching Club on 12th July 1871 and remained so until 1897. Also known as the Blue Duke. *See* Badminton Book *Driving*.

   The 10th Duke is a member of the Coaching Club today.

Beaufort Phaeton
Also known as a Hunting Phaeton. A gentleman's carriage similar to a Mail Phaeton, but accommodating six people instead of four, by having a middle seat. Sometimes there were doors let into the boot sides to facilitate entry to this central seat. It was found mainly in hunting counties and used as a convenient conveyance to hunt meets.

Bedfont Driving Club. *See* Bensington Driving Club.

Bedford Cart
A two-wheeled general-purpose vehicle suitable for farmers or dealers and for carrying goods. The square-shaped body has turned spindles along the top of each side and is hung on two semi-elliptic springs. The shafts run inside the

body. The seating resembles that of a dog cart in that two people are facing forwards and two backwards. These rear passengers put their feet against the tail board which lets down on chains to form a foot rest.

Bedford Cord
A suitable material with which to upholster the cushions and valance on such vehicles as Dog Carts and Gigs.

It is also favourable for driving aprons and rugs.

Beds
Part of the woodwork frame, known as the carriage, on which the body of the vehicle is supported. The beds consist of cross-framing timbers known as the hind-axle bed, the fore-axle bed, the hind-spring bed, the fore-spring bed or transom and the horn bar.

Beech
A wood which was not favoured for high-class carriage building. Constant exposure to the alternate conditions of air and dampness rendered it likely to warp and rot. It was, however, sometimes used by both wheelwrights and carriage builders in the 1800s as it was then extremely cheap.

Beeswax
A little, rubbed into the palm and fingers of leather gloves, particularly if they are new ones, will help to prevent the reins from slipping. This mainly applies to the holding of a team which is pulling.

Bells, Sleigh
These were worn by horses to warn other road users of the approaching sleigh as well as for the pleasant music. They were made of brass, nickel and iron and were attached to the harness. Martingale straps, quarter-straps and the belly band were frequently adorned with rows of bells. Some horses wore a girdle of bells which went right round their girth and over their back. Bells and plumes were fixed to the tops of the bridles. On heavy vehicles they were screwed to the shafts or pole. Families became recognizable by their bells, being identifiable by their sound before coming into sight. Logging teams using a single track would wear bells so that a teamster could tell, by listening, whether he could progress to the next passing point before meeting another team.

Bell Terret. *See* Fly Terret.

Bell Wagon
Also known as a Barrel Top Wagon.

Belly Band
With working and trade harness the belly band and back band are one continuous strap. The back band passes through the saddle to carry the tugs and continues round the shafts, through a loop on the girth by which time it is referred to as the belly band and buckles to the back band point below the shaft on the nearside. The belly band of single-gig harness buckles at each end to the points of the back band below the shafts. The purpose of the belly band for a two-wheeled vehicle is to prevent the shafts from pointing upwards, and the cart from tipping backwards. This is particularly important with vehicles

21

like Governess Carts when weight is put on to the rear step when entering. Without a belly band the vehicle would tip over until the rear step touched the ground. The belly band should be left loose enough to allow some play in the shafts. When in motion the points of the tug buckles should float, allowing the vehicle to ride in a balanced manner. If the belly band is too tight the balance may be upset. If it is too loose the horse will be able to jump sideways out of the shafts. This can result in an animal standing with the shafts across the top of his back. When French Tilbury tugs are used a shorter belly band is employed. It is buckled to each side after the tug points have passed through the loops on the sides of the saddle. The belly band goes through the girth loop and is buckled against the girth holding the shafts still. With pair, unicorn or team harness the belly band is buckled to the short point coming down from the trace tug buckle and is not fastened tightly. The purpose is to prevent the traces from riding upwards.

Belly Band (Farm Harness)
This is a wide leather strap, with a buckle at one end, which is attached to the offside shaft of a farm cart, below the chain backband. When the horse is put to, the belly band is passed over the girth and buckled to a leather point fixed to the nearside shaft. The belly band prevents the cart from tipping up and going over backwards.

Belly Bugle
A type of draught used in America for heavy mule carts. On either side of the pole, to coincide with the saddle pads, are fixed two semi-circular metal bands. These pass under the bellies of the mules, terminating in rings at pole height by which the belly bugles are strapped to the pads holding the pole in position. The vehicle is pulled in the normal way by traces and swingle trees.

Belly Strap
Sometimes used on a tandem leader. This is a strap with a buckle at each end which is buckled to a detachable point fastened to a dee on the lower side of each trace between the pad and the trace carrier. The strap is passed through a loop on the rear of the girth and prevents the traces from going over the horse's back if he should turn towards the shaft horse.

Benevolent Whip Club
The purpose of the club, founded in the early 1800s, was to ensure that help could be given to guards, coachmen and their families when they were in financial difficulties. An allowance of 12 shillings a week would be paid to families of men who were in prison for debt. The B.D.C. gave 100 guineas to the club, and within twenty years, £9,000 was given to the needy. This Club was later succeeded by the Cabdrivers' Benevolent Association.

Bennett
A coachbuilder of Finsbury who is said to have been the originator of the 'Dennett' gig.

Bennett, Alf
Head coachman and responsible for the running of Sir Edward Stern's immaculate stable. Said to have been precise, perfect, and polished and that, if it

were not for the fact that he was always so well dressed, he might have been mistaken for a duke!

Bensington Driving Club

Also known as the Benson Club and the B.D.C. It was a club formed in 1807 for amateur four-horse coachmen, made up from twenty-five elected members. The rules of the Club stated that members should drive, twice a year, from London to The Black Dog, Bedfont, which was fourteen miles, and from London to the White Hart, Bensington, a journey of fifty-six miles. The Club became known colloquially as The Black and White Club. To begin with, the distance to Bensington was accepted, but after sixteen years these drives no longer took place and Bedfont became the headquarters, with members driving regularly to dine there. Fortunately the initials B.D.C. still applied though the Club was officially known as the Bedfont Driving Club. It was between 1853 and 1854 that the B.D.C. finally broke up.

Benson Club. *See* Bensington Driving Club.

Bent-sided Dog Cart

Similar to a Battenberg Phaeton. The main difference being that the sides of the body are steamed so that the panels continue in one sweep to form splashboards.

Beresford Cabriolet

A gig-type vehicle with a folding hood and seating for two people. The low, cab-fronted body is hung on a combination of cee- and elliptic springs.

Berlin

A type of coach which originated in Berlin, Germany in about 1780.

Besant, John

A London coachbuilder who supplied Mail Coaches up to the time of his death in 1791.

Bian

A type of large four-wheeled Jaunting Car introduced in the early 1800s in Ireland by Charles Bianconi for transporting passengers and mail. *See* Bianconi *and* Jaunting Car.

Bianconi, Charles (Carlo) (1786–1875)

An Italian, colloquially known as Bian, born at Tregola, who was responsible for the introduction of the first public transport in Ireland. In his youth, he was reputed to be the boldest boy and the greatest dunce. In order to avoid being conscripted to the armies of Napoleon and because of his scholastic problems he was apprenticed to Faroni, a dealer in prints. They went to Dublin, where in 1802 Bianconi spent his time making frames for cheap prints, brought from Italy, which he sold in the streets. At seventeen, his apprenticeship completed, he set off with one hundred pounds (weight) of prints in a bag and some money in his pocket. The weight of the load may have made him consider the need for cheap public transport, linking up the main coaching routes which was non-existent in Ireland. He was determined not to return to Italy until he was a great man. Tiring of peddling, he directed his talents to carving and gilding, and went to Waterford and from there to Clonmel. Here, on behalf of government agents, his business turned to that of buying the hoarded guineas of the peasantry. His

23

finances improved but his inability to converse fluently gave him plenty of time for thought. He realized that something had to be done to start a horse-and-car public transport business. In 1815 he put on a single-horse jaunting car. No one was very enthusiastic but Bianconi was determined to persevere with his idea so he put on a second jaunting car in opposition, without telling anyone that he owned them both. The competition between the drivers caused excitement, the thrill caught on and both were soon in demand. At this time, a number of good horses which had been bred specifically for army use were now redundant as a result of peace following the battle of Waterloo. Bianconi was able to buy these for between £10 and £20 each. He put on a car for travellers fron Clonmel to Cahir. This was extended to Tipperary and Limerick. Within six months cars were running from Clonmel to Cashel, Thurloe, Carrick and Waterford. The result of the Waterford election in 1826 caused considerable expansion of the Bianconi business. He originally agreed to hire cars to the Beresford party. On hearing this, the opposition, Mr Villiers Stuart, wanted Bianconi for his party. Bianconi refused but this was not accepted and the Stuart regime threw two complete cars and horses over a bridge. Bianconi decided that it would be preferable to cancel his contract with Beresford and supply cars to Mr Villiers Stuart. The election was won by the latter and £1,000 was paid to Bianconi. This money was invested in forage, putting the transport business into a healthy position. The firm then grew to such an extent that, at its height, Bianconi had cars carrying passengers and mail covering 3,800 miles a day. He had 140 agents working for him. The head agent was Dan Hearn, of Hearns Hotel, Clonmel, which was the headquarters. Each agent was expected to list the exact forage used and the number of horses kept. The horses were consuming 30–40,000 bushels of oats a year and 3–4,000 tons of hay. He budgeted about 16 lb. of hay, 15 lb. of oats and 8 lb. of straw per day for each horse. No one was allowed to keep poultry as he was afraid that his corn might find its way into the chicken houses. No man was allowed to marry without first getting Bianconi's permission. He expected instant obedience and tolerated no lies. He evolved a spy system in order to check the drivers, horses, harness, vehicles and agents. Drivers soon became wise at recognizing the presence of a spy amongst the passengers and the word went round. Bianconi had, however, compassion for his men. If they became ill or disabled and when they became too old to cope with their usual jobs, they were given somewhere to live and they and their families were provided with a pension. Those that were able, were put to light work, such as that of night watchmen. In 1833 he obtained an official contract for carrying mail. The vehicle which he used was a long car known as a Bian, weighing about 16 cwt. It seated six passengers, on either side, sitting facing the sides of the road with their backs to the central boot, or well, into which the luggage was put. The driver sat at the front on a high seat on the boot from where he handled the pair or team. Doubtful horses, unwanted for other jobs, frequently found their way into Bianconi's employ. When the business was at its peak he was the largest proprietor in Europe of horses and vehicles. He showed compassion for his horses as well as for his men; when horses were in need of a rest after the hard and fast work in a car they would be turned out to grass at Longfield House, Bianconi's house near Tipperary. On occasions there would be a couple of hundred horses resting.

24

Biga

A Grecian chariot with a pair harnessed alongside the pole with yokes. *See* Chariot.

Biggar, Charles

A coachbuilder of St Martin's Lane, Westminster. It was frequent for carriage users to keep their own horses and hire the vehicle and harness from a coach-builder. This suited both parties. The carriage was kept maintained and hiring out of vehicles was a profitable branch in which some coachbuilders specialized. One recorded example was that of a new coach, built on a perch, and a set of pair horse harness, hired by Charles Biggar to John Palmer in 1787. The contract was made out for a term of four years. During that time Charles Biggar agreed to keep the coach in repair, to repaint it and supply two new hammer-cloths. John Palmer agreed to pay 36 guineas a year. This was to be paid in advance, on the first day of each new hiring year. He also had to pay for any broken plate glass on the coach and worn plated work on the harness. Any damage to the vehicle and harness was to be paid for by John Palmer. He had to agree to return everything in good order at the expiration of the four years.

Bike Wagon

A light American vehicle with a tray-shaped body, 22 inches wide and 56 inches long, hung on two elliptic springs and a perch. The wheels were mounted on bicycle axles. The forward-facing seat had railed sides, was well upholstered, and made to accommodate the driver and one passenger. The dashboard was leather padded.

Billet

The point of any strap which is buckled round part of the harness.

The point of the rein going round the bit and coming back to the buckle by the bit is known as the rein billet. These billets are subject to hard wear owing to constant contact with saliva and metal so a close watch must be kept for damage. A broken rein billet can be disastrous.

Bit Case

A case with doors containing large panes of glass.

Bits are displayed hanging on hooks set into green baize or similar cloth. In the early 1900s, when steel bits were used, they were kept covered in a fine layer of oil to prevent rust. The case was frequently placed on the harness room wall above the open fire. Pole chains and decoration flowers, as well as bits, were kept in the bit case, the whole feature becoming the focal point of the room.

Bitting

Probably as many different types of bits have been devised for driving as for riding. All of them are basically variations of the main themes. No two horses are the same and there is a key to every horse's mouth. The actions are as follows: jointed, straight bar, half moon, low port, high port, curb and gag. On these themes are devised a multitude of ideas.

A jointed bit has a nutcracker action on the tongue, and pressure is applied to the corners of the mouth when there is tension on the reins. Driving snaffles have two rings on each side. One ring is attached to the mouthpiece at each end and the other rings float on the mouthpiece. It is to these that the cheek-pieces are buckled. The reins can be buckled to both rings for a normal and fairly mild

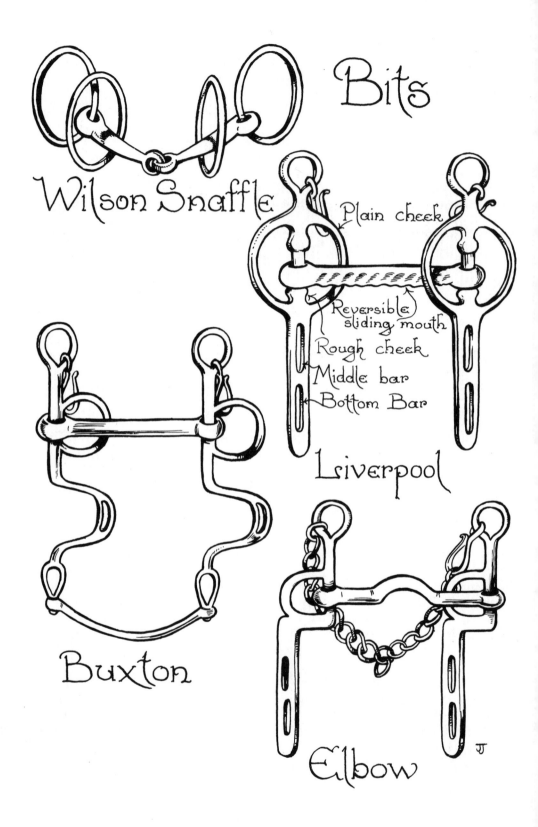

Bits

Wilson Snaffle

Plain cheek

Reversible sliding mouth
Rough cheek
Middle bar
Bottom Bar

Liverpool

Buxton

Elbow

action and to the rings on the mouthpiece for a severe action. This results in the mouthpiece jointing severely on the tongue and also in strong pressure on both sides of the jaw from the floating rings. The four-ringed snaffle comes in many variations which are generally known as Wilson snaffles.

A straight bar bit lies flat on the tongue and, in the case of a snaffle, its mildness depends on the thickness of the mouth piece. A thick rubber or leather covered mouthpiece is the least severe and a thin metal twisted mouthpiece is the most severe.

When a straight bar is incorporated in a curb bit then, of course, the severity depends largely on the curb action as well as the mouthpiece. Most Liverpool bits and some Buxton bits have varying straight mouthpieces. A half-moon or mullen mouthpiece is bent in a slight curve to follow the shape of the tongue. This permits some pressure on the bars of the mouth.

A low port accommodates the tongue and puts pressure on to the bars of the mouth. This is favoured by horses with sensitive tongues. A high port prevents the tongue from being drawn back and brought down over the top of the bit. If a tight noseband is used with a curb bit having a high port, then the port presses against the roof of the mouth. Some exceptionally severe Buxton bits were used in coaching days with ports about 4 inches high, in which a serrated ball was fixed at the top. The combination of such a bit, with a tight noseband and the reins on bottom bar, was very severe.

The curb bit varies in severity depending on where the reins are buckled. If they are buckled on plain cheek, then the action is similar to a snaffle with the severity depending on the mouthpiece and the driver's hands. If the reins are fixed to the bar, the lower they are fixed the more severe the action becomes. There is considerable leverage with the reins on bottom bar of a long-checked curb. When pressure is applied, not only does the curb chain tighten in the chin groove, with the mouth acting as an axis, but the eye of the bit tips forward, pulling on the headpiece, transferring pressure to the poll.

The gag bit is fixed to rolled cheek-pieces which run through slots on the bit. The reins are attached to the cheek-pieces below the bit. When pressure is applied, the bit slides upwards along the cheek-pieces, putting pressure towards the molars. This is very effective for horses which lower their heads or tuck their chins into their chests in order to evade control.

Black and Tan
A slang term which was used in America towards the end of the nineteenth century for a cheap cab of black and tan colour.

Black Brigade
The black horses, whose work it was to pull hearses, were generally known as the black brigade. In the late 19th century there were about seven hundred of these magnificent Flemish stallions in London. They stood in the region of sixteen hands and weighed around 12 to 13 cwt. Stallions were preferred as the geldings of the breed tended to lack the lustre in their coats and turn slightly brown. These entires were horses of tremendous character and presence, looking superb with manes and tails flowing and black plumes adorning the tops of their bridles. They were imported from Holland and Belgium as rising three-year-olds at a cost of about 100 guineas a pair. It took a year to train them, familiarize

them with their surroundings and settle them from ills caused by their sea journey, by which time those who had attained the standard required by a high-class establishment were worth £65 each. Those who had not achieved such heights were sold to second class stables for about £25. £10 was all that could be expected for those which ended up in repositories. Most of the black brigade were kept by jobmasters known as black masters. The best known of these, in London, was Dottridge. He had facilities for providing, to retail undertakers, all that was required for a funeral. His stud consisted of eighty horses. Each one was named after the famous person most discussed at the time of the animal's arrival in the yard. For every four horses there was a head man who drove them as a team and an under-groom who drove when the horses worked in two pairs. When the undertakers were busy, such as in the 'flu epidemic of the late 1800s, the horses worked up to four journeys a day, six days a week. Their working life averaged six years, after which the animal ended up at the knacker who valued him at 35 shillings. These stallions were fed on rye bread, oats and hay. Care was taken not to give food with a tendency to overheating, such as beans or too much clover. Linseed and bran mashes were fed on Saturday nights to maintain the glossy black coat which was so important in the role of a member of the black brigade. The black brigade had to be kept strictly to a yard of their own. Any attempt to put coloured horses in close proximity repeatedly proved disastrous resulting in an unhappy stable. The coal horses of London were also sometimes called the black brigade as many of them were bay or black.

Black Ribbons
On the occasion of the death and funeral of an important figure, as in the case of James Selby in December 1888, the London bus drivers tied black ribbons on to their whips.

Blacksmith
As well as shoeing horses, he played a large part in the building of vehicles as a considerable number of items for a carriage are made of iron. Door hinges, brake assemblies, tail-board chains and fittings, handles, steps, stays, seat railings, lamp brackets, roller bolts and tyres are just some of the parts for which the blacksmith was responsible.

Blackthorn
A type of wood used for whips owing to its elastic quality.

Bleeding
A veterinary application in the mid-1800s as a 'cure' for most ailments.

Blind
Also called Blinker, Winker or Blinder. *See* Blinker.

Blinders. *See* Blinkers.

Blind Halter
A west country term for a driving bridle.

Blindmaker
His work was akin to that of the trunk maker and the average weekly wage in the early 19th century was 30 shillings.

Blinds
A hood with the eye slots covered by leather discs. Blinkers are also sometimes called Blinds.

Blinkers
Also called Blinders, Blinds or Winkers. They are the leather-covered, metal plates attached to the cheek-pieces of the bridle to cover the horse's eyes. They are made in varying shapes; being round, hatchet-shaped, dee-shaped, or square. Those used on State harness are extremely ornate with metal mountings round the edge and armorial bearings in the centre. Blinkers on private driving harness should be compatible in shape to the saddle or pad. They have two or three rows of stitching round the edge and the owner's crest or monogram in metal in the centre. The purpose of blinkers is to prevent the horse from seeing behind him. The fitting is important. They should be adjusted carefully so that the widest part of the plate coincides with the widest part of the eye. If they are too low the horse will look out over the top of them and if too high he will peer out below them. An animal who has always been accustomed to working in an open bridle will be unafraid of the load behind him, but to expose the rear view suddenly to a horse who has never seen it before is likely to cause trouble. For this reason a blinkered bridle should never be taken off a horse whilst he is still put to a vehicle. The sudden sight of the vehicle close behind him, combined with inadequate means of control, perhaps just a rope halter, has caused accidents.

An unblinkered horse can become very frightened by the sight of the wheels turning closely behind him, giving the impression that he is going to be run into. When driving more than one horse it is easier to correct an idle worker if all are wearing blinkers. Without blinkers, the mere sight of the whip being unfolded will send all of the horses surging forward. Blinkers will also hide such diversions as passengers waving, or parasols being brandished. Army horses work in open bridles, as did numerous working horses in London. It was proved that these animals avoided accidents by being permitted to see clearly that which was going on around them.

Blocking-up
The block of wood which goes between the spring and the axle can be varied in depth from about $\frac{1}{2}$ inch to 3 inches, depending on how much the vehicle needs to be blocked up to fit the horse for which it is being used.

Blocks
In the case of a travelling coach or town vehicle the block was the wooden raiser that went between the bed and the spring. With two-wheeled vehicles, now in use, the height can be altered, to accommodate varying horses, by changing the size of the wooden blocks between the axle and the springs.

Blount's Spring Carriage
In 1665 Pepys wrote in his diary that he had ridden in a Colonel Edward Blount's carriage which was fitted with some kind of springing. This was a comparatively new idea at that time.

29

Blow

The coach team was given a few moments to regain its breath on reaching the summit of a steep hill, whilst the cock-horse boy unhitched the cock horse.

Blue Coach Office

One of the many coach offices in Castle Square, Brighton. This particular office had the reputation for providing coaches which were somewhat slower than the well-known ones on the Brighton road but which were safe and good. Their routes included roads to Portsmouth and Hastings as well as to London.

Blue State Harness, The

In the Royal Mews in London the two sets of blue State harness are considered to be the most historic items, since they were made in 1791. Blue harness and rosettes were always used for the Sovereign until Queen Victoria's reign. This has been superseded by crimson.

Blunderbuss

The guard, on a Mail Coach, was provided with a blunderbuss with which to protect the mails from highwaymen.

Boat Sleigh

A large boat-shaped sleigh which was used for excursion purposes and found in the New England area of America.

Bob Runner

As sleighs did not always provide the comfort required in snowy conditions, it was necessary to adapt existing vehicles, such as Breaks, for use on snow and ice. The wheels of the vehicle would be removed and bob runners, which had a hub and axle box, would be put in their place. A bob runner resembled a quarter of a wheel with a large proportion of the rim flattened to provide a reasonable bearing surface on the snow.

Bobs. *See* Bobsleigh.

Bob Sleigh

These were also known as bobs. They were made up from sleigh runners joined by metal and wooden cross-pieces to form a platform on which the body of any vehicle could be attached when winter conditions made wheeled traffic impractical. Some bobs resembled a large version of a child's modern toboggan.

Body Brake

A four wheeled vehicle used with a pair or team for country pursuits. Designs vary but most have three or more rows of seats, facing forward, over a spacious boot used for carrying everything from headcollars and rugs to picnic hampers and mackintoshes.

Body Horse. *See* Pin-Hoss.

Body Loop

A strong loop made from iron which is bolted or screwed to the body of a vehicle at the bottom corners and by which it is hung.

Bodymaker

He was a man possessing a great many skills, having to combine the ability to work in a large variety of woods, to draw and calculate geometrical problems and to create accurate angles. He was expected to make joints from every conceivable method, including scarf, mortice and tenon, tongue and groove, and lap, as well as with screws, nails, bolts and glue. It was usual for a body-maker to do piece-work, so the wages earned fluctuated according to the work achieved. In the early 1800s the average bodymaker would have earned less than £3 a week.

Bodyside
The part of the collar which goes next to the shoulders. *See* Collar.

Body Team
The pair between the wheelers and the swing team in an eight-horse team.

Bollard
A term used by the Army, meaning roller bolt.

Bolster Wagon
An American road wagon or buggy, which had no end springs but was hung on side bars and bolsters.

Bolt Hook
The bearing rein hook on the top of the driving saddle, curved to the shape of a half-ring.

Bolts
These were used extensively in carriage construction to secure heavy frame work and iron work.

Booby Hut
An American sleigh favoured by the Bostonians. The closed body is similar to that of an English coach and is entered by a half-glass full-length door and step. There are two windows on either side of the rear seat. It is driven from a high box. The body is suspended by thoroughbraces and the whole is built on two runners.

Boodge
A word derived from Saxon times meaning to bulge out, which is why the sword case was sometimes known as the boodge or booge.

Booking
When a seat was booked on a coach at the booking office it had to be paid for at the same time. A ticket would be given, stating the name of the coach and the date of the journey. The particular seat booked would be marked on the appropriate square on the ticket diagram. A time card would also be provided for passengers, with information stating the route, the stops, the times, the mileage and the fares, both overall and intermediate.

Booking Office
An office which was always staffed, such as one attached to an hotel, where seats on a coach could be booked and paid for prior to a journey. The White Horse Cellar (Hatchetts), Piccadilly, was the starting place for many London coaches up to 1889. A separate book was often kept for each coach, devoting a page for every day, stating the names of the ticket holders and the seats to be occupied.

31

Boot

The earliest boots were uncovered box-shaped projections on each side, between the front and rear wheels, of some 17th-century coaches. People of low rank travelled back-to-back, facing the sides of the roads, with their legs in these boxes which therefore became known as boots. In the 1700s some coaches had a basket fixed to the rear axle. Then a wooden open-topped box replaced this. In time the box was given a lid and became known as a hind boot. During the early 1800s, passengers sometimes rode in the lidded hind boot. In some cases this was because the guard wished to conceal their presence from the coach proprietor so that he, the guard, could keep their fares for himself.

The hind boot was known as the rumble but now the name rumble refers only to the seat above the hind boot. Hind boots of Drags, Road Coaches and Mail Coaches differ in the way that their doors hinge. The door of a hind boot on a Road Coach is hinged on the off side so that the guard could easily open it whilst in motion. The hind boot of a Mail Coach opens at the top, for security reasons, ensuring that as long as the guard was sitting with his feet on the lid, it could not be opened. With a Drag, the hind boot has a door at the back hinged at the bottom so that when it is opened the door lets down to form a table on which the lunch boxes may be pulled forward. Front boots vary in shape, design, and methods of entering, but basically the boot extends from below the footboard to down behind the roller bolts. The door is hinged at the top rather than the bottom as the latter could prove disastrous should a door accidentally open and hit the horses. Some front boots can be entered from inside the coach. Horse clothing and spare equipment is often carried in the front boot of a Drag.

Boot Tread

This is the step which is fixed to the front boot of a coach to facilitate mounting on to the box.

Boss

Also known as a rosette. It is the brass or white metal disc which is fixed at the end of the browband by means of a metallic dee. The cheek-piece point of the head-piece passes through the loop of the browband on one side of the rosette dee and the throat latch point of the head-piece passes through the other side. This prevents the browband from rising upwards. The owner's monogram or crest is frequently worked into the front of the rosette. For single, pair, tandem and unicorn, to any vehicle, and with a team to a Drag, rosettes are worn on both sides of the bridle. With a Road Coach team they are worn only on the outer sides making it easy to differentiate between nearside and offside bridles at a glance. Rosettes with outward protruding terrets through which the leaders' reins pass are often used with a tandem shaft horse or the wheelers of a unicorn or four-in-hand team. With a team they are put on the **outer** sides, and with a unicorn, on to the **inner** sides of the bridles.

At the turn of the century, rosettes were designed in many different styles and materials. As well as being made from brass and various white metals, they were manufactured with plain and patterned glass fronts. They were also produced in leather, silk and tape, when they were often large and decorative, being made up in the family or coach colours. They resembled the type of rosette which is now presented at large shows to champion horses. For those in mourning, there were large black rosettes. Any driver wishing to register his presence could do so by using a type available, known as a London Bell rosette, which had a round bell protruding outwards.

Both Sides of the Road
Also known as two sweats. Both these terms refer to a coach team being worked twice on the same day. The stage up would perhaps be driven in the morning and then the same team would be brought back over the down stage later in the day.

Bottom Bar
The lowest slot into which the reins can be buckled on a curb bit. *See* Liverpool Bit.

Bottom Bed. *See* Axle bed.

Boulnois Cab
Designed by Mr William Boulnois, in the 1830s, it was a type of closed cab resembling a small Omnibus. It was entered by a step and door at the back and the two passengers sat facing each other. The cabby drove from a seat on the front of the roof. The disadvantage of this cab was that it was a simple matter for a passenger, on nearing his destination, to open the door and slip out unnoticed, leaving his fare unpaid. For this reason, the life of the Boulnois Cab was a short one. Also known as the Backdoor Cab, the Minibus and, colloquially, as 'Slice of an Omnibus'.

Bourdalou. *See* Coach Pot.

Bow Top Waggon
A type of gypsy waggon which has a bow-shaped canvas roof. It is lighter than the Burton, Ledge or Reading waggon and therefore more suitable for touring with a single horse. Also known as a Barrel Top Wagon.

Box
The seat from which the coachman drives is called the box. The foundation of the seat is flat topped but the Whip sits on a sloping surface. This is achieved on some vehicles by a wooden box designed to slope from the back to the front, on top of which is a cushion. In others, it is the cushion which is shaped, rising gently from front to rear. The purpose of this shaping is so that the seat and legs are placed in a comfortable as well as effective driving position. A cushion which slopes too steeply is dangerous as this induces an almost standing posture from which a coachman could get pulled forward and thrown off the box. A seat which is too low and flat is equally unsatisfactory as this causes the knees to become bent at too sharp an angle and less control is maintained over pulling horses.

The passenger's seat, known as the box seat and the place of honour, has a flat cushion, somewhat shallower than that of the Whip.

Box Keeper. *See* Box Loop.

Box Loop
A large box-shaped leather keeper on the harness in which the point of a strap, having been secured by a buckle, lies. Can be found on the cheeks of the bridle,

the hame tugs, the shaft tugs, crupper and breeching. A set of harness should be uniform, either with box loops or narrow keepers (known as space loops) throughout.

Box Waggon

A light, four-wheeled, pneumatic-tyred, waggon which is used for showing hackney horses and ponies. The single, stick-back, seat is placed in a shallow box-shaped body which is hung on a perch undercarriage with two transverse elliptic springs. The shafts curve downwards to the front axle.

Nowadays better known as a Show Waggon or Hackney Show Waggon.

Brace

The bodies of some vehicles are hung, or checked from excessive motion, by means of sewn leather strips known as braces. *See* Bracemaker.

Bracemaker

Two workers were involved in bracemaking. The higher paid was the cutter whose wages, in the early 1800s, were between 2 and 3 guineas a week. His responsibility lay in the ability to calculate the relevant strengths of various parts and qualities of hides. He would be expected to know how many layers of leather were necessary to take the strain imposed on them. The sewer earned 25 to 30 shillings a week, depending on the neatness of his stitching. His job of sewing the strips of leather was unpleasant as he was continually bent over his work, and his eyes suffered from having to look at black leather all day long. This work was considered an unskilled occupation which anyone could learn.

Bradoon

A type of snaffle bit, usually jointed, which is used in conjunction with a curb bit, such as a Buxton, when a bearing rein is fitted.

A small bradoon is also sometimes used for an overhead check rein in which case it is then generally employed with a jointed snaffle.

A small ringed half moon bradoon is often used with a Liverpool bit for the bearing rein when showing a Hackney to a Wagon.

Bradoon Hanger

The straps or chains hanging from dees on either side of the head-piece to which a ring is attached through which the bearing rein passes. Also known as a bridoon hanger.

Brake

An open four-wheeled vehicle. These came into general use as gentlemen's carriages in the 1860s. They varied considerably in shape and design but were all used for country and utilitarian purposes. *See* Built-up Brake, Shooting Brake and Waggonette Brake.

Brake

Brakes first came into general use in England for private carriages in the 1860s. Up to that time coachmen had had to rely on a combination of the powers of the wheelers to hold the vehicle and skilful application of the skid pan. The brake is put on by a hand lever and, or, a foot pedal. The hand lever is positioned to the right of the Whip. The foot pedal is usually on the footboard to the left of the Whip's left foot. A series of shafts and joints connect the foot pedal or hand lever to the brake blocks. Application of either of the former results in the brake blocks being pressed against the tyres at the front of the rear wheels at, or a little below, axle height.

On the Continent, and in France, the brakes are often applied by means of a wheel-and-screw action. This method is not favoured in England as the Whip has to move his position on the box in order to apply the brake.

Some gypsy waggons in England also have the wheel system of applying the brake but as the average speed is around three miles per hour this method is then satisfactory.

A few two-wheeled vehicles built for use in hilly country have brakes working on a lever principle. It is more usual for a single horse to hold back a two-wheeled vehicle with the breeching than for it to be fitted with brakes.

Brake Block
Some were made of iron but these were not found to be entirely satisfactory as they were inclined to slip when pressed against the tyres, also the noise was considerable. Their main advantage was that they did not wear out quickly. Brake blocks of wood were made to fit iron brake block sockets, so that spares could be kept. Chestnut was favoured owing to its toughness. Soft woods wore quickly, but were easy to replace. Oak was as noisy as iron, being too hard. Wooden blocks covered with leather or strips of rubber were used and still are. Solid rubber blocks were invented by Mr I. Offord in 1885 and were made to fit the iron sockets for easy renewal. *See* Brake.

Brake Lever
The lever is one of the means by which the brakes of a vehicle are applied. It is a long-handled metallic bar, the bottom of which is jointed to a shaft leading towards the brake blocks and the top of which is rounded to accommodate the hand comfortably. The lever rests in a rack situated to the right of the coachman, just outside the seat rail. On one side of the rack is a row of ratchet teeth to hold the brake in the desired position.

The brake is released by exerting a slight outward pressure on the lever and put on or off by pushing the lever forwards or backwards depending on the design. It is claimed that a brake which goes on in a forward direction is preferable. A greater force can be applied as the arm is straightened away from the body when more pressure is needed on the brakes, than if the arm is pulled back when hard braking is necessary.

Branch
The sides of a curb bit to which the mouthpiece is fixed and the reins are buckled are called the branches. A bit with a movable mouthpiece has about an inch of square-shaped branch on which the mouthpiece can move up and down. For horses inclined to catch hold of the branch in their lips an elbow bit it used. This puts the branches out of reach.

Branch Pull
A type of pull which branches from the hame clip eye, or trace ring, to join the hames at two points, in some cases forming a kind of triangle. The designs of branch pulls are extensive and some are extremely ornate.

Brass

A copper-zinc alloy which is used for buckles on harness, handles, rein rails, catches and shaft fittings on vehicles, but should never be used for anything requiring great strength as it is likely to bend and break. Such items as hames, hame chains and tongues of buckles should be made of iron or steel and have brass plated on to them. *See* Hames.

Break

Also spelt Brake.

Breaking Cart

For the single horse this is a two-wheeled, long-shafted and strong vehicle with a low centre of gravity, suitable for the training of young horses. It is usually built to the specification of the trainer and there are numerous designs. The shafts must be made of a solid material and be long enough to keep the horse's heels well clear of the front of the vehicle should he start to kick. The forward-facing driving seat must be railed at the back and sides and there should be adequate purchase for the feet. The groom's seat must be easily accessible. For the four-wheeled version *see* Skeleton Brake.

Breaking to Harness

Almost any equine with a tractable temperament can be trained for driving. Animals which are notoriously bad in traffic or inveterate kickers are probably best left alone as they are not likely to give much pleasure for private driving, even if the trainer does manage to persuade such an individual to go in harness.

The time which it takes to break a horse to harness can vary from a couple of weeks to a year, depending on the animal's temperament.

The method which is suggested below has been well tried and tested on a large number of horses including Ali who took ten months from the onset to his first show ring appearance. His daughters who were home bred, in comparison, took fourteen and seventeen days from when they were first lunged until they were put to the breaking cart. Two Connemaras who make up the writer's four-in-hand took two and three weeks to when they were put to for the first time. They, too, had been with their trainer since they were foals and had been well handled, from the time that they were born, by their breeder.

The average family pony which has been Pony Clubbed, gymkhanaed and eventually out-grown, will probably adapt to harness quite readily. It is likely that he will have been adorned with fancy dress costume, or played cowboys and Indians, so pulling a cart is unlikely to cause much concern providing that he is carefully introduced to his new employment.

A strong and sound set of harness is essential as old harness is likely to give way under the first resistance.

A lungeing cavesson, two twenty-eight feet lungeing reins, a lunge whip and a roller are necessary.

A sound, light, two wheeled cart is also needed.

Whether the animal is already broken to saddle or being started from scratch to be trained for both riding and driving, which can be done concurrently, it is essential that absolute obedience is achieved during the early stages.

In order to obtain this, the animal should be lunged in an enclosed school which can be constructed by using two existing corners of a field and putting up hurdles, or a similar barricade, on the other two sides. The school should measure about sixty feet across. Small schools result in horses becoming unbalanced, leaning on their trainers' hands, and progressing on three sets of tracks, instead of two, in a desperate effort not to fall over. The animal stiffens and the stride becomes short and hurried instead of long and relaxed.

It is important to build up mutual confidence between the horse and the trainer and to overcome the language problem which automatically exists between equine and human. It is this preliminary training which establishes the essential ground work upon which all future training is based.

The writer is frequently asked how she teaches her animals to stand unheld whilst putting tandem to. The answer is that they were trained to halt on command as two year olds on the lunge and from there they learnt to stand whilst being put to in single harness. The obedience has become second nature.

So, the pupil is taught to walk, trot, canter and halt to left and to right. It is essential to always use identical words of command so that confusion is avoided. All forward going paces are best produced with sharp encouraging tones of walk-on, trot-on, go-on and the slowing down paces achieved with longer quieter words like ste-e-ady, wa-a-alk, and tro-o-ot. The writer always uses whoa, said in a commanding tone for stopping as it is the word which she would shout in an emergency such as coming up to a cross road and having to stop immediately.

The word of command in starting from halt is best prefixed with the animal's name so that he grows to recognize his identity. If more than one horse is being trained with pair, tandem, unicorn or team in mind, it is best if the names are dissimilar so that when, in a team, one horse is slacking or fooling around, he can be verbally chastised and will recognize his name. This can save a lot of trouble for the Whip particularly in having to unfold his whip to reach a leader.

It is a good idea, later on, when the stage of going out for drives has been reached to say, 'Are you ready?' to the horses before giving the command 'Walk on'. If more than one horse is being driven obviously there is not time to say four individual names such as Raz, Libby, Retto, Ben, Walk-on, as this would lead to confusion. However, the command 'Are you ready?' will bring all four horses to attention, in preparation for 'Walk on' and they will all go off as one saving problems for the Whip and grooms and discomfort to the passengers.

All the above should be borne in mind when the early lungeing is taking place as the words of command can then be taught from the beginning. It is for this reason that it is often so much easier to have a youngster from a foal. Mutual confidence will be built up and it is fearlessness which results in the best horses.

Frightened horses are usually the ones which cause trouble and heartache to their trainers. Confident animals can give enormous pleasure.

When the pupil is completely obedient on the circle on the lunge, in a cavesson, he can gradually be introduced to the harness. It is best to put on just one piece at a time. He should first be taught to wear a girth and for this purpose a stable roller is useful. This should be put on fairly loosely to start with. Some horses object violently to having anything round their middle and if the roller is girthed up too soon the horse may hump his back, stiffen his legs, jump forward like a kangaroo and even throw himself onto the floor. Once a horse has thrown himself down because of too tight a girth he will quite likely do it for the rest of his life. Horses may not always be highly intelligent but they do have elephantine memories. If the horse is of a type which requires the roller to be left loosely fastened then a breast girth must be added to prevent the roller from sliding backwards towards the stifles. This would cause it to act like a cinch such as is put onto a rodeo horse, to encourage bucking, which is not the object of the operation. It is quite a good plan to leave the roller on the horse in the stable for an hour or so before taking him out to work on the lunge.

Providing that the obedience has already been thoroughly established, the addition of a roller will probably not cause too much trouble.

As soon as the pupil is working calmly in a roller, he can be introduced to a crupper. This, too, is best put on in the stable. It is essential to ensure that the crupper dock is soft as a hard dock may lead to kicking. It is a good idea to cover the dock with sheep-skin if the animal is of a sensitive type. Again, the horse is probably best left in the stable for an hour or so wearing his roller and crupper before being taken out on the lunge. A roller is preferable to a driving saddle because a saddle will suffer a broken tree and bent terrets if the pupil is left alone and decides to roll to remove his uncomfortable straps.

Work on the circle is again repeated. The horse is quite likely to clamp his tail down onto the crupper. He may buck and kick but he must not be hit, or shouted at, because these resistances are being caused by fear, and chastisement will only make matters worse. It is best for the trainer to try to ignore these escapades. The pupil should be kept going forward at all costs and in time he will settle. On no account should the trainer progress to the next stage until the horse is absolutely calm and obedient whilst wearing the roller and crupper. Some equines take weeks before they fully accept these appendages whilst others do not mind and will settle in a day or so.

The next stage is to put on a full breeching. The loin strap is threaded through the crupper back strap and the seat of the breeching is placed round the hind-quarters. The breeching straps are fastened to the breeching seat rings on either side and then to the roller with another pair of straps or pieces of binder twine. It is essential to secure the breeching to the roller in this way otherwise if the pupil should start to buck the breeching will go flying upwards over his quarters. He will then have learnt, in one easy lesson, that if he wishes to remove an un-wanted appendage all he has to do is give one mighty kick and he is freed. This may then be put into practice when he is first put to a vehicle with disastrous and expensive results.

When he has accepted, fully, the girth, crupper and breeching, then a driving saddle can take the place of a roller as it will no longer be necessary to leave the horse in the stable in his breaking equipment. A collar can be put on next.

Either a breast collar or a full collar can be used, depending on availability. It is better by far to use a breast collar if a correctly fitting full collar is not to hand. Care should be taken, if a full collar is being used, that it is put on skil-fully. A young horse can become very frightened if a tight collar is forced over his eyes. The hames are put on next, and the traces passed through the shaft tugs. They can then be wound round themselves two or three times to shorten them and the breeching straps can be passed through the crewholes and buckled. This will keep the breeching and traces neatly in place. It will also give the pupil a slight feeling of collar and breeching pressure as he goes forward.

An open (riding) bridle can now be put on and the horse taught to work on the circle in all his harness, on long reins. The type of bit used will obviously depend on the age of the horse and his standard of education. A cheek piece snaffle is a useful bit for a young horse as he learns to turn more easily with the help of the cheeks. The lunge reins should be buckled to the bit and passed through the hame and saddle terrets. The position of the trainer in long reining on the circle is very important. It is essential to follow the horse with the hands and in order to achieve this the footwork is important. A dead unsympathetic hand quickly results in an overbent horse and a ruined mouth. The trainer should position himself slightly behind the centre of the horse and walk in a small circle in the centre of the school as the horse works round the perimeter. If the trainer steps towards the horse's head he will quite likely stop the young horse who will then probably turn to face him. This may be followed by a further half turn and the reins will go round the horse's chest. One more turn from the horse and the reins will rapidly pass along his body and round his quarters. The horse resembles a well tied parcel and he is in complete control of his trainer. He has only to plunge forward to free himself. This drama is avoided if the trainer keeps to the golden rule of positioning himself level with the animal's hips during the early stages of long reining. Later, when the horse is trained, he will continue to go forward regardless of where his trainer is placed because he understands what is required. It should be remembered that the inside rein on the circle governs the bend and the outside the pace. So, in slowing down, there should be slightly more pressure on the outer rein than on the inner one. However, the horse will be controlled mainly by the voice so there should not be much need for strong contact on the mouth. In fact, a calm well trained horse will go round on the circle on long reins with the reins hanging in a slight loop between the saddle terrets and the trainer's hands. The weight of the reins will create adequate contact.

When the horse is accepting the long reins, he can be taken for walks and long reined along the roads and tracks where he is likely to be driven in the early stages in a cart. The open bridle gives him a chance to have a good look at all the things which might otherwise have frightened him when he is first put to. It is so important to build up complete confidence in his trainer and surroundings.

The pupil can now begin to learn about pulling a load. The traces are passed through the tugs and on through the breeching rings. A second pair of old traces should be tied with string to the ends of the first pair and left to drag along the ground. The ends should be tied together at the crew holes otherwise the traces will fly in the air if the horse should become frightened. The breeching straps should be tied to the shaft tugs as before. The horse can be worked on the circle on the long reins and later can be taken out along the lanes dragging the traces.

When he is completely confident of the sounds and sight of the traces dragging along the ground through puddles, leaves, gravel, twigs and similar frightening noises he should be put into a blinkered bridle and the work can be repeated. If the long reins are passed through the hame and saddle terrets it is a good plan to fix an extra lunge rein onto the bridle which goes directly to the trainer's hand, as an insurance policy. Then, if the horse should get irretrievably tied up in the long reins in a moment of panic, the trainer will have the lunge in order to keep hold of the pupil. One foolproof method of fastening the lunge is, for a left handed circle, to pass the buckle of the rein through the bit ring on the near side before taking it up over the horse's head and down to buckle it onto the offside bit ring. This produces a type of gag snaffle action which is extremely effective for controlling a pulling horse. The usual methods of attaching a lunge rein to the bit often result in the bit being pulled through the horse's mouth if he should jump sideways.

It can take a young horse quite a long time to gain confidence in a blinkered bridle and the trainer is advised to execute extreme care and sympathy during the early stages. If the pupil becomes frightened it may take months before he is calm enough to progress further.

As soon as the horse can be long reined in all his harness both on the circle with complete obedience and out on roads and tracks he can be introduced to pulling a light load.

A medium sized motor tyre is a useful object and preferable to a log which if large is too heavy and if small is inclined to bounce up and hit the horse's hind legs. A chain should be passed round the tyre and secured with string. Rope round the tyre is of little use as it chafes through in a matter of minutes and the tyre is left lying on the ground. A piece of string or thin rope is passed through the chain and over the string which is tying the trace ends together. The trainer has the long reins and lunge in one hand and the rope from the tyre in the other hand. The horse is then told to walk on. Providing that he has a quiet temperament and his basic training has been correctly carried out there should be little trouble. Of course, if drama is anticipated it is helpful to have an assistant to hold the rope to the tyre and the trainer can then concentrate fully on the long reins and lunge. Work should be restricted to the walk on the circle. A faster pace can result in the tyre becoming air bound. It then swings dramatically sideways and can cause considerable panic to both the pupil and the trainer. As confidence, at the walk, is built up and the tyre can be tied to the traces with a quick release knot, the horse can be taken out along the now familiar lanes pulling his tyre. It is quite a good idea to dwell on this work for some weeks in order to build up confidence. There is no reason why a strong two year old should not be taken to this stage as there is no strain and nothing but good is done in building up a bond between trainer and horse. The pupil will learn to stand unheld whilst being put to the tyre and will later stand unheld whilst being put to his vehicle even when under the stress of a show or event. A sound basic training pays dividends in the long run.

Eventually the day comes when the horse is put to a vehicle. A two wheeler is safest owing to the fact that a four wheeler will articulate and may then turn over if the horse has to be pulled to one side, whereas a two wheeler will pivot on its inner wheel and follow the animal round.

On no account should the trainer attempt to put the youngster to a vehicle without competent help, however quiet he may appear. Things can go wrong with alarming speed and there is very little which is more frightening than a loose horse with a cart behind him. A heap of wood, a pile of straps and a ruined animal is a sobering thought.

When the time comes to put to, it is advisable to warn everyone on the premises of the proposed plan so that someone does not choose that very moment to start up a chain saw or let the dogs out.

The horse should be worked on the circle until he is slightly tired and completely relaxed. If the weather turns hostile then the plan should be postponed until another day. High winds or driving rain are unlikely to encourage calmness for the horse or the trainer.

The vehicle should be positioned facing a wall, garage door or similar high barricade.

The horse can then be brought up in front of the shafts and placed with his head facing the door. The trainer and assistant should each hold a lunge rein going directly from their hand to the bit. It is quite a good idea to attach these reins in the method earlier described so that greater control is achieved. The trainer pulls the cart forward by the nearside shaft whilst holding the lunge and the shaft is run through the tug. At the same time, the assistant must direct the offside shaft through the offside tug. The assistant should concentrate his full attention on holding the horse whilst the trainer hooks on the nearside trace, the offside trace, buckles the offside breeching strap, the nearside breeching strap and tightens the belly band, in that order. A kicking strap can be passed from one shaft over the quarters through the crupper back strap and down to the other shaft if additional precaution is deemed necessary. A piece of webbing does very adequately for a kicking strap if the proper equipment is not available.

The next step is one of greatest importance. Owing to the fact that the horse is facing a barricade, he has to start by turning when he is told to 'Walk on'. This can create problems if the management is not correct. For the first time in his life he will find that as he tries to turn he is restricted by a shaft against his right ribs and quarters and another pressing into his left shoulder. So, the trainer must be sure to get hold of the shaft tip and pull the vehicle towards him. At the same time, the assistant must push his shaft round. This will help the horse through the turn. He can then be led forward and taken for a walk along the familiar lane where he has been pulling his tyre for the past few weeks. Gradually, as days progress and all, hopefully, goes well the reins can be taken up and the trainer can quietly mount whilst the vehicle is rolling. The assistant can still hold one of the lunge reins. Eventually, the lunge can be taken off and the assistant can mount. It will probably not be long before both trainer and assistant can put to, facing the open, in the direction of the desired progression and get into the vehicle in the normal way whilst the horse stands obediently unheld.

It is important to drive at the walk to begin with so that the horse learns to keep calm. He should be made to stand quietly after everyone has mounted and must not be allowed to rush off at a fast trot as soon as he feels that his driver has sat down. If this is permitted now, he may soon be standing on his back legs the moment that the reins are taken from the offside terret and this will probably result in an accident one day.

Hills are best avoided as steep upward inclines may make an unfit horse collar shy. His neck will soon begin to ache and he will find that he cannot pull his load any further. He will then probably stop and may even lie down or at the very least jib and refuse to go forward again. Once he has learnt how powerless his driver is, under these circumstances, he may be ruined for life. Similarly, steep downward hills may frighten him when he feels that his hind legs are being pushed from underneath and he may try to gallop off or start to kick.

Some people cannot avoid hills, owing to the terrain available, in which case it is probably best to take a strong assistant on the early drives. This helper can dismount, whilst the vehicle is rolling, so that the horse is unaware of what is going on, and push the vehicle from behind up the really steep slopes. For steep descents, a rope can be passed round the axle and the assistant can lean back and take some of the weight off the breeching.

It takes several months to build up the muscles on a horse's shoulder and neck so the drives should not be too long to begin with. It is far better to go out for just a couple of miles, in the early stages, every day, than to go for twenty-five miles once a week. A long drive with an unfit horse is almost certain to result in sore shoulders, aching muscles and maybe a ruined animal. He will never forget the discomfort which was caused by his new occupation and will grow to dislike his work instead of enjoy it.

Breast Collar
Also known as a Dutch collar and used extensively on the Continent. It is a type of collar having the advantage of being easily adjustable to fit various horses of a similar size but with differently shaped necks. This saves the need to keep a large number of full collars, and solves the fitting problem which endlessly arises. A breast collar consists of a wide padded strap passing round the front of the chest with a buckle at each end to which the traces and, in the case of some pair harness, the breeching, are buckled. This is held up by a narrow adjustable strap going over the top of the neck in front of the withers to which rein terrets are fixed. It is very important that this collar be adjusted carefully. One which is fitted too low will chafe against the points of the shoulders. A breast collar provides the solution when an animal's shoulders have been rubbed by an ill-fitting full collar, and work has to continue, as the breast collar will not touch the areas effected by the full collar. The main disadvantage of a breast collar is that it is not always satisfactory when it is used with a solid splinter bar or unsprung trace hooks. The movement of the shoulders with each stride, rubbing against the breast collar attached to a fixed means of draught, frequently causes friction resulting in soreness. This can be avoided by using swingle trees or sprung trace hooks which give as the shoulder goes forward. A breast collar is not suitable when heavy loads have to be pulled, as the weight tends to be localized rather than spread over the whole of the shoulder. If a pair is to be driven, a ring to which the pole strap is buckled is sewn into the lay on the breast strap.

Breeches
The breeches worn by the coachman and groom in livery should be close fitting. They should be loose enough to permit ease of movement but there should be no tendency to bagginess above the knees. They should be pulled on in such a way that the leg buttons lie in the slight hollow on the outside of the shin bone. The top button should be as near to the knee cap hollow as is possible and some authorities state that four breeches' buttons should show above the boot.

Garter straps should never be worn with boots in livery.

Breeching
This is the means by which a horse stops the vehicle when there is no assistance

Army Breast Collar

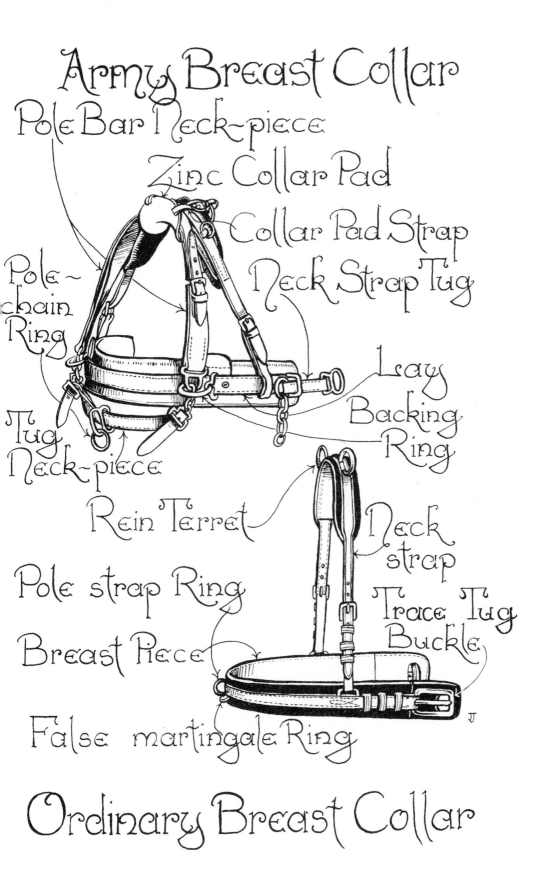

Pole Bar Neck-piece

Zinc Collar Pad

Collar Pad Strap

Neck Strap Tug

Pole~chain Ring

Lray Backing Ring

Tug Neck-piece

Rein Terret

Neck strap

Pole strap Ring

Trace Tug Buckle

Breast Piece

False martingale Ring

Ordinary Breast Collar

from a brake. Few two-wheeled vehicles have brakes, so a breeching is necessary. There are three main types of breeching. The simplest is known as a **false** breeching or Brown's patent. It consists of a fairly wide padded strap stretching across the shafts about 8 inches from the dashboard. It is fastened through the dees of the shafts by a small strap on each side passing through a figure-of-eight metal fitting at either end of the padded strap. On descending a hill or pulling up, this strap goes against the horse's quarters enabling him to hold the vehicle back. The second, and most commonly used type of breeching, is now known as a **full** breeching and used to be called 'short breeching'. It combines breeching with a kicking strap. The wide padded breeching body passes round the quarters about a foot below the dock, being held in position by a loin strap going through a slot in the back strap of the crupper. The height of the breeching is adjustable by means of buckles on each side attached to small straps coming up from the breeching body to join the loin strap. At either end of the breeching body is a ring through which a breeching strap is looped. This goes round the shaft through a dee placed halfway between the false breeching dees and the tug stops. The third type of breeching has the padded breeching body and loin strap and is known as **long** breeching. The breeching body is stitched to a breeching strap which is slightly narrower than the traces, continuing forward, alongside and under the traces. For a pair, or team wheelers, the ends are buckled to the trace tug buckles under the traces on each side. In pulling up, as the pole goes forward, the pole straps, kidney links and collars are pushed forward putting pressure on to the trace tug buckles and then the breeching. For single harness, the ends of the breeching straps are buckled to the tugs on each side and the same principle applies. This method is not fashionable now. With high-quality harness, the loin straps, breeching straps and shaft straps are made of two layers of finely stitched leather. The padded breeching body has rows of patterned stitching. Working harness is often made from one layer of thicker leather with a minimum amount of stitching. The breeching for farm horses is sometimes called the Britchin.

Breeching Body
The part of the breeching which lies against the horse's quarters.

Breeching Dee
The metal staple which is screwed on to the shafts through which the straps of the breeching pass before being buckled. The dee or staple should be of the same metal as the other shaft and vehicle fittings and should match the lamps and furniture on the harness. A square of leather is laced around the shaft before the dee is screwed into position. This is to protect the shaft from wear caused by friction. Paint alone is insufficient as this becomes rapidly worn off.

Breeching Strap
The strap which passes through the ring on the quarter-strap of the breeching and then goes round the shaft and through the breeching dee or staple before being buckled. *See* Breeching.

Brett
An American open vehicle resembling a Barouche. The shallow body was hung on two elliptic springs in front and two elliptic and two cee-springs behind. The forward-facing rear seat had a folding hood. There was another passenger seat

facing the rear one which accommodated two more people. The body was entered by a step and a door and was driven from a high box.

Brett (Round bottom)
A Brett with a shallow body which was rounded on the lower side. *See* Brett.

Brewer's Horse
Just before the turn of the century it was estimated that about three thousand heavy horses were owned by the larger breweries in London. These were the most powerful of the heavies, consisting mainly of Shires standing about 17 hands 3 inches and weighing over 1 ton. It was usual for these horses to work either in tandem or as a unicorn team to haul their load which could be as much as 8 tons. The brewer's van weighed around 2 tons and when a full load of twenty-five barrels was carried, this amounted to 7 tons. The harness and the draymen made up the rest. In some studs the first feed was given at 2 a.m. and by 5 a.m. horses were out on the roads. Particular attention was paid to the condition of the brewer's horses' feet. Shoes were painstakingly made to fit each foot, dealing with individual requirements. Some stables had shoes carefully kept when they were worn out, to be repaired with a new toe or whichever part was necessary, so that a shoe which had suited a particular horse could be renewed identically and replaced.

Brewster
America's oldest carriage-building firm which was started in the early 1800s by James Brewster after he had completed his apprenticeship with Col. Charles Chapman. The New Haven business flourished and branches were opened in other cities including New York. He was succeeded by his two sons, James Brewster and Henry Brewster who formed two more establishments. Henry's business was known as Brewster of Broome Street and later as Brewster & Co. James B. Brewster was an inventor of many notable ideas, the greatest of which was the side-bar suspension. It was Henry's company which became the better known of the two firms. Out of the forty carriage-builders in the United States there were three which dominated and took one-third of the business. They were Brewster & Co, John Lawrence, who was the sales agent for Henry Brewster, and a firm called Wood Brothers. Later, Henry's son, William Brewster, joined the business. Then came the manufacture of motor car bodies built with the same care and attention to hand-finished products as had been paid to the carriages. In 1925 Brewsters were bought by Rolls Royce.

Brewster Wagon
A type of wagon which was built on simple lines by the famous American coachbuilders Brewsters of New York.

Bridle
This is made up from a number of component parts. The crown-piece passes over the top of the head, behind the ears, terminating in two points on each side. These pass through the brow band loops, on either side of the rosette dees, before buckling to the throat lash at the rear and the cheek-pieces at the front. Attached to the cheek-pieces are blinkers, their height being adjusted by these top buckles on the cheek-pieces. The width of the blinkers is determined by the blinker stays which fasten to a buckle on the centre of the headpiece. The lower

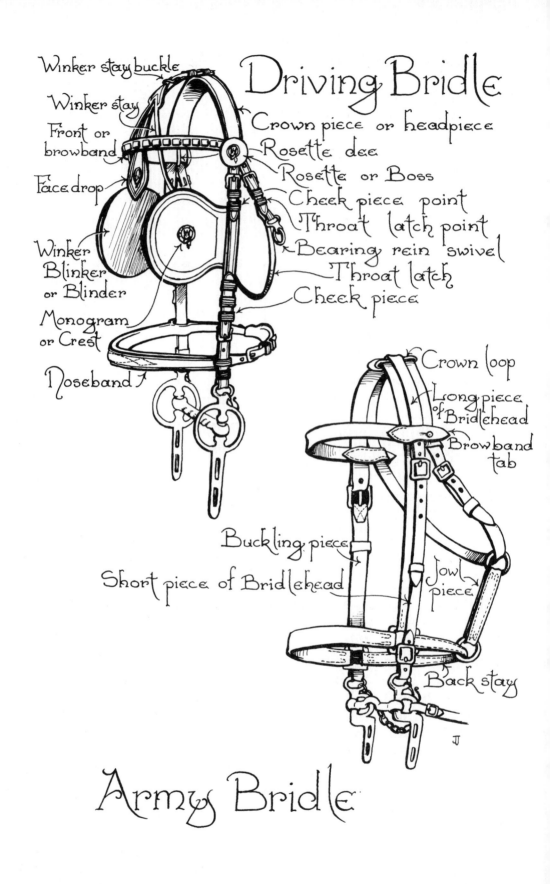

Driving Bridle

Winker stay buckle

Winker stay

Front or browband

Face drop

Crown piece or headpiece

Rosette dee

Rosette or Boss

Cheek piece point

Throat latch point

Bearing rein swivel

Throat latch

Cheek piece

Winker Blinker or Blinder

Monogram or Crest

Noseband

Crown loop

Long piece of Bridlehead

Browband tab

Buckling piece

Short piece of Bridlehead

Jowl piece

Back stay

Army Bridle

halves of the cheek-pieces are threaded through loops on the insides of the nose-band. They then go round the eyes or rings of the bit before coming up through the loops on the outsides of the noseband, after which the points are buckled. The height of the bit is altered at these lower buckles. Some bridles have bearing rein attachments, bridoon hangers and swivels. Some have a face-piece which lies between the blinker stays and is fixed to the centre buckle on the crown-piece, under the stays.

Bridlehead
The part of the bridle to which the bit is attached when referring to army harness. *See* Army Harness.

Bridoon
Another way of spelling Bradoon.

Brighton Road
During the first half of the 1800s numerous coaches ran on the Brighton Road, departing from and arriving at Castle Square, Brighton. They included the 'Regent', a heavy family coach driven by a coachman who did not like to hurry the journey and consequently took six and a half hours. Coaches from the Blue Coach Office were reputed to be safe and slow. From Snows, the White Coach Office, ran the 'Magnet'. Henry Stevenson, a gentleman coachman, who drove the 'Coronet' for the proprietor, Cripps, put on, in 1828, with Sir St. Vincent Cotton, a coach called the 'Age'. Horsed with a grey team this coach set a high standard of efficiency which was copied by some of the other proprietors. From Samuel Goodman's office the 'Times' departed at seven in the morning to arrive at Charing Cross at a quarter-past twelve. It left London at two in the afternoon to be back in Brighton five and a quarter hours later. There was also a 'Times' coach leaving both ends at four o'clock. Goodman, the proprietor, was a surly individual and his lack of civility soon cost him a considerable amount of business. In 1833 the 'Wonder', driven by a coachman called Capps, was set up in opposition to the 'Times', as it also left Brighton at seven o'clock but arrived in London half an hour before the 'Times'. The 'Quicksilver', a red-wheeled afternoon coach, was put on by the same proprietors. This was driven at one end by a fine artist, Bob Pointer, whose fault lay in an excessive liking for alcohol. To ensure that he reached his destination in a sober state all changes of horses had to take place away from public houses. The 'Quicksilver' was re-painted dark brown and re-named the 'Criterion' as a result of an accident which occurred when it was being driven by a young son of one of the coach proprietors of Castle Square. Horsed by a team of thoroughbreds, they took charge and the coach overturned. Passengers were thrown off and two landed on the spiked railings of the New Steyne Hotel. Luckily, though expensively, they survived their ordeal.

The coming of the Brighton Railway led to the diminishing of coaches on the Brighton road by the 40s.

Then came the coaching revival. A few amateur coachmen, recalling their early driving days on that road, started to put on coaches mainly for the pleasure of driving. Syndicates were formed to enable the losses sustained between run-ning costs and fares taken to be shared between these enthusiasts. In 1866 the

'New Times' was put on to the road by the Duke of Beaufort and Captain Haworth, being horsed by three or four different people who drove it whenever they travelled that way. This only lasted for a year. In 1888 the 'Old Times' coach, put on by James Selby, was running daily in sporting opposition to another daily coach, the 'Comet'. The 'Old Times' ran between Hatchetts, White Horse Cellar, Piccadilly, and The Old Ship Hotel, Brighton, going up on Mondays, Wednesdays and Fridays and down on Tuesdays, Thursdays and Saturdays. Sundays were rest days. On special occasions the return journey was completed on one day. As a result of a wager the double journey, 108 miles, was driven by James Selby in under eight hours, including all stops.

Britchin

On farm horses the britchin (breeching) is held up by two straps passing through the back strap of the crupper. The body of the breeching has short chains at each end. These are fastened by hooks on the rearmost ends of the same rectangular dees, bolted to the tops of the shafts, to which the chain backband and short hame chains are secured.

British Driving Society

Founded in 1957 to encourage and assist those interested in driving horses and ponies. The inaugural meet was held at the Royal Windsor Horse Show in 1958. Led by Mr Sanders Watney as President, the Society has grown beyond all expectation. Area Commissioners arrange meets and drives throughout the summer and film shows during the winter months. Driving classes and competitions are held at shows up and down the country every week-end during the season.

Britton Wagon

This was a modification of the Goddard buggy. The Britton Wagon was first built in 1872 to the design of John W. Britton of New York.

Britzschka

Also known as Britchka, Britzcha, Briska, Britzska and nicknamed Briskie and Brisker by post boys and coachmen of the 19th century, to get over the problems of spelling and pronunciation.

It was introduced from Austria in 1818 by Mr G. T. Adams and by 1837 was a common and popular travelling carriage. At first the body was built on a perch and hung from leather braces on cee-springs. Later, elliptic springs replaced the former. Like the Barouche it could accommodate four passengers when the knee flap was open and two when it was shut. There was a folding hood which went over the rear seat. In order to protect passengers from rain and draught a glass shutter was devised which let down between the area from the hood to the knee flap. When this was not in use it folded up into a recess in the hood. One of the main differences between the Britzschka and other carriages of that period was that the bottom line was straight instead of curved. This made it possible, once the front seat had been removed, for travellers on long and tiring journeys to lie full length. The driving seat at the front was low and could be moved if the vehicle was to be used for posting. On some there was a rumble seat at the rear which accommodated two people.

Broad-wheeled Waggon

Colloquially known as 'the snail of the King's highway', owing to its slow rate of progress which was between two and three miles per hour. This cumbersome waggon, loaded with goods and sometimes a few passengers who were unable to afford Mail or Stage Coach travel, was covered with a canvas hood to afford some kind of protection. It was hauled by four, six or eight heavy horses who were driven by a waggoner either mounted or on foot, armed with a long whip. At the front of the waggon hung a horn lanthorn. The first stage waggons were used in the 16th century. By the 1700s their numbers increased and Parliament became worried by the tremendous amount of damage that their narrow rims were doing to the roads which turnpike trusts had spent so much time and money improving. In 1753 a law was passed stating that waggon wheels had to be at least 9 inches in width. Any waggon owner found to have wheels which were narrower was fined £5 or had one horse and bridle confiscated. These 18th-century waggons were also referred to as Flying Waggons.

The name originated because this mode of conveying goods was far superior to the old pack-horse method. One waggon, or wain as they were sometimes called, could accomplish the work of five pack-horses. One, known as the Chester Original Flying Waggon, advertised in the 18th century that it left London every Saturday at 6 p.m. and arrived in Chester on the following Friday, early in the morning, taking over five days to complete the journey.

Brougham (Pronounced Brooam)

A 'close' (closed), four-wheeled, one-horse carriage which became exceedingly popular in the 1800s and which owed its name and original design to Lord Chancellor Brougham. He resolved that there was a need for a vehicle suitable for a gentleman, built on the lines of the street cabs which were, at that time, being used in London, the northern cities and Paris. He designed a conveyance which was a refined version of the street cab, stressing that it be light and handy enough for a single horse. With his plans he went to his coachbuilders, Messrs Sharp and Bland of South Audley Street. Accustomed as they were to building family coaches, Barouches and similar carriages of dignity, they were conservative in their ideas and put so many obstacles in the way that Lord Brougham took his ideas to a neighbouring firm of coachbuilders, Messrs Robinson and Cook. They accepted the commission and on the 18th May 1838 the first Brougham was completed. This original vehicle was heavy in comparison with those which were to follow in its wake. The olive green body was 4 feet long, narrower behind than in front and plated with iron to strengthen it. There was no arch between the body and the foot board. The wheels were small and heavy, the front ones being 2 feet 11 inches and the rear ones 3 feet 7 inches. There were elliptic springs in front and five springs behind. At the rear was a guard known as an opera board. The purpose of this was to protect the passengers from possible injury should the pole of a following vehicle penetrate the back of the Brougham, impaling those on the seat. This accident sometimes occurred in busy streets. There was a sword case for carrying weapons, a relic from the days of long-distance travel and the need for protection on such journeys. The inside was lined with silk tabaret. In 1840 this original Brougham was sold to Sir William Foulis who in turn sold it to Lord Henry Bentinck. He passed it on to Earl Bathurst. Mr Gladstone and Disraeli were amongst those who used it. Now this vehicle can be seen in the London Science Museum. The carriage was so much admired that the idea soon caught on and a fashion was created. In 1840 Messrs Thrupp built a similar edition.

During the ensuing years Broughams were made by all the carriage builders. They were built single- and double-seated, bow-fronted and square-fronted, the single horse sometimes gave way to a pair. Broughams appeared in lighter and neater forms replacing even the Cabriolet as a gentleman's carriage. Elliptic springs were used, as were Collinge's axles. This latter facilitated greasing which could be done quickly and easily by merely removing the hub caps. It was quite usual to have two sets of wheels. A rubber-tyred set would be used on London's wooden paving blocks and metal shod wheels for macadam roads. A luggage basket was designed for the roof. This would be removed when the passengers were to be taken to the theatre or to a party. The interior was fitted with such items as ashtrays, a clock, mirrors and a speaking tube so that travellers could convey their wishes to the coachman whilst in motion. The coachman would wear livery of an unobtrusive colour to harmonize with that of the vehicle. He might sometimes be accompanied by a footman.

Small two-seat Broughams, favoured by doctors, became affectionately known as pill boxes, partly on account of their size and partly because of their connection with the medical profession. At the turn of the century Sir Walter Gilbey had one made for postillion use. He disliked the front window being blocked by the coachman's seat. Sir Walter Gilbey also devised a means of overhead ventilation to enable tobacco smoke to escape without subjecting the passengers to a disagreeable draught.

Of all the coachbuilders, Messrs Barker were the firm most renowned for Broughams.

In 1893 it was claimed that the Brougham was the lightest of the close carriages, weighing only 17 cwt.

At that time, a single horse and Brougham could be hired from a London jobmaster for £200 a year if the hirer promised to keep within a seven-mile radius of Charing Cross. This was to prevent horses from being driven for long distances at a fast pace. The jobmasters used to claim that 'it is the pace that kills'.

Brougham Cab
A two-wheeled, single-horse, vehicle which was a cross between a Brougham and a Hansom Cab. The fully closed hansom type body could be entered from either side by curving, full-length, half-glass, doors. When these were opened they covered the front of the wheels, thus protecting the clothes from mud. The shafts resembled those on a Hansom Cab as they terminated at the front of the vehicle to which they were connected by iron brackets. The driver sat on a high seat at the rear of the vehicle which he reached by means of two back steps. The Brougham Cab was claimed to be especially suitable for medical practitioners. In the late 1800s the cost was from 60 guineas depending on furnishings and manner of building.

Browband
Also known as a front, it is the strap, going across the horse's forehead, which is

attached to the headpiece by a loop at either end. Browbands are often decorated with metal to match the mountings on the harness. The patterns of decoration are many and varied. They may also be bound with coloured tape or silk of the family or coach colours. Some are made of rolled leather. The purpose of the browband is to prevent the headpiece from slipping backwards down the neck.

Browband Tab
The flap on the outer side of the browband. *See* Army Harness.

Brown's Patent Breeching
Also known as False Breeching. *See* Breeching.

Brunswick
An American four-wheeled vehicle similar to a Surrey. The fringed top or awning over the two forward-facing seats was fixed. The body was hung on two elliptic springs and a perch. The sides only permitted the wheels to turn to a quarter-lock.

Buck
The lower part of the body of a vehicle.

Buckboard
An American four-wheeled vehicle with the seating built above and on to a single board going from the front axle to the rear axle. There are no springs but the board itself acts as a spring and the front bracing was made in such a way that jarring is minimized. Some Buckboards were built with several slats of wood instead of a single board. It is thought that the name was originally suggested by its ability to buck against uneven surfaces on the road and it was said that a Buckboard was more comfortable than imagined for long journeys and rough terrain.

Buckboards were constructed with one, two or three seats.

Buckboard Phaeton
An American hooded vehicle to seat two people. The shallow, tray-shaped body lies on a sprung board which is fixed to the front and rear axles. The wheels are of equal height and only a quarter-lock is possible.

Buckboard with Rumble
An American four-wheeled vehicle. The buckboard, which formed the floor, consisted of a single oak board, 87 inches long and 29 inches wide which was bolted to the front and rear axles. There were no springs. The front wheels were 40 inches high and only a quarter-lock could be obtained before they touched the sides of the buckboard. The rear wheels, between which was the rumble seat, were 45 inches high. The forward-facing, well-upholstered double seat from which the vehicle was driven, was mounted on a wooden platform just behind the front wheels. It was entered by a step placed inside the front wheel, which had to be turned slightly to permit easy access.

Bucket Seat Gig
A gig with two independent forward-facing seats, placed side by side and resembling the modern car-type seats.

Buckles
It is important, in the interests of uniformity, that the buckles on a set of harness should match for type, shape and metal throughout.

Buckling Piece
Part of the bridlehead. *See* Army Harness.

Budget
A leathered box, which was attached to the fore part of the carriage when the coach was to be used for travelling as opposed to town use. One containing such items as tools was known as a tool budget.

Budget Trimmer
A trimmer who specialized in leather work. *See* Trimmer.

Buggy
A four-wheeled American vehicle of which there are numerous designs. Some, like the Coal Box Buggy and Square Box Buggy, are named after their shape whilst others like the Elliptic Spring Buggy or Side Bar Buggy take their name from their suspension.

Bugle
The cross-bar which is used to hold up the pole when a pair is put to a two-wheeled vehicle such as a Cape Cart. The bugle lies just below the collars and is fastened to the harness. Also known as neck bugle, pole-bar and yoke.

Builders' Cart
A strong two-wheeled cart, made with an oak frame with elm sides and ash shafts, for transporting builders' materials. A model large enough to cart six hundred bricks could be ordered in about 1880 for between £14 and £20.

Built-up Brake
This had seating accommodation comparable to that of a Drag. The boot ran the whole length of the vehicle from the footboard to the rumble. The body was hung on a perch and telegraph springs.

Bull and Mouth, St. Martins-Le-Grand
A well-known City house owned by Mr Edward Sherman who, in the 1840s, had about 700 horses working in his own and the Mail Coaches. His coaches which included the 'Wonder', the Shrewsbury-to-London coach, were all painted yellow. He also horsed, under contract to the Post Office, the Edinburgh, Exeter, Glasgow and Leeds mails, getting other proprietors to horse them over some of the 'grounds'. The General Post Office Headquarters now stands on the site of the Bull and Mouth.

Bullet
Also called hame draught or pull. *See* Pull.

Burke
A well-known Hereford whip who, in 1839, drove a tandem team in a match against time completing forty-five miles in half a minute under three hours. The horses driven were both famous for having put up fast times in harness. The leader, Gustavus, had previously completed twenty miles in one hour and fourteen minutes. Tommy, the shaft horse, had put up a time of just four

minutes longer over the same distance. The match was driven over a five-mile stretch of road between Sunbury and Hampton which was covered nine times. To win the £100 bet the distance had to be completed in three hours.

Burnisher

When steel bits and pole chains were used they were cleaned with a combination of sand and emery cloth. This resulted in scratches which were then liable to rust easily. The solution to this was to rub the article with a burnisher, which is a pad of chain mail, mounted on a pliable backing, easily held in the hand. Energetic burnishing smooths the edges of the scratches helping to regain the original high polish of the makers' product.

Burr

The small round plate, made of iron, on the inside of the felloe, upon which the points of the iron pin is riveted after it has been driven through the tyre and felloe when a wheel is being shod.

Burton Waggon

The largest type of gypsy waggon, weighing approximately $1\frac{1}{2}$ tons. The front wheels are smaller than the rear wheels and all four lie directly under the gaily painted body. The wooden uprights between the planked sides are carved, as is the undercarriage, both for decoration and to lighten the waggon. Gargoyles frequently adorn the four corners of the roof and the rain is directed through spouts from their open mouths. Panels along the sides and below the roof are often painstakingly painted with birds and flowers. The owner's name some-times decorates the door in a painted edition of his handwriting. A small S-shaped ladder is carried to give easy access to the front door when the waggon is parked and the horse taken out of the shafts. At the back is a rack on which hay or luggage can be carried. The interior is fitted with a double bed across the rear which folds up when it is not needed. Fitted cupboards are arranged along one wall and an open range with a mahogany overmantle takes up the other wall alongside more storage facilities. The finest waggons have amber glass door handles and brass fittings.

A strong single horse is capable of pulling a Burton Waggon along level roads but additional power is needed for hills.

The brake is applied by a screw system with a handle on a small wheel.

This waggon is also known as a Showman's Waggon.

Business Buggy

An American four-wheeled, hooded buggy. The rattan-sided body had space behind the forward-facing double seat for samples.

Busman's Holiday. *See* Old John.

Butcher, Alfred

A fine tandem coachman of the early 1900s.

Butt-cap

The end of the hand-piece of the whip is covered with a plain metal butt-cap made of brass, silver or some other sort of white metal.

Butterfly

Slang term for a short-distance public coach.

Butterworth, Ninetta
A contemporary artist, well known for her delightful paintings depicting horses and carriages.

Buttons
The metal buttons on the coachman's and groom's livery should match the metal of the harness mountings. The buttons are round, about the size of a two-pence piece for the fronts and backs of the coats and a halfpence piece for the cuffs of the sleeves. They are frequently embellished with the owner's crest or monogram. A coachman's body coat is single breasted and has six buttons down the front and two pairs of two at the rear. One pair is just below the waist and the other pair is near the bottom of the skirt vents. A groom's body coat has either five or six buttons down the single-breasted front and three pairs of buttons down the back vents. One pair is a little below the waist, one pair a little above the bottom of the skirt vents and the third pair between the other two pairs.

Button Stick
A flat strip of metal or wood with a slot cut lengthways which is slid under the buttons on a livery coat to protect the cloth when the buttons are polished.

Buxton Bit
A curb bit for dressy or smart occasions with a pair or team and occasionally a single turnout. The Buxton bit has curving branches with two slots for the reins, one halfway down the bit and one at the bottom. Some have a slot just below the ring by the mouthpiece. A bar connects the bottom ends of the branches to prevent pair or lead reins from becoming caught under the bit. Mouthpieces of Buxton bits vary enormously, from the thick straight one giving a mild action to the extremely severe twisted mouthpiece with a high port surmounted by a ball with serrated edges. The outward appearance of a team in Buxton bits can be that all of the horses are identically bitted. On close inspection it can be found that all of the mouthpieces are totally different. *See* Bitting.

C.C.
Coaching Club.

Cab (abbreviation from Cabriolet)
The taxi of the 19th century of which there were many kinds. The two-wheeled Hansom Cab and the four-wheeled Clarence Cab were perhaps the most common.

Cab Drivers' Benevolent Association
Formed to provide shelters and eating places for cabmen, giving them some protection against wet and cold weather. These improvements in working conditions led to better cabmen.

Cab Fronted
Similar to the front of a Hansom Cab. The dashboard curves, as does the front

of the body, in a form which coincides with the shape of the horse's quarters. The shafts of cab-fronted vehicles usually end in front of the dash, and are frequently connected by iron supports forming a triangle from a bracket about a foot along the shaft, to the bottom of the front of the vehicle. Quite a number of vehicles were built in this way including the Morgan Cart and the Princess Cart.

Cab Horse

Towards the end of the 1800s, there were about 15,000 cab horses hauling Hansom Cabs and Clarence Cabs around the London district. A large number of these were imported from Ireland at the age of four years. They came over unshod and with their lips tied to prevent damage and noise. It took about eight weeks to acclimatize them after their journey. They were driven first in pairs, then single, around the quieter parts of London before being put to work in the heart of the City. The working life of a cab horse averaged three years. He worked a six-day week covering 200 miles, sometimes up to forty miles in one day. Brown horses were favoured for use in Hansom Cabs; greys were disliked, partly because of a whim of fashion and partly owing to the inconvenience of grey hairs getting blown back on to the dark clothing of the passengers. The only greys accepted were those for use at a stand based at a railway where cabs were hired, as they stood in order, and those greys which were outstanding in looks and action were chosen. Greys were acceptable in Clarence Cabs, however, as they were favoured by ladies. Housemaids often chose a grey, in preference to any other coloured horse, if they were going to hire a cab.

Cab Licence

All cabs, which plied for hire, had to be licensed annually. They were inspected for soundness before which they were frequently given a yearly coat of varnish. The cost of a licence in 1893 was £2 plus 15 shillings carriage duty payable to Somerset House.

Cab Man

Towards the end of the 19th century there were about 15,000 cabmen in London. They would collect the horse and cab from their cab master in the morning, leaving their licence as a type of deposit, and go out and pick up fares to return later in the day and pay their hire fee. Before being allowed to drive a cab, the cabman had to get a licence for which he was examined. The failure rate on the grounds of lack of knowledge of London was about one-third of those whom applied. The licence and driving badge cost 5 shillings and had to be displayed.

Cab Master

In the late 1800s there were over 3,500 cabmasters in London. Some owned just one or two cabs and two or three overworked horses, which they hired to cab men, whilst others had over a hundred cabs and horses. A few worked their own animals, taking a pride in their production.

Cab Phaeton

Invented and built in 1835 by Mr David Davies, a coachbuilder of Wigmore Street, London. The cab body was hung on four elliptic springs, the single horse was driven from a low seat in front of the passengers' seat. Up to the middle of the 1800s, the Cab Phaeton was a popular vehicle in England and on the Continent where it was called the Mi-lord. Then it became used as a hackney carriage on the Continent and lost its social standing. Later, a slightly altered version was brought back into favour when it became known as the Victoria. *See* Victoria.

Cabriolet

A two-wheeled vehicle which became extremely fashionable in the 1800s. It was originally imported from France and greatly improved by Count D'Orsay to whom it no doubt owed its popularity. The outline of the body was shaped like a nautilus shell with the hood to protect the driver and passenger from the weather and prying eyes. An apron of wood or leather stretched across the front of the travellers' legs adding further protection. The shafts curved considerably with the rear ends low, making access to the vehicle easier. A groom called a 'tiger' stood on a padded platform at the rear of the vehicle between the cee-springs, holding on by means of two straps. His presence necessitated that the hood be 'half struck' or 'set back' for if it were lowered there was not enough room for him. The Cabriolet was said to be greatly favoured by unmarried gentlemen for going out in, at night. It was more manoeuvrable than a four-wheeled carriage and only required one 'tiger' whereas a pair of horses needed a footman and coachman. The possession of a Cabriolet became a status symbol. Its great weight demanded an exceptionally fine carriage horse with quality, substance and showy action. For this reason, if the vehicle was used frequently it was necessary to keep two or even three horses. It was not suitable for long journeys out of town as the suspension was said to have caused some discomfort. An additional feature was a bell which hung from the horse's collar. As the Cabriolet was frequently used after dark, and travelled at considerable speed, the bell warned other road users of its approach.

Cabriolet (Four-wheeled)

Built in about 1845 in Paris and thought to be an ancestor of the English Victoria.

Cabriolet Phaeton

A four-wheeled vehicle much favoured in the early 1800s. It was built on four elliptic springs and driven from a high box. Behind was low seating for four passengers facing each other.

Cabriolet Springing

In the early 1800s this consisted of a combination of six springs. At the rear of the vehicle were a pair of cee-springs which were attached to the body by leather braces. Between the shafts and the axle were two double-elbow springs. Suspended from the shafts at the front of the body were two reverse-curved springs.

Cab Stand

A venue such as a railway station, where cabs waited to pick up fares. At the end of the 1800s there were about six hundred stands in London.

Cad

The boy who worked alongside the post boy, under the eye of the head ostler, in large stables of post horse proprietors and inn-keepers.

Calash. *See* Caleche (Canadian).

Caleche (Canadian Version)
A gig-type vehicle with a folding hood. It is driven from a small seat perched on top of the main dash, with a footboard and tiny dash in front of it. The body is hung on side- and cee-springs.

Caleche (French Version)
An elegant town carriage which is similar in design to a Barouche. It demanded superb horses, to match the grandeur of the formal work to which it was put.

Calesso
An Italian vehicle in which one horse was harnessed in between the shafts and a second horse was harnessed alongside, outside a shaft.

California
A type of four-wheeled wagon introduced by Kimball of San Francisco, U.S.A. The coal box body was hung on wooden springs and thoroughbraces.

California Mud Wagon. *See* Concord Mud Wagon.

Calkin
To give better grip on slippery surfaces, one or both heels of the hind shoes are turned downwards at a right-angle to form a small stud. If only one calkin is fitted to each shoe, then this is usually on the outer heel. The inner heel is made into a wedge shape by narrowing and thickening it, so that the heels of the shoe are level. Very often the toe, too, is thickened to the same height. Calkins used on inside heels can cause serious brushing.

Cambridge Port
A low arch in the centre of the mouthpiece of an otherwise straight bar bit.

Caned Whiskey
A two-wheeled gig-type vehicle with a scanty skeleton body which had cane sides, built by Felton at the end of the 18th century.

Canoe Landau
A Landau with a rounded-bottom profile when viewed from the side. *See* Landau.

Canopy Top
A fringed, flat-topped canopy is erected over many American vehicles, and a few English ones, to protect passengers from the sun. *See* Awning.

Cantle
The rear of the seat of a saddle. *See* Saddle.

Caoutchouc
Also called india rubber and is a gum which was imported from Ceylon and South America in the early 1800s. The gum was solidified into large squares for transportation purposes and these were then thinly sliced by a machine. Waterproof cloth was made by spreading the dissolved gum on to cotton, wool, linen or silk. This was covered with a second layer of cloth, which was heat-pressed, resulting in a water-tight and air-tight material. This was not resistant to grease and a rider's cloak would be damaged by the sweat from his horse.

Cap
Part of the collar which protrudes upwards in front of the top hame strap.

Cap Case
A large trunk which is fixed to the rear of the body of a travelling coach.

Cape
A waterproof garment covering the coachman's coat, going over the top of the apron and lying over the box cushion, so that rain is directed away from the driver.

Cape
Some collars have a flap of leather at the top to cover the sewing join. In dress harness, the cape is adorned with a crest. Working horses had their number stamped on to the cape to correspond with the number burned on to a front hoof and the number on a metal plate on the wall of their stable. This ensured that the horse always wore the correct collar and avoided sore shoulders leading to inability to work.

Cape Cart
A two-wheeled vehicle to which a pair of horses is put using cape harness. The name is derived from the Cape of Good Hope where the cart was introduced by the Dutch settlers and then extensively used by the English.

Cape Cart Harness
One method of harnessing a pair to a two-wheeled vehicle is by using Cape Cart Harness. The pole, which needs to be a little longer than a normal pair pole, is held up by a yoke made from a piece of lancewood about 5 feet long and 1 inch in diameter. The yoke can be attached to the pole about 18 inches from its end by means of a short strap with a ring at each end. The strap lies round the pole and the yoke is passed through the rings. As there is a certain amount of sideways, backwards and forwards play of the yoke against the pole, the centre of the yoke should be covered with leather to protect the wood from becoming worn. Breast collars with breeching are worn. The yoke is held up by straps running from the pole sides of the yoke, over the tops of the horses' necks alongside the breast collar straps, both of which are on leather pads, before being buckled to the outer ends of the yoke. The bridles, reins, pads, cruppers and quarter-straps are the same as with any usual type of light pair harness. This method is considered to be safer than curricle harness, as if one horse should fall he will not necessarily bring his partner down too.

Care of a Carriage
It was considered by coachbuilders of the 19th century that a carriage required as much care as the furniture in a drawing-room and that no gentleman should keep his vehicle anywhere that he would not place his wardrobe. The ideal carriage house should be kept at a moderate temperature similar to that at which the vehicle was constructed. The wooden parts of a vehicle are particularly susceptible to atmospheric conditions. If the building is too hot and dry, the wood will shrink and cracks will appear. Examples of this are in evidence with many museum-stored carriages. Dampness causes wood to swell and iron and steel to rust. Wherever the paint is chipped from metal surfaces, rust will quickly attack and work its way beneath adjoining paint surfaces. Brown rust

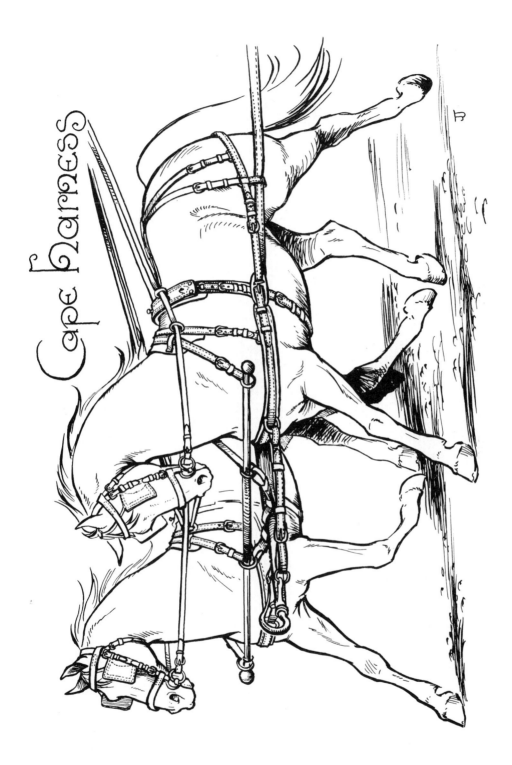

Cape Harness

lines frequently appear between the plates of the springs. If the atmosphere of the coach-house is damp, brass and other metal fittings will rapidly tarnish. Heads of vehicles should be kept up and be regularly oiled to prevent cracking as must other leather attachments such as braces and cushion straps. Axles and wheel plates should be greased at regular intervals according to the mileage covered. Cushions and soft trimmings are a delight to moths. In the 1800s it was usual to place cedar shavings and an india rubber cloth over the hammer-cloth to deter moths. It was suggested that cedar shavings could be advantageously added to the stuffing of cushions to protect them. India rubber cloth could not be used inside carriages owing to its disagreeable smell which was emphasized in warm weather. Now, the problem is easily solved with camphor moth balls which should be placed amongst the cushions and inside closed carriages which are being stored. Vehicles should not be kept near stables or manure heaps. The gases are harmful to varnish and cause it to crack. Neither should they be left by a window or open door exposed to the direct rays of the sun.

After use, the carriage should be liberally hosed to remove mud and grit. Leather parts should be kept as dry as possible as excessive water is harmful. The vehicle should then be dried with a chamois leather taking care not to get oil from shackles and wheel plate on to the chamois. It is best to keep a separate cloth for the oily parts. The wheels will benefit from hosing as this will prevent any shrinkage caused by dry and sunny conditions.

Cariole
A Canadian sleigh built to accommodate two people on the rear seat. It is driven from a small low seat in front of the passengers' feet. The driver is protected from thrown-up snow by a curving dash which is surmounted by a rein rail.

Carnation
A yellow carnation is the flower worn by British Driving Society members at their meets.

Carreto
Sicilian carts are made of exceptionally ornate design and are gaily painted. The body of the cart is carved, as are the wheels. The harness for a horse to such a vehicle is equally colourful, being embellished with decorative stones, glass and plumes.

Carriage
This refers, strictly speaking, to that part now commonly known as the under-carriage or chassis.

Carriage Association of America
Formed in 1960 and by 1973 had over 1,200 members scattered all over America, Canada and various parts of the world. The Association is responsible for the quarterly publication of *The Carriage Journal*. Every year a conference is held in a different part of America when members get together to hear experts speak on a variety of subjects ranging from the restoration of carriages to dressage driving.

Carriage Builders and Harness Makers Art Journal
A profusely illustrated periodical, published in the 1800s, in which the carriage builders and harness makers advertised their products, inventions and ideas. It also contained articles from contributors.

Carriage Clock
Numerous types of clocks, in rectangular brass cases, with a handle at the top, were in use in the 1800s. Faces varied from the ornate enamelled ones to those with plain white porcelain. As the inside of the carriage, at night, was dark, and luminous dials had not yet been thought of, many carriage clocks were made to strike at the quarter-hour. In some cases, this strike was followed by the strikes of the preceeding hour so that no doubt was left in the minds of the passengers as to what time it was.

Carriage Convenience. *See* Coach Pot.

Carriage Dog. *See* Dalmatian.

Carriage Horse
Ideally, his conformation compared favourably with that of a high-class hunter although straightness of shoulder was acceptable in a carriage horse. The size and type of horse varied to fit the work required. A pair used in a light phaeton would be smaller and better bred than a pair in a chariot when horses of seventeen hands with a considerable amount of Cleveland Bay, Yorkshire coach horse and Clydesdale blood would be mingled with that of the thoroughbred. Although many such horses came from Yorkshire, a number were imported from Germany. The élite of the single carriage horses was the Cabriolet horse who combined as near perfect conformation as could be found, with plenty of showy action. Many carriage horses were privately owned but at the turn of the century about eighty per cent of those in London were hired for the season from jobmasters.

Carriage Jack
A simple jack can be made from two pieces of iron, a chain, and an iron peg. One piece of iron, 2 inches by $\frac{1}{2}$ inch with holes punched at 2-inch intervals, about 3 feet high and mounted on a strong square base forms the upright. The lever is of the same dimensions but has a flat piece at one end which goes under the axle. Beyond this flat is a loop in the metal which passes over the upright and is secured at the desired height by a peg in holes both in the lever and on the upright. Extending from the loop is the lever and handle part. The flat part is placed under the axle, the lever is pressed down and the vehicle is easily lifted. The chain on a hook on the handle is hooked to one on the stand to hold the jack in position.

Carriage Maker
The undercarriage, as it is now called, was made by the carriage maker who was employed for £2 or £3 a week by the carriage builder. The work was heavy and required exactness although excessive delicacy was not necessary as the large scale lines absorbed any minor inaccuracies. Elm and ash were frequently used, often in conjunction with iron work prepared by the blacksmith.

Carriage Stepping Block
A block made from stone, iron, brick or wood and used for both mounting a carriage and a horse. Stepping blocks were manufactured in a multitude of designs all of which, by climbing two or three small steps on to a platform, enabled a lady to mount gracefully into her carriage. There was frequently a post with a ring to tie the horse in such a way that the carriage was lined up with the block when the horse was tethered. This left the driver free to help the lady.

Carriage Stone. *See* Carriage Stepping Block.

Carri-Coche
This was also known as a Cart Coach and was used by the natives of Buenos Aires. The closed body had sliding glass windows and was entered by steps through a door at the back. It was hung on two straight shafts and two wheels by two braces of untanned hide which was twisted into cords. For town work, one or two postillion horses were used. Sometimes three horses abreast were put to.

Carrier's Horse
Various types of van and dray horses were used for collecting and delivering goods from and to the goods' yard of the railway stations. Those animals which were used for trotting work were lighter than those used for walking. The carrier's horses were usually English, farm-bred animals selected for their good legs and feet and tough constitution. They were at least five years old before they were subjected to the rigours of heavy loads in London streets. The railway horses worked a six-day week, resting on Sundays. Owing to the strain imposed on them in starting heavy loads their working life was only about four or five years.

Carryall
A type of light Rockaway with curtained side quarters and a fixed top, which is found in America.

Carrying the Bar
When one of a pair works harder than the other, his bar is always slightly ahead.

Cart
There are numerous types of Cart, named according to the area in which they were designed or built such as Essex Cart, Norfolk Cart, etc, or by the coach-builder's name such as Morgan Cart, etc, or by the purpose for which they were to be used such as Tennis Cart, Luggage Cart, etc. Dog Carts were used for transporting sporting dogs. Donkey Carts and Goat Carts were built to be pulled by those animals. *See* details under individual entries.

Cart Horse Parade
A parade in London, which first started in 1886, of heavy horses and carts used for commercial purposes. Awards were given to those reaching the required standard of good condition and turnout with the object of improving the care of London's working horses. *See* London Harness Horse Parade.

Carting
When a heavily laden cart has to be hauled by two horses in tandem, the carter drives them by walking on the near side of the shaft horse's head. He holds the

reins of the shaft horse by the bit, in his right hand, and the reins of the lead horse in his left hand.

Cart Saddle
A heavily padded square-shaped saddle, fastened by a narrow girth on the near-side, is used for farm horses in shafts. Across the centre of the saddle is a deep wooden groove in which the chain backband lies. The horse takes the weight of an unbalanced load on his back. At the front of the saddle, on each side, is a strap to which the collar is buckled, preventing the collar from sliding down the horse's neck when he is feeding.

Carver
Workmen of varying skills at carving were employed by the carriage builder. The lowest paid were those whose job it was to carve mouldings and beadings for the body frame and undercarriage. At the other end of the scale were those highly skilled craftsmen who designed and carried out ornamental carving such as that of hind standards, blocks and the ends of timbers.

Cary
Author of *High Roads*, a map of the road for travellers of the 1800s.

Case, A
Referring to an accident in olden coaching days.

Castle Square, Brighton
A location where coach offices were as numerous as other houses. Every morning and evening people gathered to watch the arrival and departure of the coaches. *See* Brighton Road.

Catching a Double Thong
When driving a tandem, unicorn, or team, it is essential to have a whip with a thong which is long enough to reach the leader in question. When not in use, the thong has to be caught up in a double thong on the stick. This is a difficult art to achieve and is best practised on foot, before being attempted whilst sitting on the box behind a team. The aim is to have the loop of the thong hanging down about 2 feet 6 inches at the end of the whip with which the wheelers can be encouraged without the whip being unfolded. The rest of the thong is wound round the stick a few times at the top end, by the loop, and then held straight alongside the stick and twisted a couple of times round the handle where it is held under the thumb to prevent it from unintentionally unfolding. The best way to learn how to fold a whip is to draw an 'S' on a wall and stand on a platform, in front of the wall, to raise the body above ground level. The stick is held in the right hand with the end of the lash secured under the thumb. The 'S' is traced with the point of the whip starting at the bottom left hand side. The whip is then swept from right to left and upwards and then to the right and downwards. If successful, this will result in a loop at the top of the whip and a few coils of the thong round the stick from right to left. There will be a small loop at the centre of the whip with reverse coils at the handle end. These must be undone or the whip will become unfolded.

The stick is now brought down across the body and held by the left thumb whilst the right hand uncoils that part of the thong and winds the lash round the hand part of the whip. This is then held under the right thumb to prevent the whip from slipping undone.

Cattle
Coaching term applied to horses.

Cedar
A coarse-grained and exceedingly porous wood which was brought over in the 1800s from America. It was not employed for areas where a paint surface was required but could be used for panels which were to be leather covered.

Cee-Springs
First used in about 1790 as an improvement on the whip-spring. It consists of a curved spring shaped to form two-thirds of a circle. The bottom straightens out and is bolted to the block on the bed securing the spring in a vertical position. At the top of the curving spring is a leather brace by which the body of the vehicle is suspended.

Centre Framing Piece
A longitudinal member used in the attachment of the wheel plate or fifth wheel to the body of a four-wheeled vehicle.

Centre Hook
The hook on the pad, on to which the bearing rein is hooked.

Centre Terret
On the wheelers' harness of a team there is a centre terret, higher than the ordinary pad terrets, which surmounts the centre hook. It is through this terret that the lead rein passes.

Chain Backband
This chain is permanently fixed to the large rectangular dees which are bolted to the upper sides of the shafts on a farm cart. The weight of a load of a two-wheeled cart is taken on the horse's back through the backband chain, which lies on the centre of the cart saddle.

Chain Draw
The Australian term for the draught arrangement which consists of a swingle tree attached to the splinter bar by two leather straps. Chains are taken from a central ring on the swingle tree down to the axle on each side by the springs. This method of draught is far better than fixed trace hooks, which can cause chafing if a breast collar is used as the swingle tree gives with each stride.
   This is also known as a Swingle Tree Attachment.

Chain Gears
When two farm horses are working in tandem to haul a heavy load, such as a cart of mangolds, out of a muddy field, the leader wears harness known as chain, plough or sling gears. The traces, which go from the large flat hooks on the hames to eyes at the tips of the shafts are made of chain. A stretcher is placed between the traces directly behind the horse's back legs. The pad consists of a wide leather backband to hold up the traces and is fastened on the near side by a narrow girth. A strap connects the collar to the pad, on each side, to prevent the collar from sliding down the horse's neck if he should put his head down. There is also a hame rein which buckles to the bit and is looped over the horn of the hame to prevent the horse from lowering his head too much. A crupper is

used to prevent the pad from being pulled forward by the collar. A blinkered bridle and snaffle bit are usual. The bit is usually made to unhook on one side so that it can be removed when the horse is given his nosebag or a drink. The reins pass from the bit, via the pad to the carter's left hand. The shaft horse is controlled with the right hand as the carter walks alongside his head on the nearside. The above harness is also worn for such work as ploughing and harrowing. For this purpose, rope lines replace the leather reins.

Chain Horses
The swing team, or centre pair, in a team of six frequently has a chain between them instead of a pole which is why they are sometimes called chain horses.

Chain Team
The centre pair of a team of six. *See* Chain Horses.

Chair Back Gig
This vehicle was favoured at the end of the 18th century but its popularity did not last for many years. The body resembled a cabriolet and was suspended on elbow springs at the front. The rear was hung on leather braces from whip or cee-springs.

Chaise
Taken from the French word 'chair' and used generally in the naming of various vehicles such as the Post Chaise. In the 1800s numerous French designs and ideas were copied in England which inevitably led to the common use of French words in describing that which became generally accepted as an English vehicle. The Char-à-Banc is a classic example.

Chaise, Lady's
A low-two-wheeled hooded vehicle which originated in France. Its forward-facing seat and easy access made it suitable for a lady.

Change of Horses
In the heyday of coaching, no time was wasted over a change of horses between stages. On a fast coach, such as the 'Wonder', the change from an old team to a new one, was made in less than a minute. The average time for a change with the 'Defiance' was $1\frac{1}{2}$ minutes or less. At the turn of the century it was usual for the guard and two horsekeepers to be responsible for the change. If it was a wet day or an exceptionally fast change, the coachman would remain on the box. Then, in order to gather the reins he would hold his whip forward, and, one at a time, they would be thrown up over the whip by the grooms. The coachman could then retrieve each rein as he tipped the whip upwards and the rein slid down towards his hand. If only one horsekeeper was available, then the coachman had to help the guard. Two or three minutes was considered adequate time for a normal change of horses.

In 1897 at The New York Horse Show, a change was made by two contestants, in the ring, in 58 seconds.

James Selby's fastest change during his match against time, in 1888, took 47 seconds.

The record for a 'competition' change was held by Miss Brocklebank until 1963 when it was beaten during a contest held at The Royal International Horse Show at White City. The four grooms of the 'Red Rover' Road Coach, driven by Mr Sanders Watney, changed the teams in 45 seconds. The time was taken from when the wheels stopped turning with the incoming team to when the wheels started to turn as the new team was driven away.

Chapman Cab. *See* Chapman, John.

Chapman, John
Secretary of the Safety Cabriolet and Two-Wheeled Carriage Company. He was aware of the shortcomings of J. A. Hansom's early cabs and so he designed an improved cab and sold the patent to the Hansom company who put their name to the cab. It was claimed that the Hansom Cab should have been called the Chapman Cab.

Char-à-Banc
The first Char-à-Banc to appear in England was presented by King Louis Phillipe of France in about 1842 to Queen Victoria. It was a high open vehicle with four forward-facing seats, each accommodating three people. The name Char-à-Banc came from the translation 'Car with Benches'. Within a few years many were being built. They varied considerably in design but all seated a large number of people, and were used for country or holiday pursuits. One very large type was designed for public use, seating up to thirty people for sight-seeing and similar expeditions. Some of these huge conveyances had a rear staircase leading to the high seats. Some had an awning to protect the passengers from the weather. These massive vehicles were said to have had excellent road-holding capacities, resulting in popularity with members of the younger generation in trying their hand with a team. Some proprietors, over enthusiastic in their advertising gimmicks, put phoney bodies on to these Char-a-Bancs and called them coaches. These became known as Bastard Coaches.

In contrast to the huge public vehicles, were the small Char-à-Bancs favoured by owners residing in country mansions. They were used on sporting occasions when it was desirable to transport a large number of people. Easy access was provided to the central seats by means of folding steps and doors.

Some Char-à-Bancs were suspended on a perch with mail springs, others on four elliptic springs and no perch. Later, even smaller ones were made for use with a pair.

Char à Côté
An unusually designed Swiss vehicle built long and narrow for the narrow mountain roads. The three passengers sat side by side, facing the left-hand side of the road, under a hood and covered by a leather apron. The driver sat directly behind the horse's hind legs with his feet almost on the road. Luggage was stowed on a board by the rear wheels.

Chare
An early vehicle which was thought to be the forerunner of the chariot. One described by a poet, before Chaucer, was said to be covered in red velvet, and finished in gold with blue and white damask, to convey a lady out hunting.

Chariot
There are records in The Old Testament of Chariots being used. In the Book of Genesis, Joseph was said to have travelled in chariots. Later, chariots were em-ployed mainly in battle, for which purpose scythes were fixed to their wheels to

Parts of a Chariot

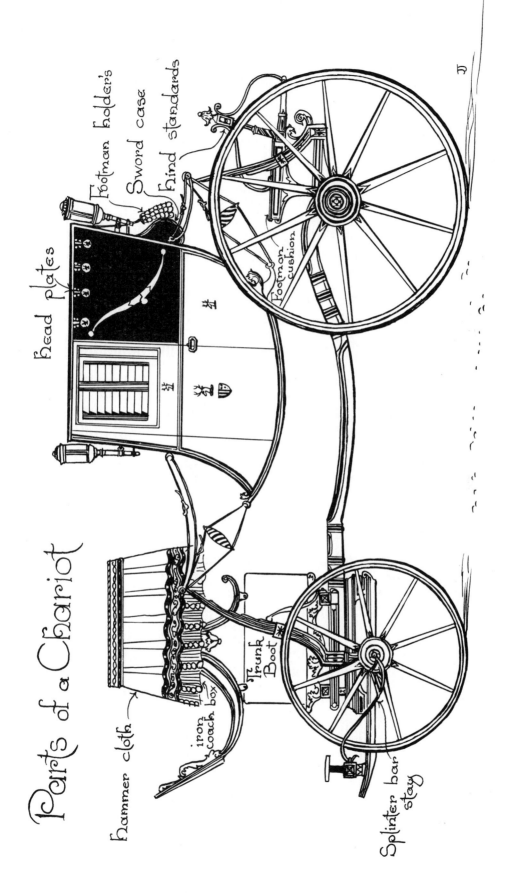

Head plates

Footman holder's

Sword case

Hind standards

Footman cushion

Hammer cloth

iron coach box

Trunk Boot

Splinter bar stay

injure anyone coming within range. The Romans and the Greeks developed chariot racing into a sport. Numbers of horses were harnessed abreast in various ways. The method of putting a pair to a chariot was similar to the method later adopted with a Curricle. Yokes were attached to the pole and secured to padded saddles on the horses. Further horses were put to, alongside, with ropes. A Grecian chariot with a pair was called a Biga, with three horses abreast a Triga, and a Quadriga when four horses were put alongside each other. Nero was said to have ridden in a Decemjugis which was a Roman chariot with ten horses abreast.

Chariots of the 18th and 19th centuries differed considerably from those just mentioned. These later Chariots were all basically uniform in shape and became known under different names according to their varying purposes and appointments. There were State or Dress Chariots, Town, Travelling and Posting Chariots. Also there was the Post Chaise and 'Yellow Bounder'. All had four wheels and were built on a perch. The body was closed and hung on four whip-springs which were later replaced by cee-springs. The Chariot was entered by a full-length, half-glass door from either side. The single seat accommodated two people and faced forwards so that the occupants could look along the road on which they were travelling. This view was only possible when the pair or team were driven postillion. When the chariot was driven by a coachman, his seat rendered the front window useless.

The State or Dress Chariot of the early 1800s was a superb vehicle of dignity and elegance used by noblemen for State and Court occasions. The vehicle was built for strength which is why quite a large number are still in existence. The panelling and doors were made of mahogany which was painted in the family colours. Arms embellished the doors and crests the quarters. The box seat was covered with a magnificent hammercloth, of a colour to blend with the body and which was trimmed with braid, fringes and tassels. The family arms were embroidered in silk or metal in the middle of this hammercloth. The body was luxuriously trimmed with Wilton carpeting and braid on the blinds. The undercarriage was decoratively carved and gilded. To this splendid Chariot would be put a pair of fine bay horses wearing heavily ornamented harness with armorial bearings on every available space such as the blinkers, pads and quarter-straps. The housings of the harness were of a colour to match the panelling and hammercloth of the Chariot. The coachman wore state livery as did the two footmen who travelled on a platform behind the body, hanging on by means of holders made from braid and tassels.

A fine example of a Dress Chariot may be seen in The Science Museum in London where one which was built in 1850 for the Earl of Caledon is on show.

The Town Chariot was similar in design but not as dressy. There was less carving and gilding, the hammercloth, though still trimmed with braid and fringes, was not as colourful. The panels of the vehicle, the harness and the liveries still bore the crest or monogram of the owner, but were of a more sombre hue.

The Travelling Chariot, or Private Posting Chariot, was an expensive and luxurious means of travel, employed by the wealthy when long journeys were to be undertaken at speed. When those of less fortunate circumstances would have travelled by Mail or Stage Coach and the poorer still by the cumbersome

68

wagons, the rich used their own Travelling Chariot. The box would be removed and luggage carried on a platform below where the coachman's seat had been. The horses were driven postillion and two servants frequently rode on a seat behind the body, between the rear springs.

The Post Chaise was a means of transport available from posting inns along main roads throughout the country for those who preferred to travel in privacy, rather than share a coach with numerous passengers. These vehicles were usually Travelling Chariots which had been cast out of a gentleman's coach house when they were no longer required. They were purchased by innkeepers and were frequently painted yellow which is why they were colloquially known as 'Yellow Bounders'. A Post Chaise complete with horses and post boy could be hired from a posting house for 18 pence a mile. If a four-horse team and two boys were required, the fee would be 3 shillings a mile. Changes were made in much the same way as with the coaches, though usually not at the same inns. Horses and postillions could also be hired by gentlemen travelling in their own Chariots. They would usually horse the first part of the journey themselves and then hire for the remainder.

Chaser
His job was to emboss the required design on to such metal parts of a carriage as the customer desired. Arms and crests on door handles and axle tree ends were common requirements. The weekly wage earned by an average chaser was 2 guineas although a skilled designer earned more.

Chatter of the Bars
The noise created by the 'dee' of the main bar, on the pole hook. *See* Lead Bars.

Check Brace Rings
With many of the early four-wheeled carriages, whose bodies were hung on whip- or cee-springs by leather braces, it was necessary to deter the body of the vehicle from swinging too violently backwards and forwards. For this purpose, there were rings on the front and back of the body, through which leather straps were passed connecting it to the heads of the springs.

Checkerboard Team
Also known as a cross team.

Check Rein
In America the bearing rein is often referred to as a check rein. Also known as overhead check, overdraw and Kemble Jackson.

Cheek
On which the box seat of a vehicle such as a Drag is constructed.
Also known as a riser. *See* Parts of a Drag.

Cheek
The branch of a curb bit which extends downwards, to which the reins can be attached in a variety of fittings according to the desired severity. *See* Bitting.

Cheek Leather
A piece of leather cut in the shape of a circle with a slit from one side to the centre, where there is a hole large enough to fit the mouthpiece of the bit. The leather is passed over the mouthpiece and laced on to the bit, either with thread

or a leather lace. The purposes of cheek leathers are: to prevent sore lips, to take up any surplus width if the bit is too wide and to deter the horse from catching the bit in his lips. Some cheek leathers have bristles on the inside to prevent the horse from leaning to that side and assist in turning away from that side.

Cheek-Piece Buckle. *See* Bridle.

Cherry Rollers
Metal balls on the mouthpiece of a bit which are made to revolve as the horse moves his tongue. They encourage salivation and assist in preventing a puller from setting his jaw.

Chopping
In turning a team, American style, the leaders are given the office to turn by either set of reins being pulled to the desired side. This is known as chopping. *See* American Stage Driving.

Chopping
When a horse was hit, with the whip, on the thigh instead of between the collar and pad in the accepted manner.

Circular-fronted Van
A four-wheeled open van with a light and strong railed body having outraves which made it a suitable vehicle for carrying brewers' barrels or similar goods. The body was hung on four semi-elliptic springs and was designed to allow the front wheels to pass under the vehicle enabling it to turn in its own length. The makers, Hayes & Son, claimed that it was impossible to overturn this van. The front of the body was rounded in a forward curve with the driver's seat attached, by iron stays, above the rail of the arc. The footboard protruded over the horse's quarters.

Towards the end of the 19th century the cost of this van was between £45 and £65 depending on whether it was built to carry 2, 4 or 6 tons and be drawn by a single or a pair of horses.

Clanwilliam, Earl of
Said to have imported from Germany the first Britzschka, a vehicle which he favoured on account of its lightness.

Clarence
A pair-horse town vehicle, which is a cross between a Brougham and a Coach. There are seats for four inside. The vehicle is coachman driven from a low box.

Clarence Cab
A one-horse version of the Clarence, in use in the mid-1800's, driven by a cabman plying for hire. It was considered more dignified to travel in this four-seater, closed carriage, than in a dashing Hansom Cab and also the roof afforded plenty of accommodation for luggage. Also known as a Growler.

Clarence Patent Loops
Harness loops or keepers which were made of either nickel or brass, instead of the more usual leather.

Clarence Rockaway
A cross between an American Clarence and an American Rockaway. The top of the closed body continues over the low box seat which is built into the front

of the vehicle. The body is hung on elliptic springs with an arch under the driver's seat for the front wheels to turn.

Clencher Tyre

The type of rubber tyre which is now used on vehicles for private driving as it is more satisfactory than the wired-on variety. The solid rubber tyre is forced into position in the iron channel which goes round the felloes and the rubber is held by the concave shape of the channel.

Rubber tyres are not recommended for the marathon and obstacle phases of Combined Driving Events. The sideways strain to which they are subjected in speed competitions and the deep ruts and sharp turns on the cross-country courses, frequently force the rubber from its channel. During the past two years, numerous competitors have come through 'the finish' with rubber tyres held into channels by hame straps and reins from the spares kit.

Iron tyres are now replacing rubber for F.E.I. and similar competitions.

Cleveland Bay

One of the oldest breeds of English horses which originated in Yorkshire. Cleveland Bays were used with thoroughbreds to produce the Yorkshire Coach horses which were favoured in the 1800s. The Cleveland Bay throws stock which runs very true to type. These clean-legged horses are strong, sound, of pleasing appearance and always bay. The only markings allowed are a small star on the face and a few white or grey hairs around the coronet or heels.

H.R.H. The Duke of Edinburgh drives a team of Cleveland Bays in F.E.I. Combined Driving Events.

Clip

Now more commonly known as 'U' bolt. It is the 'U' shaped metal fitting which is used to attach the spring to the axle. The inverted 'U' goes over the spring and axle, being secured by nuts on the threaded ends below the axle. Between the spring and the axle is a block of wood. By replacing small blocks with larger ones, the vehicle can be made to accommodate a slightly taller horse.

Closed Carriage

A general term for a carriage built to protect passengers from bad weather, such as a Brougham. One particular vehicle in the Science Museum, London, is listed as a Closed Carriage and is thought to be an example of a type of small vehicle in use during the middle of the 1800s, by professional people such as doctors. It is built like a four-wheeled Dog Cart, in many ways, with four elliptic springs and an arch under which the front wheels turn. The single horse is driven from the forward-facing seat as in a Dog Cart. The rear, backward-facing seat is covered by a solid hood in which there are two side windows and a window behind the passengers. Two doors close in front of the travellers' legs, making the rear of the vehicle resemble a two-wheeled Hansom Cab.

Close Top

A folding hood or head. Also known as a Victoria Top.

Clubs

Numerous driving clubs sprang up once amateurs began to get the taste for driving a team. In 1807, the Bensington Driving Club was formed and in 1808 The Four-Horse Club was founded. It was also known incorrectly as the Four in

Hand Club, The Whip Club and The Barouche Club. The Bedfont Club took the name of the Bensington Driving Club. The Richmond Driving Club was formed in 1856. The still-flourishing Coaching Club began in 1871 and the popular British Driving Society was started in 1957. *See* Combined Driving and Tandem Club.

Club the Reins

When driving a team, with the reins in two hands, American style, to club the reins is to take all of the reins in one hand. *See* American Stage Driver.

Clydesdale

A native breed which originated in the middle 1700s in Scotland. He is a strong animal, standing about 16 hands 2 inches with a quantity of hair about his legs. The colours of brown, bay and grey roans predominate with a lot of white on the legs, often well up to and including the knees and hocks. The blaze frequently extends over the nose to cover the sides of the muzzle. A white patch on the belly area of the girth is common with horses of this breed. Clydesdales were favoured for farm and heavy haulage work on account of their placid temperament and great strength.

Coach

It is thought that the first coach was used in Hungary in the town of Kotsee, from where it took its name. Some people claim that the first coach to be made in England was one which was built in 1555, by Walter Rippon, for the Earl of Rutland. Others say that it was the coach which a Dutchman, called William Boonen, brought from Holland in 1564 for Queen Elizabeth. The first State coach was made by Walter Rippon, and used in 1571 for the Opening of Parliament. By 1580, coaches were being used by those who could afford such a luxury. In 1601 a Bill was read in Parliament in an effort to prevent excessive use of coaches. It was thought that they were effeminate and it was feared that their use would lead to a deterioration of horsemanship if men persisted in travelling in a coach, in preference to riding a horse. The Bill was, however, rejected. By 1640 the first Stage Coaches were being used. They were excessively slow and uncomfortable owing to impossible road conditions. By 1706 the turnpikes and improved roads had led to faster journeys with better-bred horses. There was a considerable advancement in coachbuilding. Springs were introduced to make travelling more comfortable. In 1784, the first Mail Coach was put on the road and by the end of the century, the number of Stage and Mail Coaches had greatly increased. Private coaches were used by the rich. Coaching reached its peak between 1815 and 1840. This period became known as 'The Golden Age of Coaching'. Then came the decline of coaching when business gradually faded as the railways sprang to life.

Coach Box

Some coaches, built for use in towns, have an open framework, known as the coach box, fixed to the beds on which is mounted the coachman's seat and hammercloth. This was preferred by some designers to the more usual Salisbury Boot.

Coachbuilder

He was, in many ways, an engineer as well as a builder of carriages. The coachbuilder had to be capable of supplying a vehicle which was elegant, strong and light. It had to be built in such a way that it would withstand the rigours of being driven at varying speeds over rough roads, in rain, snow or sunlight whilst heavily laden, without disintegrating. Large coachbuilders very often specialized in one type of carriage, as did Messrs Barker with their famous Broughams. A coachbuilder was responsible for combining the work of many craftsmen, such as artists, bodymakers, carvers, curriers, draughtsmen, japanners, joiners, painters, smiths, sawyers, trimmers, wheelwrights and many others. All of these people worked to produce an essential part of the end product. London coachbuilders were generally considered to be superior to those in country villages. However, many country craftsmen turned out vehicles of high quality.

Coach Horn

Guards of the Mail and Stage Coaches blew a 3-foot horn, made of copper, tin or brass, to warn others on the road of their rapid approach. This horn was known as 'a yard of tin' and, the standard issue from the Post Office was made of this metal. Mail Coach guards, in particular, used it as a way of telling people to 'make way for the Mail'. Its sound warned the turnpike keeper to have the gates open so that the Mail would not be delayed. Ostlers at inns, where horses were to be changed, would hear the horn and have the new team positioned in readiness, saving valuable seconds. The horn also provided a certain amount of light entertainment, relieving boredom during the journey. Four notes could be achieved and numerous melodies were played by those proficient in the art.

During the coaching revival more people became interested in horn blowing. They discovered that by lengthening the horn to 4 feet, more notes could be blown. Horns were carried on private Drags by members of such clubs as The Four-in-Hand and The Coaching Club. Drivers of sporting tandem carts found a shorter horn a more convenient length for their smaller vehicles.

By the end of the 1800s a New Model horn was in use. The narrow tube with a bell-shaped base, replaced the original gradual tapering shape of the early Mail Coach horn of the late 1700s. The New Model was about 4 foot 4 inches long, though some were even longer.

Coach Housings

The pads made from a coloured cloth or leather which are put under the driving pads of a pair on the rare occasions when it is deemed correct.

Similar, but larger editions are used by costers for single turnouts.

Coaching Club

A revival in coaching amongst amateur four-horse whips, and the fact that the existing Four-in-Hand Club was filled to overflowing, caused Mr George Goddard and Lt Col Henry Armytage to form a committee in 1870 and the Coaching Club was founded. The opening meet was on Tuesday, 27th June 1871 when twenty-two coaches met at Marble Arch and most of the members drove via Hyde Park, Piccadilly, Pall Mall and The Embankment to The Trafalgar, Greenwich where they had dinner. Throughout the past hundred years regular meets and drives have taken place. The still-flourishing club now has Lt Col Sir John Miller as President and Mr R. A. Brown as Secretary.

Coaching Inn
The hotel upon which travellers relied for a meal, accommodation, a change of horses and the numerous other necessities during a journey in the coaching era.

Coaching Revival
The coming of the railways, gradually brought an end to coaching. Then, in the 1860s, there became a growing interest amongst amateur coachmen and the period of the 'Coaching Revival' was born.

At first, a few Stage Coaches were put on to the road during the summer months. Enthusiasm spread and syndicates were formed. Numerous subscription coaches ran on the old stage coach roads. These coaches became known as Road Coaches in order to differentiate them from the Private Four-in-Hand Coaches of the time.

Coach Makers and Coach Harness Makers Company, The
The Livery Company in the City of London.

Coachman's Coat
A single-breasted coat with buttons down the front and two pairs of buttons at the rear. The coat tails should be stitched for about 5 inches below the top button so that the tails do not fly apart. The coachman's coat has pocket flaps on false pockets just above the hips. His coat is slightly longer than that of the grooms, coming just above the knees. *See* Buttons.

Coachman's Elbow
The salute given, by one coachman to another, in passing, in which only the right elbow is raised. The whip remains in the right hand as the hat is not removed. *See* Salute.

Coachman's Overcoat
A double-breasted coat with two rows of buttons. It is made either of the same colour as the body coat or can be of drab cloth. To afford maximum protection it is long, reaching halfway down the legs.

Coach Pot
A specially designed chamber pot, carried in a closed carriage, for the use of ladies (also known as a carriage convenience), and generally referred to as a 'Bourdalou' which means 'hat band'. Since they were most probably carried by ladies' maids, in containers not unlike hat boxes, this may account for the name.

Coach Racing
A practice which developed between coachmen during 'The Golden Age of Coaching'. It was mainly carried out between coachmen of coaches leaving the same starting place at the same time and bound for the same destination. Great competition was aroused to cover the distance in a faster time than the coach of the opposition. Reports are given of Stage Coaches going at nineteen miles an hour. This inevitably led to accidents with coaches overturning and passengers being injured. Fines were imposed on coachmen for furious driving though this apparently did little to deter their sport.

Coach Retarder
Another word for Brake.

Coal Box Buggy
An American four-wheeled vehicle with a hooded forward-facing seat for two people. The profile of the body resembles a coal box from where it got its name.

Coal Horse
He was a strong heavy dray type with Shire and Clydesdale strains predominating, being similar in make and shape to a carrier's **'walking'** horse. The coal horse was five years old before he was subjected to the strains of work in London where he hauled loads of coal of up to 3 tons, six days a week. Hills were avoided if possible even if a detour was necessary. When it was essential to heave a load up a steep hill, two or three coal carts would congregate at the bottom and the horses would be put to, in improvised tandem or random, to pull each cart to the top.

Coates, Romeo
An actor of the early 1800s well known both for his hilarious rendering of Romeo on the stages of Bath and London theatres and for his Curricle, often seen in Hyde Park, which was garish in the extreme. The body of the vehicle was beautifully shaped resembling the outline of a classic sea god's car but was ruined by being made of polished copper and by being covered in shells and large brass crowing cocks accompanied by the owner's motto 'While I live I'll crow'. The harness on the pair of white horses put to this vehicle was similarly and profusely adorned.

Cockade
These were introduced into England from Germany at the time of George I and originated in the 'brooch' or fastening of three-cornered hats.

The wearing of a cockade is properly restricted to servants of the Royal Family, when it is circular and larger than that worn by other servants.

The servants of officers of the Army, Navy (and by implication, the Air Force) are entitled to wear cockades, as are those of Lord Lieutenants and Deputy Lieutenants as civil retainers of the Crown. This cockade is oval and smaller than the Royal one and only that pertaining to Army officers should have a fan. Other dignitaries holding office under the Crown, right down to J.P.s have been tacitly conceded the cockade although not strictly entitled. Retired officers are probably not really entitled to it but no one has ever disputed their continued use.

The black cockade is the badge of the House of Hanover and the white one is that of the House of Stuart, though the latter is now obsolete.

Cockades appropriate to other countries are of different colours, i.e. the tricolour for France and red for Spain, etc.

Cock-eye
The oval-shaped steel, or stainless steel, fitting attached to the end of a lead trace by which the trace is hooked on to the lead bar hook. It is so named because the profile of the metal is said to resemble the shape of a woodcock's eye. *See* also Spring Cock-Eye.

Cock Horse
An extra horse, put on in the lead at the front of a team to assist in pulling a heavy load up a hill. The harness worn was a blinkered bridle, a collar, traces, a

saddle (the cock horse was always ridden) hip straps, a crupper and a pair of straps going away from the back strap down to a bar on to which the traces were fixed. A rope was attached to the centre of the bar and passed between the leaders before being hooked to the pole hook.

Cocking Cart

A sporting, two-wheeled vehicle of the late 1700s, suitable for tandem driving on account of its high seat. The shape of the body was similar to the box seat and front boot of a coach. The Cocking Cart was said to have been used for taking cocks to the Main (cockfight) but there is some doubt about the authenticity of this theory.

Cockshoot, Messrs Joseph & Co

A Manchester coachbuilding firm established in 1844. Twenty years earlier they began as proprietors of Hackney Coaches and in 1836 started coachbuilding.

Cocktails

Slang expression for horses which have had their tails docked.

Coffin Cab

A slang term given to a type of cab used in the first half of the 1800s because its solid upright hood made it resemble a coffin. It was also noted for being a dangerous vehicle in which to travel.

Collar

The collar is the pad going round the horse's neck, accommodating the hames to which the traces are attached. It is through this that the horse is able to do his work and therefore essential that the fit is perfect. The collar is the part of the harness to which the greatest care and attention must be paid, and that which causes the most headaches to the Whip.

There are a number of points to be taken into consideration when a collar is fitted. Horses with sloping shoulders are far more difficult to fit than those with straight shoulders. The latter have a larger bearing surface for the collar to lie against and it is less likely to ride upwards when the animal is in draught. The width of the chest must be noted, as must the amount of fat and muscle on the neck. Very often, a collar which fitted perfectly when the animal was an under-developed four-year-old no longer fits when the horse is a maturing six-year-old. In fitting a collar, care should be taken to see that it is flat against the neck at the sides, but does not pinch. There should be room for the hand to pass freely between the bottom of the collar and the windpipe when the horse is standing with his head in a normal position.

Collars vary tremendously in type and shape. There is the straight collar, favoured by some who claim that it is less likely to rub. More flattering is the lighter, curved collar which follows the shape of the shoulder and then lies back towards the withers. This bent back collar gives an illusion of a greater length of rein and is preferable for showing purposes. It is more difficult to get hames to fit a bent collar. The hames lie in the groove between the after wale and the fore wale. The bend of the hames must coincide accurately with that of the collar, otherwise they will slip. If they do not fit they will tend to alter the shape of the collar which fitted until the hamestraps were tightened. With a straight collar, any straight hames, providing that they are within an inch or so of the correct length, will fit.

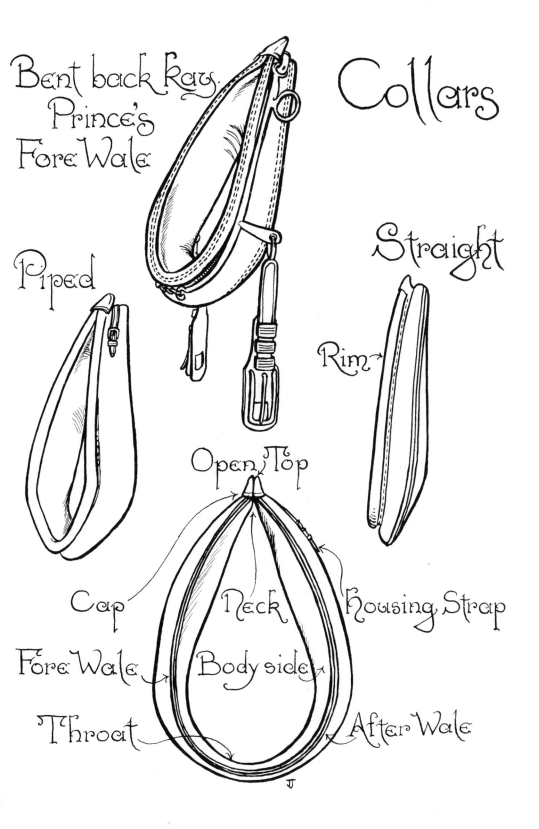

Bent back Kay.
Prince's
Fore Wale

Collars

Straight

Piped

Rim

Open Top

Cap

Neck

Housing Strap

Fore Wale

Body side

Throat

After Wale

The Kay collar, also known as the Prince's Wale collar, is the smartest type of bent collar. Viewed from the front the lining is brought round to the front of the forewale. This is met halfway by the outside covering of the forewale which is edged with three rows of stitching. The rim collar has the outside covering of the forewale continuing right round to meet the lining, forming a complete rim.

For exhibiting, when the vehicle to be pulled is light, and supreme elegance is sought, a bent Kay collar shows the horse off to the greatest advantage.

If the load to be pulled is heavy, or the distance great, a wider straight collar is preferable.

For light work, collar linings are usually of russet leather or very soft patent leather and are easily cleaned. Collars for working horses are normally lined with wool or serge. These materials absorb sweat readily, but they have to be thoroughly dried and brushed after use, otherwise sore shoulders soon occur.

Outsides of collars can be made of russet leather for use with brown harness or black or patent leather for black harness. It is quite usual for polished brown collars to be used with black harness in a Road Coach or Dog Cart.

A collar made of rush or sedge was often carried on the side of a Road Coach as a spare.

A false collar is a piece of leather, shaped to fit under a collar to protect the shoulders of a horse who is new to harness work, or unfit and soft.

During the late 1800s, an air-filled collar was in use, known as the Alpha Air Collar. It was made by the Alpha Air Horse-Collar Company, 9 Eagle Place, Piccadilly Circus, London. It was filled with air by means of a small screw opening. The makers claimed that the collar immediately adapted itself to the shape of the shoulder when in draught. It was said to be cool, resist sweating and prevent galling.

Towards the end of the 19th century, an elastic collar was patented by the Elastic Horse-Collar Company, 72 Summer Row, Birmingham. According to the makers, it was being used by the Fire Brigade, Omnibus and Railway Companies amongst others. It comprised a hame-shaped hollow collar of steel with internal springs. It was easily adjustable to fit any horse's shoulders and the springing prevented concussion from sudden jolts. The draught hooks and hame rings were fixed to the outside. The inside was galvanized with zinc. When the horse got warm, the sweat caused the zinc to give off its medicinal qualities which cooled and soothed the shoulders. This was claimed to be invaluable to horses with sensitive skins. The collar was put on by releasing a spring catch at the throat, which opened the collar, enabling it to be placed over the neck.

Injuries caused by ill-fitting collars are many and varied. Friction is the most frequent. When the horse is in motion, the collar is resting on a constantly moving surface. As one shoulder goes back, so the other shoulder goes forward. It is important that the point of draught should coincide with the part of the shoulders which moves least. If it is too low, it will be against the joint and be constantly mobile. Tremendous friction will build up, also the top of the collar will tip forward. If the collar is too wide, it will be loose on the shoulders and slip from side to side resulting in a gall. This soreness will usually occur at a place under the point of draught.

A collar which is too long will slip upwards and back when the horse is in draught.

Too short a collar will press on the windpipe and choke the animal. This condition is also known as piping. A pipe collar with a hollow to coincide with the windpipe is designed to prevent this from happening.

If the collar is too narrow, it will pinch and gall, particularly towards the top of the neck.

For a horse with a wide head and narrow neck, there is the open top collar. This can be lined and stuffed to fit the neck and as it will then be too narrow to pass comfortably over the sensitive skin above the eyes, can be put on by opening the top and slipping it over the neck. It is then closed and held together with a housing strap, before the hames are put on. The disadvantage of this system is that if the housing strap stretches, and the collar opens, the top of the neck becomes pinched.

A common injury which occurs when horses are driven alongside a pole, particularly when harness without breeching is used, is galling on the top of the neck. This is caused by pressure from the pole straps, in going downhill or pulling up. The vehicle runs forward and so does the pole. That, in turn, tightens the pole straps and the collars through the hames and kidney links are pulled forwards and downwards. Tremendous pressure is then taken by the tops of the horses' necks. It is a help to have collars for this work stuffed in such a way so as to allow a groove to coincide with the top of the neck.

When horses were working daily, and sore necks were common, zinc collar pads were frequently used. They were attached to the insides of the tops of the collars and held the collars off the injuries. The soreness was healed by the chemical qualities absorbed from the zinc whilst allowing work to continue.

In establishments where many horses were kept, every precaution was taken to ensure that they always wore their own collars. A collar being put on to the wrong horse by mistake invariably resulted in that animal being laid off work with sore shoulders. To prevent this from happening each horse had a number which was branded on his hoof, put on a metal plate in his stable and stamped in brass studs on a cape on his collar. The latter was clearly visible for his driver to check at a glance.

Collar Brace Rings
Many of the early four-wheeled vehicles, hung by leather braces on cee- or whip-springs, had rings fixed to the bottom of the body through which there passed straps connecting it to the perch to obviate excessive sideways swing.

Collar Fork
Also known as collar iron. *See* Plugging a Collar.

Collar Injuries
These are usually caused by ill-fitting collars, though they can be brought about by an unfit horse being asked to work before his skin has hardened adequately. The most usual seats of collar injuries are:
1. Three-quarters of the way down the shoulder on both sides, where too wide a collar has rocked from side to side chafing the skin until an injury develops.
2. About one-third of the way down the shoulder, where too narrow a collar has pinched and rubbed.
3. At the top of the neck, caused by downward and forward pressure from the

pole straps when the vehicle is being held entirely on the neck, if no breeching is worn.

4. At the windpipe where too short a collar has piped and bruised the neck.

The cure for all these injuries is to rest the neck and apply a lotion to heal the chafed area and harden the skin. A collar which fits properly must replace the ill-fitting one. A breast collar may be found to be a temporary solution if the area of the injury can be avoided by its use. In the case of injury number three, a breeching should be added to the harness when the horse returns to work.

Collar Iron
Also known as a collar fork. *See* Plugging a Collar.

Collar Measurer
In 1885 Messrs Spence & Storrors of Letham, Ladybank, Fife, invented a collar measurer in an effort to measure horses' necks with a degree of accuracy. The measurer consisted of a frame around which pegs were put in such a way that some semblance of the fit was assured.

Collar Pad Strap
Found in Army harness to secure the zinc collar pad to the top of the breast collar.

Collet
A metal collar used in conjunction with the Collinge's axle. *See* Axle.

Collinge's Axle
A type of axle, named after its inventor, which was first introduced in 1792, and now found in use on a great number of vehicles. *See* Axle.

Collingridge, Cork, Rowley & Co
A London coachbuilding firm.

Columbia Wagon
A type of wagon which was first made in Columbia, South Carolina, U.S.A.

Combination Carriage
This is also known as a Convertible Carriage.

Combined Driving
In 1969 a meeting was held in Switzerland of a number of representatives from many countries, under the chairmanship of Col Sir Michael Ansell. The first set of rules for combined driving were drawn. This resulted in competitions for singles, pairs and teams taking place in England. The European Championships were held in 1971 in Budapest. In 1972 the World Championships were held in Munster at which the British team took the team gold medal against six other countries. The Combined Driving Group was then formed, as a discipline of The British Horse Society, at The National Equestrian Centre, Stoneleigh, Warwickshire.

In 1975, competitions for tandems were introduced when the author became the first Whip to complete a full trial with such an equipage. This was achieved at the Lowther Three Day Trials in Cumbria with Alibi and Razali, a home-bred and home-produced team by Ali.

A full Combined Driving Event comprises of three phases known as Competition A which is divided into two sections: Presentation and Dressage; Competition B which is the Marathon; and Competition C, the Obstacle Test. *See* Competitions A, B and C.

'Comet', The
A famous coach which ran daily on the London and Brighton road.

Competition A
Section one of Competition A of a combined driving trial consists of the phase which is known as presentation.

Presentation is the equivalent to pure showing, and a very high standard of turnout is necessary if few penalties are to be written on the scoreboard. It is usually the first phase of a trial and is always judged at the halt, in or near the dressage arena. The turnouts are normally scrutinized by three judges who work individually and their scores are averaged. Judges are frequently positioned at B, C and E, and three competitors present themselves, one at a time, to each in turn. When all have been judged, another trio come forward. The order is decided by a draw and remains the same for the dressage test. It is rotated by half for the marathon.

If a large entry is forward, and time is short, then presentation is sometimes judged by different officials from those who are judging the dressage test. As this takes place concurrently, then presentation is judged outside the arena. Adequate time is allowed for working-in for the dressage test after presentation has been completed.

Each judge has a writer who takes down the marks and any constructive criticism which could be of help to a competitor for future events as exhibitors are given their score sheets at the end of the trials.

A total of fifty marks can be gained, consisting of ten marks each for: the driver and grooms or social passengers acting as grooms; the horse or horses; the vehicle; the harness; the overall impression.

Marks are based on the following lines: ten is deemed to be excellent; nine, very good; eight, good; seven, fairly good; six, satisfactory; five, sufficient; four, insufficient; three, fairly bad; two, bad; one, very bad. The final total is subtracted from fifty so that the mark is turned into penalties enabling those given for the dressage, marathon and obstacle phases to be added, resulting in the lowest overall score winning.

In judging the driver, the position on the box seat and the way in which the Whip handles the reins and whip will be noted, as will the folding of the whip if a team or tandem is being driven. Dress will be taken into consideration. Lady Whips can wear a jacket and skirt or a trouser suit. A neat, small-brimmed hat which will not fly off or distract the Whip if the wind blows is important. Gloves must be worn, and flat-heeled, clean shoes are best. Gentlemen Whips can wear a suit and bowler hat. If more formal dress is chosen then a top hat is correct in which case the accompanying grooms will probably be in livery, with breeches and boots, top hats, stocks and gloves. Grooms accompanying a gentleman in less formal dress would wear suits and bowlers. Girl grooms look very smart in well-fitting trousers, hacking or dark jacket and bowler or hunt cap. Gloves, of course, should be worn. The driving apron should blend in colour with the upholstery of the cushions and the dress of the Whip. A red hat, blue apron and yellow jacket are unlikely to be pleasing to the judge's eye.

The way in which the grooms handle the horses will be observed. Rough or incapable handling may lower an otherwise high mark. Such errors as holding pairs by the bars of Buxton bits or giving inadequate assistance in times of need may reflect on the marking.

An upright and capable looking Whip, in full command of his turnout, who is accompanied by neat and efficient grooms is bound to get a good mark.

The horses are examined for condition, cleanliness and, in the case of more than one, for match. Weeks, if not months, of careful feeding, exercise and grooming are necessary to produce a horse in peak condition. He should be fit and not carry too little or too much spare flesh. An unfit, over-fat animal will become distressed on a full marathon. The amount of corn which is fed will vary from one horse to another but the degree of fitness needed is about equivalent to that required for winning a Hunter trial. Boiled linseed added to the feed each day will help to provide an extra bloom to the coat which is also achieved by hours of strapping. White socks must sparkle, and this is best accomplished by washing with shampoo and careful drying to prevent cracked heels. A little dog chalk, which can be bought in block form at pet shops, can be rubbed on, once the legs have dried, to give extra whiteness. A smear of Vaseline round the nostrils, eyes and dock adds another finishing touch to give the professional look. Vaseline is also preferable to hoof oil for the feet as it does not leave dark marks on white socks, like hoof oil does, if the animal is inclined to move close. Action, and way of going, is not taken into account as all judging is completed at the halt.

In preparing the horse for presentation an application of fly spray or citronella (be careful because it blisters if too much is used) is a last minute must if the flies are bad.

The harness is examined for fit, condition and cleanliness. An ill-fitting collar, in particular, will be likely to result in a poor mark as this is bound to cause discomfort, if not actual galls, before the trials are completed. It is far better to have a breast collar which is correctly adjusted than a smart ill-fitting full collar. It is not essential to have harness with patent leather trim. Highly polished plain leather will gain just as high a mark. Buckles and keepers should match throughout. Brown harness is quite correct if the horse is put to a country or varnished vehicle and the turnout is of a sporting as opposed to a park flavour.

The best way to clean harness is to apply softener, such as saddle soap, to all the inner surfaces which go against the horse and to polish the outer ones either with patent leather cleaner or shoe polish. All metal furniture must be highly polished, taking care not to get metal cleaner on to the leather. Excessive saddle soap which has accumulated in holes is best removed before the harness is assembled.

The vehicle should be of a traditional type. Wire wheels and pneumatic tyres are not permitted. If the vehicle is a four-wheeler then a hand brake is obligatory. The fit, soundness, condition and cleanliness are all taken into consideration as is the height of the pole if a pair or team is being driven. Lamps have to be carried, as do rear lamps, and all should contain candles which have been lighted and blown out on the principal that it is easier to light candles which have previously been lighted. On no account should artificial flowers or coloured tinsel take their place. Certain spares, which vary according to the turnout, have to be carried. A wooden box which contains the essential equipment, cleaned and neatly displayed, gives a good impression. Teams are required to carry spare lead and wheel reins, spare lead and wheel traces and a pole strap. They also have to have a spare main and spare lead bar. Pairs must carry a rein, a trace, a pole strap and a hame strap where applicable. Tandems are required to carry a lead and wheel trace, lead and wheel rein and hame strap if full collars are used. Singles must carry a rein or rein splice, a trace and a hame strap if hames are worn. Many competitors take a great pride in laying out an elaborate spares kit with such items as shoes, hammer, buffer, nails, pinchers, candles, matches, first aid kit and a knife. These are all strictly optional and on no account should a judge ask for anything other than the specified spares. However, it is to the competitor's advantage to carry plenty of spares. If there is an accident on the marathon a good proportion of the spares carried is likely to be brought into use. The author was grateful for forty yards of nylon washing line which was used to truss up a broken cart, enabling her to drive a further six miles to complete the course. A Roger ring acted as a hame terret which had got broken in the same capsize when the shaft horse got pulled off her feet.

The final mark is given for overall impression and is usually about an average of those previously awarded.

A number of competitors take two vehicles and two sets of harness so that working equipment can be used for the marathon and show harness and vehicle employed for the presentation, dressage and obstacle competitions. No one need feel discouraged if he cannot do this. It has been found that a vehicle of medium standard which has been scrupulously cleaned and is in good sound condition and fits correctly will still gain a seven or eight out of ten.

It should be remembered that high marks for presentation are usually gained by those who take trouble and pay attention to detail. A row of nines on the score sheet spells hard work but the satisfaction resulting will more than compensate for the hours spent in polishing.

Competition A Section Two, The Dressage Test

The word 'dressage' is inclined to be surrounded by an aura of mystery which is capable of filling the newcomer to the world of combined driving with alarm. The prospect of crossing rivers, climbing steep banks and weaving between trees on the marathon holds no horrors. Driving between a series of markers with just a few centimetres to spare will be tackled without fear. It is the dressage test which can make the potential competitor hesitate when the entry form drops through the letterbox and the closing date for the event approaches.

It should be remembered that dressage is simply another word for training. A continental pupil referred to his 'dressage cart' and, when questioned about the design, answered in a matter-of-fact tone that the vehicle was long shafted and low slung like any other breaking cart!

The dressage test is purely a means of proving to the judges that the horse is obedient, calm, supple and has correct paces. Such a horse will then be capable of a high performance on the other two sections of the event. Horses which are disobedient, excited, stiff and do not have true paces will be unlikely to be pleasant to drive either across country or in the obstacle competition. Their resistances will make life difficult for their driver, cause inaccuracies and waste valuable time.

Correct basic training is the essential foundation for whatever the horse's future career is to be. He must be adjusted mentally and physically so that he is able to co-operate with his trainer. Resistances are usually caused by fear because the pupil does not fully understand what is required. The training system needs to be carefully planned and the trainer has to be patient and dedicated if successful results are to be achieved. It is quite possible to transform an ordinary looking animal into a beautiful horse by altering the top line with correct work, though it can take a very long time to build the outline into the desired form.

Different trainers have varying methods and people rarely agree on every detail. I start by building up a liaison with the horse with work on the lunge. The pupil is schooled in a cavesson in a large enclosed arena. Gradually, confidence is developed as the horse learns obedience with commands being repeated consistently. Horses are creatures of habit and learn by constant repetition. They are not generally highly intelligent but they do have excellent memories and advantage must be taken of this fact. As the horse learns to go forward freely, and cover the ground with the minimum amount of apparent effort, then the muscles over the quarters, second thighs and neck will begin to develop. The outline will improve if the work is being carried out correctly.

On no account must the horse be worked on too small a circle or on a slippery surface as this will teach him to shorten his stride and go on three sets of tracks with his quarters carried to one side. It will also make him hollow his back and reverse his neck to build up the underneath instead of the top muscles. The same will occur if he is hurried, or worked too hard, when he is over-fat or in very poor condition.

Work on the lunge must mean work and not be just a lazy method of exercising by an unskilled person. The horse will not become bored if his work is made interesting. He should be made to go with his hocks engaged so that adequate impulsion is created to propel him forward. Energy must come from behind in order that correct paces and head carriage will be formed. The head will only go into the right place if the hocks are engaged. On no account should the head be pulled into position as this will result in bending at the crest instead of at the poll and will probably lead to resistances such as overbending. As training progresses, and the forehand lightens, so the head will come naturally into the desired position.

It is essential to teach the horse to walk, trot and halt in each direction to word of command. Fortunately it is permitted to use the voice in a driven dressage test so this groundwork will prove invaluable.

Three trots are required in the driven tests. The working trot is a workmanlike pace with the horse covering the ground easily with a minimum of fuss. The hind tracks should go into those of the front. The horse should be relaxed and flow freely forward. The collected trot shows a shorter stride with the hocks well engaged. The hind track does not quite reach the front track though plenty of impulsion is maintained. The neck is raised with the head bent at the poll showing a relaxed lower jaw as the horse flexes. The speed in terms of miles an

84

hour is slower than the working trot but the hoof beats maintain the same timing so that a tune hummed during both trots would remain in tempo. The extended trot gives a longer stride with the hind tracks going well beyond those of the front. The neck is extended. The hoof beats should remain at the same timing as with the collected trot though, of course, the miles an hour are increased with the lengthened stride. On no account must the horse be forced so that his stride becomes hurried instead of extended. This is generally known as running and usually occurs when he is asked to extend before he is balanced. Extension cannot be achieved before collection and collection cannot be achieved without impulsion. It all takes time and patience.

The walk should be a pace of regular four time. Quite a number of horses have a walk which inclines toward lateral two time. This costs valuable marks in the dressage test and will, quite likely, lead to time faults in the walk sections of the marathon. It is essential to spend adequate time on establishing a true walk during the early stages of training as this is difficult to correct later if neglected in the preliminary days. A calm and free walk should be achieved with the hind legs coming well forward beyond the front tracks, to cover as much ground as possible in the minimum amount of time without appearing to hurry.

The halt should be square with the horse's weight distributed evenly over all four legs. The front legs should be together, straight under the body, as should the hind. The horse must not be stretched out as is seen in some private driving turnouts and most hackney equipages. The horse should not step back after halting. There is a tendency for the vehicle to roll back a little at the halt and the horse then takes half a step back to ease the weight off his shoulders. This is not permitted and he must be trained to hold the load on his collar and stand obediently on the bit in readiness for the command either to walk or trot forward or to rein back.

The rein back should be a pace of regular diagonal two time with the feet lifted up and put down clearly with a good stride. They must not be dragged back stiffly. The rein back should be absolutely straight as a crooked rein back results in an articulating vehicle with a four wheeler and an articulating team and vehicle with four horses.

All of this work can be carried out on long reins when the position of the head, neck, hind quarters, hocks and tracks can all be observed.

It is a good idea to mark out an arena with white boards, letters and sawdust lines and crosses so that the horse associates this with the dressage test. When he is taken into an arena at an event he will feel familiar with his surroundings and not be afraid.

If the horse can be ridden, some schooling can be done under saddle. Sometimes it is easier to teach a movement from on top than from the ground when the rider has the use of his legs and seat to back up his voice and hands. The closer contact with the horse helps to build up confidence and reward can be quickly and clearly given both verbally and physically.

Work for the test can be split up between schooling on the lunge, the long reins, under saddle and in harness. In the case of tandems, pairs and teams it is best to work each horse individually to build up correct paces, good head carriage, and smooth transitions. When they are all going properly as individuals they can be put together and worked in unison in their vehicle.

It should be remembered that a good average mark can be obtained for a correctly driven test which is calm and obedient. Full use of the arena and accuracy to the markers can make up for lack of brilliance, so the newcomer need not feel disheartened if his animal does not possess naturally spectacular paces.

The dressage test should be a happy occasion for all concerned. A well-executed test is a thing of beauty and elegance. *See* Five Minute Dressage Test.

Competition B

The marathon phase, competition B, of a combined driving trials is perhaps the one which is generally enjoyed most by competitors. From a spectator's point of view, it is the hazards in section C which present the most exciting focal points. These are usually situated within easy reach of the car parks so that onlookers can walk out to the obstacles and get a good view of the excitements which this new sport provides.

The object of the marathon is to test the fitness and stamina of the horse or horses and to test the judgement of pace and horse-mastership of competitors.

It can take several months to prepare a horse for the marathon if the course, which may be about twenty miles at a full trial, is to be completed without strain or drama. Many people, including the writer, advocate that it is preferable to train each horse individually incorporating work on the lunge, long reins, under saddle and in single harness before putting the pair, tandem or team together. This, of course, takes a great amount of time but ensures that each horse learns to carry himself correctly. It also makes certain of true paces being established. The active long striding walk, which is so essential if sections B and D are to be covered without time faults, is far more easily achieved if the horse is worked on his own in the early stages. Lengthening and shortening of the stride at the trot are necessary for sharp turns through gateways where the trotting pace has to be maintained to avoid referee faults for break of pace. Also, such bad habits as pulling away from the pole are less likely to develop if the animals are not driven alongside a pole too frequently.

A horse needs to be very fit for the marathon and this alone can take months to achieve. The standard of fitness is more or less equivalent to that required for winning a hunter trial.

It is usual, at a full trial, for competitors to assemble at a given point, in a marquee or similar, for the briefing when maps of the marathon are issued. Any alterations and amendments are discussed and intricacies of the route are explained. Bogey times for the obstacles are announced. Referees are introduced to individual competitors and then all are free to take their Land Rovers round the route. It is interesting to note that a marathon which seems rough and tedious when driven by Land Rover becomes much smoother and seems shorter when driven with a horse.

The marathon usually takes place on day two, after the dressage and presentation. The order of starting is rotated by half and competitors are given their times on the day before the marathon. Each competitor must be at the start of section A at the appointed time or risk elimination.

A judge inspects each turnout to check that the horse is safely put to and that all the correct spares are being carried.

The competitor's dress can be more casual than for the arena events. Cloth caps replace bowlers and top hats and, in hot weather, shirt sleeves are often the order of the day, though gloves and aprons should be worn and whips must be carried at all times.

Working harness is very often used instead of the patent show sets which are employed in the dressage arena. Many competitors replace their smart vehicles with ones which they care less about for the rigours of crossing rivers and scrambling down banks. The vehicle has to be of a traditional type so wire-spoked wheels and pneumatic tyres are not permitted, but competitors are rapidly designing and building all kinds of vehicles with metal shafts and metal wheels, which look like wood, in order to save their much cherished old vehicles.

The rear wheels of Mr George Mossman's team vehicle are of special interest. There are sixteen spokes which are slotted into the hub in two rows. These cross as they go down to the felloes so that no matter what angle the wheel is at, the stress on spokes, hub and felloe is direct thus saving the chance of a wheel breaking due to undue strain when it is put at an awkward angle. George's judgement in designing his vehicle, which resembles a brake, was so accurate that when it came to be weighed it was within a few grams of the stipulated 600 kilos required for horse team vehicles.

Mrs Barbara Hackett, who successfully drives a pair of Welsh Cobs, carries a small spare wheel which can be fixed by an arm to the axle to get her home should a wheel collapse on the course.

Metal poles, and wooden ones which are reinforced with ropes, are a common sight and metal bars are often seen replacing the more traditional wooden main and lead bar.

A number of single horse and pony competitors are using seat belts for traces to take the place of the traditional hand-stitched double leather kind. Some people have the belt and braces precaution of running a length of rope from the hames to the trace hook alongside their traces.

Each competitor is given a card which shows the time recorded through the start and finish of each section. It is usual for the starter at section A to count down the last few seconds as the time of departure approaches for the competitor to leave. This phase is driven at a trot of about fifteen kilometres per hour and is calculated to take about forty minutes. Naturally, distances vary according to the situation and differ from one event to another. The competitor aims to cover the distance between the time allowed and the minimum time stated proving his exact judgement of pace. Kilometre markers have now been reintroduced which simplify matters a little in keeping a close check on timing along the route.

Singles and tandems do not carry a referee because many two-wheeled vehicles do not have a third seat and it is necessary for the driver to be accompanied by a groom who is familiar with the horses. Pairs and teams carry a referee who is generally on the front seat, while grooms travel on the back. It is the referee's job to award penalties for such errors as breaks of pace which gain advantage and for halting to absorb time if a section has been driven too fast. He also has to record the length of time which has elapsed if a competitor is delayed by a third party through no fault of his own. He is responsible for seeing that turning flags are rounded and that no one dismounts in walk sections B and D.

87

On completing section A, the time is marked on the competitor's card and he proceeds to the start of section B, which is the walk. There is a definite time allowed and the section can be completed as quickly as the driver wishes. No marks are taken off for finishing too soon. Pony teams are generally given a minute extra.

Then comes a very welcome ten-minute compulsory halt. Horses are sponged down and given a mouthful of water. It is interesting to note how much they benefit from this attention and proceed to section C with renewed vigour.

Section C is the fast one with the hazards. The speed required is usually about eighteen kilometres per hour which, when hazards are taken into consideration, is very fast. This has to be completed at a trot, except at special places where terrain is difficult and cantering or walking may be permitted for a few yards. Such areas are marked with an *A* any pace or *W* walk. There are usually five or six obstacles. Competitors will have had an opportunity to inspect these thoroughly during their motorized drive round the course. Each hazard is surrounded by a penalty zone boundary which is usually marked with a tape on the ground. Once within the penalty zone, red flags are left to the right and white to the left. It is advisable to make a sketch and notes of how the hazard should be driven so that this can be studied and learnt at leisure.

Hazards may be driven at any pace, so once the competitor is over the boundary line he can drive at walk, trot or canter. He is within the jurisdiction of the obstacle judge who will award ten faults for the driver putting down his whip, twenty for a groom dismounting and twenty for disconnecting the traces or for leaving the penalty zone with part of the horse or vehicle. Sixty penalties are awarded for turning over. Failure to leave the penalty zone within four times the bogey time, having successfully negotiated the hazard, will necessitate elimination. If the competitor does not complete the hazard correctly, but leaves the penalty zone, it is quite in order for the obstacle judge to call him back to have another attempt but this must still be done within the time limit.

Obstacles vary from one event to another but often entail sharp turns through woods with trees or roots exactly where the competitor would like to place his horse in order not to wrap the hub cap of his vehicle round another tree. Some obstacles are man-made constructions with posts and rails to simulate off-set gateways. These can be built at home and it is quite easy to make a series of passages and gateways with a few jump stands and poles. Horses can then be ridden, long reined and driven in single harness around the combinations of the maze, and so get quite used to halting, facing a barrier, and backing and turning without fuss or resistance. When they are presented with the real thing at a trial the experience does not come as quite so much of a surprise.

Artificial knock-down hazards were first used at the Mellerstain trial in Scotland in 1977. They were made from large traffic cones with an extended top which held red and white plastic planks resembling a road closed show jump. Twenty penalties were given for each gateway which was knocked down, making a possible sixty penalties for knocking all three. This, being the equivalent in faults to a capsize, deterred competitors from driving carelessly in order to save time.

River crossings are always a favourite among the spectators who are usually rewarded by seeing at least one ducking during an event. Fortunately there have not been any serious injuries to humans or horses during the course of events in the seventies.

Training for water is very important and plenty of time should be allowed to accustom horses to crossing rivers before going to an event. Possibly the best method is to box the horse to several different crossings and ride or long rein him backwards and forwards until confidence is gained. He can then be driven single, when the shafts will be of great help to keep him straight, before he is finally put into pair, team or, most difficult of all, the lead of tandem. With this latter mode of driving, the Whip is rendered absolutely powerless if, on the approach, the leader decides to turn round and go back in the direction from which he has just come. Suddenly, there are about three feet of loose lead rein and trace on the inside of the turn and no contact whatsoever.

After section C there is walk section D for which the same rules apply as section B. This is followed by another compulsory halt of ten minutes when horses are thankful for a sponge down and a breather.

Section E is often driven at a similar pace to section A and is usually fairly straightforward.

The experts who have been competing in trials since the early seventies have the timing of each kilometre down to a final second and will probably come in at the end of section E exactly on time. Newcomers need not feel discouraged that their judgement of pace is unlikely to be as accurate as the pundits, and the achievement of producing a horse which trots happily through the finish is adequate. It is not winning which matters but completing the course without mishap or undue stress to the animal which is of primary importance.

Competition C

The object of Competition C, the obstacle course, is to test the fitness, obedience and suppleness of the horse after the marathon. Horses and drivers are frequently very tired after completing perhaps twenty miles across country, and this can result in numerous faults in the final phase. It is quite possible for a competitor who was well in the lead after competitions A and B to be relegated to a low placing after Competition C.

A course of between 500 and 800 metres is built in the arena where the dressage took place. A plan of the course is normally available to enable competitors to learn the track and the course is open for inspection before the start of the competition when drivers may walk round without their turnouts.

Up to twenty obstacles, consisting mainly of pairs of yellow triangular-shaped plastic markers, resembling police traffic cones, are laid out carefully to encourage a smooth flowing round with several changes of direction. A rubber ball is placed on the top of each marker and if the ball topples from the cone then ten faults are incurred. If by any chance a marker should be touched without the ball being displaced then no faults are administered. If, however, a competitor goes to one side of a marker so that it passes between the wheels of the vehicle or between the horses without being knocked, the penalties will be comparable to a displacement.

The cost of a groom dismounting for any reason, such as to adjust harness or lead a reluctant horse through a water obstacle, is ten faults which is equivalent to penalties given for the first disobedience. These are similar to refusals in show jumping. If a horse stops and steps back, circles or crosses his track in correcting a possible error of course then ten penalties are given. Twenty faults are awarded for the second disobedience, and the third results in elimination. A competitor will also be eliminated if he starts before the judge rings the bell, goes through an obstacle before the start or fails to pass between the start and finishing posts as these set off the electric timing device. Assistance from the passenger or groom, who must remain seated, with the reins, whip or brake will result in elimination as will being shown the way round the course by any third party. Taking the wrong course or exceeding the time limit also causes elimination.

The time allowed is calculated on an average speed of 200 metres per minute for teams and tandems. Singles and pairs of horses are given a minute for every 225 metres, and pony pairs and singles must cover 250 metres in a minute. Half a fault is awarded for every commenced second exceeding the time allowed.

The distance between the markers is not more than sixty centimetres wider than the track width of the vehicle. Competitors are asked to measure their wheels at ground level (which often differs from further up) and state the measurement on the entry form. Vehicles are checked during presentation, and markers on the obstacle course are altered for each competitor.

It is usual for the vehicle, harness and competitor's dress to be the same as was used for competitions A and B as the obstacle competition is deemed to be more formal than the marathon when working vehicles harness and clothes are sometimes applied. Gloves and knee rugs must be worn and the whip should be carried.

The order of the start is decided by the scores of competitors after competitions A and B with the worst marks going first. This makes the contest very exciting as the last few competitors come into the arena needing perhaps a clear round to hold their placings.

Schooling for the obstacle competition can be achieved under saddle, on long reins and in single harness before animals are put into pair, tandem or team. The training is similar, in some respects, to show jumping in that the horse must learn that no matter what angle the approach, he must go between the pairs of markers. Once he fully understands what is required he will get his driver out of trouble when presented at an obstacle from a difficult angle. He will know that he must go between the cones and will probably make every effort to do this even if he has almost to jump to the inside in order not to hit it. This applies particularly to the leader of a tandem. If the leader can be trained to go between whichever pair of markers he happens to be pointed at, he can then be dismissed by his driver who will be able to concentrate on steering the shaft horse accurately through the centre.

Competitors who do not wish to go to the expense of buying the kind of yellow cones which are used for F.E.I. competitions will find that yellow plastic fertilizer bags, as used by farmers, serve the purpose very well when they are filled with straw and tied at the top with string. They sit squarely on the ground and resemble the official cones adequately. It is a good idea to place them in pairs, allowing plenty of room to go through, around the field. The horse can be introduced to the process of going between them and soon gets the idea. When he is faced with an arena full of cones at an event he will not be taken by surprise and will realize immediately what is required.

Competitors driving clear rounds usually have a run off against the clock to decide the winner of the obstacle competition, though this does not affect the overall scoring for the whole trial.

Rosettes are normally given for each competition at a trial so it is possible for a competitor to go home with four firsts if he has won competitions A, B, C and therefore overall. But it is quite possible for a competitor who is in the lead in one competition and down in two competitions to become the overall winner with a low aggregate score.

A competitor who is eliminated in one competition is allowed to drive the other two. He is given marking comparable to the lowest score in the competition in which he was eliminated, plus 25 per cent more penalties. If, by any chance, at the end of the trials his total score is better than that of his fellow competitors, he cannot be declared the winner as he will not have completed all three phases.

Concord
A robust type of American coach which originated in Concord, New Hampshire, U.S.A., being built to withstand extremely rough road conditions. The driver's seat was joined to the unsprung body, which hung on strong leather straps attached to four iron shackles coming up from the undercarriage. The brake was applied by the driver's right foot being pressed against a cross-bar which was fixed to the lever running outside the body of the coach, going down to the bar and brake blocks. Continual pressure was needed to keep the brake on, as there was no ratchet or rack. Due to the excessive backward and forward swaying motion of the coach, on its thorough braces, and the operational system of the brake which together kept the hands, body and right leg swinging back and forth, the Concord coach could not be driven English style. It would be impossible to maintain an even, delicate feel on the horses' mouths. The American style of driving with two reins in each hand and legs apart is more suitable for such a vehicle.

Concord Mud Wagon
An American vehicle which was built on similar principles to a Concord Coach but employing far simpler joinery. Also known as a California Mud Wagon.

Concord Wagon
A simple four-wheeled runabout comprising of a seat built on to a raft-type floor which, in turn, is attached to a perch and two axles. It was built by Downing & Abbot of Concord, New Hampshire, U.S.A. amongst others.

Conestoga Wagon
A vast and tough American wagon which was first used in 1755 for conveying passengers and goods across rough country. It was noted for its ability to withstand conditions which would shake other vehicles to pieces. The Conestoga resembles a large farm wagon with a canvas top hung over bow-shaped struts. It is usually pulled by six horses. Also known as the prairie schooner.

Coning
Also known as dishing when referring to the manufacture of wheels.

Connaught Buggy
A type of low, hooded gig which was hung on side- and cee-springs. It was so

91

named because H.R.H. The Duchess of Connaught ordered one for her personal driving in India.

Continental Chaise
There is a fine example of a mid-18th century vehicle of this type in the possession of the Science Museum, London. It resembles a gig, in many ways. The ornate, yet small body is carved, gilded, has side panels decorated with pictures, and is hung on leather braces. The carved dash is built with an exaggerated curve.

Continental Posting Harness
It was usual to use breast collars for posting on the Continent. When English vehicles were taken to the Continent, swingle trees would be added to the splinter bar to accommodate the breast collar traces as breast collars used with a solid splinter bar can cause chafing and sore shoulders.

Contract Carriages
At the turn of the century, many people hired their carriages under contract from their coachmaker. Vehicles were supplied to hirers for periods varying from one year to ten years, with the hire fee reduced, accordingly, to a cheaper yearly rate for a longer loan. Hiring of carriages was particularly advantageous to ladies and those with fixed incomes. For an agreed fee, the carriage would be supplied, maintained and repaired. A replacement vehicle would be loaned, free of charge, whilst work was being carried out on the regular carriage. This system saved the worry of large, unexpected repair bills turning up and vast periodic outlays for new carriages. For some it just saved the trouble of making decisions over choosing new vehicles. The system was so satisfactory that numerous carriages used by the wealthy, and seen in the Parks of London, were, in fact, contract carriages.

Contractor (Mail Coach)
Inn keepers, or similar men of good standing were engaged, by the Post Office, to horse the Mail Coach over specific grounds of about ten miles. The contract was carefully made out, giving orders referring to the number of passengers which could be carried, the route to be taken and speed at which it had to be driven. The number of horses to be used was also specified. Contractors had to pay the wages, provide the horses, whose working life was only about three years, and rent the coach from the coachbuilder who was responsible for repairs and servicing. For operating this service the contractor was paid a mileage fee. In 1837, two pence per mile was paid in quarterly payments by the Post Office, to contractors horsing the Bristol and Portsmouth Mail Coach.
   Also known as Proprietors.

Convenience
Relevant to almost anything which made travel in a carriage more comfortable. In 1691, a method of springing was referred to as a great Convenience. By 1767 the basket in which a few passengers travelled on the tops of some coaches was known as a Conveniency. Before this idea was conceived, those on the top of a coach had to hang on as best they could and if anyone fell asleep they stood a good chance of dropping off. The modern cliché probably originated from this. *See also*, Coach Pot.

Convertible Carriage
An idea conceived in 1838 by William Bridges Adams was that of using a connecting joint to combine two two-wheeled vehicles, such as a Gig and a Curricle, with wheels of the same size, to form a four-wheeled carriage. One such vehicle was bought by the Duke of Wellington. Various designs were produced for converting carriages. One was used which, with simple adjustments, converted a two-wheeled Battlesden Car into a Victoria. Another changed a Brougham into a Char-à-Banc. It became quite usual to have more than one body for an undercarriage. In 1853 a new tax law was enforced, stating that as well as the £6 to £10 payable per year for each pair horse, four-wheeled carriage owned, an extra 3 guineas had to be paid for every additional body. *See* Equirotal.

Cook
The coachbuilder who, with Robinson, built a Brougham for Lord Brougham. *See* Brougham.

Cooper Henderson, Charles (1803–77)
An artist, famous for his coaching pictures.

Cooper, J. C.
An English coachbuilder, of the latter half of the 1800's, who is credited, by some, with having designed the Victoria.

Copal
A slightly yellow, transparent resin, which was imported from South America in the 1800s and used for preparing a hard-wearing coach varnish.

Coper
A horse dealer.

Copper
Used in carriage building, under beading, to cover joints and, on rare occasions, for panels. Horns are frequently made of copper, as are parts of the insides of carriage lamps which are then covered with silver to reflect the light from the candles.

Corinthian
A slang name which was given to young men who drove in the Georgian period. George IV was known as 'The Great Corinthian'.

Cornflower
The 8th Duke of Beaufort, who was the first President of The Coaching Club, wore cornflowers at the opening meet in 1871. At the second meet, members copied and turned out wearing cornflowers. This led to them being adopted as the traditional flower, both in the buttonhole and on the bridle, for the Coaching Club and The Four-in-Hand Club.

Corning Buggy
An offshoot of the Coal Box Buggy, hung on side bars or elliptic springs, which took its name from Erastus Corning, New York, who originated the first pattern in about 1875.
It was also known as a Corning Wagon.

'Coronet', The
A daily London and Brighton coach.

Coster
The men who sell flowers, fruit and fish from a cart in the streets take a great pride in their turnouts. A number can still be seen in their full splendour at shows and at the Van Horse Parade in London on Easter Monday, when their horses and carts are turned out to perfection. A high-stepping hairy-heeled cob stallion is favoured. His long flowing mane and tail are adorned with coloured ribbons and woollen balls. His harness is usually black, trimmed throughout with piping, to blend with the colour of the cart, and has white metal horse-shoe buckles. The vehicle, usually a flat trolley on four iron shod or pneumatic-tyred wheels, is highly painted and has the wares decoratively displayed. The white-coated, felt-hatted coster sits on a seat at the front of the cart over which the cob's blanket is draped. A water bucket and nose bag are carried on hooks under the back of the cart.

Cosy Car
A pony size, low, hooded gig which seated two people in great comfort.

Cottage Windows
The windows on the doors of Stage Coaches were sometimes made from four small panes of glass in wooden frames.

Cotton
Used in the early 19th century as a base on to which carriage lace was woven. It was also used as a foundation for making waterproof cloth with caoutchouc or india rubber.

Coupé
The American coupé of the mid 1800s was similar to a Brougham. The closed body was entered by a door on each side and had one seat at the back facing forwards and a small seat under the front box-shaped window, for a child. The carriage was driven from a box seat in front of the box window. The body hung on elliptic springs and had an arch under the coachman's seat for the wheels to turn.

Coupling
The secret of successful pair or team driving lies in skilful coupling, that is, the adjustment of the coupling reins on the draught reins. With a pair, when pressure is put on to the left rein, tension goes down to the left of the nearside horse's mouth through his draught rein and the left side of the off-horse's mouth through his coupling rein which is buckled to the left draught rein. When the right rein is pulled, both horses are brought to the right on the same principle. If both horses are exactly the same length and carry their heads in exactly the same way, then the coupling reins can both be buckled on to their draught reins halfway down the fifteen holes punched at the buckling part. If one horse, say the nearside one, tucks his head in and the offside horse stretches his out, then the nearside horse's coupling rein must be taken up the offside draught rein so that it is shortened. The offside horse's coupling rein must be let out, down the nearside draught rein so that both horses are pulling evenly. If this is not done, the horse who tucks his head in will go further forward before the bit checks him,

and he will do all the work. If both horses carry their heads outwards, then both coupling reins must be shortened. Equally, if they go with their heads turned inwards, then the coupling reins must be let out.

Coupling Buckle
The buckle on the coupling rein, which joins the rein to the draught rein, in pair and team harness.

Coupling Rein
The shorter piece of a pair rein which is buckled to the longer draught rein. *See* Coupling.

Courier
When a nobleman, or similar person, embarked on a tour on the Continent, he took with him a courier whose job it was to attend to all the details of the journey. He had to book accommodation, working out the length of each day's journey so that destinations were reached on time, settle accounts, see to luggage and, in fact, generally be responsible for the well-being of those relying on him.

It was usual for this paragon to be capable of conversing in three or four languages. For this reason, many such servants were foreigners. Frequently the courier travelled in a Fourgon so that he, and perhaps a lady's maid, could take the main bulk of the luggage in advance, ensuring that it could be unpacked and everything fully prepared for the arrival later of the gentry in their family coach. Sometimes, the courier went ahead mounted, to see that all arrangements were in order.

Court Hansom
A Hansom Cab which was built on four wheels. The body and rear wheels were similar to a two-wheeled Hansom with the driver's seat placed behind the roof in the usual manner. The front wheels were in front of the dash. Also known as the French Four-Wheel Hansom.

Covered Wagon
A general term to describe an American heavy wooden wagon with bow-shaped struts over the top of the body. A waterproof covering is put over the struts and lashed down, to protect the load from the weather. Covered wagons were used for conveying passengers and goods across rough country and were frequently referred to as prairie schooners as they were driven across the prairies in groups.

Cowburn, Mrs Anne
A Manchester coachbuilder established in 1779. Many vehicles built under her name are still in existence.

Cowlard & Selby
The coachbuilding business of which James Selby was a partner. They were the makers of the famous 'Old Times' Road Coach which was lighter than other coaches of a similar type.

Crab
The hook and cross-head at the end of the pole on to which the main and lead bars are hooked when a team is put to. The crab is bolted firmly to the end of

the pole as it is by this that the leaders draw the vehicle. It may be made of stainless or polished steel. Brass or silver plating is not satisfactory as this rapidly wears off with friction. A crab which is painted needs constant attention. At the end of the hook is a slot through which a small strap passes and then buckles on to the top of the pole. This is a safety precaution to prevent the bars falling off should the leaders start to kick.

Craddock
A London man who invented two quick-release systems which could be applied in a hurry should a horse fall whilst put to. One was a method of releasing a pole strap by pulling a peg out from where it held the strap securely, replacing the usual buckle. His other invention was a device to release the back band, which was divided, and the crupper, by pulling out a single bolt with which they were all held to a specially built pad.

Crane
An iron perch with an arch under which the wheels turn.

Crane, Double Bow
A crane with an arch at each end.

Crane Neck
An iron perch which is arched at the fore end permitting the front wheels to turn under the arch so that a full lock may be obtained. Crane-neck perches were used in pairs with one on each side of the vehicle and were first adopted to ease the difficulties experienced in turning a carriage with a quarter- or half-lock in the narrow streets. They were heavy, and considered unsightly, so when the roads improved, crane-neck perches went out of fashion.

Crane-neck Chariot
Built by William Felton, a coachbuilder of the late 1700s. It was an elegant carriage with double-bowed cranes which supported the coach box at the front and the footman's cushion at the rear. The highly decorated body, hung on braces from whip springs, was embellished with crests and handsomely finished in every detail. The carving and gilding of the carriage part could amount to £200 for a *de luxe* model.

Crane-neck Coach
One such vehicle built by Felton in the 18th century had an elegant closed body with two seats and was entered by half-glass doors at the sides. The body hung by leather braces attached to four whip-springs. It was driven from an iron coach box. A footman travelled on a rear standing cushion, holding on by means of two straps decorated with braid. This coach was built on two double-bow cranes.

Crane-neck Phaeton. *See* Highflyer.

Craven Cart
A newly designed version was introduced in 1901. It was a two-wheeled, general-purpose vehicle resembling a Ralli Car. The back let down to allow two passengers to sit facing the direction from which they had come. The forward-facing seat accommodated the driver and one passenger. Parts of the side panels, under the curving mudguards, were caned.

Crawler

The name given to a cabman who skilfully loitered with the intent to pick up a fare, instead of returning to the cab stand. He was considered a nuisance by everyone other than those wishing to hire his cab and if caught by the police was liable to be fined.

Creams, Queen Victoria's

Until the first world war, cream horses of Hanovarian blood were used for State occasions. Generations of these horses were bred in England including many at Hampton Court. Eight cream stallions were used in the Gold State Coach until 1921 when they were replaced by black horses.

By the Coronation of George V grey horses were used, and have been ever since.

The Queen's creams never appeared unplaited and their manes were also trimmed with purple ribbons.

Creasing

The decorative pattern of triangles and diamonds which is pressed on to the outer surface of a pipe loop or full safe.

Creeping Sally

A famous 14-hand trotter, who was completely blind. She was driven in a single-seat sulky in a match against time to cover fifty miles of road in five hours without breaking from a trot. Undaunted by the heavy rain and thick fog on the day appointed for the match, she easily completed the journey in four hours and forty-four minutes. This is recorded in a print after J. N. Sartorius.

Crest

These may be reproduced in metal to match the furniture on harness and displayed on such places as the blinkers, the face drop, the false martingale, the top of the pad and the loin-strap pieces. In dress harness a crest is put on to the cape on the collar. Dressy hammercloths are sometimes decorated with crests worked in metal or embroidery. Carriages may be adorned with crests on the panels and doors. Such vehicles as gigs may carry a discreet edition of the owner's crest on the rear or sides, as applicable. Crests should only be used by those entitled to do so.

Crest Panel

On a Drag, the owner's crest or monogram is painted on the tiny narrow panel immediately below the window. This is known as the crest panel. On a Stage Coach it was, during one period, obligatory for the coach proprietor to have his name and address on the crest panel. Stage and Road Coaches also had the names of the towns from where they started and finished their journey, on the door under the crest panel. The Mail Coach had the words 'Royal Mail' written here as well as its start and finish towns. The whole door panel, in this instance, was referred to as the crest panel.

Crew Hole

The slot at the rearmost end of the trace which goes over the trace hook or swingle tree. Also known as a dart hole.

Cross Head
The metal fitting at the end of the pole which has two rings on to which the pole straps or pole chain are attached.

Cross Spring. *See* Double Elbow Spring.

Cross Team
When a team is made up from four horses of two different colours, say browns and greys, they look best if put to to cross the colours, so that the near leader and off wheeler are grey and the off leader and near wheeler are brown. If the horses are put to, in matching lead and wheel, the team is made to resemble two pairs. If put to with matching sides, the team looks one-sided. On a dark night such a cross team shows up far better than a matching team.

Crossing Traces
When putting a team to, it was thought by some people that the draught from a lazy horse and a gay horse, if working as leaders, was better distributed if their traces were crossed. That is the nearside horse had his traces hooked to the left end of his bar and the left end of his partner's bar. The offside horse's traces were hooked on to the right hand ends of each bar. Experts claimed that such unevenly matched horses should be corrected with skilful coupling and bitting.

Crown Loop
The leather strap at the top of an Army bridle. *See* Army Harness.

Crown Piece. *See* Bridle.

'Crown Prince', The
A Warwick Stage Coach.

Crupper
This consists of the back strap going from the dee at the back of the pad, and the crupper dock which goes under the tail. The crupper dock may be either stitched or buckled to the back strap. For those horses who resist by clamping down their tails when an attempt is made to put on the crupper, one which buckles is more convenient as the tail can be lifted and the side of the crupper which is unbuckled can be slipped under the dock. It is essential that crupper docks be kept soft and they are frequently filled with linseed for this reason. Sheepskin or chamois leather sewn around the crupper dock will help in preventing horses with sensitive skins from becoming sore. The purpose of the crupper is to prevent the pad from slipping forwards owing to the pressure from behind by the backband or in front by a bearing rein.

Cuban Carriage. *See* Volante

Curb Chain
The small chain which is hooked on to hooks on the eyes of a curb bit and lies across the chin groove. Care must be taken when fitting a curb chain to ensure that it is not twisted. The chain is hooked on to the offside curb chain hook and the end taken between finger and thumb and turned in a clockwise direction. When the links are all lying flat the chain should be given a half-turn anti-

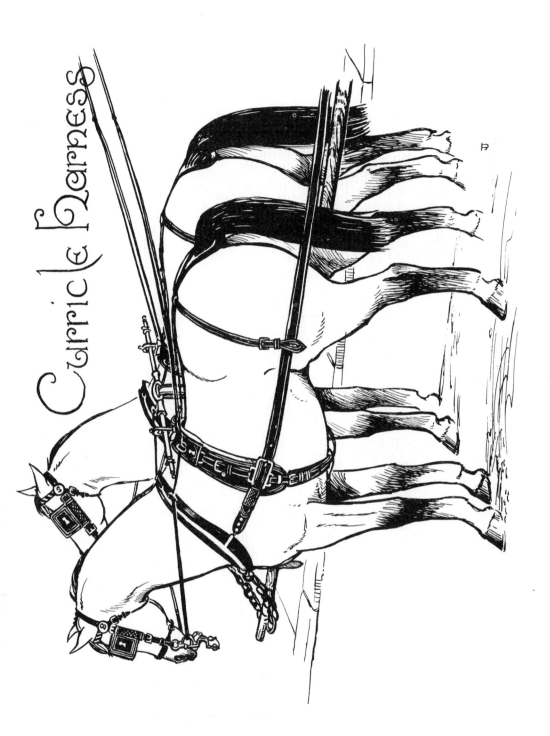

Curricle Harness

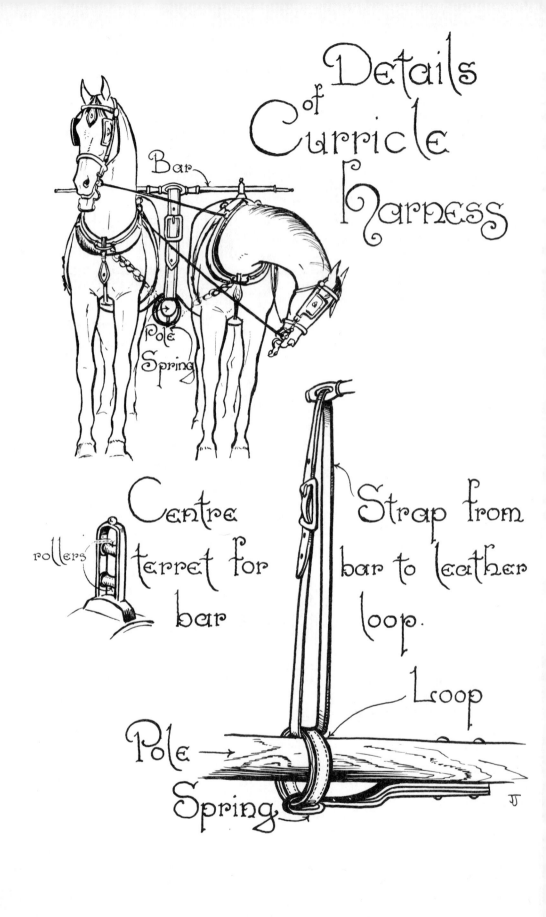

Details of Curricle Harness

Bar

Pole Spring

Centre terret for bar

rollers

Strap from bar to leather loop.

Loop

Pole → Spring.

J

clockwise, as it is hooked to the desired tightness. This makes the chain lie absolutely flat when it comes into action. It should be loose enough to allow the branch of the bit to slope backwards at an angle of forty-five degrees to the mouth before the chain presses against the chin. If it is tightened too much, the groove will become calloused and numb. When tension is put on to the bit, the chain tightens. To increase the action for a horse which pulls, the chain can be tied by a cord going from the centre link to the throat lash, putting the pressure higher up the jaw. Some 'chains' are made of leather or elastic with three links at each end to provide the necessary adjustment.

Curricle
One of the few two-wheeled vehicles to which a pair may be put. The horses should match in height and way of going as they are harnessed on either side of a pole held up by a steel bar, known as a curricle bar, fixed to their pads. The curving body of the vehicle is hung on elbow- or side-springs and has cee-springs at the rear. The groom travels on a seat between the rear springs and is important for the balance of the vehicle. The driver and passenger are protected from the weather by a folding hood. The Curricle originated in Italy, was improved in France and then considerably altered by the English. It became fashionable in the early 1800s replacing the Highflyer as a gentleman's conveyance and was used extensively for long journeys as well as for park and town driving. When properly balanced it is said to be easy on the horses.

Curricle Bar
The steel bar, which with a supporting strap, is used with curricle harness to hold up the pole of a Curricle. The bar is placed through fore-and aft-facing terrets on the centres of the pads, lying on rolling bars across the terrets to allow a certain amount of sideways play. At each end of the bar is a nut, which in turn is secured by a pin put through a slot, so that should either horse pull sideways, the bar cannot slide out of the terret. At the centre of the bar is an eye through which the strong supporting strap goes. This brace is passed under a spring on the pole, before being buckled to itself to take the weight of the vehicle when it is unbalanced.

Curricle Harness
This differs from ordinary pair harness in that the pads have a centre terret which faces forwards as well as the usual sideways-facing rein terrets. It is through these centre terrets that the curricle bar goes, lying on steel rollers to allow a certain amount of sideways play should the horses pull away from, or lean towards, the pole. It is necessary for curricle pads to be heavier and better padded than those used for normal pair harness. There are times when the horses have to take the weight of the unbalanced curricle on their backs. Great attention should be paid to the length of the traces. If they are too long, the horses will draw the vehicle by their pads and rapidly become chafed behind the saddle. In order to prevent the pole from pointing skywards, a strap with a buckle at each end is attached to the point of the girth on the outside of one horse, passed under his belly and over the pole before being brought down under the other horse's belly, after which it is buckled to the outside of his girth strap.

101

Currier

Leather was bought from the tanner by the currier. His knowledge of hides was important, as a large amount of capital was involved seasonally in the purchase of materials. Tanners would not allow any credit. The currier's job was to level the hides by a procedure which was known as shaving. He usually employed japanners to take the hides a stage further.

Curtain Rockaway

A version of an American Rockaway, fitted with leather curtains which can be let down in the window spaces if the weather deteriorates.

Curtains

These were made to cover the windows of a coach and were fitted to sprung rollers so that the curtains could be pulled down or slid up as required. The material used was frequently silk.

Cut-under Buggy

An American vehicle with an arch in the body, under which the front wheels can turn, allowing a lock which is superior to that of a number of American buggies. The body is hung on two elliptic springs. One spring is just in front of the dashboard and one is behind the rear boot. To the undersides of these are joined the perch and axles. The forward-facing seat, for two, has a folding hood.

Cut-under Phaeton

Referring to the arch in the body under which the wheels turn.

Cut-under Runabout

An American four-wheeled vehicle in which an arch was constructed in the underside of the body, enabling the front wheels to turn sharply, giving more manoeuvrability in narrow lanes. It is similar in construction to the cut-under buggy but has no hood.

Cutter

A type of sleigh. The curving and often ornate body is joined to the runners by several tall and narrow iron struts. The high dash is curved in the shape of a reversed 'S' to keep the snow, which is thrown up from the horse's hooves, from hitting the driver and passenger.

D-shaped Blinker

A blinker which is shaped like an inverted 'D'.

Dagger Pencil

A type of striping brush with which the decorative lines are painted on the wheels and body of a vehicle. The hairs are fixed to a tiny wooden handle and are cut to form a point. Also known as a sword pencil.

Dalmatian
The carriage dog whose purpose it was to run with the coach to guard parcels which were carried in the boot. As this practice has been carried out for generations, the dalmatian instinctively runs with a carriage and can be easily trained to go between the wheels with his head under the axle in the approved manner.

Dart Hole
American term for the holes at the end of the traces through which the trace hook or swingle tree goes. Also, in England, known as a crew hole.

Dashboard
The board in front of the driver's and passenger's legs to protect them from dirt thrown up by the horses' feet. The dashboard is made either of wood or of plain or patent leather sewn on to an iron frame.

Dashing Frame
The iron frame of the dashboard which is covered in patent or plain leather. Its purpose is to protect the driver and box seat passenger from the mud and dirt thrown up from the horses' feet.

Daumont or **À La Daumont**
This is a dressy method of turning out a team, which was named after the Duc D'Aumont who first used this type of equipage in the 1700s. The horses are put to a vehicle such as a Landau or a Barouche from which the driving seat has been removed. The nearside horses are ridden by postillions in full livery who also control the offside horses. Posting harness is used. The pole was often made of iron so that it could be shaped to avoid bruising the postillions' right legs. *See* Landau Grand Daumont.

Deadwood Coach
A heavy American stage coach in London in 1887 at the American Exhibition. Similar stage coaches, hung by leather braces from a perch undercarriage, were used for conveying heavy loads across rough country and were constructed accordingly.

Deal
Timber which was used extensively for the floors of carriages.

Dealer's Break. *See* Skeleton Break.

Decemjugis
A Roman chariot with ten horses abreast.

Dee
Those which are used on the shafts are known as breeching dees or shaft staples to take the breeching or kicking straps.

Dees are also used on harness to accommodate such fittings as the neck strap of the breast collar, the breeching loin strap, the false martingale and the pole strap, and therefore vary in size accordingly.

Demi-Daumont
When a pair, instead of a team, are turned out à la Daumont. *See* Daumont.

Demi-Landau. *See* Landaulette.

Demi-Mail Phaeton
The body of this carriage has a similar outline to a Mail Phaeton with a hooded seat at the front and a groom's seat at the back, allowing room between the two for luggage. The Demi-Mail Phaeton is lighter than the Mail Phaeton. It has no perch but is built with elliptic springs in front and mail springs behind. An arch in the body enables a better lock than with the Mail Phaeton. The wheels very often have Collinge's axles instead of Mail axles. In the 1800s this vehicle was favoured by gentlemen for both town and country use with a pair. It is also known as a Semi-Mail Phaeton.

Demi-Spider Phaeton
The upper outline of this carriage, which was built in 1903, resembles a Spider Phaeton with a hooded seat at the front for the driver and passenger and a railed seat at the rear for the groom. The lower outline is straight from the footboard to behind the groom's seat whereas the Spider Phaeton has a huge arch under the front seat. There is no boot along the body as in a Demi-Mail Phaeton. The vehicle is hung on four elliptic springs.

Demi Tonneau
A four-wheeled vehicle which was popular for family outings on the Continent. The front, forward facing seat accommodated two people and the rear seating resembled a governess cart to take four or six passengers.

Democrat Wagon
A square box wagon with a fixed top, used in America for conveying both passengers and luggage.

Dennett Gig
A light and elegant Gig which is thought to be a descendant of the early Whiskey. The stick-back body, outside which the shafts run, has a boot under the seat. It is hung on three springs, known as Dennett springs. The vehicle was first made by a Finsbury coachbuilder called Bennett. Somehow the 'B' became a 'D'. One theory is that the vehicle was named after the three famous dancing sisters of the period, the Misses Dennett.

Dennett Spring
Consisting of two side-springs and one cross-spring. The side-springs are fixed at their centres to the axle by two 'U' bolts. Their front ends are joined to the body of the vehicle by metal arms. Their rear ends are attached to the cross-spring by shackles. The cross-spring is joined to the rear of the body by one of a variety of methods. This system of springing is found on Dennett Gigs, Whitechapel Carts, some Dog Carts and many other vehicles.

Desborough, Lord
President of The Coaching Club from 1906 to 1935.

Designer
Very often one partner at least, in a firm of carriage builders, worked in the capacity of a designer of vehicles. The success of the business largely depended on his good taste and skill.

Detachable Tug

A strap found on Army harness to which the double hip straps and loin straps are buckled in order to support the breeching and traces. A detachable tug is a strap with a buckle at one end. The strap is passed round the trace or breeching and held in position by a keeper. The strap then passes up through its own floating keeper before buckling into itself. The buckle is uppermost and free to receive the hip strap or loin strap point coming down to it.

Devonport Mail

A Mail Coach which was also known as 'The Quicksilver'.

Diagonal Strap

When, with a Road Coach, the leaders were put to, without pads, a diagonal strap was used to hold up the traces. It ran from the top of the hames to the hame tug buckle. Such a method was used by James Selby with the 'Old Times' coach.

Dickey

The name given to the hind boot of a coach by coachmen of the 19th century. In the early 1900s it referred to the driving seat.

Digby

The Cumbrian name for a Governess Cart.

'Diligence'

The first Mail Coach which ran from Bristol to London in 1784, starting the new postal system promoted by John Palmer, was called the Mail Diligence.

Diligence

The other type of vehicle that is referred to as a Diligence was the heavy and lumbering Continental Stage Coach which ran night and day, with safety, during the 1800s and 1900s. Accommodation was divided into four apartments. Directly behind the wheelers was a closed-in cab entered by a side door and with windows at the side and front. This was known as the coupé and held three people facing forward. Leg space was limited owing to the nearness of the horses. On the roof of the coupé sat the driver and guard with their feet on a footboard in front of the top of the coupé's window. The travellers' luggage was stowed behind the driver on the roof of the main body of the coach and covered by a tarpaulin. The body was known as the intérieur and accommodated six or eight people facing each other. Behind the body, at the rear of the coach, over a hind boot containing small parcels, sat two or three more passengers with a hood to protect them. Sometimes instead of a four-horse team, a team of five was used with three horses harnessed abreast in the lead. For this purpose a sufficiently long main bar was used to spread the three horses apart. The centre horse's bar was hooked to the middle of the main bar. This in turn was fixed, not to the pole head as in English coaching, but to a rod running under the pole directly to the futchells. If the journey was hilly, then a longset was put to. That is four horses driven by the coachman and two leaders driven by a postillion.

Diligence, Handling of Reins

There were two ways of holding the reins of a four-horse team, to a Diligence, on the Continent. In both cases, all of the reins were secured in the left hand as

105

in England, but the arrangement was different. The method most like the English way had the near lead rein on top of the off lead rein, with both reins lying over the index finger. The near wheel rein lay over the middle finger and the off wheel rein over the third finger. The other method had the near lead and near wheel reins over the index finger and the off lead and off wheel reins over the middle finger. In both cases, the lead reins lay above the wheel reins.

Diligence Harness
This was tough and workmanlike, lacking the finish and elegance of English harness. The collars, which fitted perfectly, were large and heavy. The traces were made partly of leather and partly of rope. Breeching was usually worn by the wheelers. The leaders' reins passed either over the wheelers' heads or between them, and did not go through the pad terrets on their way to the coach-man's hand. The whip carried was made of an elasticated stick with a thong.

Dioropha
Invented by Messrs Corben & Rock and exhibited in 1851 at The Great Exhibition. The body was built on the lines of a Barouche from the elbow line downwards, but had a detachable roof which would be taken off or put on as required by ropes and pulleys from a beam on the coach house ceiling. If the top was not used then the hood to the rear seat and apron to the front took its place. Sliding windows were designed for the front quarters. The vehicle was at first described as being a perfect Clarence, but the developments of the Landau soon prevented any more Diorophas from being built. Their popularity lasted for less than twenty-five years.

Dishing of Wheels
Wheels are dished, that is built in such a way that the spokes slope outwards from the hub to the felloe, for a number of reasons. The axle arm is shaped so that the spokes below the hub remain vertical whilst the upper spokes slope outwards. There is less strain on both the hub and the wheel if the spokes are staggered (set into the hub on alternate sides of an imaginary line round the hub). This is also known as 'dodging' the spokes. The wheel is stronger and there is less force on the axle nuts if it is dished. The distance between the upper part of the wheel and the body of the vehicle is increased whilst the track of the wheels on the ground is not. Less dirt is thrown on to the passengers and the body of the vehicle from wheels when they are dished.

Distances
Anyone who is planning a driving holiday with a single horse, to a light two-wheeled vehicle, will find that an average of twenty miles a day can be achieved providing that the pace is slow and that lengthy stops are made in the middle of the day. The fitness of the horse and the terrain of the country largely dominate the daily mileage.

Distances Driven
Numerous long-distance drives by men of the coaching era are recorded. One of the longest was that achieved, as a result of a wager with Lord Kennedy, by Captain Barclay of Urie, a famous sportsman of the 19th century. He drove from London to Edinburgh, a distance of just under 400 miles, in $45\frac{1}{2}$ hours. His only stops were those taken when the passengers required refreshment. At the

turn of the century, seventy miles a day was considered to be a reasonable distance for a fit coachman.

Docker
Another name for the short tommy.

Docking
The cutting of the dock of the tail which, up to 1948, was carried out with harness horses and cobs to comply with whims of fashion. It was claimed that, as well as giving a smarter appearance, there was less danger of a rein getting caught under the tail of a docked horse. This practice is now illegal.

Doctor's Wagon
A light, four-wheeled American vehicle having a hooded single seat with a small seat behind. The sides of the seat are cane. The body is hung on two transverse elliptic springs from a perch undercarriage and its construction only permits a quarter-lock.

Dodging the Spokes. *See* Dishing of Wheels.

Dog Cart
A general purpose vehicle which was found in most country coach houses and used for everyday occasions when a liveried coachman was not required. A Dog Cart was often used for taking luggage to the station, for shopping expeditions, for transporting the doctor on his rounds or the lawyer to his office. The two-wheeled variety was built for a single horse or a tandem. There was a seat for two people facing forward and another for two facing the rear. The tail board lets down on two small chains to act as an adjustable foot board for the rear passengers. Early Dog Carts were built with the seating high so that the side profile was somewhat triangular. Shooting dogs for the guns or greyhounds for coursing enthusiasts were carried under the seats. The sides of the vehicle were slatted to provide ventilation. Some were hung on two side-springs, others on three or four springs. There was often some difficulty experienced in balancing the Dog Cart because if those on the rear seat were heavy, the vehicle was tipped backwards making travelling uncomfortable for everyone. Various ideas were tried to overcome this problem. One was to have sliding seats which could be adjusted as necessary. Another was the Lever Balance, patented in 1883. The vehicle was constructed in such a way that by operating a lever the driver could move the body of the carriage backwards or forwards, on its under-carriage, to balance it as he required. Doyle's Patent Safety Rail was another invention thought of for the safety of rear-seat passengers. Some Dog Carts were built of mahogany and oak and were varnished. Others were highly painted. The shafts were usually straight and ran either outside or under the body. Some had their shafts removed to be replaced by a pole so that a pair could be put to in either curricle or cape harness fashion. From these early Dog Carts were developed numerous types of Country Carts.

The Four-Wheeled Dog Cart, or Double Dog Cart, as it was sometimes called, was similar in use and design. Four people could be carried and dogs were transported under the seats. A single, pair, or even a team of small ponies could be put to. Now, Four-Wheeled Dog Carts are in great demand both for private driving and F.E.I. events.

Dog-Cart Phaeton
Alternatively and more commonly known as a Four-Wheeled Dog Cart.

Dog-Leg Stick
A whip which is shaped with a double bend almost like two right-angles, a little way up the stick above the ferrule. The shape somewhat resembles the hind leg, at the hock, of a dog.

Dog Phaeton
Better known as a Four-Wheeled Dog-Cart.

Donkey Market
In the 1890s about 3,000 donkeys were bought and sold each year at Islington Cattle Market. Irish and Welsh imports arrived both on the hoof and in railway trucks to stand in the market amongst the lowest form of London's worn-out working horses. The condition of these were so poor that the donkeys were made to look superior by comparison. Prices varied from £2. 10s. for an average animal to about £30 for an exceptional one. They were bought by costers to pull their fish, vegetable or firewood barrows.

Dormeuse
A luxurious travelling carriage used in the 1800s by the gentry and such people as King's Messengers, embarking on long journeys. The closed body, which was entered by a half-glass door from either side, was built with a long front boot to accommodate the traveller in as much comfort as possible. It was designed so that the occupant could unroll a mattress which was carried in the boot and, with the seat cushions, make up a bed for night journeys. Behind the main body of the chariot was the hooded rumble seat for the servants. This dickey strongly resembled the body of a Cabriolet and afforded protection from bad weather for these passengers. Luggage was stowed in imperials, bonnet boxes and cap boxes which were carried on top of and behind the front boot when the vehicle was postillion driven. Boxes were also carried on the roof and behind the rumble seat. A sword case was built into the back of the body with easy access from the inside.

A Dormeuse was built in 1836 for the seventh Duke of Beaufort by Adams & Hooper.

Vehicles of this type could possibly be classed as the forerunners of the Pullman.

Dos-à-Dos
A general term referring to any vehicle in which the seats are placed back-to-back.

Double Buckboard
A Buckboard with two seats, one behind the other, each accommodating two people.

Double-elbow Spring
This is the most common type of spring now found on two-wheeled and some four-wheeled vehicles. The double-elbow spring is usually fixed at right-angles to the axle by two 'U' bolts. The body of the vehicle is connected to each end of the spring by metal arms. The load of the body is taken by both ends of the

spring and supported in the centre by the axle. Dennett springs are a combination of three double-elbow springs. Platform or telegraph springs are made up from four double-elbow springs. The double-elbow spring is also known as the cross-spring, grasshopper spring, half-elliptic spring, horizontal spring, longitudinal spring, side-spring and transverse spring.

Double Hip Strap
Found in Army harness on the wheel horses where no pad or crupper is used, whether the animals are postillion ridden or driven from the box. The breeching and traces are supported by two straps, each 4 feet 9 inches long with holes punched at both ends. One end of each strap is buckled to the detachable tug fixed to the breeching and the other end of each strap is buckled to the detachable tug on the trace on the other side. The two straps cross as they pass over the loins. They are riveted at this point in order that they should lie neatly when the horse is in draught.

Double-Ring Snaffle
Also known as a Wilson Snaffle. *See* Bitting.

Double Terret
Used for a tandem and found on the wheeler's pad. A bar with a roller divides the top and bottom halves of the terret so that when the lead and wheel reins are passed through the same terret they do not stick together and can be operated independently.

Double Victoria
Said to combine the qualities of a Victoria and a Sociable. It was built to copy the outline and accommodation facilities of the Sociable and resembles the Victoria in size and weight. This carriage was also known as a Sociable without doors, though some illustrations show Double Victorias with small doors on either side. The rear hooded seat accommodates two people and the front seat takes two more, facing to the rear. Splashboards curve over the wheels to protect the passengers and step from mud. *See* Victoria.

Douga
A wooden arch which is found on Russian vehicles, fixed to the ends of the shafts and passing high over the horse's neck. Its purpose is mainly to keep the shafts apart though it also acts as a bearing rein carrier and it is frequently adorned with bells. When a Troika is put to, a douga is used on the middle horse.

Doyle's Patent Safety Rail
A device was invented in the 1800s by Thomas Doyle of The Abbey Carriage Works, Dublin, to prevent passengers from falling from the rear seat of a vehicle. A bar was fixed in two halves by hinges to the sides of the vehicle. When the passengers were seated, the bar was lowered so that the two ends met across the front of the passengers. The ends were joined together by a hook which passed over a knob. When it was in position it acted both as an arm rest and as a safety barrier to prevent travellers from being thrown on to the road if the horse should suddenly start forward.

Drab
Some driving aprons and coachman's overcoats are referred to as being made of drab cloth. This applies to the colour, which is beige.

Drag
Also known as a Park Coach or Private Coach. A Drag is used for private driving purposes and is a sporting vehicle. It should be appointed accordingly. Classes are held at major shows, and meets are arranged by The Coaching Club for teams to Private Coaches as well as to Road and Regimental Coaches. A Drag was very often built lighter than a Road Coach and has a more refined finish. There is frequently discreet carving on the undercarriage. The shackles on the spring ends are leather covered. The box seat holds the coachman on a high padded seat with one passenger to his left. The two roof seats are built to carry four passengers on each and the 'lazy backs' are designed to hinge so that they can be laid flat when passengers are not carried. The imperial is put between these seats. The rumble seat is built on iron stays and accommodates the two grooms. Behind the rumble is carried a spare main bar and a spare single bar, with the main bar uppermost. These are fixed by straps. The door of the hind boot, below the rumble seat, is hinged at the bottom and has iron supports at the sides so that when it is opened it is held in an horizontal position to form a table to support the lunch boxes. An iron ladder which folds in half is carried at the rear of the drag. It is used to assist passengers in climbing to and from the roof seats. A basket for the horn, umbrellas and parasols is buckled on to the nearside of the hindmost roof seat. A skid is carried under the left side of the body. The interior of the drag is trimmed in cloth, morocco leather or whipcord. There are holders to take the lamps when they are not in use. Very often a spare jointed whip is carried on a board in a leather case hung under the box seat. Waterproof rugs are laid on the front seat ready for use should the outside passengers require them. There is a door to the front boot, behind the back of the front seat. Here is stowed such items as rugs for the horses, head collars, and spare equipment and tools, in case of an accident. A Drag is usually painted in a sombre hue in the family's colours with the owner's crest or monogram on the crest panels and hind boot. The body and the panel of the hind boot should match in colour. The underside of the footboard and the cheeks or risers should be of the same colour as the undercarriage. The iron work, apart from the springs, is painted black so that touching up can be achieved without notice. Lining out with a single broad stripe is restricted to the wheels, hub ends of spokes, hubs, springs, pole and bars.

Drag Harness
This is superior to, and lighter in finish than, Road Coach harness. It is made of black leather throughout with double rows of stitching wherever necessary on items like the traces. The blinkers, collars, tops of pads, face drops and fronts of false martingales are faced with patent leather. Buxton bits and bridoon bearing reins are usual. The hames have anchor, or branch, pulls and the hame clips have three rivets. The wheelers' traces have quick-release ends or French loops. The leaders' traces cock-eyes are fixed so that the screw heads are uppermost. The crupper back straps are of the martingale type. Crests or monograms adorn the blinkers, face drops, martingale fronts and pads. The furniture on the

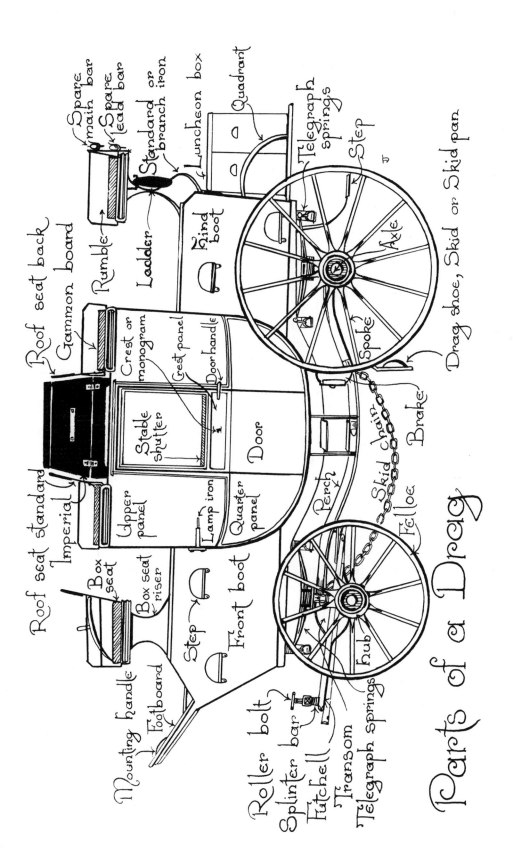

Parts of a Drag

harness should match that of the metal parts, such as door handles, of the coach. If the base of the crest is gold then the furniture will be brass. If the crest is based on a silver background then the furniture will be of a white metal such as silver plate.

Drag Horses
A Drag team should match in stride and colour and combine the qualities of good breeding, substance, showy action, presence, courage and be perfectly mannered. The wheelers can be slightly taller and have a little more substance than the leaders. Flashy white markings are not desirable.

Drag Shoe
Also known as a Skid and a Skid Pan. This is the metal device which was placed under the wheel of a heavily laden coach, by the guard, or coachman if no guard was carried, before descending a steep hill. The drag shoe resembles a piece of guttering with a flat base just wide enough to go under the rim of the iron tyre and has right-angle sides which reach to the tops of the felloe. At the front of the shoe is a hole to which the skid chain is attached. This chain is hooked at the other end to the centre of the front axle at exactly the right length to ensure that the skid remains under the wheel. When shoes became worn, new soles were welded on. Bolting of new shoes was not favoured because bolt heads soon wore out. When the drag shoe is not in use it is hooked on to the body on the nearside near to the brake arm bracket.

Drag Staff
Used on travelling carriages to hold the vehicle if the horses stopped when climbing a hill. A pole which trailed along the ground, was fixed by a hinge to the rear axle. If the carriage started to roll backwards, the drag staff dug into the road and held the vehicle.

Drag Waggon
Used in America for hauling heavy logs with a pair or a team. A strong platform is constructed on an axle between a pair of wheels. One end of the timber is placed on this support and the other end is dragged along the ground. A pole and a pair of swingle trees complete the construction of this waggon.

Draught Eye
The part of the hames to which the trace, hame tug or shoulder piece is attached. *See* Pull.

Draught Horse Collar
The name which was given to ordinary collars used by the Army for normal work. Sizes ranged from 20 to $25\frac{1}{2}$ inches, going up in $\frac{1}{2}$ inches. Collars for Army heavy transport horses were larger in every way.

Draught Rein
The longer rein, of a team or pair rein, which goes from the outside ring of the bit back to the driver's hand and to which the coupling rein is buckled. *See* Coupling.

Draught Tug
Found on Army harness. It is a short strap which passes through a dee at the

rearmost end of the breast collar. The back end of the strap has a quick-release metal fitting to which the trace is attached. The front end of the strap has a ring and four chain links to which the lead horse's trace is fixed. This gives direct draught, through the tug, from the leader to the swingle tree.

Draw Bar. *See* Splinter Bar.

Draw Bar
When horses are put to, two, three, four, five or six abreast, they are put to single trees attached to eveners, which in turn are fixed to the draw bar which is at the front of the vehicle.

Draw Iron. *See* Wheel Iron.

Dray. *See* Lorrie.

Dressage Cart
The name which is used for a training cart on the Continent.

Dressage Test. *See* Advanced Dressage Test, Competition A, Five Minute Dressage Test, and diagrams 1, 2 and 3.

Dress Chariot. *See* Chariot.

Dress Coach. *See* State Coach.

Dressed Leather
This applies to a hide which has been made into leather, smoothed and levelled, then softened with oil and dyed black or brown.

Dress Harness. *See* State Harness.

Driving Apparatus
Fairman Rogers devised a method for practising the handling of team reins in order that the muscles of the left arm could be kept in trim.

Two pulleys are made out of 'U' shaped metal. Across each 'U' are two rollers. At the round part of the 'U' is a small hook in order that the fitting can be hooked to an eye screwed into a piece of woodwork such as a door. Four pieces of leather, to represent reins, each 1 inch wide, are passed over the four rollers in the two 'U's. At the end of the reins are four rings on to which are fixed four wires. Weights of varying equal measure are hung on to the wires. It was considered that 3 lb. on each rein represented the pull taken by a light but strong-going team.

With such a driving apparatus beginners can be taught the principles of handling team reins and daily practice can be obtained without putting to.

Droitzschka
As well as applying to the Russian Droschki, this name was also given to an English vehicle of a totally different design. The English Droitzschka was similar to the Britzschka. It was a low-bodied, four-wheeled vehicle with the passengers' seat placed over the rear axle. The body was built so that it sank low at the centre to accommodate the travellers' legs. There was not much room, because in front of their feet was the arch in the body for the front wheels to turn. Two ponies, or a single horse, were driven from a front box seat, large enough for two people. The vehicle was heavy, as its design made it

necessary to reinforce the body with iron plates. It was suitable for the elderly, being low, easy to mount, and unlikely to overturn.

Drop
This is also known as a face-piece and is the decorative part of harness which lies on the horse's forehead. It is buckled into the winker stay buckle on the head-piece under the winker stays. The drop is oval in shape going to a point at the bottom. It is usually covered with patent leather and is adorned with the owner's crest or monogram. A drop is worn in show harness, drag harness and coster harness.

Drop off
Before coaches had roof seats, outside travellers had to cling on, as best as they could, to the sloping roof of the coach. If, during a journey, a passenger should by any chance fall asleep he probably lost his grip and dropped off. This was probably the origin of the present day slang term.

Droschki
A Russian vehicle on which the passenger sits with a leg each side of a padded seat as though he is riding a horse. The shafts of this extraordinary conveyance have an arch which passes over the horse's neck, acting both as a rein rail and as a way of keeping the shafts apart. Also known as a Droitzschka and a Drosky.

Drosky. *See* Droschki.

Ducker, Noel B.
President of The Coaching Club from 1946 to 1949.

Dump Cart
An American term for a cart which could be tipped backwards in order to un-load the contents. This is known as a Tip Cart in England.

Duobus
A type of two-wheeled cab of similar design to the Boulnois Cab.

Dust-cart Horse
A strong heavy horse was required to withstand the hard work entailed in hauling cartloads of refuse, sometimes with an overall weight of 3 tons, along London's wooden, granite and asphalt streets. These animals who weighed, on average, about 15 cwt., were mostly bred on English farms. Foreign breeds did not stay sound. Their tendons suffered from the concussion caused by the vary-ing surfaces. It was as important for a refuse cart horse to be capable of backing a load as it was for him to go forward. The first thing that he was taught, when he came to the vestry, was to back obediently and skilfully. Once a man was put in charge of a vestry horse, he kept the same animal for the entire period of its working life. Care was taken to match man and horse so that their strides were compatible. A liaison then developed between the two, which led to a satis-factory working partnership.

Dutch Collar
More usually known as a breast collar.

Dutfin
The name sometimes given to the bridle worn by a farm horse.

Earth Cart
A two-wheeled commercial vehicle which was built solidly with an iron reinforced oak frame. It resembled a strong farm cart and was used for carting
builders' materials. The sideboards were loose so that they could be removed
and the body was constructed so that it could be tipped for unloading. The cost
of such a cart in about 1890 was in the region of £17.

Edgeworth, Dr Lovell
In 1768 he was awarded three gold medals by The Society of English Arts and
Manufacturers for building a four-wheeled carriage which had independent
suspension on each wheel.

Eight-Horse Hitch
With an American heavy horse hitch the wheelers have the wagon pole between
them. The body team have a swing pole as do the swing team. The leaders do
not have a pole. The team is driven with eight reins. Four are held in each hand,
to correspond with the side to which they apply. In each case the lead rein
passes under the little finger and goes upwards across the palm, the body team
rein goes under the third finger, the swing team rein under the middle finger
and the leader's rein under the index finger. The ends drop down over the
thumb. Each rein is operated as required by the finger and thumb of the other
hand.

Eights
In America when a twenty-mule team is hitched to haul a heavy load, the
fourth pair from the front of the wagon is known as the eights. *See* Twenty-
Mule Team.

Ekka
A single-horse cart found in India with which no traces are used. The draught
comes through the shafts to the pad which is kept from slipping backwards by a
breast collar on to which some of the pulling power is transferred.

Elastic Curb Chain. *See* Curb Chain.

Elbow Bit
A curb bit with the cheeks, or branches, set back from the mouth in order to
prevent the horse from catching hold of them with his lips. Made with varying
mouthpieces. *See* Bitting.

Elbow Spring
A short spring resembling one-half of a side-spring. Elbow springs were sometimes used in pairs to form one spring. They were placed, one on top of the
other and joined together at one end. The other two ends were fixed to the body
of the vehicle and to the undercarriage. In this form some authorities called
them a nutcracker spring. Later, elbow springs were used for such purposes as
joining the front of the body to the shafts with some vehicles, e.g. Tilbury Gigs.
An elbow spring is used on the underneath of the pole of a Curricle where the
strap connects the pole to the curricle bar.

Elephant and Castle
A horse repository in London where, every Monday up until the late 1960s,

large quantities of horses, ponies and donkeys of every conceivable shape and size changed hands under the auctioneer's hammer, as did harness, saddlery and vehicles. Horses stood in rows of stalls and a few stood in loose boxes, before the sale started, to enable vendors to inspect them. There were four or five blocks of stables on the ground floor and a further row of stables on the first floor, which was reached by a ramp. These were only used when the ground floor stables were full. In the centre of the building was the auctioneer's rostrum in front of which the animals were run up and down, by stewards, between rows of dealers, costers and other members of the horse world in search of a bargain. A further area held vehicles and rows of harness and saddlery. This sale yard was affectionately known as 'The Elephant' to the regulars.

Elliott, Obadiah
The inventor, in 1802, of a method of building carriages without the necessity of a perch. This led, by 1804, to the introduction and use of elliptic springs which revolutionized carriage building.

Elliptic Spring
First used in 1804 by a coachbuilder called Elliot and found on numerous present-day vehicles such as Governess Carts, Four-Wheeled Dog Carts and many American Four-Wheelers. It is made up from two side-springs, one in an upwards curve and the other in a downwards curve. The whole forms an oval-shaped outline. The body of the vehicle is usually joined to the upper spring and the axle to the lower spring. The invention of the elliptic spring caused a great improvement in carriage design. Perches were no longer essential and vehicles could be made lighter and more elegant.

Elm
A wood which was used for making the naves of the wheels; also used for floors.

Embroiderer
Such people were employed indirectly by the coachbuilder to embroider the crests and similar decorations on the seats and hammercloths of high-class carriages.

Enamelled Leather
That which is coated in an elastic type of japan.

Equirotal Carriages
Vehicles of varying design, all with the prefix 'Equirotal' and built on the same basic principles, were invented by William Bridges Adams, in the 1830s, to overcome the failings which he felt existed in the majority of four-wheeled carriages of the period. His Equirotal Carriages were all built with four equal-sized wheels (from where the name is derived). They all hung on four springs which were on the same horizontal level. They all had a body which was hinged at the centre so that when the horse or horses turned, the front half of the vehicle with the driver followed the track and the rear half articulated on a central pivot. This, claimed Adams, combined the advantages of large front wheels and a reasonable lock.

The Equirotal Pony Phaeton resembled a Gig at the front and a Cabriolet at the back. Both seats were built on lockers which were used for carrying parcels and luggage. Behind the rear seat was a platform on which the groom stood when the hood was raised and sat when it was lowered. If the rear seat passengers wished to drive, the front seat could be removed. For travelling, a luggage trunk could be put in its place. This vehicle was pulled by a single horse or a pair of ponies.

The Equirotal Phaeton was similar in outline to a Mail Phaeton. The front part had a hooded driving seat and the rear part had a railed seat for servants.

The Equirotal Omnibus was designed to accommodate twelve passengers inside. It was drawn by a pair of horses which were driven from a seat on the roof of the front half of the omnibus. The two halves were connected by flexible sides, which formed a circle, providing internal access from front to rear.

The Equirotal Town Chariot had a coachman's and groom's seat at the front which was covered by a hammercloth. A large quantity of luggage could be carried in the locker between the front seat and the front axle. The lamps were placed behind the seat, in front of the chariot body. The rear half of the carriage consisted of a roomy chariot which was entered by half-glass doors situated on each side of the bow front. There were windows next to the doors. The vehicle which could seat up to six passengers, was so spacious that if only two people were travelling a table could be set up. A form of central heating was installed. Water pipes, which were heated by a lamp underneath, ran inside the carriage.

The Equirotal Mail Coach differed considerably from the Royal Mail Coach. The front half consisted of the coachman's seat with a seat for passengers behind. Below these two seats was a large luggage well which extended down beneath the front axle in order to keep the centre of gravity low to prevent overturning. The rear half consisted of a closed coach body with windows at the side. This too had a well below for luggage. The guard's seat was behind the coach. No passengers or luggage were carried on the roof. It was claimed by the inventor that if this coach became stuck in the snow then the two halves could be separated by the removal of the connecting bolts and that a pair of horses could be put to either half with a pole and harnessed, curricle fashion, to continue the journey. Two coachbuilders were constructing Equirotal Carriages in 1837, Hobson & Co of London and J. Buchanan of Glasgow, but the existence of these vehicles was short lived.

Eridge Cart

A four-wheeled vehicle which combines the features of a Dog Cart with a Pony Phaeton. The four-seat body resembles that of a low Dog Cart. In front of the driver's seat is a high dashboard. The front wheels are placed well in front of the dash to enable a good lock. The whole is hung on four elliptic springs. The vehicle came from Eridge Castle and it is thought to have been built to the design of Lord Abergavenny. It is now in the Science Museum, London.

Essex Cart

A type of general-purpose, two-wheeled country cart built with a railed-sided square body, decorated by vertical brass rods. The high, forward facing seat has a leather lazyback fastened with a brass buckle. The straight shafts run under the body which is hung on two side- and one cross-spring. The vehicle, at the turn of the century, would have probably been used for taking piglets and chickens to market during the week as well as the family out for drives on Sundays.

117

Evener

When horses are driven three, four, five or six abreast, and harnessed with single trees, they have to be put to in such a way that their pulling power is equalized no matter from which direction it is coming. This problem is overcome by using a bar between the drawbar and single bar called an evener. The horses are put to single bars which are fixed to eveners at the correct place to equalize the draught, as it goes through to the draw bar and to the load.

Excelsior Combination Carriage

A vehicle, exhibited in 1885, at the Inventions Exhibition, by Messrs Clift, which could be easily converted into a Phaeton from a two-wheeled conveyance, by the adjustment of some bolts. The idea found considerable favour.

Eyeless Team

Such a team is recorded to have been driven for a stage of the London and Basingstoke coach by the Duke of Somerset in the 1830s. The four horses, which were said to have wandered a bit on starting, were all blind.

F.E.I.

Federation Equestre Internationale. *See* Combined Driving.

Face Piece

A dressy adornment to the bridle which fastens into the winker stay buckle and lies under the browband on the forehead. It is often decorated with the owner's crest or monogram. Also known as face drop.

Faggoting

A method of producing strong metal for axles. *See* Axles.

False Belly Band

Found on pair and team harness.

It is a strap with a buckle at each end, which is attached to the two points sewn on to the dees on the lower sides of the hame tug buckles. Some harness has one side of the false belly band sewn on to the hame tug buckle and is buckled to the hame tug point on the other side. For the nearside horse this buckles on the left side and with the offside horse it buckles on the right side.

The purpose of the false belly band is to prevent the hame tug buckle from jumping up and down when the horses are in action.

False Breeching. *See* Brown's Patent Breeching.

False Collar

A flat leather pad which is shaped to fit under the collar. It has a martingale-type strap at the bottom to prevent it from working upwards and is fastened to the collar by small straps to keep it in position. A false collar was used as a protection against sore shoulders when the full collar was slightly too large and would otherwise have rocked.

False Leg
The iron guard which a postillion wore, on the outside of his right leg, to protect it from becoming injured by the pole.

False Martingale
A strap which goes from the collar to the girth. The point is passed round the collar and the lower hame strap, hame chain or upper part of the kidney link and comes down to meet a buckle just below the collar. Under the buckle is usually an oval-shaped drop which is sometimes of patent leather and decorated with a monogram or crest. Behind this, is stitched a martingale-type strap with a buckle for adjustment. The girth and belly band are passed through the loop. The purpose of a false martingale is to hold the hames on to the collar, with pair or team wheelers, and to hold the collar down.

Farmers' Draught
When the draught is taken through the short chains from the hames to the dees on the tops of the shafts.

Farm Harness
This differs in many ways from private driving harness. *See* Bellyband, Britchin, Carting, Cart Saddle, Chain Backband, Chain Gears, Dutfin, Hames, Hame Chain, Horns of Hame, Hame Rein, Lines, Plough Gears, Sling Gears, and Stretcher.

Fast Mouth
A mouthpiece which is fixed solidly to the cheek of the bit. It slides neither up nor down, nor does it allow the ring of the bit to swivel sideways.

Felloe
The wooden part of the wheel, inside the iron tyre or iron channel, into which the spokes are driven.

Felloe Pieces
Part of the bottom carriage of a four-wheeled vehicle. There are front and hind felloe pieces. They form the surface upon which the fifth wheel or wheel plate bears. These form the arcs of a circle whereas the fifth wheel, upon which they bear, is a complete circle.

Felly
Also spelt Felloe.

Felton, William
Coachbuilder of the 18th century, and author of the first book on the subject which was entitled *A Treatise on Carriages*, published in 1794.

Fender
An American term for the splashboard.

Fiddle
A slang term for a whip.

Fiddle
The name by which a round harness buckle is sometimes known.

Farm Harness

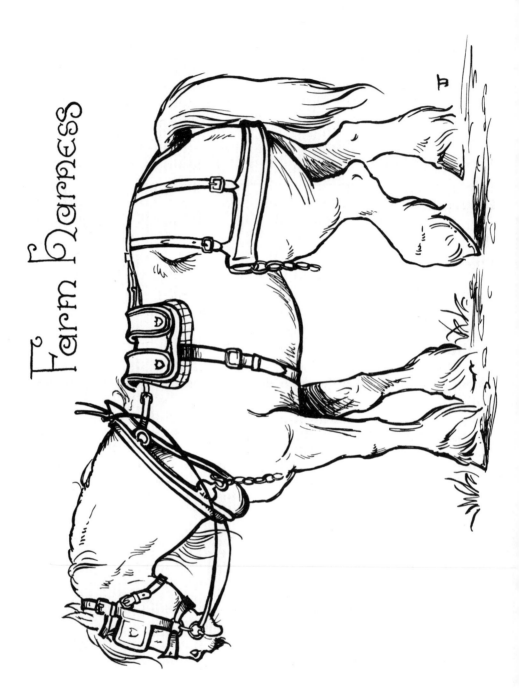

Field Cart

A two-wheeled country cart which was built on Dog Cart lines with back to back seats for four people. The shafts run outside the square body which is hung on two side- and one cross-spring.

Fifth Wheel

A circular piece of half-round iron attached to the underneath of the front of the body of a four-wheeled vehicle. It forms a bearing for the front axle and undercarriage assembly.

Fiftieth Meet of the Coaching Club

A record number of thirty-nine coaches assembled in Hyde Park for this occasion in 1894. Most of them were driven to Hurlingham Club for lunch.

Fill Gear

The single harness used on a farm horse between the shafts when carting. Also known as thiller gear and cart gear. *See* Farm Harness.

Fillet Strap

The name given to the little oval-shaped drop which hangs over both sides of the loins from the back strap of the crupper. It is worn solely for decoration and is sometimes faced with patent and bears the owner's crest or monogram. Fillet straps are now most commonly seen with coster harness, when they are brightly coloured to match the trim on the saddles and bridles. They often bear either the coster's initials or a small horse's head in metal.

Fire Engine Horse

Greys of vanner type, which were capable of galloping, were employed by the London Fire Brigade. They stood with their scanty harness suspended above them. This enabled these horses to be put to with the maximum speed when they were summoned. Diagonal straps, with bells, were worn instead of pads. The traces were already hooked to the swingle tree which could be quickly attached to the fire engine.

Fireman. *See* Axle Tree Maker.

Five Minute Dressage Test

As the author is the compiler of the 'Five Minute Test' which was used at various events including Lowther in 1977 for singles, pairs and tandems, it was felt that it might be of some help to new competitors if the writer's requirements, as a judge, were outlined.

Competitors' times are announced after the closing of declarations, and well in advance, to enable Whips to plan their day to work their horses before executing their test. The time required for working in naturally varies from one horse to another. Some animals may need over an hour before they will settle to perform an accurate test whilst others become dull if they are worked too much and go better after a brief warm up. This knowledge can, unfortunately, only be discovered by trial and error as the way in which horses go at home frequently bears little relation to how they perform under the stress of the competitive atmosphere of an event.

The judges, who sit at C, B and E, to enable three different angles to be seen of each movement, often try to permit the next competitor to drive round the outside of the arena as soon as the previous competitor has finished his Test. It is advisable to be as near to the edge of the boundary rope as possible so that no time is wasted. It is a great help to be given this opportunity to allow the horse to settle to any unfamiliar sights which might otherwise cause distraction.

Then, when all three judges are ready, the President of the Jury (sitting at C) will ring a bell, or sound his car horn, and the competitor must start his test within one minute or risk elimination.

MOVEMENT ONE A *Enter at working trot.*
          X *Halt. Salute.*

It is important to position the turnout well back from the entrance to the arena so that a bold straight approach can be made. A hesitant, weaving entry does not give a good first impression. It is best to look between and beyond the horses' ears with a single or tandem and ahead of the pole with a pair towards the President's car in order to drive absolutely straight down the centre line. This is usually marked with chalk, creosote or sawdust. A hesitant entry, to one side of the line with the inevitable effort to correct the error usually results in a series of deviations to either side which does little to enhance the competitor to the judges.

The halt is made at X when the horse is over the mark which is indicated by a large cross on the ground. He should stand attentively on the bit with his head still, bent at the poll, whilst the Whip salutes the President.

It is at this point that the stop watch is started, probably by the President's writer. Five minutes is allowed for the test and half a penalty is added for every commenced period of one second after five minutes has expired. It is the exception, rather than the rule, to exceed the time allowed and usually only occurs if the competitor forgets the test. He then has to be stopped and put right which costs five penalties for the first error, ten for the second, fifteen for the third and the fourth error results in elimination. A groom or passenger dismounting for any reason costs the competitor the same penalties. The stop watch ticks relentlessly on whilst errors are made and corrected and it is this which can cause time faults.

MOVEMENT TWO XCMB *Working trot.*

A smooth transition forward from the halt is desirable and it is important to drive straight down the centre line, towards C. The turn to the right should be calm and not made too soon or too late. A quarter circle should be enscribed with the horse looking in the direction of the turn. It is a common fault for horses to fall in which necessitates their being held out to the left. This results in apparent looking out on this turn and the following quarter circle at the corner of the arena. The trot should be workmanlike with the hoofbeats maintaining absolute regularity.

MOVEMENT THREE B *Collected trot, circle right 20 metres.*

The movement should begin as the horse comes alongside the judge at B and should be a true circle between B and X. Common faults are falling in, an irregular figure and an uneven pace which either lacks impulsion or is over exuberant with one diagonal hitting the ground harder than the other. It is quite frequent for the first half of the circle to be a correctly executed demi circle and the second half to be egg shaped.

MOVEMENT FOUR   BFAK   *Collected trot.*

Here, the judges are looking for an active collected pace with the horse maintaining an even tempo. The quarters should be well engaged with adequate impulsion. The head must be still with the profile of the front of the face on or fractionally ahead of the perpendicular. Over bending will be heavily penalized as will such resistances as being above the bit with a concave neck and hollow back.

MOVEMENT FIVE   KXM   *Extended trot.*

As soon as the horse reaches K he should be turned across the arena to execute a straight line along the diagonal, going over X on the way.

MOVEMENT SIX   MCHE   *Collected trot.*

On reaching M, the horse should be brought back calmly to a shortened stride without resistance. The collected trot is maintained to E.

MOVEMENT SEVEN   *Collected trot. Circle left 20 metres.*

The same applies here as for movement three.

MOVEMENT EIGHT   EKAD   *Working trot.*

On completing the circle, the horse must be sent forward into a longer stride. There is not much time before this movement is completed.

MOVEMENT NINE   DX   *Walk.*

This, in some ways, is the most difficult transition of the test. The horse has just executed a quarter circle at A to turn down the centre line and there is often a tendency to over-shoot and come to D off centre. D appears very quickly and is marked on the ground with a cross. To bring the horse to walk, after a turn, on the centre line, calmly and without fuss is not easy.

MOVEMENT TEN   X   *Halt. Immobility 10 seconds.*
                         Rein back 3 metres.

A square halt must be maintained for ten seconds. The head should be still and the horse must not anticipate the rein back. Resistance from the mouth usually results in a stiffened jaw and neck, hollow back and crooked rein back which will be severely penalized.

MOVEMENT ELEVEN   XG   *Walk.*   G   *Halt. Salute.*
                         Leave the arena at working trot.

The transition forward from rein back to walk should be smooth and the walk calm, forward and unhurried.

The marker G is indicated on the ground with a cross as at X and D and the final halt should be executed as the horse's body is over the mark. A calm, square halt and a cheerful looking Whip giving his salute to the President will please the judges.

At this point the stop watch will be stopped and the time recorded on the dressage sheet.

It is important to pay attention to the way in which the arena is left. Judges will be watching as the turnout goes round the perimeter of the arena to leave at A and final assessment for the 40 marks awarded for Paces, Impulsion. Obedience and Driver will be made.

Five Springs
A method of springing which is made up with a combination of two side-springs, two elbow-springs and a cross-spring. The weight of the body is transferred via the elbow-springs and cross-spring through the side-springs to the axle.

Fixed Tug
Found on a breast collar. The breast strap is held up by a neck strap whose points buckle on either side to a strap and buckle coming up from the lay of the breast collar. The strap passes round the lay and buckles into the same buckle as the neck strap. It is with Army harness that this is called a fixed tug. *See* Army Harness and Detachable Tug.

Flagging
Better known as docking.

Flange Plate
The circular iron plate to which the nave of a wheel with a mail axle is bolted. Also known as a moon plate. *See* Axle.

Flat and Laid On
The name given to reins which are made with two layers of leather. A narrow strip about $\frac{1}{2}$ inch wide is laid down the centre of 1-inch reins and secured by two rows of stitching.

Flax
This was used extensively by the carriage builder both for the manufacture of thread, cord, canvas and floor cloth as well as for making braid.

Float
A two-wheeled country vehicle. The rectangular body was built as low to the ground as possible. Many have a cranked axle. It is entered from a door at the back, on either side of which are the seats for the driver and passenger. Floats were often used for delivering milk. Churns were carried and the milk was baled out, as required for the householders, with a metal mug. This measure had a hooked handle so that the mug could be hooked on to the rim of the churn. There are a number of floats still in existence. The best-built type is the Pickering Float.

Floating Keeper
A loop of leather found on the backstrap of the crupper next to where it passes through the dee on the saddle, or pad, in order to hold the two parts of the backstrap neatly together. It is quite usual to have up to three or even four floating keepers with a martingale type of crupper backstrap.

Floating Leaders
A slang term for idle leaders of a team who do not go freely forward.

Flock
A type of stuffing used in heavy transport horse collars in the Army.

Flowers
At the turn of the century it was deemed correct for the horses' bridles to be decorated with flowers. Coachmen were presented with flowers during the summer by ladies along their road. In the winter, holly replaced the flowers.

Owners of Drags often adopted a flower which was compatible in colour to that of the coach. Artificial flowers were used by many. They were fixed by wire to the upper cheek buckles on the outer sides. On dressy occasions, flowers to match those on the horses, were worn by the Whip and grooms.

Floyd Hansom
A type of Hansom Cab which first appeared in 1885. It was built for private use and designed to give every possible comfort to the travellers. A glazed hood could be let down from the roof to the dash to protect passengers from bad weather. The back and side windows of the body could be opened. The interior was superbly finished with ivory fittings, mirrors, a rack for parcels, a holder for umbrellas, a watch case and a bell with which to signal to the driver.

Floyds, Messrs
A London coachbuilding firm whose speciality was Hansom Cabs.

Fly
Slang term for a Cab.

Fly-Head-Swing. *See* Fly Terret.

Fly Terret
The metal decoration which is worn on the centre of the crown piece of the bridle by heavy horses. The ornament is shaped like a terret and has a medallion designed like a miniature horse brass hanging from the centre by a hinge which enables it to swing backwards and forwards inside the terret. Some have a further decoration on the top of the terret. One brewery had the initials of the establishment stamped on the central swinger and a bottle-shaped emblem on the top. Some have bells in the centre and on each side. These are known as bell terrets.

Flyer. *See* Fly Terret.

Flying Coach
Coaches which travelled in the 17th century from London to Exeter, York and Chester taking four days. Six passengers travelled in the coach. They each paid £2 during the summer and an extra 5 shillings in the winter. On top of this, a tip of 1 shilling was expected by each coachman of which, on the 200-mile journey, there were five. In comparison with the time taken by these flying coaches, the ordinary coaches of the period travelled at 4 to 4½ miles an hour.

In 1754, another 'Flying Coach' was advertised. An offer was made to convey passengers on the London and Manchester road, covering 187 miles in 4½ days.

In 1755 the proprietors of a London and Exeter coach advertised a safe journey taking two weeks.

Flying Waggon. *See* Broad-Wheeled Waggon.

Folding Head
Some vehicles such as Cabriolets, George IV Phaetons and Britzschkas were built with a folding leather hood which could be put up if the weather became inclement or left down if the passengers desired to take the air..

Also known as a folding hood.

Folding Hood. *See* Folding Head.

Foot Board

The part of a vehicle on which the feet of the driver and passenger rest. An angle of 33° to the horizontal was considered correct and most comfortable for the foot board of a coach. It should be deep enough to prevent the toes from extending over the top, but not too large. The Mail Coaches had small foot boards so that the coachman could easily see the wheelers' traces.

Footboard Lamp

A small lamp which is fixed to the foot board of a coach to illuminate the pole head.

Foot Rest

It is essential to have a movable foot rest when driving a two-wheeled vehicle which has an adjustable seat. The foot rest should be made of rubber-covered wood and shaped so that the feet are placed at an angle of 90° to the legs. This provides purchase if the horse starts to pull. The foot rest is best if it is secured to the floor by two pegs which fit into a choice of pairs of holes. Some foot rests are made out of metal and take the form of a bar. Although these are quite satisfactory, care has to be taken in dismounting owing to the danger of a foot becoming caught under the rail.

Footstool

Shallow wooden boxes were sometimes placed above the front and rear boots for ladies occupying the roof seats of a coach who would not have been able to reach the floor without these. Footstools were also provided for the passengers on the outer sides of four-seater roof seats where the foot hold is incomplete.

Footwarmer

Various warmers were made for use both in carriages and sleighs. Some were filled with hot water, others contained burning coals and some were stove heated and then wrapped in paper to maintain the heat. They were made of steel, copper and stone. One type, invented in 1891, had a loose flap of carpeting which covered the feet whilst they were against the warmer. This, the makers claimed, enabled the whole of the feet, not just the soles, to be warmed. The lasting period of this warmer was given as twelve hours, in a carriage.

Forder, Messrs

A coachbuilding establishment of Upper St. Martin's Lane, which was well known for its Hansom Cabs.

Forecarriage

That part of the undercarriage which consists of the front wheels and their axle, the lower half of the wheel plate, the axle bed, the sway bar, the futchells, the splinter bar and all the intervening smaller parts which vary so much from one vehicle to another.

Fore Wale

The foremost rim of a collar.

Forger. *See* Axle Tree Maker.

Forhoss

When farm horses were driven at length, the leader was known by this name. He was also referred to as the forhust.

Forhust. *See* Forhoss.

Forty Horse Hitch
The Schlitz forty horse hitch, which made its debut in 1972, can be seen annually on the Fourth of July, taking part in the Schlitz Circus Parade in Milwaukee, U.S.A. The chestnut horses are of the Belgian draft breed and all have white blazes and light coloured manes and tails. They are harnessed four abreast and ten deep to the Schlitz Circus Bandwagon. The overall length of the horses and wagon is one hundred and thirty-five feet.

The harness is lavishly trimmed with orange decorations to match the orange circus-type uniforms which are worn by the drivers and outriders.

The team is driven by one man, Mr Dick Sparrow, on the straight. Five reins are held in each hand. They go down to the wheelers who are known as the number one team; the pole end horses, called the number two team; the fifth team from the wagon, number five; the eighth team from the rear, number eight, and the leaders, number ten.

The reins to the number two team lie under the little fingers of each hand and go up through the hand to be held between the thumbs and index fingers. The number five team reins lie between the third and little fingers and go on top of the number two reins over the palm. The number eight reins go between the middle and third fingers and lie on top of the twos and fives. The lead reins pass over the index fingers and go down the palm and the wheel reins are held between the index and middle fingers below the lead reins.

When a tight corner has to be negotiated, the leaders' reins are passed to a second driver and the wheelers' reins to a third driver leaving Dick Sparrow to hold six reins.

A further assistant sits behind Dick Sparrow to ensure that the ends of the reins are kept straight and without twists after they have been shortened to negotiate turns. When the horses straighten, several feet of rein are pulled through his hands. Any twists would inevitably result in them being wrenched from Dick Sparrow's hands.

The 'forty' is accompanied by skilled outriders, who can be relied upon to act instantly should the need arise.

Four at Length
When four farm horses were put to, one in front of the other, they were controlled by two men who walked on the offside of the forhoss and the lash-hoss with whips placed over their necks. The pin-hoss and thiller followed on their own. Displays were given at shows when the team proved their obedience in performing circles and figures. No part of the harness was used to guide the team and any commands given were whispered.

Fourgon
A four-wheeled vehicle with a hooded, cabriolet type body at the front, and a van-like back which was used at the turn of the century for conveying servants and luggage. On the occasion of a lengthy tour, when a large amount of luggage was required, this would be stowed in numbered wooden boxes at the rear and covered by a waterproof sheet. The Fourgon was taken ahead of the gentry's

party by the courier and ladies' maid, so that luggage could be unpacked in readiness for their arrival.

Four-in-Hand Driving Club
This club was formed in 1856 under the presidency of the Duke of Beaufort and originally limited to thirty members. It was agreed that coaches should meet at least two days in the season and drive to an agreed venue for dinner. The Four-in-Hand Driving Club reigned alone until 1870 when the Coaching Club was formed.

Four-wheeled Dog-Cart. *See* Dog-Cart.

French Four-wheeled Hansom. *See* Court Hansom.

French Loop
Some traces, used on a pair or the wheel horses of a team, terminate in a loop which passes over the roller bolt.

French Pole Pieces
Pole straps which are detachable for cleaning purposes.

French Tilbury Tug
These are used when it is desirous that the shafts be kept still. The comfort of travelling in a four-wheeled vehicle is greatly improved with the use of Tilbury Tugs without which the shafts jog up and down with every trotting stride. Some two-wheeled vehicles ride better when Tilbury tugs are employed. The tug is buckled on to each side of the short backband. Below the tug buckle is a leather-covered metal half-circle in which the shaft lies. On the outer side of this cup there is a metal dee to which the belly band point is stitched. The point is passed over the shaft, and through the lower half of the tug buckle before going down through a metal or leather dee on the bottom of the flap of the pad. It is then buckled to a short belly band on top of the girth, being secured more loosely than the girth though tighter than a usual belly band. The traces are passed over the outer side of the belly band point.

Friesian
A breed of horse which is found in Holland. All Friesians are black. The only white which is permitted is a small star. The average height is around 15 hands. Friesians have strong compact bodies and carry full manes and tails. The action is high and the legs are feathered. At the end of the nineteenth century these horses were in great demand in England for funeral work. In Holland they are used on the land as well as for pleasure driving. *See* Black Brigade and Friesian Chaise.

Friesian Chaise
A two-wheeled Friesian vehicle which resembles a gig with a curving dashboard. Two black Friesian horses are harnessed on either side of a pole by the belly bugle method. Breast collars are used and the harness is decorated, with white trimmings. Traditionally, the traces and reins are made of white rope. The vehicle is known in Holland as a Sjees.

128

Frog
The single loop, or handpiece, which connects the reins when the Hungarian style of driving is applied. *See* Hungarian Buckling of Team Reins.

Front
Also known as the Browband. *See* Bridle.

Front Boot
Coaches are built with a boot between the driving seat and the front axle in which items such as horse clothing and headcollars are carried. Access to the front boot varies from one coach to another. Some are reached by a door at the front which can only be opened when the horses are not put to. This door is hinged at the top so that there is no chance of its falling open downwards on to the wheelers. Some front boots are reached by a flap under the passenger's legs. Others are entered by a door behind the inside front seat.

Full Cheek Snaffle
A snaffle bit which has a cheek piece extending above the bit ring as well as below it so that when there is a sideways pull on the bit the cheek is pressed against the horse's face, forcing him to turn. Such a bit is most frequently used during the early stages of an animal's education when turning may present some difficulty.
   A Fulmer snaffle is so constructed, with egg-butt sides, and is useful for this purpose.

Full Collar
One which is shaped to fit the neck as opposed to a breast collar which can be adjusted to fit a variety of animals of a similar size.

Full Hand
A method of holding the four reins of a team which is now practised by some people and abhorred by others who say that the strength in the little finger is inadequate to hold the off wheel rein. The reins are all held in the left hand and the looping and handling is the same as with the usual English method. The near lead rein passes over the index finger, the off lead rein over the second finger, the near wheel rein over the third finger and the off wheel rein over the little finger.

Full Lock
This enables the front wheels to turn under the body of the vehicle through ninety degrees making the equipage more manoeuvrable than one with half or, worse still, quarter lock.

Full Port
A high arch in the mouthpiece of a bit which, when the curb is pulled, goes against the roof of the mouth. Some full ports have a serrated ball in the top to make them even more severe.

Full Safe
The large keeper found on harness in such places as the hame tug, shaft tug and bridle cheek, where it takes the place of two or three narrow keepers. A full safe is often decorated with patterned creasing. Also known as pipe loop and box keeper.

Funeral Horses. *See* Black Brigade.

Furious Driving
This applied, not only to coachmen who were frequently guilty of the practice of coach racing, and were fined accordingly, but to the waggoners. Drivers in the 1800s who were in charge of heavily laden wagons drawn by four or five horses frequently filled themselves with alcohol and then drove at a speed of six or seven miles an hour, down the street, endangering everyone. Such offenders were charged by the magistrates with furious driving.

Furniture
The name applies to the mountings of the harness, such as the buckles and the hames. Furniture can be made of one of a variety of metals such as solid nickel, solid brass, or metal which is plated with silver or brass. Solid brass should not be used for items such as hames, kidney links or hame chains, where strength is required, as it is likely to bend or break without warning. These should be steel, plated with brass. All the buckles on a set of harness should match in design. The metal of the furniture should match that of the lamps and the vehicle fittings. For this reason now, brass is the most suitable for private driving (unless, of course the family coat of arms contains a predominance of silver in it), and white metal for trade turnouts.

Futchell
The longitudinal pieces of wood which support the splinter bar, pole or shaft at one end and, via the axle bed, support the sway bar at the other end. With a close futchell undercarriage, two centre futchells form a casing between which the pole is placed. There may then be two outside futchells to support the extreme ends of the splinter bar near the roller bolts. With an open futchell undercarriage, two futchells spread from the sway bar and axle bed to the width desired to take the shafts, which are connected to the futchells by bolts.

Futchell Stay
The iron plate which is used to strengthen the wooden futchell on a carriage.

Gag Runner
When a bearing rein is used, a small strap with a dee and ring at its end is sometimes buckled on to the small dee on each side of the crown-piece of the bridle. The bearing rein comes up from the bridoon, whether buckled to it or via the pulley, and passes through the gag runner before going down towards the pad. This is used instead of a swivel sewn to the throat lash. The gag runner is also known as a bradoon hanger and a bearing rein drop. *See* Bearing Rein.

Galloping Ground of the Western Coaches
This referred to a straight stretch of road between Hounslow and Staines along which coachmen could spring their teams.

Gammon-Board
The name sometimes given to the roof seats on a coach and the hind roof seat in particular. In 1788 a Mr Gammon was responsible for an Act of Parliament which resulted in limiting the number of roof seat passengers to six, as well as those on the box seat. Up to that time coaches were being built to allow too many people on the roof and numerous accidents were occurring. These permitted roof seats became known as gammon-boards.

Gates
Turnpike toll gates.

Gee
Farm horses are trained to turn to the right on hearing this command.
    Various words are used in different parts of the country, both for directing horses and in referring to the parts of the harness.

Gelderlander
A Dutch breed which is popular as a coach horse. The high head and tail carriage, great presence and eye catching action make an outstanding picture when a team is put to a Drag or similar vehicle. Chestnuts, bays and greys predominate.

Gemmi Cart
A two-wheeled vehicle which was used to convey passengers over the Gemmi Pass in Switzerland. Passengers travelled, facing to the rear, on a narrow single seat between the wheels. A wind-on brake was fixed by the end of the near side shaft.

'Gentlemen, I leave you here'
It was usual for the mail coachman to receive tips from the passengers at the end of his stage of forty or fifty miles. When the time came for him to leave the coach, the passengers were politely reminded of their duty by this standard remark.

George IV Phaeton
As George IV grew older he required a vehicle for his personal driving which provided easier access and more comfort than the Highflier favoured in his youth. A low Phaeton was designed. In 1824 William Cook, his coachbuilder, produced a vehicle which became the ancestor of numerous Phaetons built on similar lines, known as George IV Phaetons. The original little Phaeton had a body which was entered by a single step with a luxuriously trimmed low-hooded seat, from which the pair of ponies was driven. The dash curved outwards towards the ponies' quarters. The front wheels, which were said to have measured only 21 inches, were placed well forward, in front of the dash and turned under a pair of light iron arches, affording a good lock. The rear wheels were 33 inches in diameter. Elliptic springs provided the suspension.
    In 1828 a similar vehicle was built for Princess Victoria. It was drawn by a team of postillion-driven ponies. This type of vehicle became known as a Victoria Phaeton.
    These two royal Phaetons were the forerunners of numerous carriages suitable for ladies to drive. They became extremely fashionable and were built with

many minor variations to the basic theme. Some had a folding hood, others had no hood. Some were provided with a rumble seat, others were not and were sometimes turned out with mounted grooms known as outriders with the horses and bridles matching those to the Phaeton. Some Phaetons had a square outline. The large editions became known as Park Phaetons or Ladies' Phaetons as well as George IV Phaetons. The small versions were also called Pony Phaetons. Those built by Peters, the coachbuilder, were called Peters' Phaetons.

The Park Phaeton was one of the most fashionable vehicles for a lady to be seen in, during the summer, for park driving. Horses of high quality with showy action and impeccable manners were essential for this equipage. The high dashboard curved towards the horses' quarters to obliterate them from the eyes of the lady Whip, thus saving embarrassment. The crinoline worn was shown to perfection by the flattering outline of the Phaeton. A parasol whip was carried to complete the turnout. This was more for effect than for use. Appointing a Park Phaeton was a costly business.

George IV Phaeton (Appointments)
When this vehicle is shown in America the appointments are taken into great consideration by the judges. A tool kit, wet weather apron, spare pair of gloves, pack of cards, and whip with a black stick are essential. The lady Whip wears a long dress, furs, elbow length gloves and jewelry.

The harness has French Tilbury tugs and full breeching. A Buxton bit and pulley bearing rein complete this dressy equipage. Reins which are about three feet longer than usual are used so that in times of stress the lady can pass them back to the liveried groom who travels on the rumble seat behind the hood.

German Posting
It was usual for four horses to be controlled by a single postillion with only one rein to the near leader and no reins at all to the off leader. Words of command and the use of a long whip were considered to be adequate aids to maintain an average speed of eight or nine miles an hour.

German Silver
Also known as Albata and white brass. *See* Brass.

Getting Hanged
When the thong or lash of a team whip becomes caught in a part of the harness or on the bars.

Gharry
A four-wheeled vehicle found in Gibraltar. The single horse is driven from a box seat at the front of the carriage. Passengers are carried face-to-face in the canopy-covered body, which is suspended on elliptic springs. Curtains are hung from below the canopy and gathered at the four corner posts to be drawn as required.

Gig
All Gigs have two wheels and, with a few exceptions, all have a forward-facing seat for two people; the driver and one passenger. The rare exceptions were those built with a single seat for the use of doctors and those built for trotting matches which, owing to their solitary seat, were known as Sulkies. The vehicle

which was known as the Suicide Gig was really more of a tandem cart than a Gig. It seated three people.

It is thought that the huge family of Gigs may owe its ancestry to the Sedan Cart. This vehicle resembles a sedan chair on wheels. The passenger travelled in the chair and the driver rode the horse with his legs on the outer sides of handles, extended from the body to form shafts. The rear ends of the shafts were joined to the axle. The conveyance was unsprung.

From this early vehicle there developed, by the middle of the 1700s, a gig-like vehicle with small, heavy wheels. The body was hung on leather straps which were attached to iron braces coming up from the rear of the shafts.

The Rib Chair Gig was an unsprung vehicle. The semi-circular seat had a rail round the back which was joined to the seat by wooden spindles. This stick-back design was the forerunner of the type of seating later to be used in many different Gigs, such as Stanhope, Tilbury, Dennett and Skeleton.

In 1790, roughly made Gigs which mostly amounted to a pair of wheels, a pair of shafts and a board for a seat, which was either completely unsprung or, at the best, was suspended by leather braces from a wooden frame, were liable to an annual tax of 12 shillings if the initial cost had not exceeded £12. These vehicles bore the words 'Taxed Cart' painted on their sides. The road tax for other two-wheeled vehicles of the period was £3 17s.

The Chair-Back Gig of the period was an improvement on the early crude Gigs. Its Cabriolet-type body was hung on cee- or whip-springs from leather braces at the back and on elbow springs at the front.

The Whiskey was also favoured at the time. It resembled a Gig with a small cane body which was joined to the shafts above horizontal springs. It was so named because of its ability to whisk along the road at great speed. It was thought to be the forerunner of the Dennett Gig.

As the popularity of Gigs grew, both the country coachbuilders and the London craftsmen were turning out Gigs of varying shapes and sizes to suit the individual requirements of their customers. Gigs were named after their design-ers, like the Stanhope Gig; after their coachbuilders, like the Tilbury Gig, and after their shape, like the Well-Bottom Gig. There were Lawton Gigs, Liverpool Gigs, Round-Backed Gigs and Bucket-Seated Gigs. There were Hooded Gigs, Skeleton Gigs and Spider Gigs. The varieties were endless.

By 1830 Gigs were used widely by bagmen, bankers and traders. Businessmen commuting from the suburbs found the Gig a useful conveyance as it only required one horse and little parking space. Most residences had their gig house as they now have their garage.

Nowadays, Gigs are very popular for private driving with both a single and a tandem. Their lightness and elegance show a free-moving horse or pony to advantage.

Girth Gall

A sore under the arm can be created either by hard leather chafing an unfit animal, or by the saddle being pushed forward in pulling up or going down hill. If breeching is not used and the crupper back strap is too long, it will be found that with a single horse the shafts push the tugs forward which in turn push the backband and saddle forward until the girth goes under the arms. The cure is to adjust the harness so that the cause will not occur again and to apply a healing lotion. A sheepskin sleeve round the girth will enable the horse to be worked whilst the area is healing.

Glass
Plate glass, owing to its strength, was used for the windows of carriages.

Glass Coach
So named because the panels, above the elbow line, are made of glass. These were introduced in the first half of the 17th century.

Glover, Webb & Liversidge Ltd
A London coachbuilding firm which was established in 1720.

Gloves
These should be of leather, dog skin is best, at least one size too large and of medium weight. Gloves which are too tight are restricting, and those which are too large, twist round the fingers should the horses start to pull. For wet weather, a spare pair of either string, cotton or wool should be available to pull on over the leather gloves which become slippery in the rain.

Go-Cart
An American form of Cabriolet on two wheels with a cranked axle.

Gold State Coach
This was said to be 'the most superb and expensive of any ever built in this Kingdom'.

It was delivered to the Royal Mews in 1762 at a cost of over £7,500. The coach was built by Butler, carved by Wilton, gilded by Pajolas and had panels painted by Giovanni Cipriani, an artist from Florence who was working in London. The 24-feet long body is hung on broad leather braces from four tritons. The frame of the body takes the form of eight palm trees with their branches supporting the ornately decorated roof. Cherubs, scallop shells and a dolphin's head are but a few of the carved and gilded figures adorning the coach.

The Gold State Coach was used for the Coronation of Queen Elizabeth II in 1953 when it was drawn by eight grey horses wearing state harness which were ridden at walking pace by four postillions in full state livery. The coach was similarly turned out in 1977 to convey the Queen in her Silver Jubilee procession.

It may be seen at the Royal Mews, London.

Golden Age of Coaching
This only lasted for the short period between about 1815 and 1840 when Mail and Stage Coaches reached the peak of their efficiency and popularity. They were then superseded by the invention of the internal combustion engine and the introduction of railways.

Gondola of London
A slang term for the Hansom Cab. The name was originated by Disraeli.

Gooch Waggon
A light and elegant four-wheeled vehicle named after the designer, Mr Vivian Gooch. It resembles a Phaeton and is suitable for showing a pair of hackneys.

The Gig-type body is hung on four elliptic springs enabling the front wheels to turn under the seat. There is a small rumble seat, at the rear, for the groom.

Good Hands
It is generally accepted that horses go better for a coachman with good hands than for a man who is not so fortunate. Good hands are those which are light and sensitive and yet at times can be strong. Suppleness of the fingers and wrist result in a yielding from the horse. A team which will pull hard against bad hands will go lightly with good hands. To a certain extent, hands are born, not made. However, good hands can be achieved if they are trained with due care and attention.

Gorst Gig
A hooded, round-backed gig with a boot under the seat. The body, which was hung on side-springs, lay between the tops of the shafts.

Governess Cart
A two-wheeled vehicle which was built in large numbers at the turn of the century. It was considered to be a safe conveyance in which the governess could take out her charges.

The round body, which has longitudinal seats, is hung low between two elliptic springs on a cranked axle. It is entered through a door at the rear, by a step. This entry prevents children from getting trodden on or being run over, if the pony should move forward unexpectedly. Once safely in, the door is shut by a handle on the outside which is placed low enough to be out of the reach of small arms. The vehicle is driven from the right-hand rear corner. Although the seat is provided with a knee recess, the driver still has to sit sideways. It is essential to have a well-mannered pony between the shafts. A pulling or difficult animal can be troublesome in such a vehicle as there is little purchase for the feet with the body twisted in this manner.

Some fine examples of Governess Carts were built by the best London makers with turned spindles and brass trim on the doors. Some were made of varnished wood and others were painted with a coach finish. A few were made of basket-work to withstand the rough treatment without paintwork becoming damaged. Governess Carts ranged in size from those suitable to be drawn by a Shetland pony to the large ones in which a horse can be put. Also known as a Tub Cart. A few were built with four wheels.

Grass Hopper Spring. *See* Double-Elbow Spring.

Great Coat (Post Boy's)
This heavy garment was designed with a slit to the waist so that it hung down on either side of the saddle. The tails were then pulled forward, covering the thighs, and tucked well under the knee to protect the postillion from rain and cold.

Great Western Horse's Collar
The railway horses' collars were taken into a drying room each evening, when the horses returned from work, so that, by the following morning, all the collars were dry, clean and warm and sore shoulders were avoided.

Greyhound
A famous trotter.

Gridiron Port

An oval-shaped metal tongue piece with circular ends which can be clipped round the mouthpiece of a bit on either side of the existing port, to provide a high port. The gridiron port lies along the tongue towards the throat and prevents the horse from getting its tongue over the bit. There is a cross of metal inside the arch of the port to prevent the tongue from becoming caught inside the port.

Grooms

When two grooms are attending to a four-horse team, the head groom should stand at the offside wheeler's head and the under groom should be positioned in front of the leaders' head. When the coach is driven forward, both grooms should mount exactly together as the vehicle passes them. This is achieved by the head groom stepping forward and the under groom towards the coach as it proceeds past them.

Groom's Coat

A single-breasted coat with buttons down the front and three pairs of buttons at the rear. There are no pocket flaps on a groom's coat. *See* Buttons and Coachman's Coat.

Grosvenor Dog Cart

A classic Dog Cart of 1884 with back-to-back seats for four people sharing the same lazy back. The body is built along the line of the shafts, which run outside. It is hung on two side-springs. The lamps were carried on the dashboard. An apron is rolled up on the dash in readiness for the use of the driver and front-seat passenger.

Ground

A term which was used in the coaching era to describe a part of the road. A coachman's or guard's ground was the forty to sixty miles which he travelled. A good ground was held up as an incentive when employing a Mail Coach guard, as it offered a regular supply of wealthy and generous passengers who would tip for services rendered. The part of the journey for which a particular contractor horsed the Mail Coach was referred to as that person's 'ground'. The high or upper ground was that part of the journey which was nearest to London. The lower ground was the section at which the journey ended; the middle ground was between the two and the part where doubtful horses might have been used, being away from the towns.

Growler

Slang name given to the Clarence Cab on account of the noise made by its progress.

G. S. Waggon

Army abbreviation for General Service Waggon. An open four-wheeled vehicle with a container back, resembling an open lorry, for conveying goods. The only seat was at the front and was suspended on two elliptic springs. A pair or team were driven on what was known as the long rein. Alternatively the horses could be ridden postillion.

Guard, Mail Coach

He was a man of great importance employed by the Post Office. He had to be recommended by a Member of Parliament who would vouch for the suitability of his character and fitness of health before he could be considered. A Mail Coach guard had to be reliable, honest, hardworking and conscientious, as he was solely responsible for the safe delivery of the mail. This was carried in the hind boot of the coach. The scarlet coated guard sat in solitary confinement on the single seat over the boot, with his feet on the lid which he kept locked. He held a blunderbuss to ward off anyone with evil intentions. He was in charge of the coachman, the coach, and the horses, though all these were provided by a contractor—not the Post Office. It was the guard's duty to see that the coach kept to its tight time schedule over the route and during the changes of horses. Before leaving the Post Office, his watch, which he carried in a leather case hung over his shoulder, was set and sealed. The timing was so strict that villagers could set their clocks by the passing of the Mail Coach. The guard blew the horn on approaching the pikes so that they were opened in advance and no delay was caused. The horn was also blown to warn ostlers to have the new team ready for a quick change of horses. When steep hills made it necessary for the drag shoe to be put under a wheel, it was the guard who had to perform the task. If the coach broke down, it was his job to render it serviceable. During his early training, to become a guard, he was sent to a coach factory to learn the rudiments of carriage repair so that engineering could be added to his list of accomplishments. If snow caused the coach to founder, then the guard had to take a couple of horses and proceed with the mail mounted. For all this, he received 10s. 6d. per week, which was supplemented on good grounds by tips from passengers which they were not officially allowed to receive.

Guard, Stage or Road Coach

His job was to attend to the welfare of the passengers. He collected the waybill from the booking office and showed travellers to their seats when they boarded the coach. He collected the tickets and, if they had no ticket, took their money. On his left side was slung a leather case containing the waybill, the key to the boot and an open-faced watch. The guard was responsible for stowing the luggage and parcels and he had to assist passengers at changes. He blew the horn to warn other road users of the approaching coach on corners and to stir ostlers on nearing the inn. When the drag shoe had to be put into place, it was the guard's task to carry out the feat. The guard had little to do with the horses, apart from at the changes. He only drove if the stables were a short way from the Inn when it was then his job to take the old team and bring back the new one for the coachman.

Guerney

A type of cab patented by J. T. Guerney, Boston, U.S.A., which was popular at the turn of the century.

Guide Terret

That which is on the centre of the wheeler's pad, to carry the leader's rein.

Gun Metal

From which axle-tree nuts were made in preference to brass which was said to corrode when in contact with oil.

Gustavus

A famous trotter. The leader of the tandem team which a Mr Burke, in 1839, is said to have driven forty-five miles at a trot within three hours. This horse is recorded on a different occasion to have trotted twenty miles in 1 hour and 14 minutes.

Gypsy Wagon

This is the gypsy's home. There are four main types of wagon, namely the Showman's Wagon, the Reading Wagon, the Ledge-Type Wagon and the Barrel Top Wagon. Skewbald, piebald or spotted horses are favoured. Black harness with red trim and white metal horse-shoe buckles is preferred.

Hackney

A descendant of the Norfolk Roadster or Norfolk Trotter.

Hackney ponies were favoured by tradesmen in the late 1800s and early 1900s. The advertisement which their high-stepping action created, was good for business.

The modern hackney is kept mainly for the show ring where he is driven to a four-wheeled, pneumatic-tyred, single-seat show waggon. Those known as Box Waggons and Viceroy Waggons are the types which are most commonly used.

The action of the hackney should be rounded and show great elevation of the knees and hocks. He should cover plenty of ground with each level and spectacular stride. Dishing and plaiting are penalized. Animals who progress in an extravagant manner upwards but do not go sufficiently forwards, are not favoured.

When hackneys are being judged they complete a few circuits of the show ring before being called in and lined up. They stand stretched out with the top rein loose. As each horse goes out to give his individual show, the top rein is hooked to the saddle by the ground attendant who stands by each exhibit.

Pairs of hackneys are sometimes shown in light Phaetons or pair-horse waggons.

The Royal International Horse Show also has a class for hackneys to Gigs.

The Hackney Horse Society holds its annual show at Ardingly, Sussex. In-hand classes are held for stallions, brood mares and youngsters. The driven events include classes for novices and amateurs, as well as the various open competitions.

Hackneys are also driven in Private Driving Classes and F.E.I. Combined Driving Events with great success. One team is, at present, being shown to a Drag, in Coaching Classes.

Hackney Coach

A horse-drawn version of the modern taxi cab which first appeared in London in the early 1600s. It was a pair-horse, four-wheeled, unsprung conveyance. People who had, up to that time, travelled by water began to patronize the Hackney Coach proprietors instead of the Thames watermen. The first Hackney stand was established in 1634. The following year the Hackney Coaches were causing such a disturbance in the narrow streets that Charles I proclaimed that they could only be used by those people who were journeying three miles or more out of London. This reduced their numbers for a few years but within a quarter of a century they were again causing jams. Hackney Coaches were no longer allowed to stand in the streets or crawl hoping to pick up fares. They had to remain in yards until they were called. By 1662 nearly 2,500 were said to have been plying for hire in the London area. In order to lessen the quantity, a law was passed and commissioners were appointed to issue just 400 licences. This inevitably led to bribery and devious practices. Some coach proprietors without licences drove into London by day and then worked in the town at night hoping not to get caught at their unlawful practice. In 1694 the number of licences which were issued was increased to 700. The cost for each one was a £50 down payment which was valid for a period of twenty-one years. An additional rate of £4 per annum was charged. Since 1662 Sunday work had not been permitted. The law was changed in 1694 and 175 cabs were allowed to work on Sundays, on a rota system, so that all got a fair chance to earn Sunday money.

The design of these early Hackney Coaches followed the same pattern as that of a gentleman's coach. When a private carriage became worn and too shabby to be seen, it was relegated to the yard of the Hackney Coach proprietor. Here it probably lasted for several years with perhaps odd wheels of varying colours, ill-fitting doors, remains of heraldic bearings still in evidence on the panels, and the inside filled with wet, germ-ridden straw. The hammercloth was either removed or tattered beyond recognition.

Progression led to special cabs being designed for public use.

Hackney Stand
The place where Hackney Coaches assembled and waited to be hired. The first stand was established at The Maypole, The Strand, London, in 1634.

Hackney Type
Private Driving Classes at the present time are frequently split into hackney-type and non-hackney-type sections. To qualify for the hackney-type section, an animal should possess true hackney characteristics both in conformation and way of going. He need not be a pure-bred hackney, which is why the word type is used.

Hair
Horse hair, preferably that from the tail, as it is longer, was used as a stuffing for cushions. In order to make it elastic and springy it was first twisted and then baked in an oven to set the curls.

Half Cheek Snaffle
A snaffle bit which has a cheek piece below or above the bit ring, to assist in turning.

Half-Elliptic Spring. *See* Double-Elbow Spring.

Half Moon
Also known as a mullen mouth piece. *See* Bitting.

Half Port

A mouth piece of a bit with an arch which keeps pressure off the centre of the tongue. It is suitable for a horse with a sensitive tongue as the pressure is taken mainly on the bars of the mouth. *See* Bitting.

Half-Struck

When the folding head of a vehicle, such as a Cabriolet, is set halfway between being fully open and completely closed. Also known as 'Set back'.

Halter

A headcollar which is made from webbing and rope or entirely from rope. It was put on underneath the bridle when it may have been necessary to tie a horse whilst delivering. During the 1939–45 War the London dairy horses all wore halters so that in the event of an air raid they could be tied up in their carts whilst their drivers sheltered from danger. Under no circumstances must the bridle be removed whilst the horse is still put to his vehicle. The animal is secured by his halter with the bridle still in place.

Hame Chain

The chain sometimes employed to connect the bottom ends of the hames. Various methods are used. Some chains are attached permanently to one hame and are fixed by passing a link, at the required tightness, over a hook at the bottom of the other hame. Some chains are loose and are hooked on to, or pass over, hooks on the hames. Whatever the method applied, solid brass chain must not be used as it is liable to break.

Hame Chain (Farm Harness)

The traces of a heavy horse in shafts are replaced by two short pieces of chain, known as the hame chains. Each chain is hooked, at one end on to the large flat hame hooks and at the other end to the hooks on the large rectangular dees bolted to the tops of the shafts. By this method, the horse pulls the cart.

Hame Clip

This goes through the pull, hame draught or bullet before being fixed by hame rivets to the trace tugs or shoulder-piece.

Hame Draught

Also called Pull or Bullet. *See* Pull.

Hame Rein

A short rein used on heavy-horse harness to prevent the horse from lowering his head excessively. It is buckled to the bit and looped over the hame horn.

Hame Rivet

Usually made of copper with brass or white metal heads. They are used for securing the hame clip to the trace tugs or shoulder-pieces.

Hames

The arms which are fixed round the collar by a hame strap passing through hame eyes at the top and a hame strap, hame chain or kidney link going through eyes or hooks at the bottom. As it is through the hames that the draught is transferred to the collar, it is essential that they fit perfectly into the groove of the collar behind the rim. If the collar is bent back, the hames must be shaped accordingly otherwise there will be a danger of them being pulled from the collar. On the top half of each hame there is a terret through which the rein

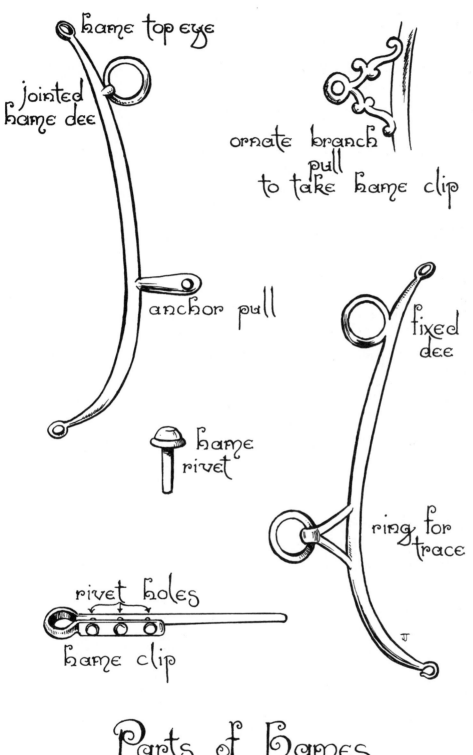

hame top eye

jointed
hame dee

ornate branch
pull
to take hame clip

anchor pull

fixed
dee

hame
rivet

ring for
trace

rivet holes

hame clip

Parts of Hames

passes. On the bottom half is a hame draught eye to which the traces are indirectly attached. Hames are usually made of steel and plated with brass or white metal. They must never be made of solid brass as these are likely to break or bend whenever any strain is applied. Farm-horse hames were sometimes made of wood and Diligence harness hames always were.

Hames (Farm Horse)
These go round the collar in the normal way, fastening with a hame strap through a choice of metal dees at the top and a chain at the bottom. Some are made of wood with metal hame strap dees and large flat metal trace hooks. Some are made of tubular metal and others are manufactured in a combination of wood and metal. The hames extend upwards on both sides, above the hame strap, to form two horns over which the hame rein is passed.

Hame Strap
The small strap which fastens the hames by their top eyes. It is essential that the hame strap is sound as it is one of the most important parts of the harness. With a pair, the pressure from the pole is transmitted via the pole strap and hames to the top hame strap and pair horse hame straps should be put on so that they are buckled from their respective outer sides with the points inwards. In an emergency, either horse can be released from the bulk of his harness by un-buckling the hame strap. With a single horse the hame strap can be fastened on either side. Some people prefer the near side to comply with fashion. Others prefer the offside, claiming that the Whip will dismount from the right and in an emergency will want to unbuckle the harness from the same side.

Hame-top Eye
The slot at the top of a hame through which the hame strap passes before being buckled.

Hammercloth
The frame of the coachman's seat is covered, on a dress carriage, with a ham-mercloth. This is made of a tough material which is hung in elegant folds and is covered with cloth such as velvet, trimmed with braid and fringes. It is decor-ated with armorial bearings, worked either in embroidery or metals like brass or silver. Some, in the 1800s, were produced with ivory embellishments.

Hammock Waggon
A vehicle which is said to have been used in the 11th century. The body re-sembled a hammock and was hung from large hooks, on posts, coming up from the axles, between the four wheels.

Hand Holder
Loops, which were made from ornate braid, known as lace, were sometimes fitted to the insides of closed carriages to provide a hand rest for travellers.

Hand Horse
When two horses are controlled by a postillion, the offside horse is known as the hand horse. The postillion has the usual riding reins on the nearside horse and a single rein to the offside horse. This rein splits into two reins which are carefully adjusted by a central buckle so that an even feel is transmitted to each side of the mouth.

Holding reins & whip for single or pair driving

near lead

off lead

off wheel

near wheel

Four-in-Hand ~how to hold reins

off wheel rein

near wheel rein

off lead draught rein

near lead draught rein

off wheel rein

near wheel rein

Hungarian Four-in-Hand Reins

Handling the Reins

The English method of holding the reins for a single or pair is to take both reins in the left hand. The nearside rein goes over the index finger and the offside rein under the middle finger. The thumb points straight and the reins are gripped by the fingers lying across the palm. The right hand, which is at all times holding the whip, assists the left in turns or in pulling up. When it is necessary to shorten or lengthen the reins, the right hand is placed with the knuckles uppermost, over both reins which are separated by the third and fourth fingers. The contact is taken and the reins altered by being pushed or pulled through the left hand.

With the English method, all four reins of the tandem, unicorn or team, are held in the same manner in the left hand. The near lead rein goes over the index finger, the off lead rein and near wheel rein between the index finger and the second finger with the lead rein on top. The off wheel rein goes under the second finger.

The hands are held in the middle of the body with the arms horizontal and the elbows close to the sides.

See Turns, for the methods of inclining and turning.

Hand-piece

The part of the rein which is held in the hand.

Handpiece

The handle of a whip which, between the cap and the collar is about 8 inches long. It is usually covered in pigskin which is either sewn with a longitudinal seam or wound round at an angle. The metal of the cap and the collar should match that of the harness furniture.

Hanging of Harness

Harness should be hung on racks in a room with a dry atmosphere free from ammonia fumes. Some harness rooms have large glass cases for storing harness away from dust and damp. It is usual to hang the collar upside down on a half-circular rack which has a rim at the front to hold the collar in position. The hames and hame tugs are laid over the top of the collar. Below the collar is placed a small rack of similar shape on to which the crupper dock is placed. At the correct distance, to coincide with the length of the back strap, is placed the rack for the pad which is shaped to fit the tree. Below the pad rack, is a bridle rack. This has a notch cut out of the centre to allow the face drop to hang centrally and often has two blinker-shaped side-pieces ensuring that the blinkers are stored in the correct position. If a bridle is hung crooked it will soon become distorted. Small hooks are placed on either side of the collar rack for the reins and traces. A set of harness hung in this way takes the minimum amount of space.

'Hang up my Bars'

This is said by a man when he retires from coaching.

Hansom

The first Hansom Cab was built in 1834 to the design of an architect, Mr J. A.

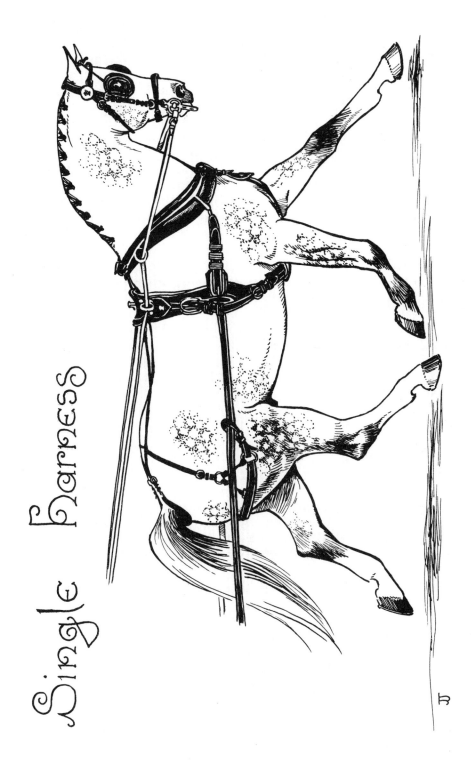

Single Harness

Hansom. It was a cumbersome vehicle bearing little relation to the superbly finished and luxuriously appointed Hansoms which were so popular forty years later. The body of this early cab resembled a box and was hung between two 7 foot 6 inch wheels which revolved on short axles sticking out of the side of the body. The single horse was driven from a small seat placed at the front of the body, level with the roof. The conveyance was entered by doors on either side, at the front, behind the shafts which curved round the horse's quarters.

Within two years, Mr John Chapman, the secretary of the Safety Cabriolet and Two-Wheeled Carriage Company, had noted the weaknesses in Mr Hansom's Cab and designed a superior vehicle on the same lines. He sold the patent to Mr Hansom so, although the cabs were Chapman's cabs, they took the name of Hansoms. The driver's seat was placed at the back of the body, level with the roof. The axle passed under the body. Fifty cabs were built to the design and launched with instant success. The words 'Hansom's Patent Safety' were painted on the sides of the cabs. The cabs were very soon copied by rival firms. In order to escape prosecution they added, in tiny lettering, the word 'not' in front of 'Hansom's Patent Safety'. Lawsuits inevitably followed.

As time passed, the Hansom was improved. The body was cut away under the seat enabling the axle to go straight across instead of being bent under the body. The windows were made larger.

The most perfect Hansom Cabs were built by Messrs Forder, coachbuilders of London and Wolverhampton. In 1873 and 1875 Forder Hansoms won prizes presented by The Society of Arts and at a cab exhibition at Alexandra Palace. They produced a carriage which had a lighter body, undercarriage and wheels than had been made before.

By 1880 the Hansom had reached perfection. The best were built by Forder and ran on rubber-tyred wheels. The apron, which formerly had been made with two doors across the front of the passengers' legs, was made into one which opened against the dash, allowing easy access. The interior was luxuriously fitted with ashtrays, matchboxes, looking-glasses and a bell to attract the driver's attention. Rubber matting covered the floor. Each window had a silk blind. Some had a flower which matched that worn by the horse on his bridle. He was likely to be an ex-racehorse, sold out of racing owing to lack of speed. The shining harness which he wore matched his quality. The cabby was smartly turned out and polite, which was a contrast to many of the cabbies of an earlier period.

Noblemen, such as Lord Lonsdale and Lord Shrewsbury, joined the ranks of cab proprietors. They set a standard of turnout which was equal to that of a private carriage. Competition in the stands forced other proprietors to follow suit.

The Hansom was thought to be a somewhat dashing conveyance. A lady hesitated to travel alone in one, preferring to use a Clarence Cab. Also, on a wet day, the door, wheel and reins of a Hansom were damaging to a lady's gown on entering and leaving.

Many immaculately finished and appointed Hansoms were privately owned and used in preference to a Brougham or Victoria for running about town. The Floyd Hansom was built for this purpose.

Court Hansoms and Victoria Hansoms were two more variations.

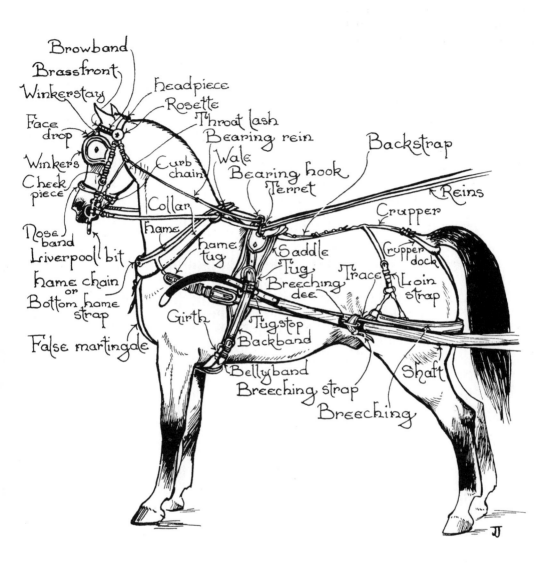

Browband
Brassfront
Winkerstay
Headpiece
Rosette
Face drop
Throat lash
Bearing rein
Winkers
Cheek piece
Curb chain
Wale
Bearing hook
Terret
Backstrap
Collar
Reins
Hame
Crupper
Nose band
Hame tug
Saddle
Crupper dock
Liverpool bit
Tug
Trace
Loin strap
Hame chain
or
Bottom hame strap
Breeching dee
Girth
Tugstop
Backband
False martingale
Bellyband
Breeching strap
Shaft
Breeching

Details of Single Harness

Harnessing

Whether the horse is to be harnessed for single, pair, tandem or team work, the same principles apply. The collar is put on first. There is a traditional super-stition amongst true harness people which rules that they must not drive a horse on to which the pad has been put before the collar. It is commonly believed than an accident will be caused by such practice. The collar is put on upside down so that the widest part is passed over the horse's eyes. If the collar is inclined to be narrow, it should be stretched by placing the knee on to one long side whilst holding the other long side in both hands. This will widen the collar temporarily. If a collar is forced roughly over the sensitive skin above the horse's eyes, he may become difficult to harness. The hames are placed over the upside-down collar and the hame strap is buckled. The collar is then turned round at the narrowest part of the neck, in the direction in which the mane lies. The hame strap is tightened next. The false martingale is buckled round the collar and hame chain, hame strap or kidney link. The pad, backstrap and crupper are put on with whichever harness is being used. It may be the back-band, tugs and belly band, with breeching or kicking strap for the single horse, or a trace bearer for tandem, pair or team, or perhaps breeching for a pair or team wheelers. The girth is threaded through the false martingale before being buckled.

If a single horse is being harnessed, the belly band is left undone until he is put to, as it is easier to pass the shafts through the tugs which are free. With a pair or team, the buckles on the shoulder tugs are secured to the points on the pads. The traces are laid over the horses' backs, with the outside one on top of the inside one, ready for putting to. With a tandem leader, the traces are passed through the pad loop and trace bearer. The reins are put through the pad and collar terrets. With a pair or team, the reins with the buckle or loop at the hand end go on to the offside and the point ends are put on the nearside. This originated from coaching days when the nearside reins were thrown over to the coachman standing at the offside. A buckle flying through the air, particularly in darkness, could damage an eye. Now, having the buckle-ended reins on the offside horses ensures that carefully adjusted couplings are not altered by being put on to the wrong sides. Particular care must be paid to see that the draught rein is put on to the outer sides in each case. Bridles are put on and the reins are buckled to the bit. With a pair or team, the draught rein is buckled on to the outer side of the bit and the coupling rein is looped through the noseband or throatlash ready to be buckled to the horse of the pair when they are put to.

Harness Loops

Also known as keepers.

Harness Makers

Names and addresses are obtainable from The British Driving Society.

Harness Measurements

The measurements given below are offered as a rough guide and should be checked with the animal concerned as they cannot be guaranteed to fit all shapes and sizes of a specified height.

Full-size Gig Harness

Bridle

Head, cut	1½ by 23in.
Head, split	6¼in.
Cheeks, cut	¾ by 30in.
Cheeks, made up	8in.
Cheeks, allow for billets . .	12in.
Noseband, cut	1¼ by 29in.
Noseband, swelled centre .	12in.
Noseband, point . . .	¾ by 6in.
Noseband, billet spaces . .	1in.
Throat, cut	¾ by 27in.
Throat, made up . . .	19½ in.
Chain Front, lining cut . .	1⅛ by 21in.
Chain Front, between . . .	13in.
Winker stay	1⅜ by 12½in.
Winker split	7½in.
Winker rounding . . .	1 by 13¼in.
Winker rounding point . .	¾ by 6in.

Hames and Traces

Hame Tugs, cut	1½ by 18in.
Hame Tugs, made up . .	9in.
Hame Tugs, safes to pattern	12in.
Hame strap (top)	¾ by 19in.
Hame strap (bottom) . . .	¾ by 18in.
Traces, made up	1½ by 72in.

Saddle

Girth, cut	2¼ by 27in.
Girth, short lay	1⅛ by 11in.
Girth, large loop	1 by 8in.
Girth strap	1⅛ by 18in.

Backband

Backband	1½ by 96in.
Backband point	18in.
Backband middle	39in.
Shaft Tugs, cut	1½ by 24in.
Shaft Tugs, between holes .	12in.
Shaft Tugs, linings . . .	12in.

Crupper

Body	1½ by 23in.
Body, split	8in.
Lay	1⅛ by 15in.
Strap	1⅛ by 42in.
Dock	3¾ by 18in.

Breeching

Seat	1½ by 42in.
Tugs (4)	¾ by 5in.
Tugs placed from ends . .	6in.
Shaft Straps	1⅛ by 32in.
Hip Strap	1½ by 52in.
Hip Strap, split	17in.

Kicking Strap

For two wheeler	1¼ by 66in.
For four wheeler . . .	1¼ by 74in.
Tugs	1¼ by 14in.

Reins

Driving Reins, drafts . . .	1 by 78in.
Driving Reins, handparts .	1 by 72in.
Driving Reins, billets . . .	1 by 13in.
Bearing Rein, middle . . .	¾ by 78in.
Bearing Rein, rounding cut .	1 by 23in.
Bearing Rein, made up . .	18in.
Bearing Rein, billets . . .	¾ by 10½in.

Short Martingale

Body, cut	1 by 36in.
Body, made up	1 by 24in.
Billet	1 by 14in.

Long Martingale

Rounding, cut	1 by 24in.
Rounding, made up . . .	22in.
Body	1 by 39in.
Patchpiece to pattern.	

Cob-size Gig Harness

Bridle

Head, cut	1½ by 21½in.
Head, split	5¾in.
Cheeks, cut	¾ by 28in.
Cheeks, made up	7in.
Cheeks, billets	12in.
Noseband, cut	1⅛ by 27in.
Noseband, swelled centre .	11in.
Noseband, point . . .	¾ by 5½in.
Noseband, billet spaces . .	1in.
Chain Front, lining cut . .	1⅛ by 20in.
Chain Front, between . . .	12in.
Winker Stay	1¼ by 11½in.
Winker Stay, split . . .	6¾in.
Winker, rounding	1 by 12in.
Winker, rounding point . .	¾ by 5½in.
Throat, cut	¾ by 26in.
Throat, made up	18½in.

Hames and Traces

Hame Tugs, cut	1⅜ by 16in.
Hame Tugs, made up . . .	8in.
Hame Tugs, safes to pattern .	11in.
Hame Strap (top) . . .	¾ by 18in.
Hame Strap (bottom) . . .	¾ by 17in.
Traces, made up	1⅜ by 66in.

149

Cob-size Gig Harness (continued)

Saddle

Girth, cut	2 by 24in.
Girth, short lay	1 by 10in.
Girth, large loop . . .	$\frac{7}{8}$ by $6\frac{1}{2}$in.
Girth Strap	1 by 17in.

Backband

Backband	$1\frac{3}{8}$ by 90in.
Backband, point	17in.
Backband, middle . . .	36in.
Shaft Tugs, cut	$1\frac{3}{8}$ by 23in.
Shaft Tugs, between holes .	$11\frac{1}{2}$in.
Shaft Tugs, linings . . .	$11\frac{1}{4}$in.

Crupper

Body	$1\frac{1}{2}$ by $21\frac{1}{2}$in.
Body, split	7in.
Lay	1 by 14in.
Strap	1 by 39in.
Dock	$3\frac{1}{2}$ by 17in.

Breeching

Seat	$1\frac{3}{8}$ by 39in.
Tugs (4)	$\frac{3}{4}$ by 5in.
Tugs, placed upon ends . .	$5\frac{1}{2}$in.
Shaft Straps	1 by 30in.

Hip Strap	$1\frac{1}{2}$ by 48in.
Hip Strap, split	16in.

Kicking Strap

For two wheeler	$1\frac{1}{8}$ by 60in.
For four wheeler . . .	$1\frac{1}{8}$ by 68in.
Tugs	$1\frac{1}{8}$ by 13in.

Reins

Driving Reins, drafts . . .	$\frac{7}{8}$ by 72in.
Driving Reins, handparts .	$\frac{7}{8}$ by 66in.
Driving Reins, billets . . .	$\frac{7}{8}$ by 12in.
Bearing Rein, middle . . .	$\frac{3}{4}$ by 69in.
Bearing Rein, roundings, cut	1 by $21\frac{1}{2}$in.
Bearing Rein, made up . .	17in.
Bearing Rein, billets . . .	$\frac{3}{4}$ by 10in.

Short Martingale

Body, cut	$\frac{7}{8}$ by 35in.
Body, made up	$\frac{7}{8}$ by 21in.
Billet	$\frac{7}{8}$ by 13in.

Long Martingale

Rounding, cut	1 by 22in.
Rounding, made up . . .	20in.
Body	$\frac{7}{8}$ by 36in.
Patchpiece to pattern.	

Pony-size Gig Harness

Bridle

Head, cut	$1\frac{1}{4}$ by 20in.
Head, split	$5\frac{1}{4}$in.
Cheeks, cut	$\frac{5}{8}$ by 25in.
Cheeks, made up	6in.
Cheeks, billets	11in.
Noseband, cut	1 by 25in.
Noseband, swelled centre .	10in.
Noseband, point	$\frac{5}{8}$ by 5in.
Noseband, billet spaces . .	$\frac{7}{8}$in.
Throat, cut	$\frac{5}{8}$ by 25in.
Throat, made up	$17\frac{1}{2}$in.
Chain Front, lining cut . .	1 by 19in.
Chain Front, between . . .	11in.
Winker Stay	$1\frac{1}{8}$ by $10\frac{1}{2}$in.
Winker Stay, split . . .	$6\frac{1}{4}$in.
Winker rounding	$\frac{7}{8}$ by $10\frac{1}{2}$in.
Winker, rounding point . .	$\frac{5}{8}$ by 5in.

Hames and Traces

Hame Tugs, cut	$1\frac{1}{4}$ by 14in.
Hame Tugs, made up . .	7in.
Hame Tugs, safes to pattern .	10in.

Hame Strap (top) . . .	$\frac{5}{8}$ by 17in.
Hame Strap (bottom) . . .	$\frac{5}{8}$ by 16in.
Traces, made up	$1\frac{1}{4}$ by 63in.

Saddle

Girth, cut	$1\frac{7}{8}$ by 22in.
Girth, short lay	$\frac{7}{8}$ by 9in.
Girth, large loop	$\frac{3}{4}$ by 6in.
Girth, Strap	$\frac{7}{8}$ by 16in.

Backband

Backband	$1\frac{1}{4}$ by 84in.
Backband, point	16in.
Backband, middle . . .	34in.
Shaft Tugs, cut	$1\frac{1}{4}$ by 22in.
Shaft Tugs, between holes .	11in.
Shaft Tugs, linings . . .	$10\frac{1}{2}$in.

Crupper

Body	$1\frac{1}{4}$ by 20in.
Body, split	6in.
Lay	$\frac{7}{8}$ by 13in.
Strap	$\frac{7}{8}$ by 36in.
Dock	$3\frac{1}{4}$ by 16in.

Pony-size Gig Harness (continued)

BREECHING
Seat	$1\frac{1}{4}$ by 36in.
Tugs (4)	$\frac{5}{8}$ by $4\frac{1}{2}$in.
Tugs placed from ends	5in.
Shaft Straps	$\frac{7}{8}$ by 28in.
Hip Strap	$1\frac{1}{4}$ by 44in.
Hip Strap, split	15in.

KICKING STRAP
For two wheeler	1 by 54in.
For four wheeler	1 by 62in.
Tugs	1 by 12in.

REINS
Driving Reins, drafts	$\frac{3}{4}$ by 66in.
Driving Reins, handparts	$\frac{3}{4}$ by 60in.
Driving Reins, billets	$\frac{3}{4}$ by 11in.
Bearing Rein, middle	$\frac{5}{8}$ by 60in.
Bearing Rein, roundings, cut	$\frac{7}{8}$ by 20in.
Bearing Rein, made up	16in.
Bearing Rein, billets	$\frac{5}{8}$ by $9\frac{1}{2}$in.

SHORT MARTINGALE
Body, cut	$\frac{3}{4}$ by 30in.
Body, made up	$\frac{3}{4}$ by 18in.
Billets	$\frac{3}{4}$ by 12in.

LONG MARTINGALE
Rounding, cut	$\frac{7}{8}$ by 20in.
Rounding, made up	18in.
Body	$\frac{3}{4}$ by 34in.

Patchpiece to pattern.

Backbands, Breechings, etc., for Gig Harness

Full-Size

BACKBANDS (Various)
French, centre	$1\frac{1}{2}$ by 39in.
French, points sewn on tugs	$1\frac{1}{2}$ by 24in.
Tilbury, full length	$1\frac{1}{2}$ by 105in.
Tilbury, with two points	$1\frac{1}{2}$ by 90 in.
Tilbury, each point	18in.
Tilbury, centre	34in.
Tilbury, reversed sewing each side of centre	13in.
Bellyband, for either French or Tilbury backband	$1\frac{1}{2}$ by 28in.
False backband for 2 wheeler, middle	$1\frac{1}{2}$ by 26in.
False backband for 2 wheeler, billets (2)	$1\frac{1}{2}$ by 24in.
False bellyband for 2 wheeler, middle	$1\frac{1}{2}$ by 32in.
False bellyband for 2 wheeler, billets	$1\frac{1}{2}$ by 24in.

BREECHINGS (Various)
Buckle Seat, cut	$1\frac{1}{2}$ by 36in.
Buckle Seat, lay	$1\frac{1}{8}$ by 36in.
Buckle Seat, between buckles	32in.
Ring points, made up	$1\frac{1}{8}$ by 9in.
Long Breeching	$1\frac{3}{8}$ by 126in.
Long Breeching, reduced for turnback to	1in.
Crupper, Martingale style	$1\frac{1}{2}$ by 50in.
Crupper, Martingale style, reduced for turnback to	1in.

BREAST COLLAR
Body (folded leather)	$2\frac{1}{4}$ by 39in.
Lay	$1\frac{1}{2}$ by 39in.
Lay, between buckles	33in.
Neck Strap	$1\frac{3}{4}$ by 40in.
Neck Strap, reduced at points to	1in.

Cob Size

BACKBANDS (Various)
French, centre	$1\frac{3}{8}$ by 36in.
French, points sewn on tugs	$1\frac{3}{8}$ by 21in.
Tilbury, full length	$1\frac{3}{8}$ by 99in.
Tilbury, with two points	$1\frac{3}{8}$ by 87in.
Tilbury, each point	17in.
Tilbury, centre	32in.
Tilbury, reversed sewing each side of centre	12in.
Bellyband for either French or Tilbury	$1\frac{3}{8}$ by 26in.
False backband for two wheeler, middle	$1\frac{3}{8}$ by 23in.
False backband for two wheeler, billets	$1\frac{3}{8}$ by 22in.
False bellyband for two wheeler, middle	$1\frac{3}{8}$ by 29in.
False bellyband for two wheeler, billets	$1\frac{3}{8}$ by 22in.

Backbands, Breechings, etc., for Gig Harness (continued)

BREECHINGS (Various)

Buckle Seat, cut	1⅜ by 33in.
Buckle Seat, lay	1 by 33in.
Buckle Seat, between buckles	29in.
Ring points, made up . .	1 by 8in.
Long Breeching	1¼ by 114in.
Long Breeching, reduced for turnback to	1in.
Crupper, Martingale style .	1⅜ by 44in.
Crupper, reduced for turnback to	1in.

BREAST COLLAR

Body (folded leather) . . .	2¼ by 33in.
Lay	1⅜ by 33in.
Lay, between buckles . . .	27in.
Neck Strap	1½ by 34in.
Reduced at point to . . .	⅞in.

Pony Size

BACKBANDS (Various)

French, centre	1¼ by 33in.
French, points sewn on tugs .	1¼ by 18in.
Tilbury, full length . . .	1¼ by 93in.
Tilbury, with two points . .	1¼ by 84in.
Tilbury, each point . . .	16in.
Tilbury, centre	30in.
Tilbury, reversed sewing each side of centre	11in.

Bellyband, for either French or Tilbury	1¼ by 24in.
False backband for two wheeler, middle . . .	1¼ by 20in.
False backband for two wheeler, billets	1¼ by 20in.
False bellyband for two wheeler, middle . . .	1¼ by 26in.
False bellyband for two wheeler, billets	1¼ by 20in.

BREECHINGS

Buckle Seat, cut	1¼ by 30in.
Buckle Seat, lay	⅞ by 30in.
Buckle Seat, between buckles	26in.
Ring points, made up . .	⅞ by 7in.
Long Breeching	1⅛ by 102in.
Long Breeching, reduced for turnback to	⅞in.
Crupper, Martingale style .	1¼ by 38in.
Crupper, Martingale style, reduced for turnback to .	⅞in.

BREAST COLLAR

Body (folded leather) . . .	2 by 27in.
Lay	1¼ by 27in.
Lay, between buckles . . .	21in.
Neck Strap	1¼ by 28in.
Neck Strap, reduced points to	¾in.

Pair-horse Harness

Full-Size

BRIDLES as Gig
HAMES AND TRACES

Hame Tugs, made up . .	1½ by 18in.
Hame Tugs, safes to pattern .	21in.
Short Tugs, to hame tug buckles	1⅛ by 5in.
Hame Straps (top only) . .	¾ by 22in.
Traces	1½ by 78in.
Traces, hand leather . . .	1½ by 5in.
Pole pieces	1½ by 60in.

PADS

Tops to pattern.

Girths, near side	2¼ by 15in.
Girths, off side	2¼ by 42in.
Girths, points	1⅛ by 18in.
Pad End Straps	1⅛ by 9in.

CRUPPERS, same as Gig

Loin Straps	1 by 50in.
Trace Carriers, cut . . .	1 by 14in.

Patent Leather to pattern.

BREECHINGS

Breechings, cut	1⅜ by 132in.
Breechings, reduced at buckles to.	1⅛in.

REINS

Driving Reins, each side . .	1 by 168in.
Driving Reins, couplings . .	1 by 80in.
Driving Reins, billets . . .	1 by 14in.
Bearing Rein, full bradoon, middle	¾ by 72in.
Bearing Rein, roundings, cut	1 by 31in.
Bearing Rein, roundings, made up	24in.

MARTINGALES

Body, cut	1 by 36in.
Body, made up	1 by 24in.
Billets	1 by 14in.

Cob Size

BRIDLES as Gig
HAMES AND TRACES

Hame Tugs, made up . .	1⅜ by 16in.
Hame Tugs, safes to pattern .	19in.
Short Tugs, sewn to hame tug buckles	1 by 4½in.
Hame Straps (top only) . .	¾ by 21in.
Traces, made up	1⅜ by 75in.
Traces, hand leather . . .	1⅜ by 5in.
Pole pieces	1⅜ by 57in.

PADS
Tops to pattern.

Girths, near side	2 by 13in.
Girths, off side	2 by 39in.
Girth point.	1 by 17in.
Pad End Straps	1 by 9in.

CRUPPERS, same as Gig

Loin Straps	1 by 48in.
Trace Carriers, cut . . .	1 by 13in.

Patent Leather to pattern.

BREECHINGS

Breechings, cut	1¼ by 120in.
Breechings, reduced at buckles to.	1in.

REINS

Driving Reins, each side . .	1 by 162in.
Driving Reins, couplings . .	1 by 78in.
Driving Reins, billets . . .	1 by 13in.
Bearing Rein, full bradoon, middle	¾ by 69in.
Bearing Rein, roundings, cut	1 by 28in.
Bearing Rein, roundings, made up	21in.

MARTINGALES

Body, cut	⅞ by 33in.
Body, made up	⅞ by 21in.
Billets	⅞ by 13in.

Pony Size

BRIDLES as Gig
HAMES AND TRACES

Hame Tugs, made up . .	1¼ by 14in.
Hame Tugs, safes to pattern	17in.
Short Tugs, sewn to hame tug buckles	⅞ by 4in.
Hame Straps (top only) . .	⅝ by 20in.
Traces, made up	1¼ by 72in.
Traces, hand leather . . .	1¼ by 4½in.
Pole pieces	1¼ by 54in.

PADS
Tops to pattern.

Girths, near side	1¾ by 11in.
Girths, off side	1¾ by 36in.
Girth points	⅞ by 16in.
Pad-end Straps	⅞ by 8in.

CRUPPERS, same as Gig

Loin Straps	⅞ by 46in.
Trace Carriers, cut . . .	⅞ by 12in.

Patent leather to pattern.

BREECHINGS

Breechings, cut	1⅛ by 108in.
Breechings, reduced at buckles to.	⅞in.

REINS

Driving Reins, each side .	⅞ by 156in.
Driving Reins, couplings . .	⅞ by 75in.
Driving Reins, billets . . .	⅞ by 12in.
Bearing Rein, full bradoon, . middle	⅝ by 66in.
Bearing Rein, roundings, cut	⅞ by 25in.
Bearing Rein, roundings, made up	18in.

MARTINGALES

Body, cut	¾ by 30in.
Body, made up	¾ by 18in.
Body, billets	¾ by 12in.

Tandem Harness

WHEELER – Same as Gig Harness	Traces, pony size . . . . $1\frac{1}{4}$ by 108in.
LEADER	Reins, full size . . . 1 by 288in. each side
Bridle, Crupper, etc., as Gig Harness	Reins, cob size . . . $\frac{7}{8}$ by 276in. each side
Traces, full size . . . . . $1\frac{1}{2}$ by 120in.	Reins, pony size . . $\frac{3}{4}$ by 264in. each side
Traces, cob size . . . . . $1\frac{3}{8}$ by 114in.	

Four-in-Hand Harness

WHEELER – Same as Pair-Horse Harness	Reins: Drafts, couplings, and billets as
LEADER	Wheeler.
Traces . . . . $1\frac{1}{2}$ by 66in.	Handparts, extra lengths added to make up to 24ft. each side.

Harness Racks
These are open racks made of iron which are sometimes covered with plastic. They are conveniently designed to accommodate the collar, pad, crupper, bridle and reins.

Harveys 'Quartobus'
A Hackney Cab, built to carry four passengers, in use in the 1830s.

Hastings, Sir George
President of The Coaching Club from 1939 to 1943.

Hatchet-shaped Blinkers
A blinker which copies the profile of the blade of a hatchet.

Hatchett & Co
A London coachbuilder of the 18th century.

Hatchetts
The White Horse Cellar, Piccadilly, London. The famous Inn from which numerous coaches started their journeys.

Having a Handful
To take the reins of a team.

Hayes & Son
Coachbuilders of Stamford and Peterborough in the 19th century who claimed to build, on average, 300 vehicles a year, ranging from carts for agricultural use to Drags.

Head Piece
The part of a bridle which passes over the top of the head.

Head Plate
Some of the smart town carriages were decorated with metal ornaments which lay flat against the top of the body. On some, there was one decoration on each side at the front and another at the back. Others had rows of three circular

discs bearing the family crest on either side of the door. Whatever form they took, these ornaments were all referred to as head plates. They were frequently made of silver.

Head Terret
A terret which is screwed into a plate fixed to the centre of the crown-piece. It was worn by the wheeler of a team, to take the lead rein. This method had gone out of fashion by the end of the 19th century.

Hearse
A four-wheeled carriage in which the coffin was carried. It was pulled by horses known as the 'Black Brigade'. Hearses were painted black except for those in which children were carried, which were finished in white. Many were handsomely carved and had glass sides.

Heavy Horse
The recognized breeds in England are: the Shire, the Clydesdale, the Percheron and the Suffolk Punch.

The Shire is the largest, standing about 17 hands and weighing about 1 ton. Black, brown, bay and grey with white legs and white markings on the face, predominate. The Shire possesses an abundance of silky feather down the backs of his legs and around the fetlocks.

The Clydesdale is smaller than the Shire, though of a similar type. He is lighter and has more length of rein. Clydesdales often have white markings on the belly and girth as well as on their legs. They frequently have a bald face.

The Percheron originated in France. He is clean-legged and strong. Grey is the predominating colour.

The Suffolk Punch is also clean-legged and well suited to the heavy clay of the Eastern Counties where he did most of his work. He is the smallest of the four breeds as his legs are short. All Suffolks are chestnut though the shades vary considerably.

Heavy Transport Collar
The name which was given to large collars used for heavy Army work. They ranged in size, at 1 inch intervals, from 23 inches to 27 inches. They were larger than the draught-horse collars and had a wider bearing surface on the shoulders, being made with an extra lining of basil stuffed with flock.

Hem Gears
The harness worn by a farm horse in the lead of tandem.

Hemp
Like flax, was used in the carriage building trade for making braid, thread, rope, and canvas.

Henderson, Charles Cooper
An artist of the 19th century who is famous for his paintings of coaching and subjects concerning 'The Road'.

Herald Painter
This artist worked for a coachbuilder and painted heraldic bearings on the panels of carriages.

155

Herring, J. F. Sen.

An artist of the 1800s who is well known for his driving pictures. Perhaps the most famous are those of the 'Cabriolet Horse and Tiger' and the 'Hackney Cabriolet Horse and Cabman'. The former depicts a faultless grey horse harnessed ready for work. He is accompanied by a liveried 'tiger'. The stable is immaculate in every detail. The other picture shows, as a contrast, a worn-out grey horse which is over at the knee. He is standing in a dingy stall, wearing old harness, with a disreputable-looking cabman by his side.

Hickory. *See* Spider Wheel.

Highflyer Phaeton

Both Crane-Neck Phaetons and Perch-High Phaetons were known generally as Highflyers owing to their excessive height, and to the speed at which they were driven. The front wheels of some were as much as 5 feet high and the rear wheels nearly 6 feet. One Highflyer was reported to have had rear wheels with a diameter of 8 feet but it is thought that this story originated from a contemporary painting in which the artist used considerable licence in order to produce a dramatic picture. The curricle-shaped hooded body was hung from whip springs behind and elbows springs in front. It was sometimes as much as 5 feet from the ground. There was a platform above the rear axle on which either servants stood, or a luggage box was carried. Some had another luggage container over the front axle. The Crane-Neck Phaeton was built on two crane-necked iron perches which permitted a full lock. The combination of the height of the body which was placed just behind the front axle, and the weight of the driver and passenger, made the phaeton likely to overturn if too sharp a turn was attempted. The Perch-High Phaeton had an iron reinforced wooden perch undercarriage and was lighter than the Crane-Neck Phaeton. The body was placed over the front axle. The perch restricted the lock and it was claimed that this made the vehicle less likely to overturn.

A pair, four or even six horses were put to Highflyers. In the latter case, the leaders were ridden by a postillion.

The height of these vehicles was so great that there are accounts of young men serenading their ladies on first-floor balconies from their lofty driving seats.

A pair, four or even six horses were put to Highflyers. In the latter case, the leaders were ridden by a postillion.

The fashion for Highflyer driving was started by the Prince of Wales towards the end of the 18th century. He was copied by other sporting young gentlemen who found the dangers exhilarating. Matches were run and race meetings attended.

There is a fine example of a Crane-Neck Phaeton in the Science Museum in London.

High Ground

Also known as the upper or home ground.

High Leader

The nearside leader of a twenty-mule team. The skinner transmitted his commands to the high leader by voice and by a single jerk line which ran through harness rings on all the nearside mules to the leader. It was essential that this mule, in the capacity of team captain, should possess a high degree of intelligence.

156

High Port
A type of mouth piece. *See* Bitting.

Hind Boot
In the 1700s, this took the form of a basket, over the rear axle, in which passengers travelled. Straw was placed inside the boot to keep them warm. Later, a wooden box replaced the basket and soon a lid with a seat was placed on the top. The door of the hind boot of a Stage and Road Coach was hinged on the right hand side so that the guard, who sat on the left-hand rear seat, could reach down and open the boot to get at the parcels. The hind boot of the Mail Coach contained the mail and had its lid opening upwards under the guard's feet. The Drag had the door of its hind boot hinged at the bottom so that it could be let down on quadrants to form a table on to which the picnic boxes could be pulled out. At one time, the hind boot was called the rumble. This now refers to the rear seat.

Hind Footboard
The leather-covered platform, at the rear of a town carriage, on which the servant stood, hanging on by braid or webbing holders fixed to the rear of the vehicle.

Hind Standard
The ornate framing on each side of the hind footboard of a vehicle such as a Town Chariot or Town Coach. Hind standards were made of a combination of delicately carved, small wooden pillars and carefully worked ornamental iron. Their purpose was partly decorative to balance the profile of the carriage and partly functional as they acted as mounting handles for the footman when he climbed on to his footboard.

Hip Strap
Also known as Trace Bearer or Trace Carrier.

Hitch and Hop
A slang term which is used to describe the action of a hackney, when he breaks momentarily in his trotting stride to a half-canter and then hesitates as he puts in a short stride before continuing his elevated and cadenced pace.

Hobson, Samuel
A coachbuilder of the 19th century who earned a name by decreasing the size of carriage wheels.

Holder
When a servant travelled on the hind footboard of a town carriage he held on by means of braid or webbing holders fixed by staples to the back of the vehicle. These holders were frequently trimmed with tassels or other ornamentation.

Holland & Holland
A coachbuilding firm, famous for the production of Road Coaches. Many are still in existence.

Holly
A wood from which many whips are made. The second-growth shoot of holly is best cut when it is six or seven years old. The stick is then hung with a weight at its end and thoroughly seasoned before being stained, varnished and mounted with a suitable handle, quill and thong. The diameter of the quill end should be

about three-tenths of an inch and the collar end about three-fifths. The length of the stick, for team driving, should be about 5 feet.

Holmes, Oliver Wendall
Author of the famous poem, the 'One-Hoss Shay', which tells, so vividly, the one hundred years' life story of the Shay from its building, with details of the types of wood used, to its collapse a century later.

Holyhead Mail, The
This coach regularly completed 260 miles over difficult roads in under twenty seven hours. Stops for twenty-seven changes of horses, and dinner and breakfast were included in the time.

Hooded Gig
A Gig with a folding head. Sometimes called a Buggy.

Hooper, G. N.
A famous coachbuilder of the 19th century. He supplied numerous superb carriages for the Royal Family and the nobility of England as well as to the Continent. Great importance was paid to safety and comfort in the construction of these vehicles. Many were very heavy, needing six horses. This was of little consequence to those rich enough to order such carriages, when comfort on long journeys was essential and the cost of horses unimportant.

Hoop, Nave
A narrow iron hoop fitted round the nave on either side of the spokes.

Hoop Tyre
The name given to the tyre of an iron shod wheel. It referred to the hoop of hot iron which was placed on to the wooden wheel. As the tyre cooled, it shrank and held the felloes and spokes firmly together.

Hopkinson, Luke
A London coachbuilder known for the production of a Briska Landau.

Hopping Bobs
A game played by American boys in the early 1900s. They stood in the snow on the curb waiting for a bob sled to come along the road. As it passed, the child would hop on to the rear runner. Then, clinging to the side of the sled, a hazardous ride could be enjoyed.

Horizontal Spring. *See* Double-Elbow Spring.

Horn Bar
A transverse wooden member used to secure the after-part of the wheel plate, or fifth wheel, to the body of a four-wheeled vehicle.

Horn Bar Plate
An iron strengthener for the horn bar.

Horn Case
A horn-shaped leather case in which the coach horn is stowed. It is strapped to the rear of the coach on the right-hand side where it is within the reach of the head groom.

Horns of Hames
The upper parts of the hames, used on farm horses, over which the hame rein is secured.

Horse Guards Parade
Members of The Coaching Club first met here in 1895 before driving to Ranelagh Club. There were twenty-six coaches present. The last meet on Horse Guards Parade was held in 1911.

Horsing the Mail Coach
Those who contracted with the Post Office to provide suitable horses for the Mail Coach over one or more stages of the journey were said to 'horse the coach'. The rivalry between contractors resulted in an efficient service.

Hostler
Now better known as an ostler.

Hounds. *See* Wings.

Hour of Coach
The arrival time of the coach at the end of a stage. The recorded time taken to complete a stage was from arrival to arrival apart from the first stage which was from departure to arrival.

Housen
The large leather flap, behind the hames, on a heavy horse's collar. In bad weather it is folded back to protect the area below it, but otherwise it remains upright as is featured in most of the old prints.

Housing Strap
A small strap with holes at each end which buckle on to small buckles placed either side of the top of the collar behind the hames. It is used for holding the bearing rein down.

Howlett, E.
A 19th-century coachman who was said to be one of the finest Whips that had ever been seen. He was born in Paris of English descent and was established in France as a teacher of driving and adviser to many members of the nobility. He was credited with the success of the art of four-in-hand driving in France. His book *Driving Lessons*, is quoted from frequently.

Howlett's methods were adopted and publicized by Benno von Achenbach so that they became known as the Achenbach school of driving on the Continent.

Hub Cap
The cap on the wheel, frequently made of brass or plated, on which the carriage makers' name is often stamped. It is made to screw into the threaded part of the axle box. The purpose of the hub cap is for storing oil to lubricate the axle arm and axle box, and to prevent dirt and mud from working their way into these parts, causing damage through abrasion. *See* Axle.

Hungarian Buckling of Team Reins
The leaders' reins merge into two single draught reins in the usual way (English style), as do the wheelers' reins. The near wheel draught rein ends in a buckle

159

which is fastened to the near lead rein. The off wheel rein also terminates in a buckle on the off lead rein so that the reins are coupled together to form two reins. A short loop of rein, known as a frog, is buckled between the two single reins and the short ends of the reins hang down beyond the loop.

Hungarian Handling of Team Reins
All of the reins are coupled together to form two reins which are joined by a handpiece loop called a frog. The coupling and adjustment requires extreme accuracy to enable the required steady contact to be maintained.

The handpiece is taken in the full left hand which is placed on the rein with the knuckles uppermost. In pulling up and turning, the right hand is put in the same position, on the frog, alongside the left. Gradual turns to left and right are made by taking a stronger contact on the part of the handpiece which is nearest to the side of the direction required. This increases the tension on the inner sides of the horses' mouths. At the same time, the pressure on the side opposite to the turn is lessened which decreases the tension on the outer sides of the horses' mouths and permits them to turn.

Sharp turns are made by placing whichever hand is nearest to the side that the turn is being made, forward to the buckle where the wheel rein is coupled to the lead rein. Points are then made as required. The other hand remains on the centre of the handpiece.

At all times, the hands are held well forward.

Hungarian Team Harness
This is usually light, ornate and hung with fringes, known as sallengs, and patterned leather or metal decorations from the back strap. A bell is sometimes worn hanging from the centre of the throat lash. Breast collars are employed, as are yoke straps. Double-ringed snaffle bits are worn. The reins are coupled and buckled together to form a single loop at the handpiece.

Hunting Phaeton. *See* Beaufort Phaeton.

Hurlingham Club at Fulham, London
Members of The Coaching Club have driven there on regular occasions for lunch, tea or dinner, since 1880.

Hyde Park, London
Members of The Coaching Club assembled at the Magazine in Hyde Park for their inaugural meet in 1871. This meeting place has been used, amongst others, for over a century.

Ice Skid
A skid which was designed to hold the coach on an icy hill. It took the form of a 2-foot 4-inch iron link with protruding teeth. It was placed under the tyre and felloe of a hind wheel and the teeth dug into the ice. A floating ring was secured on to the link to which the chain was attached and hooked to the axle.

If an ice skid was not available and road conditions were bad, a makeshift ice skid was made. A chain was passed round the felloe and over the ordinary skid which was placed in position against the wheel. The links of the chain bit into the icy surface.

Imitation Cane Work
Various Gigs, Phaetons and similar vehicles have imitation cane either stuck or painted on to the side and back panels, to give a lightening appearance to the body.

Imperial
This is a box which fits between the passenger seats on the roof of a Drag and contains the requirements for a lunch party, in addition to those stowed in the hind boot. It is also known as a lunch box. The box for luggage on a Travelling Coach or Chariot was also called an Imperial.

Imperial Mercury
An unusual coach which was patented in 1780, by Mr Crispus Claggett, to carry sixteen inside passengers. It was divided by doors and glass into four separate compartments, each with its own door.

Improved Cart
Hayes & Sons who were anxious to produce the best possible carts, carriages and waggons, frequently prefixed the name of a vehicle with 'Improved'. On offer, in the 1870s, were, amongst others, The Improved Cranked Axle Cart and The Improved Parcel Van. Their improvements no doubt went a long way towards their successes at exhibitions in London and Paris where they were awarded prize medals and Honourable Mentions and with the Royal Agricultural Society of England and other Societies whose prizes they frequently won.

Incline. *See* Turns.

Indian Cart Yoke
A method of harnessing a pair to a two-wheeled vehicle. The pole is made of wood and is shaped with two right-angle bends to bring it level with the tops of the saddles. A steel yoke, or bar, lies in a groove on each saddle and is prevented from coming out by a small strap across the top of the groove. The pole is passed through a ring in the centre of the yoke. There are two pins going through the pole on either side of the yoke ring, about 8 inches apart. The rear one prevents the cart from running forward on to the horses, as no pole straps are used. The front one prevents the yoke from coming off the pole. The distance between the two allows a certain amount of leeway for the draught which might otherwise be taken through the saddles instead of the traces. The ring on the yoke ensures that if one horse should fall, the other will not be pulled down, too, as the ring allows the yoke to pivot on the pole. At each end of the yoke is a rein terret through which the draught reins pass. The coupling reins go under the yoke.

India Rubber. *See* Caoutchouc.

India Rubber Apron. *See* Apron.

India Rubber Balling Pads
Pads of rubber which were nailed between the foot and the shoe to prevent the snow from balling in the feet. It was found that soap or tallow, packed into the foot also prevented balling, if pads could not be fitted in time. Vaseline is also moderately effective.

India Rubber Loin Cover

A rubber quarter-sheet, lined with cloth, which is used in wet weather. There are two straps and buckles at the front which are fixed to the backband or tug buckles. Commercial horses, like those working on a milk round, always wore loin covers if they had to stand around for any length of time in bad weather. When a block of flats was visited, there could be a two-hour wait whilst milk was delivered to all the occupants. The horse would stand in his cart, untied, with his head in a nosebag and a loin cover to keep him warm and dry.

India Rubber Pads

Horses were shod with rubber pads between the sole and the shoe to give some purchase on slippery roads.

India Rubber Tyres

By the end of the 19th century, most high-class carriages were fitted with india rubber tyres. They could only be used on good surfaces as they were soon cut to pieces on stony roads. Rubber tyres found particular favour with aged, sick and nervous passengers, as the progress of vehicles was rendered silent. The springy capacity of rubber made travel more comfortable causing less jolting to the carriages. This reduced repair bills and gave vehicles a longer life. At first, the wired-on variety was used. This consisted of a solid rubber tyre held into a straight-sided iron channel by one or two strands of thick wire running longitudinally through the tyre. The ends of the wires were joined to hold the tyre into its channel. Wired-on tyres were superseded by clencher tyres. With these, the solid rubber tyre is held by a curved channel and is far less likely to spring out of place. It has, however, been proved that clencher tyres too, are only suitable for good road conditions. Attempts have been made to use them for F.E.I. Competitions but the severe sideways strain applied when cornering at speed over rough terrain during marathons sometimes levers the tyres from their channels, as does the strain of sideways skid in obstacle tests.

Infirmary

In large stables, where hundreds of working horses were kept, there was usually a building set aside to act as an infirmary where sick horses could be placed. This ensured a degree of isolation. Specialized care was more practical if all patients were housed together. It was normal practice to have a chart by the stable door stating the horse's name, or number, his illness, his treatment and the food allowed.

Inside Car

An Irish vehicle not unlike a Governess car in construction and so called since the seats were inside, as opposed to the more usual Outside or Jaunting Car. The driver sat on a forward-facing seat in the centre of the front of the vehicle.

Inside Passenger

He was considered to be superior to an outside passenger on a coach. If an outside passenger wished to continue his journey inside, he had to gain permission from an inside traveller and then sit next to that person.

In the Cheek

When the reins are buckled on to the mouthpiece rings of a Liverpool, Buxton or similar bit. Also known as plain cheek. *See* Bitting.

In the White
The term used to describe the state of a carriage when the building was completed and it was ready to be trimmed and painted.

Irish Car
The traditional two-wheeled vehicle of Ireland. The passengers sit facing the sides of the road, back-to-back, with a lidded luggage well between them. Footrests which resemble shelves are let down on hinges at the edges of the seats and hang over the outsides of the wheels. On the centre of each footrest is a step by which the narrow seat is reached. When the vehicle is not in use, these rests can be turned up and the width of the car is reduced considerably. At the rear of the body, which is hung on side springs, are frequently a pair of iron props on which the vehicle rests when it is stored with the shafts in the air. The jarvey drives either from a forward-facing central seat on top of the luggage well, or perched in a precarious position on one of the side seats.
  Also known as Jaunting Car, Side Car and Outside Car.

Irish Slide Car
A wheel-less cart which was still in use in 1900 in Ireland. It was similar to the early conveyances used by the Ancient Britons. Two poles formed the shafts to the rear of which a type of large laundry basket was fixed. The load was carried in the basket. The ends of the poles slid along the ground as the single horse dragged the car by a collar and rope traces which were fixed to the shafts. These were held up by another rope lying over a crude saddle.

Iron Cart
A box-shaped, two-wheeled cart made from cast iron plates which were bolted and cemented to render the cart waterproof. It was used for carting water or liquid manure for agricultural purposes. An outlet valve, a pump and a hose were fitted for spreading the contents. The large-sized Iron Cart, which held 200 gallons, cost, in the 1870s, £26, plus 7 guineas for the pump and hose if required.

Iron Quadrant
On which the door of the hind boot of a Drag is let down so that it is held firmly in an horizontal position to form a table. Sometimes, chains are used instead of iron quadrants.

Italian Handling of Reins
Two of the methods of handling team reins which were practised in Italy at the end of the 1800s, are similar to each other but different from the English method. In each, both nearside reins lie over the index finger and the off lead rein lies over the second finger with the off wheel over the third finger. The only difference between the two Italian methods is that with one the near lead rein is on top of the near wheel rein and, with the second, the order is reversed.

Ivory
This was used for carriages with a luxurious finish. Crests would sometimes be carved out of ivory as would buttons, studs and various interior fittings.

Ivory Worker
He was indirectly employed by the coachbuilder whenever work was required.

Jack. *See* Carriage Jack.

Jackson Wagon
A type of wagon which was first made in Jackson, Mississippi, U.S.A.

Jagger Wagon
A type of square boxed buggy, used in New York, which had no springs but was hung on bolsters.

Japan
A coating put on to leather to give it the shiny surface known as patent leather. Another method of japanning can be used which is more pliable and allows the leather to be folded without becoming cracked. This is called enamelling.

Japanned Leather
Also known as patent leather. This is made from carefully tanned hides which are specially treated and then varnished.

Japanner
A workman who was employed by the currier and who was responsible for glazing and enamelling leather to produce patent and enamelled leather for carriages and harness.

Jarvey
The man who drives a Jaunting or Irish Car.

Jaunting Car. *See* Irish Car.

Jenny Lind
A light, four-wheeled American vehicle which was named after the singer. The forward-facing seat was protected by a canopy and placed in the centre of the box-shaped body which was only 2 feet 6 inches wide. It was hung on transverse springs and a perch. The front wheels were just under 4 feet high and the rear wheels 3 inches larger.

Jerk Line
The rein by which the 'skinner' controls his mule team. It passes through rings on the harness of all the nearside mules to the high leader. The aid to the leading pair of mules to turn to the right is a series of jerks on the line. A turn to the left is achieved by a steady pull.

Jerky
A four-wheeled, American, single-horse vehicle.

Jersey Van
A gaily painted dray which is common on the Channel Island of Jersey and used for carting such goods as potatoes from the farms down to the merchants on the coast before being shipped to the mainland. Jersey vans are also employed for transporting sightseers around the island. There are longitudinal seats along each side. The suspension is a combination of Telegraph springs and semi-elliptic springs. The single or pair of vanner type horses are driven from a transverse seat at the front. Strong and ornate harness, plentifully decorated with brasses, is worn. The collar is thick and the lining covers a wide area in order to distribute the load over as much of the shoulders as possible.

Jibbing

A habit adopted by some ungenerous horses who stop and refuse to go forward in any direction. The causes are many and varied. Sometimes too heavy a load, sore shoulders or unsympathetic hands on a sensitive mouth can result in a normally kind horse resorting to jibbing as a means of defence. Some horses jib from pure nappiness.

Reputed cures are as varied as the causes. One method is to place the known jibber alongside a heavy and strong horse who will effectively drag his reluctant partner, even if he lies down, in the desired direction. Some people say that after tying up a front leg for a considerable time and leaving the animal without water and food the jibber will move forward when asked. Others advocate the use of a hose. One desperate driver, anxious to progress, lit a bonfire under his stationary horse. The animal moved forward; but only far enough to place the gig over the fire!

Jingle

A long-shafted cart.

Jingle

A single-horse vehicle used for hire in Ireland.

Jingle

The name which is given to a Governess Cart, in Somerset.

Jinker

A two-wheeled vehicle, resembling a gig, which is commonly used in Australia.

Job

To jerk the horse in the mouth with the reins.

Job Horse

One which is hired out by a jobmaster.

Jobmaster

The man from whom horses, harness and vehicles of every type for any job could be hired. Many were hired by the month, for the summer season or by the year and charges varied accordingly. At the end of the 1800s, the hire fee was about 100 guineas a year for a pair if they were kept and shod by the person who was hiring them. If the jobmaster kept and shod them the fee was about 180 guineas. At the end of the 19th century, one of the largest jobmasters' establishments was that of Thomas Tilling in London. His 2,500 horses were to be found all over England. Some pulled trams, others drew vans or brewery drays, some worked for the Fire Brigade. Many were put to town carriages.

Jobmasters kept good-looking horses to satisfy those who wished to hire. About eighty per cent of those horses which drew fashionable carriages to smart London drawing rooms and state balls were jobbed from a master.

Jocky Stick

The pole which is fixed between the leaders of a twenty-mule hitch. *See* Twenty-Mule Team.

Jogging Cart

A light, two-wheeled American vehicle which was used for jogging or exercising trotters. The seat was built for either one or two people whose feet rested on a slatted floor.

Joiner
Also known as a bodymaker. He was employed by the carriage builder.

Joint
One of the metal stays on a leather hood. Each of these joints takes the shape of a flattened 'S'. Their purpose is to keep the leather stretched to its proper shape.

Jointed Bit
This refers to the mouthpiece, and in some cases to the bar across the bottom of the branches of a bit, which is jointed in one or more places. A single central joint is most common and works on the tongue with a nutcracker action. *See* Bitting.

Jointed Hame Ring
The rein ring on some hames is made so that it is free to move fore and aft in its branch from the hame.

Jointed Whip
A whip which is jointed in the middle with a metal screw and socket. It can be carried in halves on a board, in a case, and kept as a spare.

Jowl Piece
Part of a bridle. *See* Army Harness.

Jump Seat Carriage
Any American vehicle which has one or more adjustable folding seats which can be hidden when not in use is frequently referred to as a Jump Seat Carriage. A jump seat quickly and conveniently converts a two-passenger vehicle into a four-seat carriage.

Jump Seat Wagon
A four-wheeled American wagon with a canopy over the two forward-facing seats. It could be converted into a single-seater by folding the front seat down and jumping the rear seat forward. It then resembled a Jenny Lind, although the body was 10 inches wider.

Junky
A general term used in parts of Australia for a two-wheeled cart.

Karrozin
A curtained, four-wheeled vehicle, which is driven from a box seat and used as a tourist conveyance in Malta.

Kay Collar
Named after the inventor. *See* Collar.

Keeper
A loop of leather found on the harness to keep the point of leather in position after it has passed through a buckle. Some people prefer to have the solid type of box keepers on their harness whilst others favour narrow loop or space keepers. For the sake of uniformity, the type of keepers which are chosen should match throughout a set of harness.

Kemble Jackson. *See* Overhead Check.

Key Bugle
A copper horn which was favoured by Stage Coach guards in the 1830s. The six or more brass keys enabled a large range of notes to be played. The rendering of melodies was a pleasurable pastime for both the guard and the passengers. The Post Office did not permit its use on the Mail Coaches. Perhaps the reason for this was because two hands were needed to play the key bugle and this left the guard unarmed. Undeterred, some Mail guards carried their own key bugles, as well as the regulation horn issued by the Post Office.

Kicking
A slang term for tipping of guards by passengers. Also known as shelling and shouldering.

Kicking Strap
A strap which passes over the loins through a slot in the back strap of the crupper. The point is buckled at each side to a short strap which goes through a shaft staple and round the shaft. The point of the little shaft strap goes into a buckle and lies below the point of the kicking strap going into the same buckle. It is secured further, by a keeper beyond the shaft strap buckle. A kicking strap will help to keep the quarters down if the horse is likely to kick. It should not be fastened too tightly, as the feeling of restriction may start kicking instead of preventing it.

Kidney Link
A kidney-shaped metal link which takes the place of a bottom hame strap or hame chain with some pair and team harness. The link sometimes opens at the top, in the centre, so that it can be passed through the bottom hame eyes. The kidney link ring is put on to the lower part of the link. To prevent the hames from being pulled off the collar, by the pole straps, the false martingale is buckled round the top half of the kidney link as well as the collar.

Kidney Link Ring
The metal ring which hangs from the lower side of the kidney link. It is to this ring that the pole strap or pole chain is fastened for a pair or the wheelers of a team. Some competitors in F.E.I. events have their team leaders joined by a strap passing between the kidney link rings. For normal work with a team, the leaders would not wear rings on their kidney links.

King Bolt
Also known as perch bolt.

Kings of the Road
The name given to The Royal Mail and the Stage Coach men owing to their dignity.

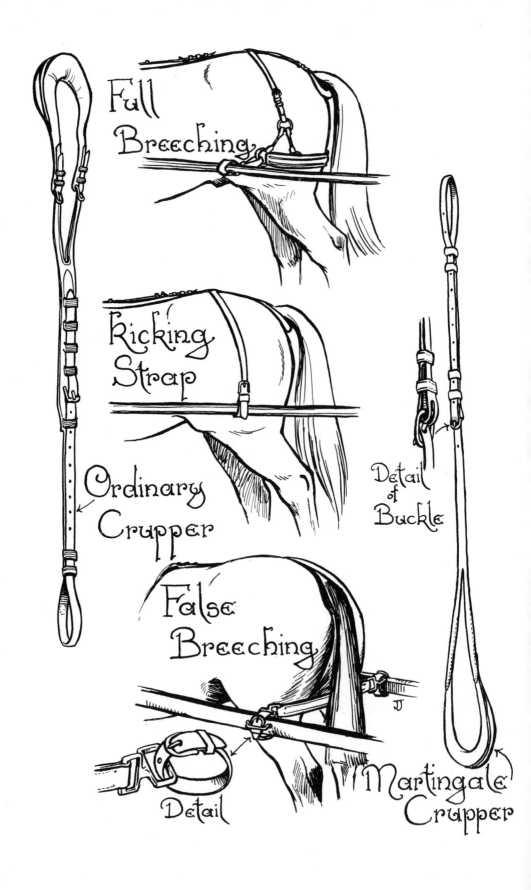

Full Breeching

Kicking Strap

Ordinary Crupper

Detail of Buckle

False Breeching

Detail

Martingale Crupper

Knacker
The horse slaughterer and the harness maker were, many years ago, run as the same business. The harness maker dressed and tanned the horses' hides for his own use in his profession. Because of this, harness makers were referred to as knackers.

Knacker's Brandy
Harness oil. *See* Knacker.

Knee Action
The rocking, up-and-down motion, created by a trotting horse in an ill-sprung or badly balanced two-wheeled cart.

Knee Boot
The apron which is sometimes attached to the dashboard and rolled up when not in use. If protection against bad weather is required, the boot is unrolled and pulled up over the legs.

Knee-flap
A cover which can be drawn up, if so desired, to give protection to passengers or upholstery on a vehicle such as a Barouche or a Britzschka.

Knife Board
Some of the London coaches had a seat in the centre of the roof to accommodate three passengers. It was said to make the coach top-heavy and was not favoured.

Knifeboard Omnibus
In the middle of the 19th century, some London Omnibuses had two longitudinal seats on the roof. Passengers sat back-to-back, facing the sides of the road. These roof seats were reached by steps at the rear of the bus. 'Modesty boards' were fixed to the sides of the roof to prevent pedestrians having a glimpse of the ankles of lady passengers. These boards were subsequently used for advertising.

Knight, Capt. Morley
Author of the book *Hints on Driving* published in 1905 and recently reprinted.

Knob Hook
The type of bearing rein hook which takes the form of a decorated knob shaped object, such as an acorn or a ball. Behind the knob is a hook on to which the rein is fixed.

L.F.H.C.
The Ladies Four-in-Hand Club was founded in 1901 in America. Ladies drove their teams at their Club's regular meets and drives, some of which were as long as forty miles. They paraded each spring and had a Father's day when parents rode on the box seat alongside their daughters. The Club uniform was a tan coat with blue trim. Grey beaver hats with cut-down crowns were worn. In 1910, The Arrow, a public coach, was put on the road and driven by the ladies.

Lace
The braid with which the edges of the material in the upholstery of carriages was trimmed or the unsightly parts such as a row of tack heads was covered. It was also used for trimming hammercloths, for footman's holders and for the frames of carriage windows.

Lace was woven individually for each family.

Lacemaker
The interior of many carriages was trimmed with lace and it was often used for the footmen's holders and for the edges of hammercloths. Lacemaking was a skilled art at which men, in London, in the first part of the 19th century could earn £3 a week. As the carriage trade escalated, lace began to be made wholesale in many of the big towns. The London lacemaker gradually became redundant.

Ladder
A folding ladder with about five steps is carried for the benefit of ladies wishing to mount the top of a coach. The little ladder has either a platform, or hooks, or both, at the top which fit into the open steps on the side of the coach. When it is not in use it is hung underneath the hind boot on a Road Coach and under the rumble seat on a Drag, in readiness for the servants to unhook it and assist passengers.

Ladders for Drags were usually made of iron and those for Road Coaches of wood.

Lade, Lady (Letty)
Wife of Sir John Lade. She shared her husband's love for driving and was as at home on the box as she was as a passenger during Sir John's speedy excursions. She owned a colourful vocabulary which she no doubt acquired from the highwayman with whom she was associated before she married.

Lade, Sir John, Bart.
One-time friend of George IV and considered to be one of the best coachmen of the period. His admiration for the stagecoachmen was carried to such an extreme that he adopted their speech and dress. He even filed his teeth so that he could copy their ability to spit. One of his favourite occupations, whilst he was at the Royal Pavilion stables, was to drive as fast as possible along Brighton's narrow lanes. Stories of his coaching feats became somewhat muddled with those of George IV.

Ladies' Phaeton. *See* George IV Phaeton.

Lady
A 15-hand English roadster out of Cheshire Cheese Lass by Matchless, who was famous for her ability to trot at speed. In 1834, carrying 12 stone, she trotted 17 miles in 55 minutes and continued a further mile to her stable within the hour.

Lamp Bracket, Iron or Socket
The circular metal fitting into which the stem of the lamp is placed to hold the lamp in position on the vehicle. The ring has a metal arm to keep the lamp away from the vehicle and the end is shaped either with a 'T' or a right-angle bend in

which holes are drilled. Bolts are passed through these holes to secure the bracket to the carriage.

Lamp Bracket Plug
A well-appointed Drag had wooden plugs, which were carefully finished with rounded tops, to place in the lamp socket when the lamps were not carried. They protected people's hands from the sharp edges of the metal brackets which were sometimes held when mounting and dismounting the coach and they gave a neat appearance.

Lampmaker
In the first half of the 1800s he earned 25 to 30 shillings a week. He worked mostly with thin metal which required a neat but not minutely accurate finish, as the joints were soldered.

Lamps
They were first used on carriages in about 1700. Those on 19th-century coaches were oil-powered and had wicks which required daily trimming. This design was later abandoned as being dirty and troublesome. By the end of that century, candles were usually providing the light from lamps.

Lamps were made in many shapes and patterns on the same basic design. The main body of the lamp has a box-like form with four, six or eight sides of glass joined by strips of metal, or a combination of glass sides and metal sides. They have square, round, oval, horse-shoe and numerous other shaped fronts. Dial faces were said to give the best light and were favoured for use on Drags. Mr Johnson of Edinburgh perfected such a lamp which became known as a Scotch Dial. Some fronts are surrounded by a narrow metal trim. Others have a deep brass rim. Lavishly decorated lamps were made for use on State occasions with Royal carriages.

The top is designed to allow ventilation and the patterns vary considerably. Some have an oval or round top which is fluted. Others have two or three diminishing layers of squares. These are known as pagoda tops. Some are surmounted by golden eagles or crowns.

The most usual lamps are those with a glass front and glass outer side. The side which is nearest to the vehicle is of metal, as is the rearmost side which often has a small circular red glass in the centre to act as a rear light. The insides of these metal surfaces and of the base, is often of silver-plated copper. These plated surfaces effectively reflect the light sideways across the road and forwards towards the horses.

The candle is fitted into the stem of the lamp which is made of brass, white metal or painted metal and goes on top of a longitudinal spring. The top of the candle is held down by a circular metal fitting which is attached to the base of the lamp with a groove running over a small protrusion. There is a hole in the centre of this attachment through which the wick rises. As the candle burns down, so the spring expands and the candle is pressed up against the fitting. The candle is lit by opening the lamp at the back. A new candle is fitted by opening the lamp and pulling a small lever which releases the stem downwards to free it from the lamp.

Coaches carry their lamps in sockets near the front of the body. A footboard lamp is sometimes used. Road Coaches had a portable lamp by the hind boot on

171

the near side so that the guard could read the names on the parcels and see the waybill. This lamp was also used by the guard when he had to go ahead to inspect the road if there was any doubt about its condition.

At the end of the 19th century, it was not correct to carry lamps on coaches during daylight hours. This probably originated from when oil lamps were used and left at the inn in the morning to be filled and trimmed in preparation for the night journey.

Now, lamps are always carried as part of the correct appointment of private driving vehicles. These lamps should be plain and the metal trim should match that of the furniture on the harness and the fittings on the vehicle. One or two rear lamps can also be carried. These are miniature editions of ordinary lamps but have just a single red glass and the rest of the lamp is metal. The candles should have been lit and immediately blown out. The reason for this is that there may be difficulty in lighting new candles on a windy night. If the supply of matches is limited this could cause a real problem.

Coloured candles and artificial flowers should never be put into lamps though it is a habit which some costers adopt in dressing up their London trolleys for parades.

Lamps are not usually carried on Drags during daylight. They are frequently stowed inside the coach in readiness for an evening journey.

Lancashire Bit
Used on heavy horses. The half-moon mouthpiece has ends which curve to form hooks by which the bit is fixed to the rings on the cheeks of the bridle.

Lancewood
A straight-grained wood, grown in the West Indies, which can be shaped by boiling. It was used mainly for making shafts owing to its elasticity. Some sticks of whips were made of lancewood, for the same reason.

Landau
Opinions differ regarding the exact date in the 1700s when the Landau first appeared in England. The vehicle was of German origin, taking its name from the fortress town.

This four-wheeled conveyance gained popularity as it was well suited to England's uncertain climate in that it could be converted from an open to a closed carriage with little trouble. The leather heads could be raised over the two seats and the window pulled up to form a coach-like body if the weather changed. Early Landaus had leather heads which required frequent greasing and blacking, giving off a disagreeable odour and being unpleasant to touch. Furthermore they did not open completely but lay at an angle of 45 degrees. Early examples of Landaus were heavy, as well as expensive to maintain. They were built on an iron-strengthened perch and the body was reinforced with a substantial amount of iron. It was hung first on braces, then on whip springs and later on cee-springs.

In 1838 an English coachbuilder, Mr Luke Hopkinson, made numerous improvements to a vehicle called a Briska Landau. The heads were made to fold right back and the seats were raised 6 inches to give the passengers more air and further elbow room. Cee-springs, in some cases, gave way to four elliptic springs, or to a combination of two elliptic springs in front and five springs at the rear.

These five springs consisted of two elbow springs, two side-springs and one cross-spring. The Landaus of the 1860s weighed at least three-quarters of a ton and needed two strong horses to draw them.

Soon though, they were being built with numerous improvements and the weight was reduced. This immediately increased the demand. Messrs Hooper built a light canoe-shaped Landau for the Earl of Sefton which could be drawn by a single horse. Landaus shaped thus became known as Sefton Landaus. Blood horses began to take the place of the Yorkshire carriage horses whose strength and size had been necessary for the heavy carriages.

A squarer, angular version of the Landau was built for the Earl of Shelburne. Landaus with this angular outline, having a well-shaped centre by the doors, became recognized as Shelburne Landaus.

Towards the last quarter of the 1800s it was claimed that no carriage had been improved upon to such an extent in twenty years as the Landau. Great ingenuity from English craftsmen went into perfecting it. The weight and size were reduced tremendously. Heads were designed so that they folded as easily as a parasol. Landaus were made in large numbers. In a modest establishment where only one vehicle and horse were kept, a Landau provided the answer to combine the qualities of a Brougham and Victoria in one carriage. It was suitable for use in summer or winter and in town or country. By the end of the 19th century, canoe-shaped Landaus far outnumbered the Shelburne Landaus, whose heavier lines were favoured by the wealthy who were more able to afford to horse them.

One of the most formal ways of turning out a Landau was called Landau Grande Daumont. It was drawn by four horses driven postillion and attended by two outriders on matching horses, wearing livery similar to that of the postillions. The purpose of these outriders was to protect the occupants of the carriage from possible danger. To find six horses, all of the same colour, action and stamp, was an expensive business. The bridles, which were all blinkered, and the cruppers on the six horses, were identical in shape and in adornment.

The State Landau was a large and magnificent vehicle, similar in lavish appointment to the State Coaches and State Chariots. The body was painted in the family colours with heraldic bearings on the panels and the hammercloth. The undercarriage was painstakingly carved and gilded. The harness on the upstanding horses was heavily encrusted with metal ornamentation. State Landaus can be seen in the Royal Mews, Buckingham Palace, from where they are turned out for the State Opening of Parliament, amongst other duties.

At the other end of the scale in the Royal Mews are the light Ascot Landaus with basketwork sides to their bodies which are hung on elliptic springs. They are used at Ascot when the Queen drives up the course. On this occasion they are driven postillion and drawn by teams of bay or grey horses.

Landau Grande Daumont
A Landau, driven postillion, with outriders in attendance, named after a French nobleman — Duc d'Aumont. *See* Landau.

Landaulette
Also known as Demi-Landau. This was to the Landau as the Chariot was to the

Coach. It only had a rear seat. When required the hood folded to form an open carriage and the front pillars were designed to fall across one another.

Landau Sleigh
An American Sleigh with a Landau-shaped body. The passengers entered by small doors between the two face-to-face seats. The Sleigh was driven from a high box seat at the front.

Landau Waggonette
A Waggonette with a leather hood which opened longitudinally to lie back towards the sides of the road. Such a vehicle was presented, in 1893, to the Duke and Duchess of York on their marriage, by Lord Lonsdale. Vehicles built to this design became known as Lonsdale Waggonettes, and there is one in the Royal Mews today.

Lapping Traces
When putting a team to, some people prefer to lap the leaders' traces. One leader is put to with his traces going directly from his collar to his lead bar. The other horse has his outside trace fixed in the normal way and his inside trace passed through his partners trace, between the pad and the bar. There are two reasons for this. One is to help to keep the leaders together. The other is to keep the inside traces away from the horses' sides, thus lessening the chance of sore sides caused by a combination of grit and sweat. The disadvantage of this method is that if a horse should fall or start to kick, the problem of sorting out the muddle is greater.

Lash
This is joined to the end of the thong and made either of leather to match the thong, or of whipcord which is plaited to a fine finish. Thick or coloured thongs are not desirable though these are often found on modern whips.

Lash-Hoss
When a team of four farm-horses is driven at length, this is the horse which goes behind the forhoss.

Latten Bells
Bells which are used on heavy harness.

Laurie and Marner, Messrs
London Coachbuilders of Oxford Street. Known for producing the first Clarence in 1842 and for building the Sovereign which was a similar vehicle.

Lawrence Wagon
A type of American buggy which was named after its designer James W. Lawrence of Brewster & Co., New York.

Lawton Buggy
A name given to a Lawton gig which had been fitted with a hood.

Lawton Gig
An elegant Gig, built by Lawton, with a square body.

Lay

The part of a breast collar which is sewn on top of the padding of the breast piece to the tug buckle on each side. The pole strap dee and neck piece tug dees are sewn into the lay.

Lazy-Back

A movable back rest. It is sometimes placed on the rumble seat of a Drag when this seat is occupied by passengers instead of grooms. Some Gigs and similar vehicles have a padded lazy-back which can be fitted for the comfort of passengers. Some are designed with two supports which drop into slots at the rear of the seat to hold it in position.

Lazy Leader

Though it is preferable not to have such a horse in the team, if this does occur it is better to have the lazy horse on the off-side where he is more easily reached with the whip.

Lazy Wheeler

Such a horse is probably best placed on the nearside where he is under the whip and it is therefore easier to persuade him to go into his collar if he is thus positioned. The disadvantage of having a lazy horse in the near wheel is that it is this horse which has to pull the hardest to get the coach away from the side of the road. An idle horse may not be willing to exert the necessary strength for such work.

Lead Bars

When a pair of leaders is put to in front of a pair of wheelers a main bar is hooked on to the pole hook and two single bars are hooked on to either end of the main bar. These are called the lead bars. The main bar is about 3 feet 4 inches long and is made of wood. It is attached to the pole hook by either a 'D' shaped metal fitting or a small metal eye shaped fixture. The advantage of the large dee is that it cannot get twisted sideways on the hook whereas the smaller ring can. The disadvantage is that the dee is so large that it is inclined to rattle and be noisy. It was favoured on coaches of the 1900s because on a dark night the coachman could tell by 'the chatter of the bars' whether or not his leaders were working. If they were up to their collars there was no chatter. On each end of the main bar is a hook with a spring going from the bar to the point of the hook. The wooden single bars are hooked to the main bar ends by their centre metal eyes which are set at right-angles. These bars are about 2 feet 11 inches long and have a hook with a safety spring at each end on to which the lead trace cock-eyes are hooked. All the metal parts on the three bars are held in position by screws or bolts. If screws are used, the bars should be put on with the screws' heads uppermost so that if a screw should come out its loss will be seen. Another type of lead bar occasionally used is that which is made from a long single bar attached to the pole hook by a centre ring. It has four trace hooks along its width. The disadvantage is that if one horse goes forward more freely than the others, the bar is at a permanent angle. Collars then become twisted sideways and sore shoulders are inevitable. Mail coaches frequently carried this type of lead bar amongst their spares.

175

Lead Rein

The rein of a tandem, unicorn or team which passes through the terrets on the harness of the intervening horses between the leader and the coachman.

Best-quality leather should be used for reins. Inferior leather will stretch and wear at the place where it passes through the wheeler's pad terret. The width of a rein is a matter of personal taste. Generally speaking, a rein which is $\frac{7}{8}$ inch wide is favoured by women and that of 1 inch by men. The thickness also varies. Four reins amounting to between $\frac{1}{2}$ and $\frac{3}{4}$ inch are quite thick enough for the average hand.

Lead reins are made up out of three or four lengths of rein and joined by being spliced. It is important to see, when the reins are made, that the splices are not put so that they coincide with where the rein goes through a terret. The edges of the splice will catch in the terret and prevent free running. This is particularly dangerous with a tandem leader. Also, the stitching will become worn by the friction against the terret. Care must be taken to ensure that the rearmost splices are not near to the hand. Four splices, coming at the place where the reins are held, make delicate handling difficult and pointing almost impossible.

The average length of a full-size tandem leader and team draught rein is about 24 feet from the bit to the end.

Lead Traces

With the leaders of a team, the trace ends have metal cockeyes stitched on to them. These are placed over the hooks on the lead bars.

Tandem leader traces are much longer than single horse traces. They terminate in spring cockeyes which are hooked on to the leading eye buckles on the shaft horse. If tandem bars are used, ordinary single harness traces are employed as lead traces.

Leading Eye Buckle

The hame tug buckle worn by the shaft horse in a tandem. On the lower front edge is a protrusion with a slot through which the tandem bar trace cockeye or lead trace cockeye is hooked.

Leading Eye Rosette

A rosette which is worn on the bridle of a tandem or team wheeler. A ring, resembling a terret, protrudes at right-angles from the outside of the rosette to carry the lead rein. A version of this without the rosette is known as a Roger ring.

Leaning Against the Pole

A disagreeable habit which some horses develop. It must be stopped as soon as there is any suspicion that it may be starting. A hedgehog skin tied to the pole may act as a deterrent. Placing the offender on the other side of the pole is sometimes effective.

Leather Bit

A bit with a mouthpiece made entirely of leather. Horses with sensitive mouths will sometimes go more kindly in this type of bit which, on salivation, becomes soft and adapts itself to the shape of the tongue. It is particularly suitable for young horses who will not accept a metal or vulcanite mouthpiece.

Leather-covered Bit
It is sometimes found that horses who will not accept a metal bit will settle if a layer of chamois leather is wound round the mouthpiece and stitched to keep it in position. The stitches should be away from the side which rests against the tongue.

Leather Curb Chain. *See* Curb Chain.

Leconfield, The Lord
President of The Coaching Club for 1935. He owned, drove and ran 'The Old Times' Coach.

Ledge Waggon
A type of Gypsy Waggon which has its four wheels under the body. A ledge extends over the top of the wheels which forms a longitudinal seat on each side of the interior.

Leeds Wagon
Also known as a Barrel Top Wagon.

Left-handed Coachman
If a coachman was desperately left-handed, it was possible for the coach to be built with the brake lever between his seat and that of his box seat passenger.

Leg Guard
Used by postillions to protect their right leg from damage caused by the pole.

Leicester Car
A two-wheeled country cart with a forward-facing seat for the driver and passenger. There are two inward facing seats at the back which are reached by a rear door and a step. This is a more comfortable arrangement for rear passengers, in a two-wheeled vehicle, than the usual backwards-facing rear seats which are often narrow and tipped at an angle.

Lemoine Brake
An effective brake which was used on omnibuses in Paris and was found on some coaches. It worked by means of a cord running from a foot-pedal which was operated by the coachman, to a pulley by the hub of the hind wheel Pressure on the foot brake caused the cord to tighten, the pulley to take up slack cord, and the brake to be strongly applied.

Lever Balance
A device patented in 1883 by Messrs Maskey & Co of Washington which enabled the driver to move the body of a two-wheeled Dog Cart on its undercarriage by the use of a lever, to overcome the problem of it being unbalanced by heavy people on the rear seat.

Liberator Roller and Trace Bolt
A quick-release system devised by Woolnough's, 2 Elizabeth Street, London. In an emergency, the head of the roller bolt could be unscrewed enabling the trace to be freed.

Lignum Vitae
A type of wood which is so heavy that it sinks in water. When horses were tied in stalls, their headcollar ropes or chains were passed through rings on the manger, or a ring at manger height, and then through a hole drilled through a lump of wood known as a log or a ball. Lignum vitae was frequently used, owing to its weight.

Linchpin
A pin which was made either of wood or metal. It was passed through a hole in the axle arm, beyond the hub of the wheel in order to hold the wheel on to the arm.

Lincolnshire Cart
A strong two-wheeled tipping farm cart. It was built with an oak frame and had panelled sides which could be made to take out if that model was desired. The iron-shod wheels had tyres which were $3\frac{1}{2}$ inches wide. The cart, which was built by Hayes & Son of Stamford, won prizes at the North Lincolnshire Agricultural Society from 1857 to 1864. Models were offered at between £14 and £20. Harvest ladders were an optional extra.

Lincolnshire Wagon
Also known as a Barrel Top Wagon.

Line
American name for the rein.

Line Mule. *See* High Leader.

Lines
Reins which are made of ropes and replace the leather ones on farm horses for such work as ploughing.

Linseed
The seed of flax which has many uses.
   Harness makers fill the docks of cruppers with linseed, in order to render them permanently supple.
   Carriage painters add linseed oil to some varnishes and paints.
   Paint brushes, which are being used for varnishing a vehicle can be stored overnight in linseed oil to save washing and drying.
   Linseed is particularly valuable as a supplementary horse food for conditioning and making the coat shine. It acts as a mild laxative. Linseed must never be fed raw, but always cooked.

Litter
A conveyance used in the 16th and 17th century which was built on the lines of a horse-motivated sedan chair. The handles were extended to form shafts and the two horses were harnessed in front of and behind the body so that the horses had to take both the weight of the litter and that of the passenger. Litters were used to transport the sick and the aged as they were more comfortable than the unsprung coaches of the period. Some Litters were luxuriously trimmed with satin and velvet. They were carried by ornately harnessed horses who were attended by magnificently dressed grooms. These Litters were used for occasions

of state to carry high-ranking ladies whilst people of less importance travelled in Coaches.

Liverpool Bit
A curb bit with up to five variations of severity according to the position of the reins. If buckled to the ring, the fitting known as plain cheek, the action is that of a straight bar snaffle. If to the branch of the bit, directly below the mouthpiece, on rough cheek, a slight curb action is obtained. The positions in the slots down the bars of the bit, known as top bar, middle bar and bottom bar, have increasing severity as the rein is put lower. Not only is the curb chain leverage increased but so is the pressure on the horse's poll as the top of the bit is tipped forward. Some Liverpool bits are reversible enabling either the rough or smooth mouthpiece to be put against the tongue. Some have fixed mouthpieces for use with pairs and teams so that when the reins are coupled on to plain cheek the front part of the ring does not twist from the sideways pull and press against the side of the mouth. For pair, team, or, tandem-shaft horse a bar bit should be used. Liverpool bits are suitable for sporting turnouts. *See* Bitting.

Liverpool Gig
A square-bodied beautifully finished Gig which was similar to the Lawton Gig.

Livery
This is the clothing which is worn by servants with a carriage on formal occasions. Coachmen and grooms wear a coat of black, dark blue, dark green or dark maroon to blend with the bodywork of the vehicle. The coat buttons have a suitable crest or monogram and are made of a metal to match that of the harness and carriage fittings. The black top hat is decorated with a cockade if the owner is entitled to use one. White cloth or buckskin breeches, top boots, gloves and stock complete the livery. All should be spotlessly clean and fit perfectly. Such livery is worn at the present time by some grooms accompanying their employers with smart private driving turnouts whether single, pair, tandem, unicorn or team, at large shows and F.E.I. events. It is in order for a groom to sit beside the owner on the box if the vehicle is a Gig or has a similar seating arrangement. If the vehicle is a four-wheeler, with rear seats, then it is more usual for grooms to occupy this hind seat.

Her Majesty The Queen's Royal Coachmen wear Full State Livery for State occasions such as the Opening of Parliament and Royal Weddings. A black and yellow tricorne hat with red ostrich feathers is worn over a white wig. The magnificent frock coat which reaches to just above the knees is made of scarlet and gold and has buttons down the front. The knee breeches are scarlet and the stockings, which reach to the knees, are of pink silk. Black shoes with gold buckles and white gloves complete the livery. Decorations are worn. This livery is worn by the coachman of a State Coach turned out with horses in State Harness.

The Royal Postillions' Full State Livery consists of a hunt-type cap over a white wig, a waist-length jacket elaborately designed in yellow and scarlet with scarlet, yellow and black striped sleeves, buckskin breeches, top boots, leg guard and gloves. The postillion carries a small whip with a thong to control the offside horse. This livery is worn for State occasions with a State Coach.

179

Semi-State Coachman's Livery consists of a black top hat with gold lace round the base of the crown and a scarlet frock coat with black and yellow collar and cuffs. Blue knee breeches and white stockings with black, gold buckled, shoes complete the livery.

Scarlet Livery for Royal Coachmen consists of the same type of top coat and top hat as Semi-State Livery but buckskin breeches and top boots replace the knee breeches and shoes.

The Queen's coachmen wear what is known as black livery or undress livery for everyday occasions. This is a black top hat, with a cockade, a black top coat with black buttons, buckskin breeches, top boots and gloves.

Royal Postillions wear Ascot livery for the Ascot processions. Breeches, boots, gloves, whip and leg guard are the same for all postillion livery but the jacket worn for the Ascot Race Meeting is colourfully designed in the Queen's racing colours. The main body is purple. This is decorated with a gold front and scarlet sleeves. A hunt-type cap is worn.

Royal Postillions in Semi-State Livery wear a dark blue jacket which is plentifully decorated with gilt buttons. A black top hat with gold lace replaces the cap.

Everyday black livery for Royal Postillions consists of a black waist-length jacket with black buttons and a black top hat.

Living Margin
The tip which the person hiring a cab was duty bound to pay on top of the sixpence or shilling a mile, in order that the cabman had adequate income on which to live.

Log. *See* Lignum vitae.

Loin Rug
A small rug, resembling a quarter-sheet, which is put over horses' quarters if they are required to stand in cold weather for any length of time. The loin rug must always be placed under the reins. If it is put over the reins and the horse goes forward, the weight of the rug hampers the reins and an accident may result. In coaching days, loin rugs were considered only to be necessary at the ends of the road when horses were kept waiting whilst travellers mounted the coach. It was thought that stable rugs were adequate for the rest of the road. Providing that the coach ran on time, horses were not kept waiting. The new team stood in position with stable rugs on and as the coach arrived the rugs were pulled off, the horses changed and the rugs put on to the old team to go back to the stables. On a smart coach, some owners used matching loin rugs for all the changes along the road. *See* India Rubber Loin Cover.

Loin Strap
The narrow strap which passes through the back strap of the crupper and goes over the loins. The points at each side are buckled to the breeching tugs coming up from the breeching body. Also called a hip strap.

London Bell Rosette. *See* Boss.

London Coachbuilders
The large London firms were noted for turning out carriages from their factories which in design and finish were second to none.

London Van Horse Parade Society
Founded in 1904 to encourage the horse owners of London to maintain a higher standard of horse management. Each year, on Easter Monday, a parade was held in Regent's Park, London. First-class awards and merit badges presented by the Royal Society for the Prevention of Cruelty to Animals, were given to all exhibits who reached the required standard of care and turn out. This resulted in a great improvement in the health of London's horses.

Winning awards were proudly displayed along the shafts and on the horses' bridles, for weeks after the event, as the working horses of London went about their daily rounds.

In 1966 the Society amalgamated with the London Cart Horse Parade Society and became known as the London Harness Horse Parade Society.

A parade is still held on Easter Monday in Regent's Park.

Now, private driving turn-outs line up, alongside London's remaining working horses, for inspection.

In 1974, a total entry of 273 horses and ponies was received for the parade.

Long Breeching. *See* Breeching.

Long Car
This vehicle was used in Ireland. The private version was driven by a coachman from a centre seat. The passenger seats, which ran along each side of the car, faced the edges of the road and it was usual for the family to be accommodated along one side and the servants on the other side.

Long cars were also used, by Bianconi, as public passenger vehicles. *See* Bian.

Longitudinal Spring. *See* Double-Elbow Spring.

Long Price
A term used to describe the cost of an expensive horse.

Long Rein
A term used in the Army when driving a pair or team from the box on a vehicle such as G. S. Waggon.

Longset
When six horses are put to a vehicle such as a Diligence, to haul it up a hill, four were driven by the coachman and two leaders by a postillion.

Long Waggon
Also known as Flying or Stage Waggon.

Lonsdale, the Fifth Earl of 1857-1944
A great all-round sportsman. He was a perfectionist in appointing and turning out his carriages. His stable contained chestnut horses and his coach house was filled with yellow vehicles. One of his ventures was that of Hansom Cab proprietor and his cabs were turned out to the same high standard as that of his private carriages.

Perhaps Lord Lonsdale's most famous sporting achievement was his match against time when he drove four different equipages to cover twenty miles in fifty-five and a half minutes.

This event was originally scheduled to be run as a match for a £100 wager between Lord Lonsdale, who was to drive his horses, at the gallop, against Lord Shrewsbury who claimed that his horses could cover the ground faster, at a trot. The match was to be run over a five-mile stretch of road between Reigate and Crawley with a single, a pair, a four-in-hand team and a postillion pair.

Lord Lonsdale put his nine, carefully selected horses, into a training programme equal to that of race-horses. Harness and vehicles were specially made. The vehicle for the first phase was imported from America. Lord Lonsdale also went into strict training.

On the day of the race, 10th March 1891, thick snow covered the route and a heavy grey sky threatened more falls. Enthusiastic crowds lined the route but it was decided to postpone the match until the following day. Although more snow had fallen, a snow plough had cleared the road. Even more spectators arrived and bets were made. The officials were in position. Lord Lonsdale had two turnouts at the Crawley end of the road and two at the Reigate end. The word began to go round that Lord Shrewsbury had decided not to start. Lord Lonsdale was determined that neither he, nor the crowd should be disappointed and made the decision to run the match against time.

The first phase started at Reigate and was galloped with 'War Paint' to an American Buggy. In spite of a spectator's jibbing horse momentarily blocking the road and the Law doing its duty and briefly warning Lord Lonsdale that he was 'committing an offence', the five miles was covered in a little over 13 minutes and 39 seconds. At Crawley, Lord Lonsdale changed to the pair-horse American vehicle in three seconds and set off with 'Claire Soteil' and 'Vagonette' taking 12 minutes and 52 seconds to get back to Reigate. Thirty-seven seconds after pulling up, he was mounted on the Holland & Holland Brake and away behind four galloping horses with their heads pointing towards Crawley. The wheelers had worked in a fire-engine and 'Eveston King' and 'Stella', two thoroughbreds, were in the lead. The distance was completed in a fraction under twenty miles an hour. Forty-one seconds later, Lord Lonsdale was astride 'Royalty' with 'Violetta' as his hand-horse to an American Buggy. They arrived at Reigate 13 minutes and 56 seconds later.

The story created world wide interest.

Lonsdale Waggonette
In 1893 Lord Lonsdale presented a Landau Waggonette to the Duke and Duchess of York and the vehicle became known as a Lonsdale Waggonette. Disagreement arose regarding who should receive the credit for the idea. Mr Robertson claimed to have made a similar vehicle in 1864, Mr Kinder said that he had made one in 1865 and Messrs Morgan had built such a vehicle in 1870. Mr Hamshaw exhibited a Lonsdale Waggonette at the Royal Agricultural Society's Show in 1896 and built others under that name for Royalty.

Loop
The iron fitting by which the vehicle is suspended. The manufacture of loops

required great skill owing to the variety of curves desired for the shaping, combined with the accuracy required for the loops to be bolted in position.

Looping a Rein
Also known as pointing a rein. *See* Turns.

Loop Keeper
A narrow keeper or loop which is sewn onto various parts of the harness wherever a point strap needs to be secured after going through a buckle. It is usual to have two or three loop keepers alongside each other to secure the point firmly.

Lorrie
A strongly built, flat-topped, four-wheeled cart, which was hung on four side-springs. It was used for transporting heavy goods such as sacks of coal or corn and could be pulled by a single horse with shafts, or a pair with either a pole or two pairs of shafts. The cost of a new lorrie in the last quarter of the 19th century was between £27 and £35.

Lower Bar
When the rein is buckled on to the bottom slot of the branch of the bit the horse is said to be driven on lower bar. Also known as bottom bar. *See* Bitting.

Lower Ground
The last part of the road, or the furthest from home, on a coach journey in the nineteenth century.

Low Port
A type of mouth piece. *See* Bitting.

Lunch Boxes
These boxes were made of oak or mahogany and fitted into the hind boot of a drag. Some were lined with zinc or tinned copper and had watertight compartments to hold ice, salads and bottles. Others were designed to take plates, dishes, glasses and table linen. Sometimes the 'Imperial' on the roof is referred to as a lunch box.

Lynch Pin
An early method of securing a wheel to its axle. *See* Axle.

Macadam, John Loudon (1756–1836)
He was responsible, in conjunction with Thomas Telford, for creating roads which led to vast improvements in communications. In 1818 Macadam's idea of carefully laying stones of uniform size, in that none should exceed 6 ounces, to a depth of 6 inches as a foundation, was accepted. His surveyor carried scales and a 6-ounce weight and his road workers were armed with hammers to break the stones. A grant of £10,000 was paid to Macadam and in 1827 he was given the position of Surveyor General of Roads.

These improved roads led to the Stage and Mail Coaches making better times. Coachbuilders designed lighter vehicles to match the faster horses which were being driven.

The Golden Age of Coaching was due mainly to macadamized roads.

'Mad Woman'

The name which was sometimes given to a Stage Coach when it had no passengers.

Magazine

Members of The Coaching Club have been meeting, with their coaches, at the Magazine in Hyde Park since 1872 before departing on various drives, organized by the Club.

Mahogany

This wood was widely used for panelled areas of carriages when a high quality surface for a superb paint finish was required. It was also used for vehicles which were varnished. The red and yellow of mahogany and oak make an agreeable combination for a varnished country cart or similar type of vehicle.

Mail Axle

A type of axle originally used with the Mail Coaches. *See* Axle.

Mail Cart

A scarlet, two-wheeled, single-horse cart which resembled a mobile cupboard. It was painstakingly painted with about sixteen layers of paint and varnish. McNamara's, the contractors, built Mail Carts for the Post Office.

Mail Coach

Mr John Palmer, a theatre manager of Bath, was largely responsible for the introduction of Mail Coaches, which resulted in improved communications. He was dissatisfied that his mail took two days to be delivered to London by a mounted postboy. These boys were supposed to average six miles an hour, but rarely did. Numerous excuses were given for delays along the route and the chance of being accosted by a highwayman was considerable. Palmer claimed that it would be quicker and more efficient to send the mail by coach with a guard. He put forward a scheme which was opposed by the Post Office authorities who felt that their existing service was adequate. Palmer suggested that the coach should be horsed by contractors who were chosen by the Post Office, and to whom they, the P.O., should pay a mileage fee. Revenue from passengers and parcels should be kept by the contractor. The coachman would be selected by the contractor. The coach would be hired from the coachbuilder, by the contractor, for a mileage fee. The coachbuilder should be responsible for supplying, maintaining, servicing and repairing the coach, as required. The guard should be employed by the Post Office.

The Prime Minister was on Palmer's side and agreed to allow a coach to run from Bristol and Bath to London, at Palmer's expense.

On 2nd August 1784, a Mail Diligence carrying Mail, with a coachman, a guard and four inside passengers left Bristol at 4 p.m. and reached London sixteen hours later. It cut the time taken by the Stage Coach of the period, by 1 hour, as Palmer had predicted that it would.

Rapidly, more coaches were put on, to cover different parts of the country.

In 1786, by which time Palmer was getting short of money having financed the Mail Coaches for two years instead of the originally intended few weeks, he was given the position of Surveyor and Comptroller General of the Post Office. He was paid £1,500 a year and a rebate on a proportion of his initial outlay. He was also offered a percentage of the income from the now flourishing Mail Coach system.

John Besant was given the contract to supply the coaches. In 1791, this was taken over by John Vidler, a partner in Besant's London establishment. Vidler's continued to build and maintain Mail Coaches until 1836.

By 1804, outside passengers were carried, on a front seat behind the coachman, to obtain more revenue.

The Mail, as it was known, was built on a perch undercarriage with two sets of platform springs. The wheels were on mail axles. The coachman sat over the front boot with a passenger on the box seat alongside him. Three more passengers travelled outside, on the forward-facing seat behind him. Four people rode inside. The guard sat on a single circular seat at the back, with his feet over the lid of the hind boot. A tool kit, which also contained weapons such as a blunderbuss and a pair of pistols, was fixed to the roof in front of him. The coach horn was kept in a holder near to hand, as was a lamp which he used to read the names on the mail bags.

The Mails were all painted identically. The panels of the body were maroon. The sides of the front boot were black and carried the letters G.R. or V.R. in gold script writing. The hind boot was also black and displayed the number of the coach. The four upper-quarter panels were black and decorated with the four stars of the orders of knighthood. The stars of the Garter and the Thistle were on the near side and the Bath and of St. Patrick on the offside. The two towns between which the coach ran were painted on the door panels as were the words Royal Mail. The Royal Arms were painted in gold on the doors. The undercarriage and wheels were scarlet.

The Mails ran by day and by night, keeping to a split-second time-table for which the guard was responsible. They had the right of way over all other road users. They were untaxed and paid no tolls.

By 1835, there were about 700 Mail Coaches travelling at ten miles an hour along the improved roads built by Telford and Macadam.

Mail Coach Halfpenny

At least five types of token were struck in the 18th century in relation to Mail Coaches. It is thought that some were handed out for advertising purposes and others as a token of gratitude to John Palmer for all he had done in improving communications.

Three were struck as compliments to Palmer. One token depicts a galloping team to a coach with the words 'Mail Coach Halfpenny' above and 'To Trade Expedition and To Property Protection Payable in London' below. On the other side are the words 'To J. Palmer Esq., This is Inscribed As A Token of Gratitude for Benefits Rec'd from the Establishment of Mail Coaches'. Entwined leaves form the border on this side. The date 1798 is written at the bottom.

A second token is identical but has the initials J.F. in place of the date.

The third token, struck in relation to Palmer, has the words 'Halfpenny Payable in London' above the galloping team and 'To Trade Expedi and To Property Protection' written below. On the reverse side are the words 'To J. Palmer Esq., This is Inscribed' written around the edge. In the centre are entwined the letters A.F.H. surrounded by a wreath of leaves.

It is thought that these three halfpennies were struck, in gratitude, by Bath businessmen.

A Mail Coach Halfpenny was issued by the coaching proprietor William Waterhouse, whose headquarters were established at the famous London Inn 'The Swan with Two Necks'. This shows a picture of a coach and team with the motto 'Speed, Regularity and Security' written on one side. On the other side is printed a swan with two necks, one head is facing forward and the other looks to the rear. The words 'Payable at the Mail Coach Office' form the border. The address 'Lad Lane, London' is stamped below the swan. Under the address are the proprietor's initials, 'W.W.'

Another was circulated by the proprietor of 'The George and Blue Boar', a Holborn coaching inn. On one side of the coin is stamped St. George killing a dragon with a blue boar above them. The address 'Holborn, London' and the landlord's name, 'C. Jbberson', is written on the same side. On the reverse is inscribed 'Mail and Post Coaches to All Parts of England'.

The Mail Coach Halfpenny is also known as a Mail Coach Token.

Mail Coachman

He was supplied and paid by the contractor to drive the Mail for a certain number of stages along the route. This usually amounted to forty or fifty miles. He returned later, driving on the other side of the road. A coachman's wages in the 1830s were about £2 10 shillings a week. His pay was increased by tips which sometimes amounted to as much as £6 a week. On top of this, shouldering was practised, to gain more income. Relations between the coachman and guard were sometimes strained. Cold and wet weather led to habitual hard drinking by coachmen. The guard was responsible for the correct time-keeping of the Mail and was blamed if the coachman was guilty of bad driving resulting in loss of time. It was the guard's duty to report, to the Post Office, any incidents which occurred.

When the Mail reached its heyday, many sporting young men, who were artists at handling a team, bribed the professional coachmen to allow them to take the ribbons.

The breed of drunken, obese, coachmen of the earlier period thus disappeared.

Mail Horse

A workmanlike animal who was not employed in London until he was five or six years old. He worked a seven-day week in the Mail Cart and was likely to be called upon to collect foreign mails from the railway at unexpected times as well as to cart the regular Inland mails. His only guaranteed rest period was between 10.30 a.m. on Sunday and 4 p.m. the same day. In spite of his irregular routine, he lasted for an average of six years in Post Office work. This was mainly due to the care, attention and good food which was lavished on to him by his keepers at both ends of his journey. Those at the railway checked to see that those at the stables were doing their job properly and vice versa. The mail horse benefited from such rivalry. *See* McNamara's.

Mail Phaeton
A dignified and large Phaeton which became fashionable in about 1830. The rectangular body restricted the vehicle to a quarter-lock and was hung on an undercarriage resembling that of a Mail Coach. It had a perch, two sets of telegraph springs, mail axles and a pole with a hook for lead bars. A pair or team was usually driven by the gentleman owner from a comfortable hooded seat over the front wheels. There was a railed groom's seat at the rear which, on some mail phaetons, could be exchanged with the driving seat so that the groom could drive when the owner wished to rest. Between the two seats was an extensive boot providing a large amount of luggage space which made this phaeton popular for travelling both in England and on the Continent. Light and fast post horses were sometimes used for such expeditions. When the vehicle was employed for Town or Park driving, the Road Coach flavour was dominant. Then, a pair or team of upstanding coach horses was put to, in road coach harness with brown or straw collars. Pole chains were always used. If a pair was put to, it was quite normal to use wheeler coach harness.

The paint finish was usually of a sombre hue with little or no lining on the wheels as this was thought to be rather feminine for such a masculine carriage.

From the ancestry of the Mail Phaeton grew such descendants as Demi- or Semi-Mail Phaetons, Stanhope Phaetons, T-Cart Phaetons, Beaufort Phaetons, Hunting Phaetons and Shooting Brakes.

Mail Spring
Also known as a Telegraph Spring.

Main Bar
The bar by which the single bars for the leaders of a team are connected to the pole hook. *See* Lead Bars.

Main, Col. A. K.
President of The Coaching Club from 1949 to 1956.

Malle Poste
Two kinds of French Mail Coaches ran in the early 19th century. One type of vehicle carried four passengers inside and the guard travelled either in a hooded dickey at the rear or a cab seat at the front. The four horses were often driven from a small front seat. The other Malle Poste was a four-horse carriage resembling a Britzska. The two passengers travelled under a fixed half-hood in the centre of the vehicle which was entered by small doors on either side. A solid apron could be pulled up to cover the occupants' legs for which there was adequate space. Luggage was restricted to one case and one small item of hand baggage. The guard sat in a hooded dickey at the rear. The four horses were frequently driven by one or two postillions at an average speed of between nine and ten miles an hour as the stages were of only five miles. Changes of horses were completed in 45 seconds which was said to be too fast for the convenience of travellers as it did not allow time for them to disembark, even briefly, except at stops where mail had to be unloaded.

Malvern Dog Cart

A two-wheeled dog cart which is hung on two side springs with the shafts underneath the body. The floor and sides show an almost triangular profile. The top of the body and seat rails are rounded and this outline is followed by the splashboards. The lamps are hung on the front of the dashboard.

Malvern Phaeton. *See* Sporting Phaeton.

Manchester Market Cart

A robust two-wheeled vehicle which was as suitable for the servants' use, as it was for carting luggage or game, or being employed as a trade cart. The back-to-back seats accommodated four people. In place of a dash was a low board at the front to prevent goods from sliding forward on to the road. The panelled sides were railed at the top. The cost of this cart, towards the end of the 1800s, was £12.

Manchester Team

Also better known as a Trandem.

Marathon

Drives of from about four to ten miles are organized by horse show committees running both Private Driving and Coaching Classes. A standard time is set and there is no advantage in completing the course under this time. The marathon is arranged both for the enjoyment of competitors and to enable the judge to assess the suitability of the turnouts for pleasure driving on the road. *See* Combined Driving, Competition B.

Marche Donc

A slang name for the Canadian Calash which originated from the driver's cry to the horse to increase the pace. The shout was 'Marche', followed by 'Marche-donc', meaning 'Walk' and 'Go on, walk'.

Martingale Crupper

Used on team leaders and for the sake of uniformity they are very often worn all round. If ordinary cruppers are worn, the coupling of the rein is likely to get caught in the point of the back strap which protrudes from the rearmost keeper. It is also safer to use this type of crupper on a tandem leader for much the same reason. The back strap of a martingale crupper is designed like the girth loop and lower half of a riding martingale. The back strap goes through the dee at the back of the pad. One part ends by going round the back of the back strap buckle and is held in place by the buckle tongue passing through a slit in the leather. It is rarely secured by stitching so that it can be taken apart for cleaning. The upper part of the back strap continues from the dee on the pad, through the backstrap buckle, and then towards the crupper dock as a single strap. The double layers of backstrap between the buckle and the pad dee are held together by two or three floating keepers. The length adjustment is carried out in the usual way by the buckle being altered along holes in the top part of the back strap.

Mason's Improved Patent Axle

In use during the first half of the 19th century. It had three oil grooves running longitudinally along the axle box in which oil was retained.

Master Coachbuilders Benevolent Institution
This was formed as a result of the international exhibitions where coach-builders frequently met. Money was collected from professionals and distributed amongst less fortunate members of the trade. Pensioners were regularly assisted and those in need were helped through difficult financial periods.

Matches
Numerous matches were run during the 19th century both between driving enthusiasts and against the clock. Perhaps the one which was most reported and illustrated was Lord Lonsdale's famous match against time in 1891. *See* Lord Lonsdale.

McNamara's
A Finsbury contractor who, in 1893, had over 600 horses. This firm horsed the Mail Carts and some Stages of the parcels coaches. McNamara's were self sufficient in the running of their establishment. They chopped their own hay to make chaff and then carefully mixed it with oats and beans by machinery. Both harness and carts were made by the firm, as were the wheels for the carts and the shoes for the horses.

McNaught Dog Cart
A country cart made by McNaught.

Measuring a Collar
The ruler should be placed inside the neck of the collar and the measurement taken from where the lining joins the back of the fore-wale at the uppermost point to the inside of the fore-wale at the throat. This measurement will be about 21 inches for an average 14 hands horse.

Meet
Since there have been driving clubs there have been meets at which members have assembled with their turnouts to share the thrill of a drive with fellow enthusiasts. The Coaching Club has been holding meets for over a century and continues to do so.

The British Driving Society hold two official meets each year. One is held at The Royal Windsor Horse Show in May and the other at The British Timken Show in August. Unofficial meets are held throughout the year all over England, organized by the Society's Area Commissioners.

Melton Cloth
A suitable material for driving rugs and aprons as well as for the upholstery on a vehicle.

Melton Port
An arch in the centre of an otherwise straight bar bit. It is higher than a Cambridge port but not as high as a half-port.

Melton Rein
Also known as flat and laid on.

Metal Cantle
Some saddles which were employed for commercial purposes had a metal rim round the cantle, or back, to protect this edge from tears caused by rough treatment.

Metal Seat
Driving saddles which were made for commercial use sometimes had an entirely metal seat. This is the uppermost area and can be compared with the seat part of a riding saddle.

Mexican Quarter Coach
An American coach, built in about 1850 by Wood Brothers of New York.

Middle Bar
The centre slot on the branch of a Liverpool or Buxton bit which has a choice of three slots into which the rein can be buckled. Middle bar gives a medium amount of curb action. *See* Bitting.

Middle Ground
The part of the road on a coach journey which was between the upper ground and the lower ground. It was here that doubtful teams were used where they were out of sight of crowded towns. 'Three blind'uns and a bolter' was a likely combination for a middle-ground team.

Midland Wagon
Also known as a Barrel Top Wagon.

Miller, Lt-Col. Sir John, K.C.V.O., D.S.O., M.C.
President of the Coaching Club since 1975.

Milling
Another word for kicking horses in the 1800s.

Milord. *See* Cab Phaeton.

Milton Waggonette
A type of waggonette which was made by Hayes & Son in the late 1800s, for between £55 and £70. It was designed so that one of the longitudinal seats could be moved to a transverse position across the rear of the vehicle to convert the carriage into a Stanhope Phaeton. The four elliptic springs permitted a full lock as the front wheels passed under an arch in the body.

Minibus. *See* Boulnois Cab.

Modesty Board. *See* Knifeboard Omnibus.

Mogg
Author and compiler of *Patterson's Roads*.

Mohawk
An attachment which can be put on to a straight curb bit and was said to prevent horses from pulling. Six small hard rubber balls are placed along a bar

having a hook at each end which goes through the eyes of the bit. The mohawk is held above the mouthpiece of the bit. The balls circulate on the bar which is connected to the mouthpiece of the bit by a thick rubber band. The movement on the mohawk mouthpiece causes salivation which results in a more relaxed jaw and neck.

Monogram
If a crest is not used, then the initials of the owner can be entwined to form an agreeable design to decorate the turnout. Neat monograms are made of metal and fitted by prongs to the harness on the blinkers, face drop, false martingale and pad. Discreet matching monograms can be painted on the side and rear panels of the carriage. A small edition can also be embroidered on the apron or rug.

Moon Plate
The circular plate to which the wheel of a vehicle with a mail axle hub is attached. *See* Axle.

Moped
A horse was said to be moped when a shield was placed over his eyes so that he could not see forwards. This practice was applied to difficult horses in an effort to bring them to their senses.

Moping a Leader
A practice which was frequently carried out on difficult horses. *See* Moped.

Moray Car
A two-wheeled vehicle which was first introduced by the coachbuilder, Thrupp. It has back-to-back seats for four people and a tail board which lets down on chains. The shafts run outside the body which is hung low, on two side-springs. The profile given by the side rails of the seat and the body, forms a semi-circle to coincide with the wheels. The splash boards follow the same line and extend to protect the low front steps and the dress from mud off the wheels. The vehicle was ideal for ladies, as the generous amount of room between the dash and splash boards afforded easy access when dressed in a voluminous skirt.

Morgan
A breed of horses which originated in Vermont, U.S.A., in the late eighteenth century. The original bay stallion was named after his owner, Justin Morgan. This entire stamped all his progeny with his lovely head, compact tough body and outstanding action, causing the breed to be named after the foundation stallion. Bays, browns, blacks and chestnuts around 15·2 hands with the same attractive heads, cresty necks, strong bodies and clean legs are plentiful in America.

Morgan Cart
A two-wheeled vehicle, built by Morgan around the turn of the century. The cab-fronted, Gig-type body is hung on Dennett springs. The tail board lets down so that a luggage box or picnic basket can be carried or an occasional rear seat fitted. The front steps are bucket shaped, with leather toe-pieces.

Morocco Leather

This is made from goat skin. By about 1870 morocco leather was replacing silk for the inside linings of carriages, though State coaches were still lined with silk. Leather was considered to be smarter, easier to keep clean and to last longer.

Mosenthall Cart

A rectangular-bodied country cart built on the lines of a low Dog Cart. There is a seat for two facing forwards and another facing the rear sharing the same backrest. The tail board lets down to form a foot board for the back seat passengers. The shafts run inside the body, which is decorated with cane panels and hung on two side- and one cross-spring. The tops of the sides of the body extend outwards at an angle over the wheels and have splash boards joined to them by iron brackets.

Mounting

Before mounting a carriage, whether it be drawn by a single, pair, tandem, unicorn, team or whatever, the routine is basically the same. First of all, an inspection should be made to ensure that the horses are correctly put to. In the case of a single, it is necessary to see that the traces, breeching, belly band, hame strap, reins and bit are fixed as desired. With a pair, a quick look should be taken at everything just mentioned, the pole pin and a check made to see that the coupling reins are properly buckled. It has been known for an inexperienced groom to buckle both the coupling rein and draught rein to the same horse so that the horses may be stopped but never turned! A tandem needs the same check as a single. If bars are used, a look to see that the hook strap is fastened and a glance at the lead reins to note that they are running through all the terrets is advisable. The same thoughts which apply to a pair and tandem leader also concern a unicorn. With a team, just about everything must be checked. Coupling reins, bitting, hame straps, pole chains, traces, lead reins and pole pin should all be seen before mounting.

In preparing to mount, the reins are taken in the left hand whilst standing by the offside horse's quarters. The reins are placed in the correct position whether there are two or four and then the offside rein, or reins, is, or are, pulled out from about 4 inches with a single or tandem to about 12 inches with some pairs or teams depending on the vehicle. The reins are then transferred to the right hand, in the same order, in preparation for mounting. The ends are either placed over the arm or hooked over the little finger to prevent them from getting caught on a step or roller bolt. Some people have a small piece of cord fixed to the rein buckle for this purpose and the cord is secured over the little finger. The whip is picked up in the right hand if, as with some teams, it has been lying over the wheelers' backs. Some vehicles have a whip socket by the driver's seat and the whip is put there before mounting. Others have a whip socket by the dashboard which makes it impossible to mount with the whip in position as it fouls the reins on the way. Some vehicles have their whip socket at the bottom of the dash, fixed at such an angle that the whip slopes across towards the seat, blocking the way for the coachman. With such arrangements, the whip is best laid between the driver's and passengers' seats. On a coach, the disadvantage of leaving a whip in its socket is that passengers mounting and dismounting are inclined to catch hold of it to steady themselves. This invariably results in a broken whip.

The footwork employed for mounting a coach is first to put the left foot on to the wheel hub. Then to place the right foot on to the roller bolt. Next the left foot goes up to the step and finally the right foot reaches the footboard. During the ascent, the left hand holds on to any available support. The right hand secures the reins. The coachman should sit down and transfer the reins, which will now be found to be level, to the left hand. If the horse or horses should start forward at least the vehicle can be kept straight. The apron is adjusted and the whip taken. The coachman, after another quick glance at the harness, is now ready to drive forwards as soon as the passengers have mounted.

Mountings
The buckles and other metal parts of the harness. Also known as the furniture.

Mounting Wagon
An American vehicle which was built to carry four people. It was hung on two side springs and one elliptic spring and used in the Rocky Mountain area.

Mullen
A type of mouth piece which is also known as a half moon. *See* Bitting.

Mulliner
Three coachbuilders of London, Liverpool and Northampton, were all related and traded under this name.

'Multum-in-Parvo' Pick
A type of folding hoof-pick which was designed as an all-purpose tool for rendering emergency repairs. It was made to form a claw hammer, which held three strap-repairing screws and their metal sockets in the handle, a bradawl and a screwdriver. The gadget was carried in a shaped leather case.

Murrieta Gig
Designed by Mr G. J. de Murrieta. The hooded body resembled a Curricle. It was hung on two transverse springs, running parallel to the axle, which were shackled to two side-springs bolted to the axle.

Museums and Carriage Collections
ENGLAND
Bedfordshire
1. Shuttleworth Museum, Old Warden, Biggleswade, Beds.
   Principally a museum of aircraft, but vintage motor cars and a sizeable collection of carriages are also on show. Illustrated catalogue on sale.
2. Mr G. C. H. Mossman, Bury Farm, Caddington, Nr Luton.
   Viewing of this large and comprehensive collection is by appointment only.
Devonshire
Arlington Court Museum, Nr Barnstaple, Devon.
   About thirty carriages are on view, and a descriptive guide is on sale.

Gloucestershire

Dodington Park, Chipping Sodbury, Glos.

　The stables of this beautiful house make an ideal setting for the superbly presented two dozen carriages on show. A lavishly produced illustrated catalogue is on sale at the gift stall, and drives by carriage are available during the summer.

Hampshire

Breamore House, Nr Fordingbridge, Hants.

　About a dozen of Mr S. Watney's carriages are contained in the stables of this Elizabethan manor house which also houses an agricultural museum. Books, post cards, and table-mats are on sale in the gift shop.

Kent

Tyrwhitt-Drake Museum, Maidstone, Kent.

　One of the first carriage museums to open in this country. Coloured slides and an illustrated catalogue on sale.

Lancashire

Royal Umpire Exhibition, Croston, Lancs.

　Among other exhibits there are sixty coaches and carriages on view.

London

1. The Royal Mews, Buckingham Palace Road, S.W.1.

　Open every Wednesday afternoon (also on Thursdays during the summer months); State, semi-State coaches and carriages, as well as smaller vehicles are on view, as well as horses, harness and saddlery. Illustrated guide and post cards on sale.

2. Hampton Court Palace, Hampton, Middlesex.

　Smaller collection of Royal carriages on show.

Yorkshire

1. Carriage Museum, Aysgarth Falls, Nr Hawes, Yorks.

　About a hundred vehicles are owned by Mr G. W. Shaw, some of which take visitors for drives.

2. Shibden Hall, Halifax, W. Yorks.

　A most attractive illustrated catalogue describing the small collection of carriages is on sale.

3. Transport Museum, Hull, Yorks.

　Illustrated guide of carriages is on sale.

SCOTLAND

Transport Museum, Glasgow.

　Coloured post cards on sale.

ULSTER

Transport Museum, Belfast, N. Ireland.

AUSTRIA

Kunsthistorisches Museum, Vienna.

　Coloured post cards on sale.

BELGIUM

Musée des Carosses, Brussels.

DENMARK
Sparresholm.
  Not far from Copenhagen, this is a newly opened museum containing over a hundred vehicles of every sort, housed in farm buildings of a delightful moated manor house belonging to Mr and Mrs Garth Gruner.

EIRE
Luggala, Roundwood, Co. Wicklow.
  A private collection of nearly a hundred carriages collected by the Hon. Garech Browne, to whom applications to view should be made.

FRANCE
1. Musée de la Voiture, Château de Compiègne.
2. Musée des Voitures, Versailles, Nr Paris.

GERMANY
1. Deutsches Museum, Munich.
2. Marstallmuseum, in Schloss Nymphenburg.

HOLLAND
1. Leek, Dutch National Carriage Museum, Nr Groningen.
2. Arnhem Dutch National County Museum.
3. Het Loo Palace, Nr Apeldoorn.
  Small collection of Royal carriages. Open in the summer.
4. Buren, 35km from Utrecht.
  Museum of farmers' waggons and equipment.

ITALY
Leonardo da Vinci, Milan.

PORTUGAL
National Coach Museum, Lisbon.

SWITZERLAND
Museum of Transport, Lucerne.

U.S.A.
1. Suffolk Museum, Stony Brook, Long Island, New York.
2. Shelburne Museum, Vermont.
3. Early American Museum, Silver Springs, Florida.
4. Hawthorn Mellody Museum, Libertyville, Illinois.
5. El Pomar Carriage House Museum, The Broadmoor, Colorado Springs.

U.S.S.R.
The Armoury Museum, The Kremlin, Moscow.

Mytton, John
A character who was noted for his mad driving exploits in the early 1800s. He lived in Shropshire, as squire of Halston.
  There are many stories told, giving examples of his eccentricity which was perhaps created by the large quantity of brandy consumed. One day, he was trying some horses in tandem and on coming up to a turnpike gate asked the luckless dealer, who was in the unfortunate position of accompanying him, if the leader could jump timber. Then, deciding to confirm the answer, he put

the horses at the gate. The leader sailed over, without hesitation, leaving the shaft horse, the two men and what was left of the Gig on the take-off side. Another story is told of how, one day, he had a passenger who had never been upset out of a Gig. Mytton was surprised to hear such news and soon rectified the matter by running a wheel up the bank. On another occasion, in search of amusement, he put a team into a gallop and when they were well out of hand he baled out into a hedge and left them to continue alone. He frequently abandoned his horses at his front door if no one was there to attend to their well being. They were left to dash back to their stables on their own with the vehicle bouncing behind them. One night, he drove a tandem across country over hedges and ditches for a bet of £25.

When in a saner frame of mind he drove stages of the Holyhead Mail.

He died, in prison, at the age of thirty-eight.

Mytton's biography was written by C. J. Apperley.

Names of Carriages

The modern desire to apply names to vehicles often creates a problem. Carriages for present-day owner driving tend to fall into the basic categories of Coaches, Brakes, Phaetons, Dog Carts and Gigs from which there are many descendants. In the 18th and 19th century there were also many types of vehicles which were coachman driven for town use, and coachman or postillion driven for travelling. All carriages were designed and built for a specific purpose.

Vehicles were sometimes named after their designer, as was the Lonsdale Waggonette. Others took their name from their builder, as did the Peter's Phaeton. Some were known by their shape like the Round-Back Gig, or the purpose for which they were built, like the Shooting Brake.

Names of Coaches

The same name was frequently given to several coaches running on different roads. There were, for instance, at least four lines of coaches which were known as the 'Red Rover'. The one which is now so familiar with spectators at major shows is the Southampton 'Red Rover'. Others were known as the Manchester 'Red Rover', the Bristol 'Red Rover' and the Brighton 'Red Rover'.

The only Mail Coach to be given a name was the 'Quicksilver' London–Devonport mail.

Names of Horses

Not all horses were given names. Some large establishments issued each horse with a number which was stamped on to the hoof. A corresponding number was engraved on a metal plate high above the manger in the stall and often in brass-headed tacks on the cape of the collar. Naming was left to the delivery man and known, very often, only to him and his horse.

Some stables gave all horses which were bought in the same year names starting with the same letter. This was useful in referring back to when a horse came into the yard. Other horses owed their names to personalities or happenings in the news on the day of arrival at the stable and even the state of the weather influenced some proprietors in the naming of horses.

Christian names, which were likely to coincide with stable or establishment staff, were avoided owing to likely confusion which could result.

Names of Towns on Road Coaches
The two towns between which the coach ran were painted on both the hind boot panel and the crest panel. The word 'and' was written on the hind boot but not on the door. Other towns, along the route, were painted on the boots. The name of the coach was often painted on the underneath of the footboard and on the back of the rumble above the hind boot panel.

Napoleon's Military Carriage
A Chariot which was fitted with every conceivable convenience for comfortable travelling. The dark blue body, with bullet-proof side panels, was hung from cee-springs on a red undercarriage. Above the sword case at the back was a lamp which lit up the interior of the carriage. At the bottom of the back was a panel which could be let down for the purpose of removing chamber pots without passengers being disturbed. The interior could be made into a kitchen, dining room, bedroom, dressing room or an office. A collapsible bed was carried under the coachman's seat which could quickly be made up with the mattresses and bedding which were stored in other compartments. A writing desk, pens, ink and numerous solid gold fittings were available so that correspondence could be dealt with, whilst travelling. Coffee and tea pots, plates, candlesticks and sugar basins of gold and silver, all embossed with the Imperial arms and the letter 'N' were conveyed for Napoleon's use, as was a liquor case. Pistol holsters with loaded pistols, a telescope and maps were all to hand. After the battle of Waterloo, this carriage was exhibited to the public in London at Bullocks Museum, Piccadilly in 1816. It ended its days in 1925 when it was destroyed by fire in Madame Tussauds, London.

Nave
The central block of the wheel. *See* Axle.

Near Side
The left side. This originated because the person in charge of a team walked on the left-hand side and this was nearest to the waggoner's right hand.

Nearside Rein
The rein which is on the left side and does not have the buckle at the hand end. *See* Lead Rein.

Neck Bar
The Army term for the bar which is used in conjunction with the pole for a pair, to a two-wheeled vehicle, when Cape harness is worn.

Neck Bugle. *See* Bugle.

Neck Piece
A part of the Army harness.

Net
A nose net can be effective in preventing a horse from pulling. It is usually only a short-term cure, as when the horse becomes accustomed to wearing it he reverts to being a puller.

New Collars
Even a perfectly fitting collar, which is new, has to be worn for some consider-able time before the combination of leather and straw moulds to fit the neck comfortably. Care should be taken not to drive the horse too far with a heavy load until the collar has adapted itself to the shape of the animal's shoulder.

Newhouse, C. B.
Well known for his coaching pictures which he produced mainly between 1830 and 1845.

Newlands, Lord
President of The Coaching Club from 1902 to 1905.

Newmarket Strap
Found on the pad of a Road Coach horse. This single strap connects the dee on the top of the hame tug buckle with the ring below the terret at the top of the pad, to hold up the trace. It is used instead of the point strap and buckle method found with Drag harness. The buckle end of the strap is looped round the dee on the hame tug buckle. The strap passes through a keeper on its inner side, to secure it to the buckle, before going upwards and through the ring on the pad. The point of the strap is then brought downwards to be buckled. Also known as Newmarket Tug-Bearer.

Newmarket Tug-Bearer. *See* Newmarket Strap.

New Model. *See* Coach Horn.

Newport Pagnell, Improved
A two-wheeled country cart with a panelled body having turned spindles round the top. The back-to-back seats accommodate four people. It is hung on two side-springs and the shafts go underneath the body.

'New Times', The
A Road Coach. In 1894 it was driven at a meet of the Coaching Club by Walter Schoolbred.

Next Pair Out
The familiar order for which post boys waited in the inn-yards of posting houses. The next postillion on call was ready with his boots, spurs and false leg strapped in position. The pair of horses which he was to drive were harnessed and waiting on pillar reins, so that there was no delay.

Night Cab Horse
The majority of the horses who hauled the cabs around London at night, towards the late 1800s, had spent part, if not most, of the day working in some other capacity.

Nimrod (C. J. Apperley)
A prolific writer of sporting events. Many well known 19th-century characters of *The Road* are colourfully illustrated by his words. Accounts by Nimrod include Mytton's biography, *The Life of a Sportsman* and *The Road, The Turf and The Chase*.

Non-Hackney Type

Private Driving classes are very often divided into two sections of hackney type and non-hackney type before being sub-divided into heights. An animal of non-hackney type is one which has no characteristics of a hackney, either in con-formation or action. A high-stepping cob, of perhaps Welsh origin, qualifies for the non-hackney type section if his conformation bears no resemblance to that of a true hackney. An animal is not put into the hackney section purely on account of his action. A horse which is part-bred hackney usually competes in the hackney-type section.

Norfolk Bit

A jointed mouthpiece, with a serrated edged port which lies over the tongue. On the inner sides of the port are two spikes which act when pressure is applied to the bit.

Norfolk Cart

A two-wheeled country cart which was built on Dog Cart lines with back-to-back seating for four people. The tops of the sides of the body were slatted to provide ventilation for animals, like piglets or chickens, which were being taken to market, or dogs conveyed to a shoot or coursing meeting. The shafts ran under the body which was hung on two side-springs. Many fine Norfolk carts were built of mahogany and oak. These were often varnished instead of painted.

Norfolk Roadster or Trotter

A strong, general-purpose, animal which was favoured by farmers. The Norfolk roadster could cover long distances at great speeds. One was said to have com-pleted a journey of 100 miles in under ten hours.

The coming of the railways put these Norfolk breeds into redundancy until the Hackney Breed Society was responsible for their revival.

Nosebag

A bag made of hemp, webbing, or similar tough material in which the horse's food was carried if he was to be out working all day. Nosebags were made in many different designs. The most common types were rectangular. Others were circular, resembling a waste-paper basket. Some were made with an oval bottom so that there were no corners in which the food could get caught. The bag was placed over the horse's muzzle and held in position by a strap going over the top of the head above the bridle. Working horses were frequently left, untied and unattended, to eat their lunch outside a pub whilst their driver had his, inside. It was a common sight to see an expert with a nosebag hurling his food con-tainer upwards in the hopes of releasing a stray oat from a corner.

Nose-Band

A strap going round the nose. It is usually held in position by a keeper and a slot on each side. The cheek-piece of the bridle goes down through the slot, passes through the eye of the bit and comes up through the outside keeper before being buckled to the cheek buckle. The nose-band is adjusted for tightness by a buckle at the back which should generally be fastened on the near side. In the case of a pair or a team, the offside horses have their nose-bands buckled on the offside. The purpose of a nose-band is to prevent the cheeks, and consequently the blinkers, from gaping and to keep the mouth shut if the horse should pull.

Nunters. *See* Tongue Pieces.

Nutcracker Springs
Some authorities state that when four elliptic springs are used together on one vehicle, they make a set known collectively as nutcracker springs.

Other authorities say that when two elbow springs are used, one above the other, joined to each other at one end and to the vehicle body and undercarriage respectively by their other ends, this is known as a nutcracker spring.

Oak
This wood was used extensively by wheelwrights for the spokes of wheels.

Obstacle Test. *See* Combined Driving, Competition C.

Offord, Gordon
A member of the family of coachbuilders since the 18th century, who were responsible for many fine vehicles.

Mr Offord still renovates carriages at 264 Brompton Road, London.

Off Side
The right-hand side.

Ogee
The curved body shape of a vehicle like a Curricle or a Cabriolet.

Oil Axle
Mail and Collinge's axles were known by this name owing to their capability of storing a limited amount of oil, or grease, whilst they were in use.

Old Heavy
Slang term for the early Mail Coaches of the 1700s.

Old John
Thought to be the originator of the busman's holiday. He was a coachman of a pair-horse suburban coach who may have been looked down on by the four-horse mail and stage coachmen, which is probably why he was called a busman. For eighteen years, Old John drove forty miles on the Exeter and Teignmouth road. Eventually he was persuaded to take a day off. This created the problem of how to spend such unaccustomed leisure time. After great consideration, he bought a ticket on the opposition coach and took what became known as a busman's holiday.

Old Lal
The legless pauper who, wearing layers of waistcoats, and a hunt cap, frequented the Great North Road, driving a team of well-turned out foxhounds, either three abreast or four-in-hand. His vehicle was made of four wheels, springs and a plank of wood. Old Lal earned a living by the sporting venture of overtaking the fast coaches with his speedy equipage; he would then pull into the yard alongside the coach at the end of the stage and beg from the passengers.

Old Phaeton Springs
A collective name which was given to the combination of six springs which were frequently used on early Phaetons. The vehicle was hung in front on four elbow springs and behind on two whip- or cee-springs.

Old Ship Hotel
A Brighton hotel, famous for its coaching connections. The Brighton end of the 'Old Times' coach was at 'The Old Ship'.

Old Slow Coach
A term given to coaches of the 1700s when they averaged about four miles an hour. One authority states that the 'Telegraph' took nineteen hours to travel the eighty miles to London from Gosport in 1798.

'Old Times', The
A subscription coach which was built by Cowlard and Selby and ran on the Brighton and London road during the last half of the 1800s. It was managed by James Selby who drove when none of the subscribers was on the box. The 'Old Times' started from Hatchetts on Tuesdays, Thursdays and Saturdays and from 'The Old Ship' at Brighton on Mondays, Wednesdays and Fridays. The horses rested on Sundays.

On a few occasions the return journey was driven on the same day. One day, the double distance was completed in just over eight hours after Selby had promised his passengers that he could cover the 108 miles in nine hours. This led to a bet being laid that Selby could not drive the distance within eight hours. On 13th July 1888, the Selby Run took place and he proved that it could be done.

Subsequently, this coach was owned by Lord Leconfield. The 'Old Times' coach is now in the possession of Mr Bernard Mills. *See* Selby Run.

Olive Draught Eye. *See* Pull.

Omnibi, An
A slang term for Omnibus.

Omnibus
A public vehicle which was first used in Paris in 1662. It was put on to the road by Blaise Pascal and known as a 'Carrosse à cinq sols'. The venture only lasted a year or so.

In 1819 a Monsieur Jacques Laffitte decided to try to revive the idea of producing a public vehicle as an alternative to the existing coaches and carts. At that time Baudry was using coaches to convey passengers to public baths owned by him. Across the road from the baths, was a shop owned by Omnes. Above the door there hung a sign saying 'Omnes Omnibus – All Things for Everybody'. Baudry borrowed the idea and had the name Omnibus put on the sides of his coach. The vehicle then became known as Baudry's Omnibus.

Laffitte liked the thought and he too called his public vehicle an Omnibus. Over the years, the name was accepted.

George Shillibeer, an ex-naval man, who was then a Parisian coach-maker, built an improved version of the Omnibus for Laffitte. Shillibeer decided that he would try to make his fortune from a public transport venture with buses in

London. On 4th July 1829 he put his first Omnibus on the road. It was a large affair with twenty-two inside seats. Three magnificent bay horses were put to, to draw the conveyance from Paddington Green to The Bank. The builder's name was written in large letters on the side. The idea caught on and these buses soon became known as Shillibeers. At first, fellow shipmates manned the buses but soon grew bored and had to be replaced by professional coachmen. Shillibeer dressed his men in velvet suits. A high standard of manners had to be displayed to patrons. A library was provided to relieve boredom during travel. However, the business soon began to go downhill. The driver's dishonesty led to pilfering of fares. Meters were put on to the buses and other devices tried, but all failed. Even the books were stolen by passengers wishing to finish a story. Rival firms sprang up all over the country and Shillibeer was forced off the road.

As more and more Omnibuses were put on, so they were painted with colours which depicted their line. Passengers knew, at a glance, to where the bus was going.

There was tremendous competition between firms to cover equal distances at a greater speed than a rival company. A certain amount of dishonesty was practised. Some buses had the word Shillibeer emblazoned on the side. Passengers hurried to catch the bus confident that they would be treated with the comfort and civility expected from George Shillibeer's employees. In their haste, they did not always notice the small words 'not the original' which preceded the main word.

Smaller, pair-horse buses seating twelve inside passengers were being used. One or two more people could travel alongside the driver but this was not generally popular.

By 1850 knifeboard seating for outside passengers was introduced. These longitudinal back-to-back seats were reached by an iron ladder at the rear of the bus.

Firms up and down the country began making take-over bids to form larger companies. In 1856 London's largest Omnibus Company was started. A group of French businessmen were quietly engaged in buying most of the London firms. By 1858 they were collectively named as The London General Omnibus Company. This vast concern owned three-quarters of London's buses. By 1904 the company had over 17,000 horses and over 1,400 Omnibuses in use.

Wheels of Omnibuses had, in the past, varied in colour. Now, all were painted yellow, which simplified repairs and replacements.

By 1890, a new design of Omnibus was being used. It was known as a garden seat Omnibus. The knifeboard seats were replaced by transverse garden seats. An open curving staircase, at the back, afforded easy access to the upper deck. This made it popular with ladies who found that they could take the air and enjoy the view. It was preferable to the crush of the inside seats where toes got trodden on.

Omnibus Horse
This animal, usually a mare, was of the heavy vanner type. She came to London as a five-year-old and was probably introduced to the traffic alongside an old horse in a Skeleton Brake. She was then found a suitable partner, with whom she always worked. Together they covered twelve miles a day. The continual

stopping and starting was hard on horses and their working life was usually about five years. They were well fed, on about 17 lb. of corn and 10 lb. of roughage hay and chaff a day. Towards the end of the 19th century there were well over 10,000 horses working for The London General Omnibus Company.

Omnis, An
Slang for Omnibus.

On the Lock
When the front wheels of a vehicle are turned so that they cannot go any further without hitting the body.

Open Lot Wagon
A type of Gypsy Wagon which has its body and bowed canvas top built on to a four-wheeled dray or trolley.

It gets its name from the open frame front which is fitted with canvas curtains which can be drawn across as required.

Opera Board
A guard which was fixed to the back panel of some carriages to protect passengers from injury which might otherwise be caused by the pole of a following vehicle penetrating the rear panel and stabbing the occupants. Such accidents were known to happen in overcrowded streets, if the vehicle in front was forced to stop suddenly and the carriage behind was following too close and unable to pull up in time.

Opera Bus
Better known as a Private Omnibus.

Opposition. *See* Turns.

Orleans Club at Twickenham, Middlesex
To where members of the Coaching Club drove, from Hyde Park, on a few occasions between 1878 and 1883.

Ostler
A horse keeper.

Outraves
Extension rails which were fixed by iron supports and protruded outwards from the tops of the sides, and sometimes the front and rear, of some commercial and farm carts. They enabled a top load to be carried.

Outrigger
The extension beyond the shafts to which an outspanner is harnessed, by a swingle tree, such as in a Troika.

Outside Car. *See* Irish Car.

Outside Passenger (Outsider)
One who travelled on a seat on the top of a coach and because the fare was cheap, the derogatory term, 'an outsider', came into use. *See* Inside Passenger.

Outspanner
One of the outer horses of a troika, or a horse put to, on an outrigger, alongside the shaft horse.

Overcheck. *See* Overhead Check.

Overdraw. *See* Overhead Check.

Overhead Check
A type of bearing rein used with American fine harness and with harness used for trotting racing, when it is desirous to raise the horse's head to a stargazing angle where his breathing will be unimpeded. The two ends of the overcheck are buckled on to the front of the rings of a jointed half-cheek snaffle. They then join together to pass over the poll between the ears and down the neck before being hooked on to the bolt hook at the front of the pad. Also known as Kemble Jackson, Overdraw and Check Rein.

Oxford Dog Cart
One of the earliest forms of Dog Cart with very high wheels which was said to have made it popular with tandem drivers.

Pacer
A type of horse, which is distinguished by his action, and driven to a Sulky in trotting races. A pacer moves in lateral two-time whereas a trotter moves in diagonal two-time.

Pad
Used with pair and team harness and sometimes for a tandem leader. It is lighter than a saddle for single or curricle harness as no weight is taken on the horse's back. There are many different designs of pad. Some are straight-sided and only about 2 inches wide, others are built with a swell. The fit is important. Too wide a pad will bear down on the spine and chafe. This is particularly applicable if a bearing rein is used, causing the pad to be pulled forward. A pad which is too narrow will pinch. Point straps are sewn to dees on each side at the base of the pad body. It is to these that the buckles on the small straps coming up from the upper dee on the hame tug buckles are attached. These act as trace carriers. Rein terrets are screwed into the pad on each side. A wheeler pad also has a centre terret through which the leader's rein goes.

   The pad is attached to the horse either by two girth straps, one on each side, to which a short central girth is buckled, or by a single wider band which terminates in a buckle. This is then fastened to a girth strap coming down from the outer side of the pad. It is made to buckle on the left-hand side for the near-side horses and the right-hand side for the offside horses.

Pad Cloth
A decorative patent leather, or cloth, pad which went under the harness saddle,

Pair Harness

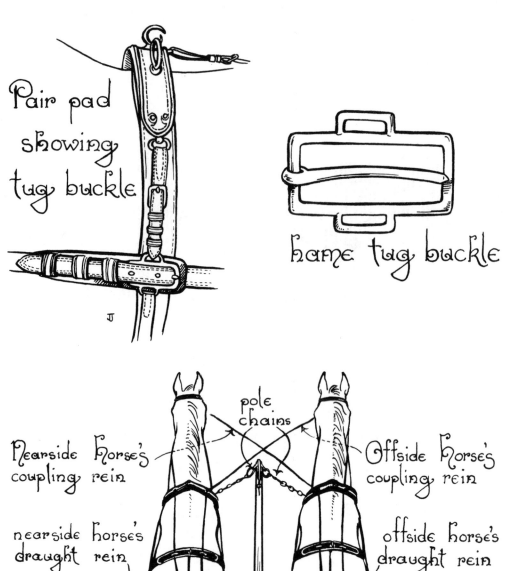

Pair pad showing tug buckle

hame tug buckle

pole chains

Nearside Horse's coupling rein

Offside Horse's coupling rein

nearside horse's draught rein

offside horse's draught rein

roller bolt

pole

bar

Details of Pair Harness

or pad, to form an auxiliary lining. It was made to correspond in shape with the driving pad and in colours with the vehicle. It was bound with braid or similar ornamentation which was known as a lace border at the turn of the century. Pad cloths are still used occasionally with State carriages and by costers.

Pagoda Top Lamp. *See* Lamp.

Painter
It was usual for the large carriage-building factories to employ painters. They were an important section of that community, as the whole appearance of the finished article depended upon the skills of these men.

The foreman had to possess a thorough knowledge of paint colours. He had to know the likely effect that a coat of varnish would have on a given colour and how a shade would change over a period of months. Such problems as the accurate matching of colours on panels, after a repair job had been completed, were his to solve. During the first half of the 19th century, he earned between 2 and 4 guineas a week.

Ordinary painters varied in capability. The most skilled were those who were able to 'line out' the wheels, shafts and body, with perfect narrow lines. Wages varied between 25 and 35 shillings a week, in the early 1800s.

Even with modern, quick-drying high-gloss paints, a first-class coach finish is still a job for the expert.

Names of coach painters can be obtained from the British Driving Society.

Palmer, John
The man who was mainly responsible for starting the Mail Coach system in 1784. *See* Mail Coach.

Palmer, Lynwood
A sporting artist at the turn of the 19th century who lived at Heston in Middlesex. Equine characters of the turf, the chase and the road were all subjects of his work. He kept an immaculate establishment. His coachhouse contained a fine collection of blue carriages. His stables were filled with thoroughbreds which he frequently drove at night, as this was the only time that he had free from his work. Palmer's harness room was full of gleaming sets of team and tandem, pairs and single harness. All was a perfect example of how things should be done.

Panel Cart
A two-wheeled country cart, which was built on Dog-Cart lines, with back-to-back seats. The sides of the body are panelled. They are surmounted by an iron rail which forms mounting handles for the passengers at the front and back and supports the splash boards along the sides. The shafts run under the body which is hung on two side-springs.

Parasol Whip
A decorative appointment which was sometimes carried by a lady driving her Phaeton. The light stick was fitted with a small sunshade to protect her face from the rays of the sun. It is unlikely that such a whip could have been used on the horse, as the thong was usually very short.

Parcel Carter
A type of light vanner suitable for a parcel van.

Parcel Van
A four-wheeled delivery van. The roof and mahogany-panelled sides were removable so that the van could easily be converted into an open vehicle. The forward-facing driving seat was placed under the front of the roof. There were oval side-windows in the front of the body. The firm's name and address was painted on the sides of the body which was hung on four elliptic springs and had an arch to enable a good lock.

The cost of a Parcel Van in the late 1800s was between £40 and £60.

Parisian, The
A four-wheeled open carriage which was made by Hayes & Son and cost about £31 10s., towards the end of the 1800s. The angular skeleton body was hung on four elliptic springs and entered by steps, in the middle, on each side. The Parisian was driven from a rear, forward-facing, stick-back, bootless seat. More passengers sat on a railed seat, facing the driver. There was a small railed seat behind the driver, between the rear wheels, for the groom.

Park Coach. *See* Drag.

Park Drag
A private coach, commonly known as a Drag.

Park Phaeton. *See* George IV Phaeton.

Parliamentary Horse
In an attempt to reduce the number of accidents caused by reckless driving, a law was passed which made galloping a team an offence. In order to avoid breaking the law, one horse would be put into the team which could trot fast enough to keep up with the other three which galloped. This trotting horse became known as the parliamentary horse.

Part-Covered and Plated
Harness furniture which was partly leather covered and partly brass or silver plated. The large buckles, terrets and hame rings were plated, enabling them to be polished. The small buckles such as those on the bridle, crupper and breeching were covered with leather. This was fashionable in the 1880s.

Passenger Fares
In the early 1800s, the cost of travel varied enormously depending on whether it was by the privacy of a postillion carriage, by the fast Mail Coach or by the Stage Coach. Coach fares varied with inside and outside seats. Posting was the most expensive, at about eighteen pence a mile. An inside seat on a Mail Coach cost between eight and ten pence a mile, and half that for an outside seat. Cheapest of these three modes of travel was the Stage Coach, on which an outside seat cost between two and a half and three pence a mile and an inside seat between four and five pence a mile.

Patent Leather

This is leather which has been coated with a covering of japan to produce a shiny surface. It is used for various parts of the vehicle such as the dash and splash-boards, when wood is not employed. The leather is stitched on to an iron framework. It is also used on shafts under the breeching dees and tug stops where friction would otherwise scratch the paint and damage the wood. On show harness the outer surfaces of the winkers, face drop, false martingale, collar and pad are usually covered with patent leather. This should not be used for any surfaces which bend, as cracks will rapidly appear. Patent leather is best cleaned either with patent leather cleaner or a little cream rubbed in and polished off with a non-abrasive cloth. Patent both scratches and dents easily and should be packed carefully if harness is being stored in a box. If it is wrapped in cloth with a coarse weave the shiny surfaces will become permanently marked.

Patterson's 'Roads'

A comprehensive guide which was published in the 1900s for the benefit of travellers. Its pages contained a variety of useful information for those embarking on a long journey. A map showed the Mail Coach roads of England, Wales and part of Scotland with a schedule of arrival and departure times at all the towns. Inns were catalogued and those where post horses could be obtained were clearly defined. The presence of toll-gates was marked. To add interest to travelling, all the country seats adjoining the roads were named. The population number and the industries carried out in the towns were also listed. Even the monuments and natural objects of interest were included in the information given.

A copy of *Patterson* probably transformed what might have been a dreary journey into an interesting and educational venture.

'Peacock', The

The famous coaching inn at Islington where passengers, bound for northern districts, were picked up by the Mail Coaches.

Pearl Shell

This was used by carriage makers for such items as buttons and for parts of the decorative armorial bearings.

Buttons on Coachmen's coats were huge – often the size of a five-shilling piece.

Perch

The longitudinal member, between the front and rear axles, forming a foundation around which the undercarriage is constructed. Mail Coaches were built on a perch undercarriage. The minimum length for such a perch was 6 feet.

The invention of the elliptic spring opened a new field for carriage designers, enabling vehicles to be built without perches. These are generally lighter and have a better lock. With a perch, the horses draw the vehicle by the undercarriage part, and every bump, which is hit by a wheel, is transmitted to the horses' shoulders. Carriages without perches are more inclined to take the vibration, from pot holes, on the springs. The pole on such a vehicle is likely to bounce up, if the road is rough, and knock the horses in the teeth. A perch helps to keep the pole steady.

Many American vehicles are built on a light perch undercarriage with two transverse elliptic springs.

Perch Bolt
The bolt upon which the front wheel assembly and undercarriage of a four-wheeled vehicle rotates.

Perch High Phaeton. *See* Highflyer.

Perithron
A type of waggonette invented in 1869, by a Mr Samuel Smith of Suffolk, which provided easy access from the rear seats to the box seat. The driving seat was cut in half. This enabled the left-hand side to be raised, permitting a passenger to change from the back of the vehicle, to the front, without dismounting.

'Perseverance', The
On 30th May 1891, this Dorking coach was driven by Mr E. Brown to the only meet for Road Coaches organized by the Coaching Club. The meet was held on Horse Guards Parade.

Peters & Sons
A coachbuilding firm which was founded in 1798 and combined with Offord & Sons in 1931. Peters built many fine carriages for Royalty. They were responsible for outstanding examples of craftsmanship with their travelling carriages and for the Peter's Phaeton which was a variation of the George IV Phaeton.

Peterschuttler Wagon
A covered wagon similar in design to the Conestoga wagon.

Peter's Phaeton. *See* George IV Phaeton.

Phaeton
An open carriage, with four wheels, which is suitable to be owner driven from a forward-facing seat. Some are built large enough to take a team of coach horses. Others are small enough to be drawn by a donkey.
    The name is said to have been derived from Greek mythology when Phaeton, the son of Helios, the sun god, wanted to drive his father's sun chariot. The horses took off and almost set fire to the earth before they were stopped.
    The earliest Phaeton appeared at the end of the 18th century in the form of the Highflyer. The Prince of Wales set a fashion by driving these high vehicles at speed. The idea caught on and from these early ancestors there descended a variety of Phaetons built to satisfy every need.
    For gentlemen Whips, there were the Mail Phaetons. George IV had a low Phaeton which took his name. Ladies used their Pony Phaetons. Perhaps the most elegant of all, was the Spider Phaeton.

Piano Box Buggy
An American four-wheeled vehicle with a square shaped body. It was said to have first been introduced in 1855 by R. M. Stivers of New York.

Pick-Axe Team

Some authorities state that this is made up from a pair of leaders and one wheeler or three leaders and a pair of wheelers.

Others say that a pick-axe comprises one leader and a pair of wheelers. *See* Unicorn.

Pickering Float

A two-wheeled country vehicle. *See* Float.

Pigskin

It is sometimes used for the seats of a carriage. The outside seats of a Drag were often trimmed in pigskin.

The handle part of a whip is frequently covered with pigskin. It is secured either by a longitudinal seam or wound round at an angle. The latter method is effective for preventing the whip from slipping in the hand in wet weather.

Piker

A driver who contrived to get past a toll-gate without paying.

Pikes

Slang term for Turnpike Gates.

Pilentum

An open four-wheeled vehicle, invented by Mr David Davies, the London coachbuilder, which was popular in the 1830s. The low body, similar in outline to a Victoria, was hung on four elliptic springs and entered from either side by a small door. Sizes of Pilentum varied for conveying four or six passengers and could be drawn by a single or a pair of coachman-driven horses.

Pillar Reins

When horses are harnessed and ready for work but the time has not come for them to be put to, they can be turned round in their stalls and left on pillar reins. A leather or rope rein is attached to the ring on each of the pillars at the back of the stall. Each pillar rein has a spring hook at the end which is clipped on to the bit. The horse is unable to pull back as he soon comes up against the manger. If he tries to step forward, he is held by the pillar reins. This method enables horses to be harnessed and left for a reasonable period without the harness getting broken by being rubbed or chewed and is particularly useful when a team is being harnessed by only two grooms.

Pill Box Brougham

A small edition, of this popular Victorian vehicle, which was favoured by doctors from where the nickname probably originated.

Pill Box Phaeton

A slang term in America for a physician's or pedlar's vehicle.

Pin Hole

The hole which is drilled through the carriage end of the pole to take the pole pin.

Pin-Hoss

When farm horses are driven four-at-length, this horse goes in front of the thiller. Also known as the body horse.

The pin horse is also generally known to be the middle one of three horses which are driven abreast.

Pinned Ribbons

Reins which are buckled at the hand end.

Pipe Collar. *See* Collar.

Pipe Loop. *See* Full Safe and Box Keeper.

Pipes

Also known as pipe loops and box keepers. *See* Full Safe.

Piping

Harness which is used by costers is frequently trimmed with piping of coloured leather along the edges of the saddle, breeching seat, and any other suitable surfaces. Red and yellow appear to be the favourite colours to blend with the paint on the trolley.

Pirate Cabs

When Hansom's Patent Safety Cabs were put on the roads, a number of rival proprietors soon had copies of the original cab built. These afforded serious competition to the Hansom Company who prosecuted the guilty parties. The ensuing law suits proved fruitless and expensive, so the presence of pirate cabs had to be accepted.

Pit Pony

Ponies ranging from 11 to 14 hands which pulled the tubs of coal along tracks in the mine-shafts. They were protected by a law passed in 1911 which stipulated, in detail, the permissible working hours and conditions for these ponies. This resulted in the life of a pit pony being preferable to many of his contemporaries.

Plain Cheek

This is the least severe position on to which the reins can be buckled with a Buxton, Liverpool or similar curb bit. *See* Liverpool Bit.

Plater

His job was to make such parts of the carriage as the door handles. He also prepared metal furniture for the harness. The average wage in the first half of the 1800s, for a plater, was 30 shillings a week.

Plates

Parts of some vehicles, such as the shafts on cab-fronted gigs and many four-wheeled vehicles, are reinforced by strips of iron running underneath to give additional strength. These plates are usually bolted or screwed to the adjacent wood which they are supporting.

Platform Boot

A luggage box, which was fixed above the front axle on a travelling carriage, in place of the coachman's seat. Such a vehicle would have been postillion-driven.

Platform Spring. *See* Telegraph Spring.

Plough Back
Part of plough harness. It is the strap which goes from each side of the top of the collar to the crupper. A short connecting strap passes over the loins to join the two plough straps. The rein goes through a metal dee which is fixed to the outer plough back of each horse, with a pair.

Plough Gears
Also known as Sling Gears. *See* Chain Gears.

Plow Handle
Also known as a Pump Handle.

Plugging a Collar
When a collar is made, it is filled with straw. This is wetted and pushed into the leather body of the collar with an iron tool called a collar fork. This process, known as plugging, is continued until the lining of the neck is shaped to the form required for the horse in question.

Plumes
Coloured plumes made from ostrich feathers, horse hair or carefully worked materials were often worn by horses drawing sleighs. The plumes were fixed to the tops of the bridles and centres of the pads. Some were incorporated with bells on swingers or fly terrets. Black plumes were frequently worn by members of the Black Brigade.

Pointers
The pair of mules who were in front of the wheelers in a twenty-mule team.

Pointing a Rein
Also known as looping a rein. *See* Turns.

Point of the Whip
More commonly known as the lash.

Point Strap
The small strap which is sewn to the dee at the bottom of the body part of a pad. It receives the buckle which is attached to the strap sewn to the upper dee of the hame tug buckle.

Pole
The horses are harnessed on either side of the pole. It is by this that the vehicle is steered and held back if a brake is not used.

The end of the pole fits between the futchells. It is secured by a pole pin which is put through the futchells and the pole. As it is at this point that the pole is most likely to break, it is sometimes plated to about a foot in front of the futchells.

At the pole head there is a metal mounting with a ring on either side to which the pole straps or pole chains are fastened. If a team is driven, there is a crab for the lead bars.

Both the length and the height of the pole is important. For horses of about 16 hands, the pole head should be approximately 3 feet from the ground. It should be about 9 feet long from the front of the splinter bar to the pole head.

If the pole is too long, the pole chains will lie almost parallel to the pole. If is is too short, they will pull sideways on the collars. A horse may get a leg over a pole which is too low.

Pole Cart
An American term at the turn of the century, for a pair-horse road cart.

Pole Chain
The steel or stainless steel chain by which the horses hold back the carriage when going down a hill and in pulling up. Painted or plated pole chains are unsatisfactory as both of these coverings wear off rapidly but pole chains of Road Coaches are now painted black.

Pole chains have either a hook at each end or a ring at one end and a hook at the other. The chain is fastened to the pole head, either by a hook or by the chain being passed through its own ring. The other end of the chain is put through the kidney link ring, from the pole side, before going back towards the pole head. It is then hooked either into one of the links or back to the pole head. The hook, or hooks, should be fastened with the backs uppermost so that the bar of the bit does not get caught. If open hooks are used, instead of spring hooks, a rubber ring is passed over the open end for the same reason.

Pole chains should not be fastened too tightly. This causes pressure on the tops of the collars.

At the turn of the century it was usual for owner-driven carriages to be turned out with pole chains and for coachmen driven vehicles to use pole straps.

Pole-End Horses
The middle pair in a six-horse team. Also known as the swing pair.

Pole Head
The steel fitting which is bolted to the end of the pole. For pair-horse work, there is a ring on each side to which the pole chains or pole straps are fastened. For team work the pole head also has a large hook at the centre in to which the main bar is hung. *See* Crab.

Pole-Head Slip
A quick-release system devised to free horses from the pole head if they should fall. The two links at the pole head were replaced by branches with screws. In case of emergency, the screw was undone and the horse was freed as the branches were released.

Pole Hook
Also known as a crab.

Pole Pieces
More commonly known as pole straps.

Pole Pin
The small metal fitting which holds the pole in position at the vehicle end. *See* Pole.

Pole Strap

The strap by which each horse of a pair holds the carriage when pulling up, or going down hill. The pole strap is put through the ring on the pole head and through its own leather keeper to hold it in position with the buckle on the outside and the strap on the pole side. When the horse is put to, the strap is passed through the kidney link ring from the pole side and fastened to its own buckle. When it is tightened the pull goes to the rear from the outside.

Pole straps should not be fastened too tightly, otherwise unnecessary discomfort is caused to the horses by constant pressure from the tops of their collars.

Pollard, James (1792–1865)

A prolific artist of coaching pictures. He has left numerous meticulous records of everyday scenes for future generations to relive. His pictures show coaches being driven under every conceivable condition.

Reproductions of Pollard's work appear regularly in books, on table mats, and in vast numbers each year as Christmas cards.

Polo Cart

A low-hung type of Dog Cart which was originally used for taking polo ponies to a game.

Ponsonby Gig

An elegant, low, cab-fronted Gig. The hooded body is hung between springs which are a combination of three-quarter elliptic and cee-springs.

Pony Buckboard

A small edition of a Buckboard for children and ponies.

Pony Cart

At the turn of the century, a pony cart could be bought for about 18 guineas, as could a pony to draw it. The man who acted as a groom gardener, on the estate, was expected to look after such an equipage as part of his work.

A four-wheeled carriage for a single pony cost from about 28 guineas to 80 guineas, depending on the finish. One with a hood, and suitable for a pair, could cost up to 140 guineas.

Pony Phaeton. *See* George IV Phaeton.

Poor Man's Concord. *See* Concord Mud Waggon.

Port

The arch is the mouthpiece of a bit into which the tongue fits. This permits the mouthpiece of the bit, on either side of the port, to act on the bars of the horse's mouth. Many horses are happier with such a bit and pull less than with a straight mouthpiece.

High ports can be extremely severe if they are combined with a tight noseband and a pair of unsympathetic hands. The port presses against the roof of the mouth and causes considerable pain. *See* Bitting.

Portable Seat

Folding seats, made with an iron frame and resembling a camping stool were sometimes placed on the floor as additional accommodation for children travelling in a sleigh.

Portland Cutter
One of the oldest types of Cutters to be found in U.S.A. It was originally made in about 1816 by Peter Kimbal of Portland.

Portland Waggonette
A large, hooded, pair-horse version which was inaugurated in about 1894 by the Duke of Portland and designed by a Suffolk coach builder. It was used for driving to covert.

Post Boy
The name given to the man who carried the mails on horseback before the introduction of Mail Coaches.

He later rode postillion to a Post Chaise.

Post Chaise. *See* Chariot.

Postillion
It was not always desirable to have a coachman or for the traveller to drive himself. On these occasions the horses were ridden and driven. They would be put to a four-wheeled vehicle and the nearside horse was ridden by a man known as a postillion, or post boy, who also led the offside horse. He ensured that the passengers were conveyed to their destination whilst they rested or slept.

Some of the State carriages are drawn by two, four, six or eight horses with one, two, three or four postillions.

In France, it was customary for one postillion to manage four horses. *See* Daumont and Posting.

Postillion Dress
Post boys in England wore breeches, top boots and a short coat which extended only as far as their waist. This coat was traditionally yellow in the South and blue or red in the North of England. A choker which reached to the chin was worn. The beaver hat was usually white, though some proprietors put their boys into black beaver hats so that they could be easily distinguished. A drab top coat was worn in bad weather. This was slit to well above the waist and designed to wrap over the thighs and protect the postillion from the wet and cold. An iron leg guard was strapped to the outside of the right leg to protect it from the pole. This was sometimes called a false leg.

Postillion Harness
The offside horse wears normal pair harness apart from the reins. These are short and are carefully adjusted at a central buckle ensuring that an even contact is taken on each side of the mouth. They then join together to form a single rein which the postillion holds in his right hand.

The nearside horse wears a riding saddle instead of a pad. The crupper backstrap is attached to a dee at the cantle. The traces are made so that the buckle does not go under the saddle to cause discomfort to the postillion. The collar, crupper and loin straps are the same as with normal pair harness. Blinkered bridles are worn by both horses.

216

With postillion teams, lead bars are not used. The traces of the leaders or swing teams are longer than when bars are employed, and are hooked on to the swing or wheelers' hame tug buckles.

Postillion Horses
Instead of being driven by a coachman, each pair of horses is ridden and led by a postillion.

The Ascot Landau in which Her Majesty The Queen's party leads the procession down the course at Royal Ascot is drawn by four postillion horses who are controlled by two postillions.

On some occasions, with six-horse teams, four horses are driven by the coachman from the box and the two leaders are postillion-driven.

Posting
This was a more expensive form of transport than the Mail or Stage Coach. A traveller who desired privacy could hire a Post Chaise, complete with post boy and pair, from post houses along the road. These 'Yellow Bounders' were frequently old and battered, badly sprung and noisy, dirty and draughty. The floor was covered in straw. The traveller who was rich enough to afford both comfort and seclusion could use his own luxuriously fitted Dormeuse, Britszka, Posting Chariot or similar carriage and just hire the post boys and horses.

The cost of posting was about eighteen pence per mile for a pair with one post boy and was double for two post boys with four horses.

Dr Johnson is reputed to have said something to the effect that 'if he had no other duties, he would spend his life in a post chaise with a pretty woman'.

It was also said that the right-hand seat was preferable in a Post Chaise. From there, the view was of the offside horse and the country. The left-hand seat offered only the sight of the rear of the post boy rising up and down for mile after tedious mile.

Posting Chariot. *See* Chariot.

Posting House
An inn where postillions and post horses could be obtained. At the larger posting houses, the post boy stood ready in the yard and the pair of horses waited on pillar reins in preparation for the shout of 'Next pair out'.

Posting Match
One in particular was in 1812 when two post boys drove a team, to a Barouche containing passengers, seventy-two miles from Portsmouth to London in one minute over five and a half hours, including changes. The time allowed for this match had been seven and three-quarter hours.

Post Office Horse. *See* Mail Horse.

Pot Cart, Four Wheeled
This was originally known as a Potter's Cart because it was used by gypsies who bought and sold cheap pottery. Roofing canvas was hung on to the rounded frame which slotted into the floor. The cart was mainly used for conveying goods and for additional sleeping facilities if the need arose.

Pot Cart, Two Wheeled
A lighter version of the four-wheeled Pot Cart with a similar roofing frame and canvas tilt. There are canvas curtains which can be drawn across the front for privacy. The match board wall at the back has a window which gives some light to the interior. There are supports fixed at the front and back so that the cart can be propped up when the horse is taken from the shafts.

Potter's Cart. *See* Pot Cart.

Powell, Sir R. Leonard
President of The Coaching Club for 1938.

Prairie Schooner
Slang term for the Conestoga or Covered Waggon.

Presentation. *See* Combined Driving, Competition A.

'Present Times', The
In 1894, Mr. Jones drove this road coach at the Coaching Club's only meet for Road Coaches.

Pricked Tail
A method employed in the early 1800s. The sinews under the dock were cut in order to make horses carry their docked tails high. This gave what was then considered to be a smart appearance.
   Also known as nicking.

Prince of Wales
Who was later King George IV. In his youth, the Prince of Wales was probably largely responsible for encouraging the art of driving as a sport. During the last decade of the 18th century he took a great delight in driving a team, at speed, to a Perch High Phaeton. Race meetings were attended and park driving became a popular pastime. The young bloods of the period soon followed suit. Progression of time forced George IV into a lower and safer conveyance in the form of his little Phaeton.

Princess Car
A two-wheeled, cab-fronted, vehicle designed in 1893 by Messrs Taylor of Ipswich, Suffolk. The Governess Cart shaped body is hung low, often between elliptic springs, on a cranked axle. Unlike the Governess Cart, it is entered from either side of the cab front, by a step, and is driven from a movable transverse seat at the rear. This can be slid forward to adjust the balance when no passengers are carried on the inward-facing side seats.

Private Coach. *See* Drag.

Private Drag. *See* Drag.

Private Omnibus
A closed four-wheeled carriage which was first used in the 1860s. The pair, or single horse, was usually driven by a coachman from a high box seat in front of the closed body. The passengers entered from a rear door and sat on inward-

facing seats. There were windows along both sides and at the front. Luggage was stowed on the roof which was railed for this purpose. The overall practicality of this carriage made it an essential vehicle for all large establishments. It was extensively used both for station work and for visits to the theatre. For this reason it was also known as a Station Bus and an Opera Bus.

There were many variations of the main design. Some were built enabling a team to be owner-driven. Race meetings were attended and the Omnibus acted as a portable grandstand. Two seats were fitted, on either side of the rear door, for grooms. A seat was placed behind that of the drivers for outside passengers. Some even had a folding table inside so that lunch could be served in comparative comfort.

Proprietor
Also known as a Contractor.

Pull
Also known as a hame draught eye or a bullet. This is the metal protrusion on the lower part of the hames through the eye of which, in the case of Gig and carriage harness, the hame clip passes before being riveted to the trace tug or shoulder piece. With van harness, or Road Coach harness, the pull has a ring to which the trace is sewn. French cab harness, of the early 1900s, used an olive draught eye. The hame tug was attached to the pull by an olive shaped metal fitting sewn to the tug which was passed horizontally through a similarly shaped link on the pull. The tug was then turned through an angle of 90° so that the olive was secured in a perpendicular position in the horizontal slot.

Pulling away from the Pole
A dangerous habit which sometimes develops when pairs of horses are over-driven and fear that they may slip, or become overtired. Some will lean so far away that their bodies are at an angle of 45° to the ground. They are then held up by the coupling reins, pole straps and outside traces.

Pump Handle
The projection at the rear of a carriage which supports the footman's standing cushion.

Pung
A term used in New England, U.S.A., for a light business vehicle either on wheels or runners.

Putting to
The rules for putting a horse or horses into a vehicle are simple and should be strictly adhered to. If a system is always followed, then accidents can be avoided.
SINGLE. The horse stands harnessed with the belly band undone and the reins looped through the offside terret on the saddle, in preparation for mounting.

The vehicle is brought up from behind and the shafts are put through the tugs.

The horse should never be backed into a private driving vehicle. This can result in a broken shaft tip, if he treads on it whilst the shafts are resting on the ground.

The traces are hooked on to the trace hooks.

219

The breeching straps are fastened round the shafts and traces, going through the shaft staples.

The belly band is buckled last.

TANDEM. The above also applies to a tandem shaft horse.

If tandem bars are used, these are now hooked and buckled on to the hame chain ring on the shaft horse's collar and hame tug buckles.

The leader is led into position. His reins are passed through the leading eye and saddle terrets on the shaft horse. Someone should stand to the left of the wheeler's head in order to hold both horses. The leader's reins can be taken in the left hand and the shaft horse's reins in the right hand. The lead traces are hooked on last, either to the bar or to the shaft horse's hame tug buckle. Some experts advocate that the traces should be attached before the reins are attended to.

PAIR. The horses are led up from the rear and to the side of the pole.

The pole straps which are already on the pole head are fastened loosely. The outside traces are secured and then the inside traces are fixed. The coupling reins are buckled and the nearside rein is thrown over to the offside, ready for mounting. The pole straps are tightened last.

TEAM. The above also applies to the wheelers of a team but a pole with hook and bars will be used and the bars will be in place.

The leaders are brought into position and their reins are coupled and passed through the leading eye and pad terrets on the wheelers' harness. The reins are thrown over to the offside in preparation for mounting. A groom should stand at the near wheeler's head. The outer traces are hooked on to the lead bars. The inner traces are secured last.

Some people prefer to hook the traces to the lead bars before they attend to the reins. This largely depends on the number of available grooms and the training of the horses.

Quadrem

Four horses harnessed one in front of the other.

Quadriga

A Grecian chariot with four horses harnessed abreast. The two strongest animals were put on either side of the pole, under yokes. The other two were put to with ropes on each side.

Quarter Lock

A number of four-wheeled vehicles are built to permit a very limited turning arc before the wheels come into contact with the buck. Such a turning radius is known as quarter lock and a vehicle of this type can create difficulties if space is limited. *See* Angle of Lock.

Quarter Rug. *See* Loin Rug.

Quick-release Attachment
The wire traces of Army harness are joined by passing one metal shackle through another metal shackle. The two are secured by a leather strap. When the strap is removed, the traces can be instantly released.

Quick-release Mechanism
A system was devised, at the end of the 18th century, which enabled the leaders of a team to be released from the pole hook if they got out of hand or if a postillion fell off. Once released, they were free to go, coupled together with the lead bars clattering on their heels and the lead reins, (presuming that they were unbuckled at the hand end) flapping behind.

Quick-release Trace
Similar in principle to the Army quick-release attachment for wire traces. At the end of the quick-release trace there is a square metal shackle. Next to this, is a small leather keeper. Loose on the trace is a smaller square metal shackle with a metal bar down the centre. One half of this shackle is on the trace. The other half receives the trace end shackle. This larger shackle is passed over the smaller shackle after the trace has been taken round the roller bolt. It is then secured by a point of leather which is sewn to the outside of the trace about a foot from the end. After the larger shackle has been put over the smaller one, the leather point is passed through the keeper and the outer side of the smaller shackle to prevent the larger one from jumping off.

'Quicksilver', The
A famous Mail Coach which ran on the London and Devonport road. Most Mail Coaches were known by their numbers. This was the only one to be known by name, which was given to it on account of its speed.

Quill
Part of an English driving whip. Between the stick and the thong are bound the quills of goose feathers. A bow shape, resembling that of a shepherd's crook is formed by the quills and the top of the thong. This makes the thong easier to catch and the whip more pleasant to hold and use. In order to maintain the desired shape, the whip should be hung from a whip reel.

Rabbit-Bitten Holly
Some holly becomes nibbled at the base whilst it is growing. If the resulting stick is made into a whip, it is known as 'rabbit bitten'. The chewed area, which forms the handle part, is considered to be decorative and is not covered with leather as is usual with other holly whips.

Racing
There are numerous records of stage coachmen racing each other in order to cover the road more quickly than the coach of the opposition. Large fines were

imposed but this did little to deter them from their sport. Passengers frequently suffered injuries from coaches overturning as a result of rocking and rolling caused by galloping.

Ralli Car

A descendant of the Dog Cart which became very popular in the late 1800s. Ralli Cars were built with numerous variations to the main theme. The distinguishing feature is that the side panels curve outwards over the wheels to form splash boards. This is achieved by steam-bending the wood. Some curve completely in one panel. Others curve part of the way and have splash boards bolted on to them. Some Ralli Cars are built on two wheels and seat four back-to-back travellers. The methods of suspension vary. Some are hung on two side-springs, some are on Dennett springs, some are on cee-springs and others are on elliptic springs. The shafts run outside or under the body on some Ralli Cars and inside the body on others. A few were even made so that the shafts could be removed and a pole fitted to enable a pair to be put to in Cape or Curricle fashion.

Ralli Cars were also built on the lines of a Four-Wheeled Dog Cart, suitable for a pair or even a small team.

It was named after a member of the Ralli family who lived at Ashstead Park.

Randem

Three horses which are harnessed one in front of the other.

Ranelagh Club at Barnes, South-West London

In 1881 twenty-three members of The Coaching Club met in Hyde Park and drove to Ranelagh Club. This tradition continued until 1938 when seven coaches were present to drive to Ranelagh for dinner.

Rat Tail

A small piece of leather, resembling a boot lace, which is used to secure the trace on to a wooden-ended swingle tree. A hole is drilled on the inner side of the indentation on the swingle tree where the trace lies. The rat tail is threaded through the hole and knotted on either side of the swingle tree to keep it in place. After the trace hole is passed over the swingle tree, the rat tail is placed over the trace and the end is threaded down through a second hole which is drilled at the outer end of the swingle tree.

Rat-tailed Horse

He grows a very limited amount of hair from his dock. In the days of working horses, those with rat tails were reputed to be a tough breed which possessed a longer working life.

Rawhide

A strip of rawhide is an effective and simple first-aid kit for an emergency repair to a broken part of a vehicle. It should be wetted before being used to bind the damaged area. It will contract on drying and this will result in a strong mend.

Reach, The

Another name for the perch of a carriage.

Reading Cart

A general-purpose two-wheeled vehicle which was an offshoot of the Dog Cart. The panelled body is railed at the top and has back-to-back seats for four people. The sides extend with a low panel to join the dash, so that this has to be stepped over, on mounting. It is hung on side-springs with the shafts bolted to the underneath of the body. The vehicle had numerous uses which probably included that of Market Cart, Delivery Cart, Shooting Cart, Game Cart and Luggage Cart.

Reading Lamp

With which some travelling carriages were fitted for the convenience of passengers journeying through the night.

Reading Waggon

A type of gypsy waggon which has its rear wheels outside the body. Those at the front are smaller than those at the back. The body slopes outwards from the floor to the roof.

Rear Lamp

This is shaped like a miniature edition of an ordinary lamp. The single glass is red.

Rear lights have to be carried on vehicles for Competition A of an F.E.I. Combined Driving Event.

Reckler

An American Sulky which is fitted with a pole.

'Red Rover'

A London and Southampton coach which was built by Shanks. Until 1843 it ran between the Bolt-in-Tun Inn in Fleet Street and the Red Lion, Southampton. Then, in about 1890, during the coaching revival, the 'Red Rover' was put on the road from Margate to Herne Bay as a summer coach by Mr Craig McKerrow. It continued to run until the outbreak of World War I in 1914. In 1948 it was acquired by Mr Sanders Watney. Between 1952 and 1965 this coach ran for four days each summer, alternately to Brighton and Southampton. It was also driven with consistent success in coaching marathons, drawn by chestnut, piebald and grey teams. Now, the 'Red Rover' with a grey team, driven by Mr Sanders Watney and Mr James Corbett, continues its winning run in coaching classes at major shows.

Reducing the Width of a Collar

This is achieved by adding more straw in the appropriate places. The amount is limited by the size of the lining, which has to be renewed if a great reduction is necessary. *See* Plugging.

Regimental Coach

Regimental Coaches are Park Drags owned by the officers of a regiment or an association of officers within a corps. Their construction, colour scheme and turnout is the same as that of a private Park Drag, although the actual colours, being those of the regiment or corps concerned, may be brighter and more contrasting. The regimental or corps badge is displayed on the hind boot, door

223

panels, and harness, and grooms wear normal livery with military cockades and regimental buttons.

Regimental Coaches have attended meets of the Coaching Club since its foundation, but, prior to 1874, were always driven by officers who were full members of the club in their own right. From this date onwards each regiment owning a coach has been permitted to pay a regimental subscription and to nominate one officer to represent it as an *ex officio* member.

At the turn of the century and generally until 1920, some forty Regimental Coaches were in existence but only three, those of the Royal Horse Guards, the Royal Artillery and the Royal Corps of Transport (formerly the Royal Army Service Corps) remain today.

The coach of the Royal Horse Guards is now the only Regimental Coach still on the road; since 1958 it has been maintained jointly with the Life Guards and turned out in the ownership of the Household Cavalry.

'Regulator', The

A Stage Coach which ran on the London and Portsmouth road between Hatchetts at the London end and The Fountain Inn at the Portsmouth end.

Rein Holder

A spring clip which can be fitted to the dashboard, or as part of the rein rail. The reins can be secured under it when the passenger and Whip dismount.

Rein Rail

A brass or white metal rail which is bolted to the top of the dash board to support the reins and prevent them from getting caught under the horse's tail.

Rein Ring

The rosette on a wheeler or shaft horse's bridle through which the leader's rein passes.

This also refers to a Roger ring.

Reins

With which the horse is driven. They are best made of russet leather. It is normal to have brown reins with both black and brown harness. The dye from black reins would mark the clothing. The exact width of the reins is a matter of personal preference, depending on the length of the fingers. Many women find that reins of seven-eighths of an inch are comfortable to hold. Wider reins become too much of a handful and narrow reins are unsatisfactory if the horse starts to pull or if it rains. Some reins are made with a plaited or laced hand-piece to prevent them from slipping. Others are made with a strip of leather laid and stitched down the centre. This is known as 'flat and laid on' or 'Melton'. Some have the hand part folded and sewn.

Reins must be kept pliable. Stiff ones are unpleasant and a delicate touch cannot be achieved. Billets should be checked for wear. Saliva tends to cause this part to rot. A broken rein is almost certain to result in a nasty accident.

Reins which are too short are dangerous. If the horse stumbles the end may be snatched from the hand. Those which are too long are a nuisance as they get caught in the Whip's feet.

The ideal length of a single rein for a 15-hand horse in a Gig, or similar vehicle, is 13 feet from the billet to the end.

The reins must always be on the horse before he is put to a vehicle. Failure to keep to this rule can lead to disaster. *See* Lead Reins.

Reliance Slip Link

A quick-release slip link which was sometimes used on pole straps and pole chains. If a horse should fall, he could be easily freed from the pole by pressing a spring on the link. This released the catch and left the horse, unimpeded, to get to his feet.

Resin

It was said that if a small amount was put on to the gloves it acted as a preventative against the reins slipping if the team started to pull.

Restoration of Carriages

This is really a job for the experts whose names can be obtained from the British Driving Society.

For the amateur, who is considering 'having a go', the following advice is given.

If a first-class finish is being aimed for, then the vehicle should be completely dismantled. The painted metal parts such as springs, steps, trace hooks, lamp holders and mounting handles are probably thick with rust. These should be sent away for shot blasting and zinc spraying. This removes the rust and helps to prevent it from starting again too rapidly. The frames for the leather dash and splash boards should have the same treatment before being taken, after painting, to a saddler for new leather. For showing, patent leather is best.

Brass fittings are removed and labelled ensuring that each is returned to the same place with the same bolts and screws to maintain a good fit.

Wheels can be sent away to experts, for repairs, re-channelling and re-tyring, before any painting is considered.

For a good surface it is best to remove all the old paint down to the wood. Paint stripper and a paint scraper, followed by 'wet and dry' paper is effective. A blow lamp, in the hands of an amateur, can result in scorch marks.

When all the paint has been removed and repairs have been attended to, painting can begin. Aluminium primer is best for bare wood. It fills and seals many tiny crevices. Two thin layers, with light sanding between, are preferable to one thick coat which could take days to harden. The first undercoat is put on next. This is followed by as many layers as are considered necessary to fill the uneven areas. Each undercoat must be allowed to harden completely before any attempt is made to sand down the surface. Eventually, after several layers of paint have been applied and sanded, a glass-like surface is obtained. A dust-free and warm room is essential for top-coat work. If an outside building is used, the floor should be swept the previous day and then damped before painting starts, to avoid dust. Damp or freezing atmospheric conditions are unsatisfactory as the paint might then dry with a dull or even milky finish. Sometimes it is possible to bring the body of a vehicle indoors for top-coat work, where the dust-free, centrally heated atmosphere is ideal. Two or three top coats can be applied as required. Each is rubbed lightly with fine glass paper.

Lining out is for the experts. Usually a sign writer or yacht painter will oblige.

Last of all, one or two coats of clear varnish are put on, to protect the paint and give an extra glow.

The vehicle is then ready to be assembled and proudly taken out on the road.

Reversible Cushions
Some were made with leather on one side and melton cloth on the other side, so that they could be reversed in accordance with weather conditions.

Ribbons
Another name for reins.

Ribbons
Coloured ribbons to match the colours of the coach were sometimes worn on the bridles and pads of the horses to a Road Coach on its last stage on the last day of the season. *See* Black Ribbons.

Rib-Chair Gig
An unsprung two-wheeled vehicle of the late 18th century. Above the shafts was fixed a semi-circular-shaped seat with a similarly formed back rest, supported on wooden spindles.

Richmond Driving Club
A four-in-hand club which was formed in 1838 by, and under the presidency of, Lord Chesterfield. Some of the members drove Coaches and others drove Barouches. Lord Chesterfield expected his members, when they drove from his house to the Castle Hotel at Richmond for dinner, to look like gentlemen and only ape the old stage coachmen in their way of handling the ribbons. This club came to an end by 1845.

Rig
A slang term which, at the turn of the century, was sometimes used in America to describe a light or dilapidated vehicle.

Rim Collar
A type of collar with which the fore-wale extends round from in front of the hames, to form a rim, before it meets the lining on the inside of the neck. *See* Collar.

Ring Draught Eye
This is the way in which some traces, such as those used for commercial harness, are fixed to the hames. The trace is sewn directly to a ring which is secured through a pull on the hames. Adjustment is made at the other end which is frequently made of chain. *See* Parts of Hames.

Ringing the Bell
A slang term used to describe a method of driving which is practised by those not possessing good hands or a feeling for the art. An aid to turn is given with a rough jerk, as though pulling a bell, instead of a light and steady hand with consideration for the mouth on the receiving end.

Rippon, Walter
He was reputed, by some people, to have made the first coach, in 1555, to appear in England. This was built for the Earl of Rutland. It was said that, in 1564, he made a coach for Her Majesty Queen Elizabeth I.

Riser. *See* Cheek.

Rivet
Some hame tugs are secured to a hame pull by a clip which is fixed with copper rivets having brass or white metal heads. For pair and team harness it is usual to have three rivet heads on top of the clip. For single harness two rivets are used. On some harness, the clip is inside the tug and only the rivet heads are shown.

Road, The
These words are the traditional toast amongst 'Coaching Men'. Glasses are raised to 'The Road'. It is always the final Toast at a coaching dinner.

Road Cart
An American single-seat vehicle, used for exercising trotters. The driver sits between the two four-foot-high wheels with his feet on a slatted foot board. The shafts curve down to the axle, inside the wheels. These road carts were used for racing until they were superseded by the modern Racing Sulky.

Road Club, The
Instigated in the 1880s by Major Furnivall for the benefit of coaching people by whom it was, at first, used and enjoyed. The club was, however, soon abused and its original purpose faded until it had nothing whatsoever to do with coaching.

Road Coach
The opening of the railways brought a gradual end to the Stage Coaches.

Towards the last quarter of the 19th century, the 'Coaching Revival' began. It started with a few enthusiasts running Stage Coaches during the summer months. The idea caught on and the revival flourished. Subscription coaches were organized and those such as the 'Old Times' were running daily over regular roads. They became known as Road Coaches, in order to distinguish them from the Private Coaches.

Many fine examples were built by Holland & Holland, and Shanks & Co. Road Coaches were more robust than Private Coaches and weighed just over a ton. They had to be strongly built to withstand the heavy daily mileage which was covered in all weather conditions. Such parts as the futchells and splinter bar were left plain, whereas on a Private Coach these were lightened by a small amount of carving. The Road Coach seated twelve outside passengers as well as the guard and coachman. A Private Coach accommodated two less, as the rumble only seated the two liveried grooms. The rear seat on a Road Coach transported four people including the scarlet-coated guard. He sat on the left, as the hind boot was designed to open from that side. Iron rails ran between the roof seats to which a net of leather straps was fixed on top of the roof. This held the passengers' coats and small pieces of luggage. The lazy backs of the roof seats were permanently fixed in an upright position. On a Drag they were made to fold down when the seats were not being used.

To complete the flavour reminiscent of the Stage Coach, the Road Coach was often painted in bright colours with place and inn names written in gold on the panels and boots. The name of the coach was painted on the back panel. A Private Coach was finished in a more sombre hue with discreet crests or monograms on the crest panels. On a Road Coach, the folding ladder was secured under the hind boot in readiness for the guard to erect, in order to assist those wishing to mount to or dismount or from the roof seats.

The inside trim was plainer than with a Private Coach. The windows were often made up from four small panes instead of one large glass. These smaller windows were presumably less likely to get broken with a coach in everyday use.

In 1894 The Coaching Club held a meet, purely for Road Coaches, when fifteen were present. These were 'The Age', the 'Brighton Comet', the 'Defiance', the 'Excelsior', the 'New Times', the 'Old Times', the 'Perseverance', the 'Present Times', the 'Quicksilver', the 'Reliance', the 'Rocket', the 'Sporting Times', the 'Venture', the 'Vivid' and the 'Wonder'.

Now, coaching marathons are held at many of the larger shows. The classes are often divided into three sections for Private Coaches, Road Coaches and Regimental Coaches.

Road Coach Harness

This was made for practical everyday work and differs considerably from Drag harness. Road Coach horses tend to be tougher and heavier than their counterparts in a Drag who need light and elegant harness to compliment their quality.

Road Coach harness can be either brown or black whereas Drag harness is always black. Polished brown collars look very smart with black harness on Road Coach horses. Road hames have ring draught eyes on the tugs and Drag hames have clips and rivets. The traces on a Road Coach often have French loop or chain ends. A Drag has traces with quick-release ends. The bridles have rosettes on the outer sides only so that in the bustle of harnessing a road team, each bridle can be quickly distinguished. Metal or metal and leather browbands to match the colour of the coach are worn by Road Coach horses. The initial of the coach, such as R.R. in the case of the 'Red Rover', or an emblem, such as a set of bars, decorates the blinkers and pads instead of a crest or monogram. Open pole chain hooks, with rubber rings, are used on a Road Coach whilst spring hooks are preferred with a Drag. It is permissible to drive Road Coach leaders without pads and cruppers if bearing reins are not worn. Short trace bearers, known as diagonal straps, from the hame rings to the tug buckle are then used.

If bearing reins are worn with a Drag team, they should be put on all four horses. With a Road Coach a single bearing rein can be used, as necessary. Liverpool or Elbow bits with a bar across the bottom of the branches are usually worn by Road Coach horses, whereas Buxton bits are used with a Drag.

Road Cribbage

To relieve boredom during long journeys the passengers might watch different sides of the road for such objects as cows and pigs. Points would be scored for the number viewed. This game was also referrred to as the Road Game and Road Piquet.

Road Game. *See* Road Cribbage.

Road Phaeton
A name which was sometimes given to a Four-Wheeled Dog Cart.

Road Piquet. *See* Road Cribbage.

Roadster
A type of horse which was originally bred in Norfolk and to whom the modern hackneys owe their ancestry. The bloodlines go back to Arab and Yorkshire stallions. The Norfolk Roadster was a tough, all-round animal, capable of great speed. One is recorded to have covered two miles in four seconds over five minutes.

Robinson & Cook
The London coachbuilders who, in 1838, made the first Brougham.

Rochelle Waggon, New
An American four-wheeled vehicle with two seats, one behind the other, on a rectangular base.

Rockalette
A small American Rockaway with a movable top.

Rockaway
An American four-wheeled general purpose vehicle which was built in numerous variations and given names to match the description like the Curtain Rockaway on account of its leather curtains.

'Rocket', The
A London and Brighton coach. It was driven by Mr J. Bolding at the Coaching Club's only meet for Road Coaches in 1894.

Rocking
The term which is given to the sideways motion of a coach caused by a galloping team. *See* Rolling.

Roger Ring
The rein terret on the wheeler's bridle through which the leader's rein passes. Also known as wheeler terret.

Rogers, Fairman
The author of *A Manual of Coaching*, published in 1900. He advocated the use of the 'Driving Apparatus' for practising the handling of team reins without a team.

Roller Bar Terret
Used on the saddle of a tandem shaft horse. The terret is divided into an upper and lower half by a bar which rotates on a transverse pin. The shaft horse's reins go under the bar and the leader's reins lie on top of the bar. This prevents the two reins from sticking together.

Roller Bolt

An upward circular protruberance on the splinter bar to which the trace is attached. Each roller bolt is surmounted by a leather or metal flange to prevent the trace from coming off. Those on the outer sides of the splinter bar sometimes have larger metal flanges, with treads, which act as steps. The inner roller bolts often have a strip of leather wrapped round them to take up some of the length of the inside trace which needs to be fractionally shorter.

Also known as a Bollard.

Roller Wheel Waggon

The damage which was caused by the wheels of heavy waggons on muddy roads was considerable. The use of wide tyres was encouraged by lower tolls being charged. In 1763, Mr Daniel Bourn invented a waggon which had wheels like garden rollers. Their bearing surface was 16 inches and they were only 2 feet high. They were attached to the vehicle in such a way that each took a different track. The front rollers were placed inside the hind rollers. The result was that the waggon almost performed the task of a road roller.

Rolling

When a coach is driven fast, it sometimes starts to rock laterally from side to side. This is known as rolling and can result in overturning if the pace is not checked.

'Romance of the Road'

A coaching book which was written and illustrated by Cecil Aldin, published in 1928.

Roof Seat

A seat on top of the roof of a coach. Also known as an outside seat.

On early coaches, there were no seats on the roof. Travellers perching there, had to cling on to the roof with their toes and fingertips to prevent themselves from falling off. In order to make roof travelling less hazardous, seats were added. The idea was exploited. Vehicles were overloaded and numerous accidents were caused by coaches overturning because they were top heavy. In 1788 an Act was passed, due to Mr Gammon, in which roof seat passengers were limited to six, with one roof seat facing forward behind the box and the other facing the rear in front of the forward-facing guard's or groom's seat. Three people, including the coachman, sat on the box seat. Later, wider roof seats were made each to hold four people. This resulted in the seats extending slightly beyond the sides of the coach. The box was then built to accommodate just the driver and one passenger. *See* Footboard.

Rosette. *See* Boss.

Rough Cheek

The position where the reins are buckled to a Liverpool bit when they are passed round the branch of the bit, below the mouth piece. *See* Liverpool Bit.

Roulette

A type of sedan chair on wheels, in use in France in the 17th century. *See* Brouette.

Round-cornered Waggonette, Low Hung
A four-wheeled carriage which resembles a Governess Cart with a box seat. The rear half of the vehicle has a Governess Cart body hung on a cranked axle between elliptic springs. The inward-facing seats are reached from a rear door with a step. The box seat is mounted on a boot in front of the Governess Cart body. It is hung on elliptic springs above a straight axle. An arch in the body behind the box seat permits a good lock.

Rowlandson, Thomas (1756–1827)
A prolific artist with a great sense of humour which protrudes through his drawings. Many of his coaching and driving scenes depict caricatures of grotesquely overweight travellers coping with a crisis of some kind.

Royal Agricultural Society of England
In the last half of the 19th century this Society held meetings at which coachbuilders exhibited the finest examples of their work for the judges to examine Reports were written and money prizes awarded.

At the present time, a show is held by the Society each year at Stoneleigh, Warwicks, with numerous classes for cattle and pigs as well as for horses. Also included are coaching, Private Driving, and F.E.I. Combined Driving events. A win at 'The Royal' is a much sought-after award.

Royal Mail. *See* Mail Coach.

Royal Messenger's Carriage
It was important for a Royal Messenger to have his own travelling carriage which was always available at a moment's notice. One was kept at Calais so that there was no delay in his journey, with post horses, to Paris or where ever he might be directed to deliver secret papers at speed.

Royalty Cart
The name which Hayes & Son gave to a vehicle which was similar in design to a two-wheeled Dog Cart. One was built for Prince Rohan of Bohemia by them.

Rubbed Dock
The skin underneath the dock can become sore and chafed if the crupper is not kept soft. This condition most frequently occurs to young horses whose skin is soft and consequently reacts adversely to the unaccustomed presence of a crupper. It can result in kicking, so must be avoided. A layer of sheepskin, stitched in position round the crupper dock, is a simple solution.

Rub Iron
The cigarette-shaped metal bar which is often found on vehicles of American design. It is fixed to the lower side of the body on some quarter-lock vehicles and to the perch of some with a cut-under body. When the front wheels are turned to the full extent of their lock, the inside tyre contacts the rub iron which then rotates on its central pin.

Rug
Some people prefer to use a rug in preference to an apron. Cotton or linen rugs of Tattersall check, bound with a matching braid, are suitable for the summer.

For winter driving, a dark or fawn-coloured box cloth or waterproof rug with a wool lining is the most practical. Bright-coloured rugs are best avoided. They generally clash with the vehicle and the Whip's clothing. The rug should be wide enough to allow a generous tuck-in and deep enough to reach the floor from the waist, in order to protect the wearer from the cold and wet.

Rumble

The rearmost seat on a Private or Road Coach. On a Drag, the rumble is built to accommodate two grooms. It is supported by iron branches above the hind boot. If passengers are carried on the rumble, a lazy back is put on for them to lean against and a valance is hung from the front of the seat to protect them from draughts.

On a Road Coach, the rumble is built on a solid wooden support above the hind boot. The seat back is permanently fixed. The width varies to take either three or four people.

Rumble Tumble

The rear basket on an early coach in which some passengers travelled. *See* Boot.

Runabout

An American four-wheeled general-purpose vehicle to accommodate two people on a forward-facing seat. Some had parasol tops. The body was hung on a perch undercarriage with two elliptic springs.

Runner

Unless the two leaders of a team are held together by a connecting strap between their collars, there is nothing to prevent one leader from shying violently away from his partner. If this occurs, he may pull his coupling rein with such a jerk that the coupling buckle and even part of the draught rein is dragged through his partner's pad. In order to prevent this situation from happening, a runner resembling the stop which is put on a riding rein to prevent the ring of a running martingale from getting caught over the rein buckle, can be used. The runner is made from a piece of flat metal which is about $3\frac{1}{2}$ inches long. This is covered in leather, with a slit, so that it can be passed over the coupling rein in front of the buckle. If a leader should shy, then the runner comes up against the terret and prevents the rein from being pulled any further.

Running Gear

The American term for the undercarriage of a vehicle.

Running Loop

The type of trace end which is sometimes used with pair or team wheeler harness. Sewn to the end of the trace is a curving square metal fitting through which the trace is passed so that a loop is formed. At the other side of the square fitting is sewn a short leather tag. The trace loop is placed over the roller bolt and pulled tight when the horses are put to. When they are taken out, the loop is loosened by pulling the tag. For this reason, the traces are put on to the hame tugs in such a way that both traces on the nearside horse have the tags on the nearside and the tags of the offside horse's traces face the offside.

Russet Leather
A high-quality leather from which reins are made.

Rustic Cart
One of the many descendants of the two-wheeled Dog Cart. This was a general-purpose slat-sided vehicle with back-to-back seats for four people.

Rutland, The Earl of
For whom in 1555, Walter Rippon is said to have made the first coach to be seen in England.

Saddle
A driving saddle is used in preference to a pad whenever the horse is likely to have to take part of the weight of the vehicle on his back. For this reason saddles are worn for most work with two-wheeled vehicles including by a pair to a Curricle. Saddles are not necessary with a Cape Cart as any weight is taken on the top of the neck.

Pads are worn by pairs and teams to four-wheeled vehicles when their purpose is purely to act as trace and perhaps breeching carriers, and as an anchor for the bearing rein and crupper back strap. A single horse to a four-wheeled vehicle usually wears a saddle to take the weight of the shafts.

A saddle differs from a pad in many ways. A saddle is more substantially built and has a greater amount of stuffing. The stuffed panels extend well down against each side of the horse's ribs.

Saddles which are now used for private driving, with gigs and similar vehicles, are elegant in shape and light in weight. The form of the panels varies considerably. They are usually narrow. Some are straight-sided whilst others have a swell. They have a girth strap going down from each side to which is buckled a small girth. The backband, to carry the tugs and belly band, is passed through a slit between the seat and the lining. Brass or white metal rein terrets are screwed into threaded slots on each side of the seat. A bearing rein hook is fastened to the centre, at the front, and a crupper dee at the rear.

Saddles which are used for showing are frequently covered with black patent leather, if the remainder of the harness is black with patent trim. Plain black leather, which can be polished, is frequently used for everyday work. Brown leather saddles are often used with brown harness for ponies in varnished vehicles for country driving.

Horses which are engaged in heavy work in two-wheeled carts, such as farm horses, wear large square-shaped saddles so that the load is distributed over a wide area. These have a metal or wooden ridge across the top in which the chain backband, from the shafts, lies.

Commercial saddles had wider panels than the modern private driving saddles. Some had a metal-covered cantle. Others had a metal seat to protect them from damage. These working saddles were made with a girth resembling part of a surcingle which passed under the horse from the offside panel and buckled to a point strap fixed to the bottom of the nearside panel.

The fit of a driving saddle is as important as that of a riding saddle. One which has too wide a tree, or lacks stuffing, will bear down on the spine and cause a sore back. One which is too narrow will perch above the back and pinch.

The saddle should not be placed too far forward or it will press on the withers. Girth galls can also be caused by the saddle being pushed forward, on going downhill, if the breeching straps are too loose and the crupper backstrap is too long.

Safe

A leather lining which follows the same form and is stitched on to the back of some hame tugs to prevent the tug buckle from pressing against the trace, thus causing wear. A hole is cut in the safe, directly behind the buckle. The trace is passed through the hole before being buckled. The buckle then rests against the safe instead of on the trace. When a heavy load is being pulled, a deep indentation will appear on the safe which would otherwise have dented the trace. Safes on black harness are frequently faced with patent leather, if other parts such as the pad, collar and blinkers are covered with patent. They vary in length. A full safe extends from the hame pull to just beyond the buckle. A three-quarter-safe ends about halfway between the buckle and the hame. A half-safe goes behind the buckle and ends just beyond where the buckle is stitched to the tug.

Safety Chain

When a steep hill had to be descended with a heavily laden coach, a safety chain was used in case either one or both of the drag shoes were displaced. One end of the chain was fixed to the front axle alongside the drag shoe chain. At the other end was a leather-covered hook which went over the felloe and iron tyre. Sometimes, instead of the hook, the chain, which was leather covered at this point, went round the rim and hooked back on to itself.

Salisbury Coach Box

Carriages built for town use in the 1700s and early 1800s were sometimes equipped with a Salisbury boot. This took the form of an oval-shaped frame which was covered in leather and placed on the front beds. It was surmounted by a coachman's seat which was shaped for his comfort and safety with high sides. An ornate hammer-cloth was placed over the top. The decorated footboard was fixed to the front of the boot.

It is believed to have been named after the Earl of Salisbury.

Sallengs

The fringes on Hungarian harness.

Salute

When a turnout first enters the show ring, a coaching salute should be given to the occupants of the Royal Box on passing. This is repeated on the last lap before leaving the arena. A gentleman Whip should take the reins and whip in his left hand and turn his head slightly towards the Royal Box as he raises his hat with his right hand. A lady Whip should turn her head slightly and give a small bow. At the same time, the whip, which is in the right hand, should be raised to an horizontal position so that the elbow is tipped upwards. Male passengers should raise their hats and female passengers should bow. Grooms in livery should look straight ahead and keep their hats on their heads. If a Whip is addressed by Royalty or the occasion is formal, then the liveried grooms, who are seated in the carriage, should place their hats on their knees.

Sark
Also known as 'The Island of Carriages'. It is the smallest island in the British Commonwealth, being 3½ miles long by 1¼ miles wide. No motor transport is used on Sark other than the tractors which attend to some of the farm work. Horse-drawn vehicles provide the transport. In 1973 there were sixty-six horses on Sark and forty-four horse-drawn vehicles of which the waggonette type predominated. The vehicles are tested each year, to ensure that they are maintained in a roadworthy condition. Visitors to the island frequently hire a carriage, to go sight-seeing, so the reliability of these vehicles is important.

Savile, Capt. Hon. George
President of The Coaching Club for 1936 and 1937.

Sawyer
It was said that those men who did not possess much skill as carpenters, sunk to the job of a sawyer in a coachbuilding factory. It was tedious work for which a man was paid about 30 shillings a week in the early 19th century.

Scalded Shoulder
Caused by an ill-fitting collar. *See* Collar Injuries.

Scarborough Phaeton
A carriage which resembles a four-wheeled Dog Cart in that the two seats are placed back-to-back. The body is hung on four elliptic springs and has an arch under the front seat to permit a full lock.
   This vehicle is believed to have been named after the Earl of Scarborough.

Scarf
It was usual for the servants of a Drag to wear a white collar and white scarf which together resembled a hunting stock. At the turn of the century, the scarf and collar could be purchased as a complete unit.
   Also known as a Newmarket tie.

Scarf Pin
These are worn by grooms in livery, to pin their stocks. It was considered correct, with a Private Coach, for the pins worn by both men to match in design.

Schlitz Circus Bandwagon
The wagon to which the Schlitz forty horse hitch is driven at numerous parades throughout U.S.A. including the Schlitz Circus Parade in Milwaukee which is sponsored by the Jos. Schlitz Brewing Company.
   The five ton, twenty-two feet long wagon is over twelve feet high when the sky boards are raised. It is painted gold and white and the carvings on the body are covered with gold leaf.
   The bandwagon carries twelve to fifteen piece bands which play circus type music when the hitch appears at major events.

235

Schoolmaster

A reliable horse next to whom a 'green' horse is put in a vehicle such as a Skeleton Break. If the youngster tries to run away or is reluctant to go forward, the schoolmaster holds him back or drags him along as necessary.

Scoop

A type of Side Spring Buggy, with a scoop-shaped body, found in America around 1873. It later received favour in the carriage building shops around New England.

Screw

A slang term for a broken-down, unsound or useless horse.

Screw-heads

Bars should be put on to the crab with the screw-heads uppermost. Then, if a screw should come loose and drop out, there is more chance that its absence will be seen. The loss of such a screw could result in a hook dropping off the end of a bar.

Scroll Pull

A type of V-shaped pull, on the hames, to which the trace tug is attached. This also is known as a branch pull.

Seals

Sometimes the wooden hames of farm-horse harness are referred to as the seals.

Seat Box

A wooden box with a hinged lid which was designed to fit exactly under the inside seat of a closed carriage. It was used for storing such items as linen.

Second Man

When two grooms are carried on a Drag, the head groom travels on the offside of the rumble and the second groom sits on the nearside. It is his job to stand by the leaders when the coach is stationary. If the drag shoe has to be applied, it is the duty of the second man to perform this task.

Sefton Landau

Also known as Canoe Landau. *See* Landau.

Segunda

A type of half-port on the mouthpiece of a bit which has the lower sides narrower than the uppermost arch.

Selby

A short, double-breasted overcoat worn by James Selby and copied by other driving men who referred to coats of this type as 'Selbys'. It was made of almost waterproof box-cloth and was large enough to keep the wearer both warm and dry when weather conditions were bad.

Selby, James (1844–88)

A well-known and respected coachman. He was both a coach proprietor and a partner in the coachbuilding firm of Cowland & Selby. He was responsible for putting the 'Old Times' subscription coach on the London and Brighton road during the coaching revival. Selby is perhaps best remembered for his famous match against time in July 1888 known as The Selby Run when he drove the 'Old Times' coach 108 miles in under eight hours. He died of bronchitis at the age of forty-four in December of the same year. The sadness was in evidence on the days of his death and of his funeral, by the black ribbons which were tied to the whips of bus drivers.

Selby Run, The

A famous match against time in which James Selby drove the 'Old Times' coach 108 miles from London to Brighton and back, in seven hours and fifty minutes. A bet of £1,000 was laid that he could not cover the ground within eight hours and Selby was determined to prove that he could.

Extra horses were put to work and the teams to be used were prepared to a fit and hard condition for the galloping which was to be required of them. Rivalry developed between horsekeepers of stables along the route as each hoped to outdo the others by performing their change in a record time.

At ten o'clock in the morning of 13th July 1888, Selby ordered the ostlers to 'Let 'em go' and the team flew away from Hatchetts, Piccadilly. The first change, at Streatham, was completed in forty-seven seconds. This time was never bettered on the run, and only once equalled, at Patcham. More changes took place at Purley Bottom, Merstham (here, the wheel plate was greased causing the change to take two minutes), Horley, Peas Pottage, Cuckfield and Patcham. The last four miles to Brighton were completed in a quarter of an hour. Telegrams of good wishes were picked up at The Old Ship Hotel. The fifty-four miles had been completed with four minutes in hand. The team was rapidly turned for London. At Patcham, both Selby and the passengers dismounted briefly before dashing away again. There were six more changes along the return route. The plate had to be greased both at Friars Oak and Merstham. At five-fifty in the evening, the team galloped into Piccadilly. The journey had been completed with ten minutes to spare.

The 'Old Times' continued to run on that road and was popular with passengers after this great feat. Models of the coach were sold in London. A picture, now famous, was painted by Harrington Bird of the team being sprung by Lowfield Heath at twenty miles an hour. The original is in possession of Mr Bernard Mills who also has the 'Old Times' coach at his home. Many prints were made of the picture and one, presented by Mr Mills, can be seen at the National Equestrian Centre, Stoneleigh, Warwicks.

A tablet was erected in London on the fiftieth anniversary of the death of Selby. This was thought to have been destroyed by bombs during the second world war but was later recovered and returned to Mr Bernard Mills. It is now set in the wall of the coach house alongside the coach.

Semi Elliptical Spring

Also known as a double elbow spring.

Semi-Mail Phaeton. *See* Demi-Mail Phaeton.

Servants. *See* Grooms.

Service Harness. *See* Army Harness.

Set Back. *See* Half-struck.

Set Stick
Also known as the stretcher.

Seven-spring Gig
More commonly known as a Tilbury Gig.

Shackle
These are used for joining springs together.

Shadowing
The sharing-out, between the guard and the coachman, of dishonestly gained short fares. These were not entered on the waybill.

Shaft Horse
Wheeler in a tandem or random.

Shafts
The two longitudinal timbers between which the horse is harnessed. It is by these, with a two-wheeled vehicle, that balance and steering are obtained. With a four-wheeled vehicle and a sleigh, the shafts prevent the conveyance from running forwards on to the horse. They also act as a means of steering.

Shafts are frequently made from lancewood owing to its elastic qualities. Many, now, are also made from ash which can be steam-bent to the required shape.

Shaft Staple. *See* Breeching Dee.

Shaft Strap
A strap, or light chain, which is attached to the shaft tips and lies in front of the horse's chest. The purpose is to prevent the reins from getting caught on the ends of the shafts. The shaft tips are specially designed with a small hole through which a spring clip, strap, or rat tail is put to secure the shaft strap or chain.

Shandrydan
A rough type of float which is used in Ireland.

Shanks & Company
A coachbuilding firm of Gt Queen Street, London, who were well known for their Drags and Road Coaches. Many coaches built by them are still in existence, including the present-day Southampton 'Red Rover'. Unfortunately, it is not possible to trace details of their coach designs as in 1898 all their records were deliberately destroyed in a bonfire party when the firm was forced to close down – due to the advent of the motor car.

Sharp & Bland
Coachbuilders of South Audley Street, London, who were famous for their large family carriages such as Barouches, Chariots and Landaus. They were approached by Lord Brougham with the commission to build the first Brougham. They rejected the job on the grounds that it was too far removed from the usual heavier carriages which they were accustomed to building.

Shayer, W. J. (1811–60)
Noted for his accurate renderings, on canvas, of Mail and Stage Coaches which ran on the southern roads. His pictures record, for future generations, useful details of harness and appointments.

Shebang
A slang term used in the western states of America to describe an equipage comprising of a rough carriage and a poorly fed horse.

Shelburne
A type of Landau, designed by the Earl of Shelburne, with a square, angular profile. *See* Landau.

Shelling. *See* Kicking.

Shelter Fund Society
Many of the old cabmen, in connection with their Society, directed that shelter be erected, complete with restaurants, at some of the cab stands.

Shepherd's Lock
A patent safety device, used commercially, for joining the pole chain to the ring on the kidney link. It could be quickly released by inserting a finger into a ring. These were sometimes also used for attaching the ring through which the head rope was passed in a stall, so that horses could be immediately freed in case of fire.

Sherman, Edward
One of the largest coach proprietors in London who kept the Bull and Mouth Inn. Sherman painted all his coaches yellow and set a high standard of turnout. Perhaps the most celebrated of his Stage Coaches, was the 'Wonder'.

Shifter
A type of single-horse sleigh found in New England, U.S.A., which was designed with the shafts directly in front of the runner enabling the animal to use the track of a pair horse sleigh thus avoiding the roughness of the centre of the road.

Shillibeer, A
An Omnibus, named after George Shillibeer.

Shillibeer, George (1797–1866)
An Englishman, living in Paris, working as a coachbuilder, at the time when M. Laffitte decided to put an omnibus on the road. Shillibeer built an improved version for Laffitte. He then sought to try his hand at the omnibus business in London. Shillibeer had been in the Royal Navy and when his first bus was launched in 1829, it was manned by fellow shipmates who were intrigued by the prospect of this new and amusing occupation. Unfortunately, the enthusiasm wore off and professional coachmen had to be employed, which was the beginning of Shillibeer's downfall. He was eventually defeated by the dishonesty of his drivers who pocketed a large proportion of the fares. Rivalry from other firms springing up all over the country and the opening of the railway put an end to Shillibeer's project. After about six years, he abandoned the scheme and set up as an undertaker. His hearses, with 'Shillibeer's Funeral Carriages' written in gold letters on the side became a familiar sight.

Before the advent of the funeral business, people had talked of 'taking a

Shillibeer' when they meant 'catching a bus'. Now, embarrassed that this meant a hearse, they said that they were going by Omnibus, Omnis, or Omnibi.

Although Shillibeer no longer ran any omnibuses, his idea had caught on thoroughly and so it is he who can be credited for the introduction of buses as a form of public transport.

Shooter
The guard of a Mail Coach was sometimes known by this name because he always carried a blunderbuss.

Shooting Brake
A sporting carriage built on Dog Cart lines. The high box seat accommodated two people and the two rear seats a further four passengers. These latter seats were often reversible so that the four passengers could either sit back-to-back with two facing forward and two facing the rear with the tailboard forming a footboard, or they could sit face-to-face. The dogs were carried in two venetian-slatted boots, one of which was under the driver's seat and the other between the rear seats. The whole was hung on four elliptic springs.

Shooting Cart
A four-wheeled sporting vehicle. The high driving seat from which a pair, or a team of ponies, could be driven, is placed over the front axle. At the rear of the slatted body is a forward-facing seat for two passengers. The body is entered by two steps and a central door on each side. There is adequate space under both seats for carrying dogs and game. The vehicle is hung on four elliptic springs and is shaped to permit a full lock.

Shooting Phaeton
This vehicle was built at the end of the 18th century by William Felton.

The forward-facing driving seat accommodated two people. On shooting expeditions, it was here that the groom sat whilst the gentleman rode in the forward-facing, leather-covered, single seat at the rear from where he could shoot. If the owner wished to drive, then this hind seat was useful for the groom. Between the two seats was a shallow, box-shaped, well for carrying game. The shooting dogs travelled in a railed compartment under the front seat which was fitted with a sword case. Over each axle was a boot under which was the perch.

The cost of Felton's Shooting Phaeton was about £61.

Short Breeching. *See* Breeching.

Short Harnessed
This refers to when the wheel-horses of a team are harnessed as close to the carriage and the leaders as near to the wheelers, as is practical. Such a team is easier to drive and does not take up as much space as a team which is harnessed loosely with long pole chains and long traces.

Short Stages
Hackney Coaches were often used by businessmen who did not keep a Gig. These public conveyances were convenient in which to travel, from a surburban residence to a city office, each day. The short-stage Coaches carried six passengers and were drawn by four horses.

Short Tommy
A whip made up from a short stick with a short thong. It was used, on night stages, to persuade the reluctant wheelers to put more effort into hauling a heavy coach up a steep hill. A similar persuader was applied by the guard, who was on foot, to the leaders. This whip was also known as a 'docker'.

Short Wheel Rein
A method which was sometimes used up to the first quarter of the 19th century. The leaders' team reins were of a normal length. The wheelers' reins terminated in a loop which lay over the second and third fingers. The adjusting buckle was placed to one side (on the off-rein) so that it did not come into the hand. The disadvantage of this short wheel rein was that it had to be of exactly the correct length and this was difficult to achieve. Also, the coachman could be dragged off the box seat if a wheeler should stumble badly.

Shoulder Collar
The metal plate which is welded to the rear of a mail axle. *See* Axle.

Shouldering
A slang term referring to the dishonest practice applied by the coachman and guard in allowing travellers not listed on the waybill on to the coach for short distances. As there was no record of such passengers their fares were pocketed by the driver and his guard. The coach proprietors were well aware of this unprofitable habit but were unable to stop it. At the dinners held by the proprietors of the great coach companies, the toast was 'Shouldering – but don't let me catch you at it'!

Shouldering the Pole. *See* Leaning against the Pole.

Shoulder Sticks
The name given to passengers travelling on a coach without having entered their names on the waybill and therefore responsible for shouldering.

Shoulder Tug
The name given to the hame tug buckle and the leather which joins it to the hames. With a pair or team, this also includes the point strap which is sewn to the lower dee on the hame tug buckle, to take the false belly band, and the strap and buckle sewn to the upper dee on the hame tug buckle, to which the point strap on the pad is fixed.

Showing
Show classes, for private driving turnouts, are held at numerous horse shows during the summer months. At the larger shows, these classes are usually divided into hackney-type and non-hackney type. They are then frequently subdivided into sections for pairs and singles of non-hackney type. If there is a large entry, the single non-hackney type is sometimes split into two height sections at 14 hands.

The judges of a private driving class have to consider many factors which, when combined, result in their decision. The horse must be of the right type for the vehicle to which he is put. A robust Welsh cob is no more suitable for a light

241

Phaeton than an Arab or thoroughbred for a substantially built Market Cart. The horse is closely examined for make and shape and way of going. He should be as perfect in conformation as possible.

A straight mover who covers plenty of ground with each stride is more desirable than one with showy action who makes a little progress and a lot of fuss. Above all, he must be suitable for an amateur to drive and yet be full of courage.

The harness should fit and be clean and soft. The vehicle must be clean and sound. The paint finish should be of a high quality and the tyres in good order. Appointments should be suitable for the equipage. The dress of the Whip, passengers and grooms should be neat and in keeping with the vehicle.

At some shows, a marathon is held as part of the private driving class. Turnouts are sent out along a pre-arranged route, of between five and ten miles, after preliminary judging. Speed is not taken into account and the suitability of exhibits for private driving is specially considered. The judge is driven round the course in a car and he stops, at intervals, to watch the class as it drives past. Animals which are traffic shy, excitable, or excessive pullers are noted as not being ideal for amateurs to drive. Exhibits return to the main ring for final judging.

The judges sometimes drive some of the exhibits, if they consider that this is necessary, before a final decision can be made.

Showman's Waggon
A type of gypsy caravan. *See* Burton Waggon.

Show Phaeton
This vehicle is built purely for showing a single horse or a pair of light horses such as hackneys. Under the single seat is an arch for the wheels to turn. The body is hung on four elliptic springs.

Shows
Many different types of competitive events are arranged for harness enthusiasts. The most common are the private driving classes when the turnout is judged purely on a showing basis. There are 'combined driving events' when the equipage is judged on presentation and dressage and accumulates further penalty marks for the marathon and obstacle courses. Some shows have 'driving competitions' when the Whip has to negotiate his horse or horses through a course of obstacles against the clock. 'Ride and drive' show classes are held for owners with an all-round animal. The horse is judged as a show-riding horse and then as a show-harness horse. The winner is the one who is considered to be the best overall. If there is doubt, preference is given to the better harness horse. There are ride-and-drive classes run against the clock, when changes from harness to saddle and back, are completed in seconds. The two harness sections are driven over an obstacle course with seconds added for markers displaced. The ridden section is over a show-jumping course and seconds are added for jumps which are lowered.

For those people who like to share their sport with fellow enthusiasts but do not wish to compete, there are non-competitive meets and country drives held by British Driving Society Area Commissioners throughout the summer months.

Shrewsbury, Lord

It was he who challenged Lord Lonsdale that the speed of galloping horses in harness was not as great as that of trotting horses in harness. This resulted in a bet of £100 which led to Lord Lonsdale's famous match against time being run.

In 1888 both Lord Shrewsbury and Lord Lonsdale went into the Hansom Cab business as proprietors.

Siamese Phaeton

An unusual Phaeton in that instead of there being the traditional groom's seat behind the driver, it was built with a second seat of an identical shape and size to the front one.

Siamese Victoria

A type of Double Victoria. *See* Victoria.

Side Car. *See* Irish Car.

Side Irons

The metal frames of the sides of the roof seats on a coach. *See* Baggage Net.

Side Rein

An emergency method which was used if one horse of a team started to pull badly. A side rein was buckled, either to the puller's nose band or to his bit. It was then passed through his partner's hame terret before being fastened to that horse's hame tug buckle. If the side rein was attached to the bit, it had two points and two buckles which were fastened to each side of the bit. A single rein was then fastened to the centre of this coupling to ensure that a straight pull was maintained.

Side-seated Platform Waggon

An American four-wheeled vehicle which was used when large numbers of people had to be transported. The 9-foot long body had a forward-facing seat at the front from which it was driven. Numerous passengers were accommodated on the inward-facing bench seats behind the front seat. A fringed top was provided to protect the occupants from the weather. It was hung on two sets of three springs. Each set consisted of two side- and one cross-spring.

Side-spring. *See* Double-Elbow Spring.

Silk

This was used extensively for the interior trim of high-class carriages.

Silk Hat

The black top hat which is worn by coachmen and grooms should fit perfectly and be placed squarely on the head. One which is worn at a jaunty angle detracts from the smartness of an equipage.

If a silk hat gets wet, it is best to wipe it all over with a damp cloth on returning home. It must then be allowed time to dry gradually, before being brushed. The final polish is achieved with a piece of velvet.

Silver

Used for plating the insides of lamps owing to its high powers of reflectivity. It is also sometimes employed for plating harness furniture and for ornamentation on carriages.

Single Bar
The bar to which the lead horse's traces are hooked when a team is driven. *See* Lead Bars.

Single Tree
Also called swingle tree.

'Sit Fast'
The warning shout which is given by the coachman before moving off. Passengers are then not taken unawares and accidents are prevented.

Sixes
The third pair of mules from the front of the waggon in a twenty-mule hitch.

Six Horses, Handling of the Reins
When a team of six horses is driven, English style, all six reins are held in the left hand. The handling and positioning of the reins is similar to that of a team of four. Points are made in the usual way. The near lead rein goes over the index finger and the off lead rein under the same finger. The near swing rein lies under the off lead rein and on top of the middle finger. The off swing rein goes under the middle finger. The near wheel rein lies over the third finger under the off swing rein. The off wheel rein goes on top of the little finger.

As it is not possible to reach the leaders with the whip, it is essential that they are free moving and know their job.

Six-horse Team Harness
This is almost the same as for a four-horse team. The leaders' reins run through the swing horses' bridle rosettes and pad centre terrets. Then, both the swing horses' reins and the lead horses' reins pass through the wheelers' divided bridle rosettes and pad centre terrets so that all of the reins are separated.

The leaders' traces can either be long and fastened to the underside of the hame tug buckles of the swing pair, or be of normal length and hooked to lead bars from the swing pole or swing chain.

Size of a Road Coach
One which was built by Shanks measures about $12\frac{1}{2}$ feet from the front of the foot-board to the lazy back on the rumble seat and the height from the ground to the tops of the lazy backs is about $7\frac{1}{2}$ feet.

Sjees. *See* Friesian Chaise.

Skein
A conical tube of thin iron covering the axle arm of simple waggons and carts. *See* Axle.

Skeleton Break
This vehicle, also known as a Dealer's Break, was kept by companies, dealers and any large establishment where a great number of horses were working. It was used for breaking and training when a youngster would be put in alongside an older schoolmaster or brake horse. The combination of a strong vehicle and solid companion restricted the newcomer's tactics. The break had a high box seat to accommodate two people and a small platform behind, on which the groom stood ready to jump down when the need arose. The four wheels were

dished, large and set wide apart. The perch was heavy and there was no body. The pole and splinter bar were covered with leather for dual protection.

Skeleton Gig
A light Gig with a curved open stick-back seat which is suspended by iron stays on two side and one cross-spring. The shafts run outside the bootless body.

Skeleton Wagon
A light four-wheeled American vehicle with the seat supports fixed to the frame.

'Sketches of the Road'
The name which was given to a set of three prints after Herring. They are, the 'Royal Mail Coach', 'Coach Horses' and 'Post Horses'.

Skid. *See* Drag Shoe.

Skid Chain. *See* Drag Shoe.

Skid Pan. *See* Drag Shoe.

Skijoering
A Swiss racing sport in which horses wearing breast collar harness are galloped over the snow, pulling their drivers who are on skis.

Slat Bottom
This refers to the type of footboard on some light exercising carts. It is constructed with a row of slats which are bolted at each end to a strip of metal fixed to the splinter bar at the front and under the seat at the rear.

Sledge
Also known as a Sleigh.

Sleigh
There are many varieties which differ from one country to another. The two-passenger type, with or without a rumble seat behind, are frequently set on one pair of runners. The larger varieties often have two sleds with a fixed frame at the rear while the forward one is designed to revolve like the forecarriage of a wheeled vehicle.

Slice of an Omnibus. *See* Boulnois Cab.

Slide Mouth
A bit, such as a Buxton or Liverpool, with a mouthpiece which is designed to move up and down on the narrow part of the branch to which it is attached. The play is limited to about $\frac{1}{4}$ inch above and below the mouth-piece as it then comes up against a shoulder. Many horses prefer a mouthpiece with which they can play. It keeps the saliva running and results in a relaxed jaw.

For pair work, if Liverpool bits are employed, those with fast mouths should be used. A slide mouth is not satisfactory, because the coupling rein pulls the back part of the bit sideways. This causes the front part of the ring to press painfully into the front of the face.

Sling Gears. *See* Chain Gears.

Smiths, Coach

Three types of coachsmiths were sometimes employed in the large carriage-building factories. They were the fireman, the hammerman, and the viceman.

The fireman was the highest paid. In the first half of the 19th century, he earned between £2 and £4 a week. His job was to produce iron-work of the various shapes and forms, which were required by the builders, to fix to the wooden parts of the carriage. The iron bars with which the fireman worked were heavy and the conditions hot, so he needed to be of a robust physique. A good eye was essential in order to produce accurately shaped pieces which had to be strong and yet give the appearance of lightness.

The lowest paid of the three smiths was the hammerman who worked alongside the fireman. His job was to wield the large hammer, as directed, and to work the bellows to keep the fire going. For this, he was paid 25 to 30 shillings a week.

The viceman earned between 30 shillings and £2 a week for which he had to put the finishing touches to the ironwork. Dents made by the hammers had to be filed away. Screw bolts, nuts and joints were his responsibility.

Snaffle

A bit with a mouthpiece which may be plain or twisted, straight or jointed, and made of metal or some other substance. The reins are attached to a ring or rings which are fixed directly or indirectly to the mouthpiece. Some snaffles have a full or half-cheek to prevent the bit from being pulled sideways through the mouth.

Snail of the King's Highway. *See* Broad Wheeled Waggon.

Snow Book

A book kept by the guard of a Mail Coach in which he entered, for the information of the Post-master General, any incidents on the journey which entailed expenditure. An occurrence such as the coach becoming snowbound in a drift could result in extra horses having to be hired to get the mail forward. Details would be recorded for submission to the Post Office.

Snow Plough

A wedge-shaped contraption which was used to clear the snow from the roads to enable the Mail Coaches to get through. The plough was made of wooden boards and horsed with a pair. Two boards which were 6 feet long and 4 feet high formed a point at the front to penetrate the snow. A pair of horses were harnessed alongside a pole which was fixed to the centre of the point. Behind the horses' 4-foot-wide splinter bar was a 3-foot wide board to which two 6-foot longitudinal boards were attached at each end. These spread out to be joined by a 7-foot wide board across the rear. The driver sat on a railed seat above this rear box-shaped part of the plough. As the horses pulled, so the pole pushed the forwardmost point through the snow and cleared a path which was then widened by the sides and rear.

Snow, Robert

A stage-coachman of the early 1800s who was noted for his knowledge in the art of handling a team. His manners, dress and whole outlook set a high example for others to follow. He drove the London and Manchester 'Defiance' and then, on the Brighton road, the 'Comet', the 'Dart', the 'Rocket' and the 'Sovereign'.

Snow Shovel
One of the essential appointments of a Mail Coach during the winter. The shovel was strapped to the rail of the guard's seat.

Sociable
An angular type of Sociable was used in about 1700. The body was hung on braces from a perch undercarriage.

Towards the end of the 18th century, elegant sociables were built by William Felton at a cost of just over £100. These vehicles were said to be as suitable for Park driving as for transporting the servants. The bodies of some of Felton's Sociables were built in such a way that they could be fitted on to existing Coach or Chariot undercarriages in order that the vehicles could be alternated as required. Two different carriages could then be obtained for the price of one extra body, though an annual tax of £3 was payable in the 1820s for each additional body.

These early Sociables hung on elbow- and whip-springs on a crane-neck perch. The open-caned body, in which the passengers sat facing each other, was entered from the centre of each side. A large knee-flap buttoned across the space between the seats, at elbow height. Further protection was given to those on the rear seat, by a folding hood and to passengers on the opposite seat by a jointed umbrella. One-half of this was shared by those on the driving seat, which was built at the same level. A leather sword case was fitted into the back of the vehicle, just below the hood.

By the last quarter of the 19th century a modified version of the Sociable had become popular.

The coachman drove a 15-hand to 15·2 pair from a low box seat which was placed over the front axle. The open body seated four people and those on the rear seat had the protection of a folding hood. The low carriage was entered by a single step and central door placed on each side of the well shaped body.

Some Sociables were built with a curving profile and others with more angular lines. The suspension was provided by four elliptic springs.

By the end of the 19th century, the Sociable had found favour as a lady's summer carriage for Park driving.

Sociable Landau
A smart town carriage which was usually horsed with a 'quality' pair and turned out with quiet dignity. The footman travelled alongside the coachman on the low box seat over the front axle.

The Landau-type body was entered by central doors and seated four people facing each other.

Sore Back
This can be caused by an ill-fitting pad or saddle or by one which has been placed too far forward and is pressing on the withers. The cure is to rest the affected area, to remove the cause so that it does not re-occur and to bathe in a healing lotion. Once a scab has formed then a healing cream can be applied to remove the hard scab and encourage the hair to grow.

Sore Neck. *See* Collar Injuries.

Sore Shoulder. *See* Collar Injuries.

Sovereign
A four-wheeled carriage which resembled a Clarence, but was much more ornately finished.

'Sovereign', The
A London and Brighton Stage Coach which was, at one time, driven by Bob Snow.

Space Loop
Also known as a loop keeper.

Spare Pole
One which could be used in an emergency was sometimes carried alongside the perch of a Drag or Road Coach by those embarking on a long journey. It was made from three sections which screwed together. Collars were designed to pull over the joints for additional strength.

Spares
It is essential to carry some kind of emergency repair kit, even when driving a quiet single horse. The minimum spares always known as a 'knife, a shilling and a piece of string', should be a leather bootlace, a pen-knife and a tenpenny piece. For F.E.I. Competitions the 1972 rules laid down that the following spares be carried: one lead trace, one wheel trace, one lead rein, one wheel rein, one main bar, one lead bar. Competitors frequently added to this hame straps, a bit, shoeing equipment, ropes and a first aid kit.

Speaking Tube
An accessory which was fitted to the insides of some closed carriages, such as Broughams, which enabled the traveller to communicate with his driver.

Speed
A comfortable average speed for a horse to trot is eight miles an hour. Greater speeds are frequently obtained but 'it is the pace that kills' and averages of fourteen or so miles an hour cannot usually be maintained for long distances or be repeated daily for weeks on end. Such practice will dramatically shorten a horse's working life.

Mail Coaches averaged about nine and a half miles an hour.

The French Malle Poste averaged between ten and ten and a half miles an hour but the stages were short, being about five miles.

Sections A and E of Competition B in an F.E.I. Driving Event are trotted at fifteen kilometres per hour and Section C is driven at between sixteen and eighteen kilometres an hour depending on the length of the course with the faster speed being required for the shorter course. The walk sections of B and D are driven at seven kilometres per hour.

Sperm Oil
Used as a fuel for lamps on such vehicles as the Mail Coaches. The Post Office

supplied sperm oil to their contractors for which they charged 4 shillings and 6 pence a gallon.

Spicy Jack

The nickname given to Jack Everitt, who was a character noted for his dashing appearance. He drove the Yeovil Mail Coach and the Warwick 'Crown Prince' Stage Coach. The equipage which he tooled for his own amusement, to such events as race meetings, was in keeping with his name. He had a showy pair who wore silver-mounted harness with red leather collars and they were put to a bright yellow Phaeton.

Spider Phaeton

Perhaps the most elegant of the Phaeton tribe. It first became fashionable in the last quarter of the 19th century. The hooded front seat resembles the body of a Tilbury Gig. An iron framework connects the front to a single groom's seat behind, which is suspended on curved iron branches. It is hung on four elliptic springs. Spider Phaetons were used, with a pair of high-couraged horses, for Town and Park driving, when all eyes would be drawn towards the showy spectacle. Now, they are ideal for exhibiting a pair of elegant horses to full advantage in a private driving class and the lightness of the vehicle permits freedom of action.

Spider Wheel

An American wheel with narrow spokes which are made of an elastic wood such as hickory. This enables the spokes to be thinner and lighter than those on English-made wheels. Dishing is unnecessary as the elasticity in the spokes allows them to bend slightly and then return to their straight form as soon as the pressure is removed. This treatment would render an oak spoke loose in its nave and felloe, in a short time.

Spike

Two-wheelers and one leader. Also better known as a unicorn team.

Spindle Wagon

An American Buggy in which the lower section of the body is panelled and the upper half is fitted with spindles to give a light appearance.

Splashboard

The mudguards which are fitted to the sides of the vehicle to protect the passengers from water and dirt which is thrown up by the wheels. Some splashboards are made of wood. Others are constructed with an iron frame which is covered in patent or plain leather.

Splinter Bar

The stiff bar, at the front of a vehicle, by which it is drawn.

Various arrangements for the fitting of traces are used. Sometimes, swingle trees are attached to the splinter bar.

For a single horse, to a two-wheeled vehicle, the trace hooks are usually bolted to each end of the splinter bar or to hooks on the extremities of a spring which is bolted through the centre of the splinter bar. For a pair, to a four-wheeled vehicle, if swingle trees are not used, there are usually four roller bolts attached to the splinter bar. There is one at each end and one on either side of the pole.

Also known as draw bar.

Splinter Bar, Movable
This enables the traces to give in accordance with the alternate forward movement of each shoulder, which reduces friction and lessens the likelihood of sore shoulders.

It was usual to take swingle trees with the splinter bar on English carriages which were being used for travelling on the Continent. There, breast collars were employed with posting harness and were unsatisfactory if used on fixed splinter bars.

One design used on coaches gives the outward appearance of the usual splinter bar and roller bolt arrangement but has the advantage of a swingle tree. A $\frac{3}{4}$-inch diameter bolt is passed through the splinter bar and a swingle tree which is made to resemble part of a coach splinter bar with a roller bolt at each end. Lying between the swingle tree and the splinter bar are two metal arms which are welded on to each side of the bolt. These hold the swingle tree in the desired horizontal position and allow the outer roller bolts to be used as steps in the normal way. The securing bolt acts as a pivot on which the swingle tree can move back and forth with the alternate pull of the traces. It is prevented from excessive movement by a strap which is passed round the splinter bar and swingle tree on the inner side which allows about $1\frac{1}{2}$ inches of play.

Splinter Bar Stay
Found on early carriages. This iron stay went from the outer ends of the axle, outside the wheels, to the end of the splinter bar.

Also known as a wheel iron.

Splintrees
Another name for lead bars.

Split Pin
Found on the ends of a Collinge's axle as a safety measure to prevent the nuts from coming off. These small split pins are frequently submerged in thick grease and a careful check should be made to see that they have been taken out before there is any attempt to remove the nuts.

Split Quarter-strap
A strap which passes over the loins, going through the back strap of the crupper, to hold up the breeching. At a point about halfway between the back strap and the breeching, the quarter-strap divides into two straps so that the breeching is supported towards the rear as well as at the front.

Split Strap
Also known as a winker stay.

Spoke Brush
A narrow brush for cleaning between the spokes of a wheel. It was said that the use of such an implement should never be permitted, owing to the resulting damage. If the brush was used, before all the mud and grit was removed, the scratches reduced a shiny surface to a dull one in a very short time.

Now, this problem no longer exists. The modern hose-type brushes used for washing cars are also excellent for cleaning carriages.

Spokes
The timbers on a wheel which are set into the nave at one end and the felloe at the other. *See* Dishing and Spider Wheel.

Sporting Phaeton
Similar to a four-wheeled Dog Cart. The two seats are placed back-to-back. The body, which has an arch under the front seat to allow a full lock, is hung on four elliptic springs. The side profile at the top is straight and slightly narrower than the line of the floor, which gives this vehicle the triangular impression seen with many Dog Carts.

Also known as a Malvern Phaeton.

Sporting Vehicle
One which was originally used for conveying the driver and passengers to a sporting event. Coursing meetings, cock fights, race meetings, shooting expeditions and meets of hounds were all attended by people driving sporting vehicles like Dog Carts.

Carriages of this type, were not suitable for formal occasions such as visits to State ballrooms or the opera.

Spring Cock-eye
A cock-eye consisting of a spring hook by which the lead trace of a tandem leader is hooked on to the specially designed tandem hame tug buckle. *See* Tandem Hame Tug Buckle.

Spring Curtain
Some closed carriages were fitted with curtains which could be rolled up above the window, on a spring-operated cylinder, when they were not required.

Springing
The earliest form of carriage suspension was provided by leather thoroughbraces. The body of the vehicle hung on leather straps attached to four solid pillars on the undercarriage. In about 1700 the whip spring came into general use. By 1790 cee-springs were taking their place. In 1804 the elliptic spring, invented by Obadiah Elliott brought a revolutionary change in carriage construction. Vehicles could be built without perches. Outlines became more elegant and the weight of carriages was reduced.

Spring Maker
Like the fireman, he also had the help of a hammerman, when he was making his springs, and a viceman to finish the work. The springmaker needed great skill in order to make the curving springs which entailed layers of accurately shaped plates. His wages ranged between £2 and £6, in the first half of the 1800s. *See* Smiths.

Spring the Team
To gallop the team. In order to get a heavily laden coach up a hill, it was quite usual for the coachman to 'spring the team'.

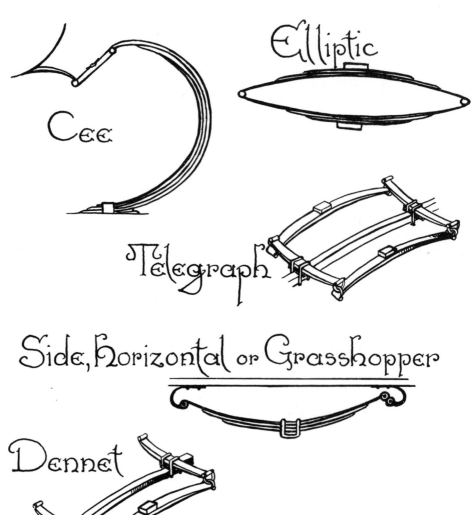

Cee

Elliptic

Telegraph

Side, Horizontal or Grasshopper

Dennet

Springs

Whip

Spring Waggon
An American four-wheeled vehicle with a long shallow box-shaped body which enables a reasonable quantity of goods to be transported. The forward-facing seat is placed towards the front, behind a dashboard. It is built on a perch undercarriage with a transverse elliptic spring at the front and two longitudinal elliptic springs at the rear. Unlike many vehicles of this type, it is fitted with a hand-brake.

Squab
A small cushion which was sometimes kept in a closed carriage. It was hung on strings or buttons and acted as a head or shoulder rest.

Square Lamp
One with square-shaped sides and a square front. The top, too, is very often square shaped of the pagoda design.

Square Pattern Blinker
If square blinkers are used, then the buckles on the harness should also be square at their ends, not rounded.

'S' Spring
Also known as a whip spring.

Stable Shutters
The wooden shutters which are fitted to pull up over the glass windows of a coach. When a Drag is driven by an employee of the owner, it is usual to have these shutters pulled up. At the turn of the century, when a coach was being driven from the stables, to the starting place of the journey, it was customary to have the stable shutters closed.

Now, it is usual for the windows, or stable shutters of Drags to be kept up and those on Road Coaches to be kept down.

Stage
The distance between coaching inns, along the route, where the horses of Mail and Stage Coaches, or postillion travelling carriages, were changed. The lengths of stages varied considerably. They depended on the terrain, the condition of the road and the availability of inns. Distance ranged between five and fifteen miles. A stage which was shorter than five miles was not economical for the time taken to change horses. Long stages were too much for horses to repeat daily. The length also depended on the speed at which the horses were driven. Horses could travel further at a steady pace than at a fast one. It was always said that it is the pace that kills.

Stage Coach
A public coach which ran on a given road at a regular time to convey passengers and their luggage. The long journey was made up from numerous stages and horses were changed at coaching inns along the route. The coach was usually driven by a professional coachman. Occasionally amateur enthusiasts took the ribbons. A scarlet-coated guard attended to the welfare of the passengers.

Stage Coaches first appeared in the early 1600s. They were limited to the summer months. Even then, the muddy tracks which passed for roads made travel hazardous and the likelihood of being accosted by highwaymen was an additional danger. It was no wonder that wills were written, and prayers were said, before travellers embarked on a long journey. Gradually, roads were improved by systems put forward by Telford and Macadam. These resulted in better coaches and faster horses.

Competition between the Mail Coaches and the Stage Coaches led to a higher standard of long-distance passenger transport than had been experienced before this 'Golden Age of Coaching'. Speeds averaged about ten miles an hour. Fares were charged both by the mile and for the overall distance. The cost of inside seats was about double that of those outside.

Stage Coaches were painted in gay colours, with the main towns along the road written on the side panels and boots.

Stage Waggon. *See* Broad-Wheeled Waggon.

Staggering the Spokes. *See* Dishing of Wheels.

Stall

Working horses frequently stood in rows between partitions. They were tied with head collars or neck straps to logs through rings fixed on the manger, hay rack and water bucket unit at the front. Very often, the partition was higher at the head end than further back. This prevented horses from trying to bite one another. Some stalls were separated by solid wooden partitions with railed tops. Others had swinging bales which are hung by chains from the roof timbers or ceiling. Stalls were found to be convenient where large numbers of horses were kept. They took up less space than loose boxes as they only had to be wide enough to permit a horse to lie down and long enough to accommodate the animal.

Stamping the Footboard

Some coachmen battered their feet on the footboard of the coach to make a noise at the same time as they applied their 'short tommy' to their wheelers. The horses soon learned to associate this stamping with the slicing of the whip and would surge forward as soon as the warning sound was given.

Standard

The back of the seat on a Road Coach or Drag.

Standard Bred

An American breed of horse which is used extensively for harness racing in sulkies. Some are produced to trot whilst others move laterally and pace.

Stanhope Gig

This vehicle is a direct predecessor of the Tilbury Gig and was first built in about 1815 by the London coachbuilder, Tilbury, to the design of the Hon. Fitzroy Stanhope. By 1830, Stanhope Gigs were the most usual two-wheeled vehicles to be seen on the roads.

The rib chair seat had a spacious boot underneath, which provided valuable storage space. For this reason, Stanhope Gigs were favoured by bagmen. They were also popular with commuters who drove from their homes in the suburbs to their offices in the City. Only a single horse was needed and the vehicle was easily stored in the Gig house which adjoined their suburban residence.

The suspension was adequately provided by two longitudinal springs and two transverse springs. The ash shafts ran right round the back of the body and were plated with iron. This made the Gig unnecessarily heavy and difficulties were experienced in keeping the plates sound. Later, lancewood shafts replaced the ash ones. Gradually more improvements to the original design took place. Rubber tyres succeeded the iron tyres. A swingle tree with chains from the centre going down to each side of the axle provided a better draught than that which was obtained from solid trace hooks.

Many modern gigs now seen, can claim their ancestry from the early Stanhope Gigs.

Stanhope Phaeton

Originally designed by the Hon. Fitzroy Stanhope and first used in about 1830. It is a smaller and lighter version of the Semi- or Demi-Mail Phaeton and could be used with a single horse or a pair. The hooded front seat has an open, curved, stick-back. The groom's seat at the rear is rectangular and railed. Between the two seats is a boot running the whole length of the vehicle. The body, which is hung on four elliptic springs, has an arch enabling a full lock to be obtained.

Starting a Team

The wheelers should be asked to move off fractionally before, or at exactly the same time as the leaders in a four-in-hand team. Disaster is likely if the leaders pull forward before the wheelers have begun to move. The leaders, on finding that the vehicle is not moving, will stop, by which time the wheelers will have begun to move. The result will be that the leaders will get hit by the bars and the pole will either go between them or hit one of them if, by now, they have swung to one side.

This same rule applies to starting a unicorn team and a tandem team.

State Carriage Horses

Until about 1914, cream Hannovarian stallions were used to draw the Gold State Coach. In the early 1920s, black horses were used. Now, both grey horses of Irish and German breeding and bay horses of German and Cleveland Bay blood are used for the State Carriages. Stallions are no longer kept for harness work at the Royal Mews, London.

State Chariot. *See* Chariot.

State Coach

The building of these superb carriages reached its height at the time of Queen Victoria's coronation. They are fine examples of the outstanding craftsmanship and finish which was executed by high-class coachbuilders of the period. State Coaches were built for formal use by the nobility on occasions of State and are still used at such times as the State Opening of Parliament and Royal Weddings. The elegantly painted coach body hangs on cee-springs from a perch undercarriage. It seats four passengers who can be clearly seen through the large glass windows on either side of the seats. Tasselled blinds are fitted to the windows and usually kept rolled up. The interior of the body is luxuriously trimmed with cloth and silk. The lamps are large and ornate, many being six- or eight-sided, or rounded, and surmounted by elaborate decoration. The coachman, wearing full State livery, drives the pair or team from a box seat covered by an ornate hammer-cloth which is profusely decorated with fringes, tassels and

255

armorial bearings. These bearings are repeated on the panels of the coach and on the heavily ornamented harness. Two footmen, also in full State livery, travel on the platform at the rear of the coach. Sometimes a State Coach is drawn by a team of four horses which are driven from the box and two leaders which are driven by a postillion. On other occasions State Coaches are used with four, six or eight postillion-ridden horses. Upstanding bay horses with Yorkshire bloodlines were favoured but now grey horses are used as well as bays. By tradition, grey horses are for the use of the Sovereign only, as in former years the creams were used.

Amongst the State Coaches which may be seen in the Royal Mews, Buckingham Palace, London are The Irish State Coach, The Glass Coach, Queen Alexandra's State Coach and The Gold State Coach. The latter named was built much earlier so differs considerably from those first mentioned.

State Harness
Used with Her Majesty The Queen's State Carriages on formal occasions. State harness is heavily decorated throughout with armorial bearings and ornamental buckles of gilt or brass. One set alone can weigh over 100 lb. The bridle is often decorated on the blinkers, face drop, noseband and sides of the bit. The pad is richly embellished and crowns surmount the terrets. The five or six loin straps going from the crupper back strap to the breeching are covered with ornamentation. Some harness is made of blue leather, some of scarlet and some of black. The blue harness is Georgian and the oldest in the Mews.

Station Bus
Better known as a Private Omnibus.

Stay
Brackets made of iron which are used to join various parts of the body of a carriage. The groom's seat on a vehicle such as a Spider Phaeton is frequently supported by branch-shaped stays.

Steadying a Team
Before a turn is made, whether it be with a single, pair, tandem or team, the horses should be held together so that they are on the bit and well balanced. A smooth turn can then be executed.

Step-piece Body
A term which was sometimes used to describe the arch, in the body of a vehicle, under which the front wheels turned.

Steps
These vary enormously in shape and form. The steps on country vehicles can be square or round, rectangular or oval. Some are solid and others are made with a grating. Designs are cut in some and others are 'roughed' to give a grip. A rear step is frequently made from just a single bar. Many early Gigs have 'bucket' steps which are hung on a stirrup-shaped bracket. These have either a metal or leather toe-cap to protect the step surface from mud thrown up by the wheels. High vehicles were sometimes built with two or three steps which folded up and disappeared into the body when they were not needed. Four-wheeled carriages like Broughams and Landaus, which have a central step, often have a step cover

fixed to the door to protect the step from mud. When the door is opened, a clean surface is revealed. Others have two or three folding steps for the same reason. Many ingenious designs were devised. In 1855, a 'Perfect' step was patented. This was rubber covered to give a better grip.

Stevenson, Henry
A one-time 'gentleman professional' coachman of the London and Brighton 'Coronet'. He then put the 'Age' on the same road and set a high standard of turnout and efficient service which others on that road were forced to copy in the interests of their own business.

Stevenson died at the age of twenty-six, in 1830.

Stick Basket
Also known as an umbrella basket.

Stick-seat Slat Waggon
An American four-wheeled vehicle. The forward-facing seat has a stick-back and sides and is supported on iron braces. The floor is slatted. The body is hung on two inverted longitudinal springs, known as Concord springs, each of which extends from the front axle to the back axle.

St. Martin's-le-Grand
The London terminus for Mail Coaches which were bound for the North, the South and the East. Those for the West went from the Gloucester Coffee House (now the Berkeley Hotel), Piccadilly. It was from the railed courtyard of St. Martin's-le-Grand, in the City of London, that the Mails departed at eight o'clock every night. Mail bags were loaded and the mail guard's slamming of the boot lid was the signal to 'let 'em go'.

Stolkjaere
A Norwegian two-wheeled vehicle with two facing forward seats for passengers and a rumble seat behind for the driver or groom.

Stopping
When pulling up, whether it be with one, two, three or four horses, the right hand is placed on the reins in front of the left hand and both resist when the command to slow down or halt is given. The right hand lies a little below the left with the second and third fingers between the two single or pairs of reins. The left hand is raised slightly and the right hand, taking most of the pull, is lowered a little.

Straddle
An Irish word for a driving saddle.

Straight Bar
A type of mouth piece of a bit.

Strake
The piece of iron which is placed on the inside of a felloe to cover the joint.

Before wheels were shod with hoop tyres, they were shod with short pieces of iron known as strakes.

Straw

This was used by the carriage builder for stuffing the leather padding which was put on some poles.

The harness-maker used straw to stuff collars, and still does.

Straw Collar

This is made from rush. Some Road Coaches in coaching classes carry a spare straw collar hanging on a lamp holder, which gives the coach a very sporting appearance.

Straw collars are useful for long-distance work as they mould themselves easily to the shape of any horse's neck.

Stretched out

A number of horses are trained to stand with their front feet together, slightly ahead of the perpendicular, and their hind feet together as far behind as they can stretch. This originated from when it was essential that a carriage horse should remain stationary whilst passengers mounted and dismounted. A horse which is stretched out in this manner is unable to move forwards or backwards until he has pulled himself together.

The tradition has remained and hackneys and many other types of horses are trained to stand stretched out. It is not desirous in the halt for an F.E.I. Combined Driving Dressage Test when the horse should stand with all four legs underneath his body, ready to move off when asked.

Stretcher

The bar, used with chain, sling or plough gears, on farm horses, which is hooked between the chain traces, behind the back legs, to hold the chains apart. The traces are then kept away from the horses' sides and thighs, preventing the friction which would cause sore sides from a combination of mud and sweat.

Striping Pencil

A narrow brush which is used for painting the lines on the wheels and body of a vehicle.

Stubbs, George (1724–1806)

A famous artist who unfortunately lived before the coaching era. His two best-known pictures concerning harness subjects, both depict High Phaetons. One painting is of a Crane-Neck Perch Phaeton drawn by a pair of black horses. They are wearing wide breast collars and breeching. The position of the buckles on the neck-piece suggests that, at that time, the point of the strap went upwards from the breast part instead of downwards towards it. Presumably, the neck-piece of some 18th-century breast collars had a buckle at each end instead of a point as is now the case. Perhaps this was to enable the neck strap to be released with a downward pull, giving more leverage, should an emergency arise. The pole is very long and pole straps are used although the vehicle is being driven by the gentleman owner.

This picture may be seen in the National Gallery, London.

The other picture hangs at Windsor, in the Royal collection. It shows the Prince of Wales's gaily painted Highflyer. The black body is elaborately trimmed with ornate black, red and yellow lace (braid). The high red wheels are extravagently dished. Thomas, the state coachman, is standing resplendent in a red coat, black breeches, white stockings and buckled shoes between two superb black carriage horses who are about to be put to. The angle of the short-docked tail, visible on one, suggests that it had also been nicked. The State harness consists of a full collar, narrow pad and wide breeching set high on the quarters. The ornately embossed bridles are trimmed with huge red rosettes, red brow-bands and protruding red winker stays.

Studebaker
An American carriage-building firm.

Studebaker Wagon
This vehicle was introduced by the Studebaker Brothers and widely used in the western states of America by farmers.

Studs
Some people have their horses shod with studs, which are made from small knobs of very hard metal fitted into the heels of the shoes to prevent the horse from slipping. These are best confined to the hind feet of harness horses as if they are shod with these in front, the slight forward slide, which normally occurs, will be prevented so that extra concussion will be occasioned. This is likely to result in loss of action and a possibility of eventual lameness.

An alternative to studs is the use of calkins on the outer sides of the hind shoes. The type of studs, used by the jumping fraternity, which screw into the shoes, are not used for harness horses.

Subscriber. *See* Subscription Coach.

Subscription Coach
During the last half of the 1800s a number of coaching men, remembering the thrills of 'The Road', were keen to revive the 'Golden Age of Coaching'. Others wanted to learn, from the older experts, the art of tooling a team. Syndicates were formed by proprietors, who were the professional coachmen and always travelled on the coach, sometimes driving a stage or two, and other men who paid to be allowed to drive. Coaches were put on to the road. There was some income from passenger fares. The losses in running the coach were rectified by the subscribers, in exchange for the privilege of having a handful. Horses and appointments of these subscription coaches were of a high standard.

The 'Old Times' was a subscription coach managed by James Selby.

Suicide Gig
A type of Cocking Cart which had a groom's seat about 3 feet higher than the driver's seat.

Sulky
A low single-seat vehicle which is built of tubular steel and has two small pneumatic-tyred wheels. It is used for trotting and pacing races. Early Sulkies were built with a single seat on a high framework above large wheels. They were so named because of the solitary confinement of the driver.

Sunday Cab Horse
This was very often one of the lowest forms of cab horse. He was frequently an animal who spent the rest of the week in some other occupation. He was hired

out for Sunday cab work wearing hired harness and put to a hired cab. On some occasions it might be found that the cab driver's badge was hired too.

Not all Sunday cabs fell into this category. Some were properly turned out with horses who rested on an alternative day.

Surrey
A four-wheeled American vehicle. The two forward-facing seats are identical in design and are placed one behind the other in the shallow box shaped body. Some Surreys have a fringed canopy whilst others have a more solid top which can be folded back when the weather permits. Curving splashboards follow the front line of the rear wheels and rear line of the front wheels, down to a central step which they protect from mud. The suspension is provided by a transverse elliptic spring at each end of the perch.

Surrey Clarence
A formal version of a Brougham. A hammer-cloth was placed on the box and a platform on which the footmen could travel, was built at the rear of the body.

Suspension Braces
The leather linings on the convex sides of cee- and similar springs.

Swallowing
This referred to the dishonest practice, which was carried out by some guards, of putting the short fares into their own pockets instead of handing them to the proprietor. The ill-gained loot was then shared with the coachman, ensuring an amicable silence. This, dividing of the prize, was known as Shadowing.

Swan Neck
Another name for the pole hook.

Swan with Two Necks
An important coaching inn which was situated in Lad Lane, in the City of London.

Some of John Palmer's early Mail Coaches were horsed by Wilson, one of London's larger contractors, who was based at 'The Swan with Two Necks.'

William Waterhouse, as landlord, operated a contracting business of considerable size from this inn. He issued a Mail Coach halfpenny which was payable at his office in Lad Lane, with the slogan promising 'Speed, Regularity and Security' stamped on one side.

Later, William Chaplin used the inn as the headquarters for his contracting concern. A vast number of horses filled the underground stables.

The name 'Swan with Two Necks' is probably derived from a swan with two *nicks*, i.e. one of the Royal swans, which were marked by nicking their beaks.

Sway Bar Plate
An arc, approximately a quarter of a circle of half-round steel, sometimes fitted to the top and bottom carriage of a four-wheeled vehicle behind the fifth wheel as an extra bearing for the front axle and bottom carriage assembly.

Swell
With high quality traces, a third layer of leather is placed down the centre of the two outer layers before they are sewn which swells the shape of the traces. *See* Traces.

Swing Bars
Also known as swingle trees.

Swing Chain
Sometimes, when a six-horse team is being driven, the leaders' bars are attached to a chain, instead of a pole, between the swing pair. It is by this that the leaders are connected to the vehicle. The chain is fastened to the pole head at one end. A strap, or chain, connects the other end of the swing chain, and the lead bars, to the swing pair's collars. A further strap lies between the hame tug buckles of the swing pair on which the swing chain lies.

Swinger. *See* Fly Terret.

Swing Holder
A loop made from decorated braid, known as lace, which was sometimes fitted to the inside of a closed carriage to enable the traveller to rest his arm. The height could be adjusted as required by moving the holder on to a different button.

Swinging of a Coach. *See* Rolling.

Swingle Bar
Also known as swingle tree.

Swingle Tree
The bar which is sometimes used to transmit the draught from the traces to the vehicle. Some swingle trees have a hook at each end to receive the traces. Others have metal fittings at the extremities over which the crew holes are passed. Some are shaped so that the crew holes go over the wooden ends of the swingle tree and rest in indentations. The traces are prevented from slipping off by rat tails.

There are various methods of attaching swingle trees to vehicles. One is by a central bolt which goes through both the swingle tree and the splinter bar. Some are held by a central ring or dee which pivots on a fitting on the vehicle. Others are connected by a central ring to which leather-covered chains are attached. These chains go down to the axle where they are connected to slots by the springs. This method produces a direct draught. Straps are passed through dees both on the swingle tree and on the splinter bar, to hold up the swingle tree. These must be long enough to ensure that the draught is taken by the chains and not by the straps.

The mobility afforded by a swingle tree makes its use preferable to that of a solid trace attachment, particularly if breast collars are used. As the horse progresses, so his shoulders move alternately. The constant friction from side to side caused by a collar which is held firmly by unyielding traces frequently results in sore shoulders. Some vehicles, with solid trace attachments are swung to right and left in time with each stride. This is both tiring for the horse and for those in the vehicle. A swingle tree prevents all these discomforts. The draught connection goes forward in accordance with the forwardmost shoulder and the horse is able to work more easily. The vehicle rides better.

Other names given to a swingle tree are a bar, a single-tree, a swing bar, a swingle bar, a whiffle-tree and a whipple-tree. *See* Movable Splinter-Bar.

Swingle Tree Attachment. *See* Chain Draw.

Swing Pair
The central pair in a team of six.

Swing Pole
The light pole through which the leaders' draught is transmitted to the vehicle when a six-horse team is being driven. It has a ring at one end which goes over the pole hook and under the main bar. At the front end is a crab to carry the leaders' main and lead bars. The swing pole has to be light as both the pole end and the bars, are carried by the swing horses on their collars.

Swing Reins. *See* Six-Horse Team Harness.

Swivel
The ring which is sewn to the throat lash or bearing rein drop, through which the bearing rein passes. It may take a round, oval or rectangular form and has a smaller similar form at right-angles at the top by which it is attached. This ensures that the swivel is set at the correct angle to take the bearing rein. Some swivels are made up from two or three interlocking rings of varying sizes. These also then lie at the desired angle.

Sword Case
Some of the early carriages were built with a sword case at the rear. Builders sometimes claimed that this bulge, at the back of an elegant vehicle, spoiled its profile.

Sword Pencil. *See* Dagger Pencil.

Taglioni, The
A Stage Coach which was put on the road in 1837 by Lord Chesterfield and magnificently horsed with his own teams and those of Count Bethany and Mr Harvey Aston. The standard of turnout was exceptionally high but the venture only lasted for two summers and one winter. It ran from Chesterfield House on the Windsor road.

Tail Board
The rear of a vehicle, such as a Dog Cart or Ralli Car, which lets down on chains to form a foot rest for rear seat passengers.

Tail over the Rein
If the leader of a team should get his tail over a rein an attempt can be made to release it by touching him with the whip. This may cause him to lift his tail and drop the rein. On no account should the Whip try to free the rein by pulling at it, as this will almost certainly result in the horse clamping his tail firmly down. He may even start to kick. *See* Docking.

Taking off
A slang term meaning to run away.

Taking off
The system for taking a horse, or horses, out of a vehicle should be exactly the reverse to that practised in putting to.

A method should be devised and adhered to. Everyone then knows exactly what is to be done. This results in speed, efficiency and a reduction of accidents.

Tallow
This was packed into the horse's feet to prevent the soft snow from balling. *See* India Rubber Balling Pads.

Tally-Ho
An American term, of the late 1800s, for a coach. A dictionary stated that a Tally-Ho was 'a four-in-hand pleasure coach, probably so called from the horn blown on it!'

'Tally-Ho'
There were several coaches so named in England – the most famous being the London–Birmingham Coach which was depicted by James Pollard.

Tandem
Two horses, one in front of the other. The shaft horse is put to between the shafts and the leader is harnessed in front of the shaft horse.

Tandem Bars
Two bars are sometimes used instead of long lead traces and these assist the Whip considerably in the handling of a tandem team.

The lead bar resembles a swingle tree. For a 14-hand team, it is about 2 feet 5 inches long with a trace hook at either end. The centre ring goes over a long hook on the middle of the rear bar which is about 1 foot 11 inches long. On each end of this bar is a ring to which 1 foot 9 inches of trace is sewn. There is a spring cock-eye at the end of each short trace which is hooked on to the shaft horse's hame tug buckle. At the centre of the rear bar is a 9-inch chain with a hook at the end which is fastened to the kidney link ring or hame chain ring on the shaft horse's hames. A small strap goes from the underneath of the centre of the rear bar through a slot at the end of the centre hook and buckles on a small buckle on the bar. This is put on as a precaution to prevent the lead bar from jumping off, and to stop the shaft horse from catching the bar of his bit, or his rein, in the hook.

Tandem Cart
A two-wheeled sporting vehicle with a high box seat which places the Whip in a commanding position above his tandem team. Some Tandem Carts have a forward-facing seat, behind the driver's seat, for the groom to enable him to react in a flash if trouble should arise. Others have a servant's seat facing the rear. Many Tandem Carts are built on the lines of a two-wheeled Dog Cart.

Tandem Club
After some young Army officers had returned to Woolwich from Crimea, they grew bored by the lack of activity and began to search for excitement. This was

adequately provided when one young officer harnessed an ill-assorted pair to a Dog Cart in tandem. The resulting muddles created the necessary challenge and other young bloods were quick to recognize the thrills of the sport and followed suit.

A Club was formed in the 1860s. The rules were simple. They were made by the President. Club members abided by whichever rules they wished. The entrance fee to the Tandem Club was nil and the annual subscription was under no circumstances to exceed the entrance fee.

The parade ground at Woolwich provided a spacious meeting place for members. They would assemble, with their tandem teams, to be surveyed by their President, Col Fane, from the box of his Drag. It was he who took on the responsibility of training these young Whips. They would then drive off, in an orderly manner, to an appointed venue for dinner. After dinner everyone set off for home having been plentifully charged with food and wine. It was said that it was fortunate that the Army horses knew their way back to the stables.

In the late 1800s, the members of the Tandem Club met annually in Hyde Park. Here could be seen some of the best-turned-out tandem teams of the period.

Tandem Club

A Tandem Club was founded in 1977 by the author and Lady Cromwell with Mr Sanders Watney as Patron.

The first meet was held on 13th August at The Manor House, Great Milton, Oxford, when ten Whips tooled tandems on a twelve-mile drive to qualify for membership.

Tandem Driving

This probably originated when a trace horse was put in front of a shaft horse in order to apply additional pulling power to haul heavy loads out of the snow, through the mud, or up a steep hill.

The young bloods of the 19th century found excitement in driving a tandem team and the art became a sport. Matches were run and clubs were formed. The remark from a horse dealer of that period was probably sufficient challenge to encourage those upon whose ears it fell. He said that 'I always look upon a man as drives a tandem as a fool. He makes two horses do the work of one and most likely breaks his silly neck.'

It was quite usual for a hunter to be taken to a meet in the lead of tandem where he could jog along quietly without exerting himself.

The art of tandem driving requires an alert brain and sensitive fingers. It has been compared with playing a harp. It is, in many ways, more difficult than driving a team. Whereas the leaders of a team balance one another and keep each other straight, there is nothing other than the skill of the Whip to prevent a tandem leader from turning to face his driver.

For a lady who wishes to get hold of four reins, but is not in a position to keep four horses, then perhaps a tandem is the answer. Less muscle and more delicacy is required than with a team.

The handling of the reins is the same with a tandem as with a unicorn or a team. *See* Handling of Reins and Turns.

Harness

Tandem

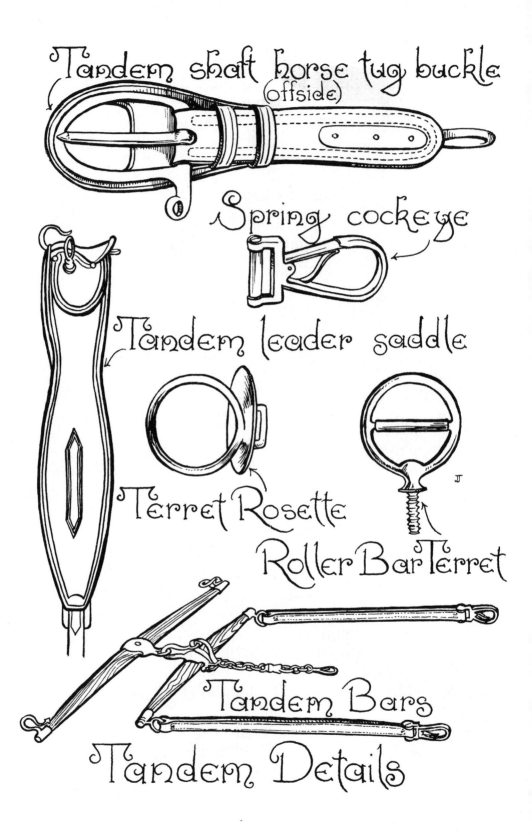

Tandem shaft horse tug buckle
(offside)

Spring cockeye

Tandem leader saddle

Terret Rosette

Roller Bar Terret

Tandem Bars

Tandem Details

Tandem Hame Tug Buckle

The hame tug buckle on the shaft horse in a tandem is designed to receive the spring cock-eye of the tandem lead trace, or tandem lead bar trace. It has a protrusion on the lower side with a slot through which the spring cock-eye is hooked.

Tandem Harness

The shaft horse of a tandem team wears a set of single harness with a few additions. Roller bar terrets replace the ordinary terrets on the saddle. Leading eye rosettes or Roger rings are put on to the bridle. The hame tug buckles have an eye protruding from their lower sides to take the spring cock-eyes of the leader's trace or tandem bars.

The leader wears the usual bridle and collar. A breast collar is acceptable for a leader. The saddle has no back band or slot under the seat. A strip of leather is sewn to the outer side of the panel to carry the trace. Some people use a side of a set of pair harness and buckle the hame tug buckle tug to the point on the pad instead of using a tandem leader saddle. A trace bearer is often added as a safety guard against the leader getting a hind leg, or the shaft horse getting a fore leg, over the leader's traces. A belly strap can also be worn to prevent the traces from going over the top of the leader's back if he should turn to face the shaft horse. This strap passes through a keeper at the back of the girth and buckles to two detachable points fixed to dees towards the rear of the traces. If long lead traces are used, then the spring cock-eyes at the heel are hooked on to the shaft horse's hame tug buckles. If tandem bars are used, single horse traces with dart holes, to go over the hooks on the lead bar, are employed. The reins go from the leader, through the rings on the shaft horse's rosettes and through the upper half of the roller bar terrets to the Whip's hand. A bit with a bar across the bottom is used on the shaft horse. For the sake of uniformity bits with bars look best on both horses.

The addition of a trace bearer, a belly strap and tandem bars, takes a little of the difficulty from tandem driving. A leader wearing long lead traces and no auxiliary straps requires the most skill to keep straight. *See* Putting to.

Tandem Horn

A shorter edition of a coach horn which is carried in a horn or stick basket. It was sometimes used to warn other road users, of the lengthy equipage, when approaching a sharp corner on a narrow road.

Tandem Lamps

Those who drove a tandem regularly advocated that a leader lamp should be carried on the dashboard in addition to the lamps which were placed in holders on the side of the vehicle.

'Tantivy Trot', The

A popular coaching song of the 19th century.

Such songs were sung, very often to the accompaniment of the guard with his key bugle, to relieve boredom on long journeys by coach.

Tattersall Check

The type of check design which is commonly used in material for summer sheets for horses, waistcoats for men, linings for farm horse's collars, driving aprons and numerous other purposes. It is made of red, blue and yellow on a white background with a bold check of about 1 inch square and smaller checks of about a $\frac{1}{4}$ inch square.

Tattersall's
A horse repository which moved from Hyde Park Corner to Knightsbridge Green in 1865. Although Tattersall's dealt mostly in hunters and hacks, carriage horses and vehicles were also sold. The Knightsbridge repository was closed in 1939, but sales of bloodstock are held to this day at Newmarket.

Taxed Cart
In 1790, the annual tax which had to be paid for a cart, which cost less than £12 to build, was 12 shillings. The vehicle had to display the words 'Taxed Cart' painted on its side.

Taxes
In 1888, numerous facts were taken into consideration when the amount payable to the Government in carriage tax was decided.

The size and number of horses, the number of passengers, the number of wheels, whether the vehicle was closed or open or had a hood, the weight and the purchase price were all carefully assessed.

The annual tax for an open two-wheeled, two-seat, pony cart weighing between 3 and 4 cwt. and costing between 20 and 50 guineas, was 15 shillings a year.

A four-in-hand Dress Coach weighing between 18 and 24 cwt. and costing between £320 and £650 to purchase, was taxable at 2 guineas a year, as was a pair-horse Omnibus.

These taxes caused large numbers of the bigger carriages to be rejected and preference was given to the smaller conveyances in order to save 27 shillings a year.

T-Cart Phaeton
This vehicle was first used in the last quarter of the 19th century. It was a lighter edition of the Stanhope Phaeton. The front seat had a curving rail with a stick-back but, unlike the Stanhope, had no hood. The rear seat was built for only one groom as T-Cart Phaetons were always used with a single horse. The name originated because the bird's eye view of the vehicle with its double seat at the front, the long boot and single seat at the rear, resembled a letter T.

Team
An American term for a pair of horses. In England the word applies to four or more horses.

Team Driving. *See* Handling the Reins.

Tees
A name which was given, in some parts of the country, to the hames worn by farm horses.

'Telegraph'
There were various coaches which were known by this name. One was a fast

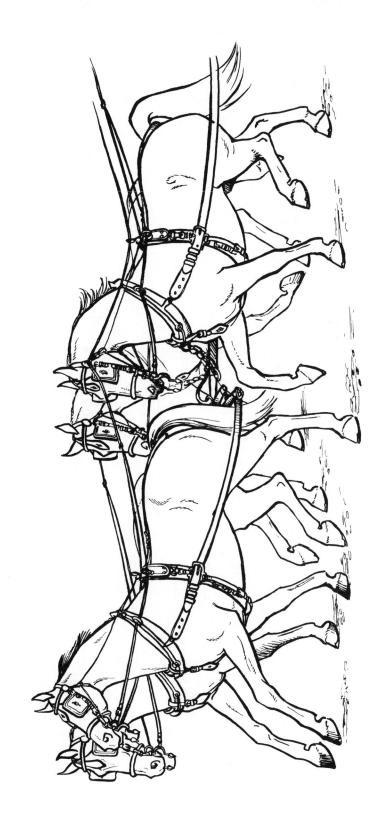

Team Harness

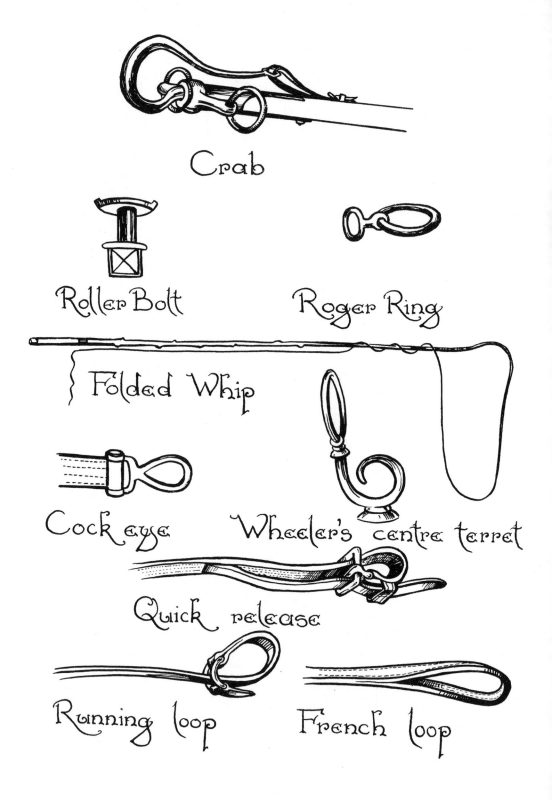

Crab

Roller Bolt

Roger Ring

Folded Whip

Cock eye

Wheeler's centre terret

Quick release

Running loop

French loop

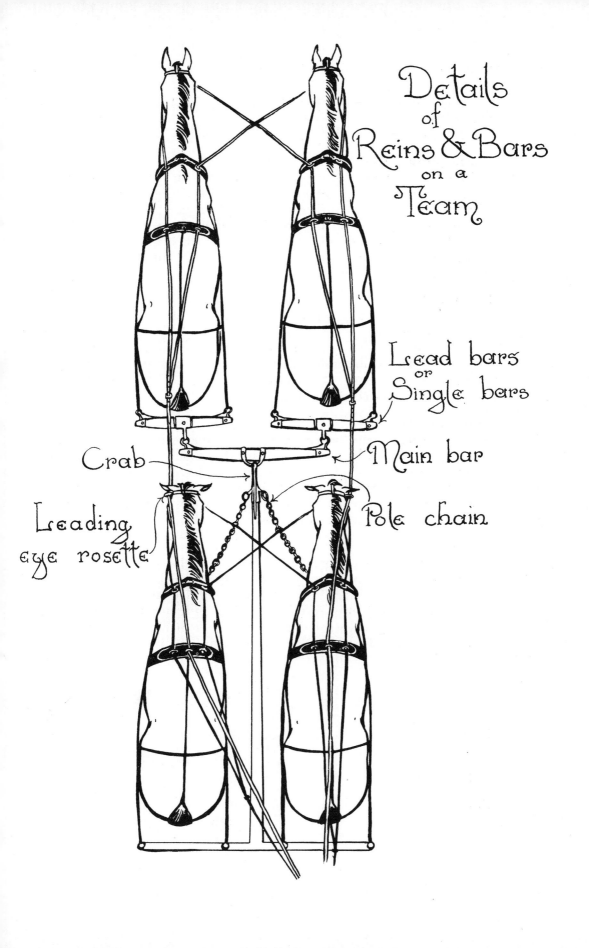

Details
of
Reins & Bars
on a
Team

Lead bars
or
Single bars

Crab

Main bar

Leading
eye rosette

Pole chain

Stage Coach which ran on the London and Exeter road before the coming of the railways.

Another Stage Coach known as the 'Telegraph' ran on the Manchester and London road.

The Sheffield 'Telegraph' is now in the possession of Mr John Richards.

Telegraph Springs
So named because the first ones in England were on the 'Telegraph' Coach. Telegraph springs are a combination of four double-elbow springs, two going sideways and two crossways. The cross-springs are fixed at their centres to the body of the vehicle to take the load. The side-springs are joined to the cross springs by shackles and to the axle by 'U' bolts.

Telegraph springs are found on Mail Coaches, Mail Phaetons, Stanhope Gigs and many other vehicles.

Telford, Thomas
The engineer and bridge builder who, with Macadam, was responsible for creating roads which resulted in faster coaching. Telford organized that roads, which had, for years run over hills, should be levelled so that no slope exceeded one in thirty. The combination of flatter roads with macadamized surfaces made travelling less hazardous. Carriage builders produced better vehicles to take full advantage of the improved conditions.

Tellier's Rods
In 1828, Mr Jean Tellier, an American, invented a device to prevent carriages from overturning. It took the form of a rod which was hinged to the top of each side of the vehicle. At the end of each rod was a large rowel which hung a few inches from the ground. If a wheel should drop off, or the vehicle tilt sideways for any other reason, the rod dug into the ground or the rowel ran along and an overturn was prevented, or at least eased.

Terret
The ring on the hames, pad or saddle through which the rein passes.

Some hame terrets are jointed so that they can move back and forth, on their connector, whilst others are fixed in a permanent sideways position. The reins are put through the hame terrets to prevent them from getting caught on the shafts or, in extreme cases, under a horse's leg. There are two more terrets on the pad or saddle. These are made to screw into slots on each side of the seat. The wheelers of a team also have high central terrets, through which the leaders' reins pass.

The shaft horse of a tandem has roller bar terrets, to take both the leader's reins and the shaft horse's reins. *See* also Head Terret.

Thiller
The shaft horse in a farm cart.

Thiller Gear. *See* Fill Gear.

Thong
That part of a whip which is between the stick and the lash. *See* Whip.

Thoroughbrace
The strong leather strap on which the body of an early vehicle was sometimes suspended. The carriage rested on thoroughbraces which were fastened at each end to standards.

Three Abreast
Known as a Trandem.

Three-horse Lead Bars
To enable all three horses to do the same amount of work, a combination of five bars is used when three leaders are put to. The main bar is longer than usual and has its dee placed to one side at one-third of the overall distance from the end. A single bar, with hooks at each end is secured to the shorter end of the main bar. Two lead bars are fastened to each end of the single bar. The third lead bar is attached to a long hook coming from the long end of the main bar. This ensures that all three lead bars are level.

Three-rein Principle
This applies to tandem driving when the right hand is placed on the reins in front of the left hand. The second and third fingers lie over the two offside reins, making them virtually into one, except when a sharp turn is to be executed. This simplifies considerably the handling of four reins.

Three-seat Surrey
An American vehicle. A Surrey with three forward-facing seats which are identical and placed one behind the other.

Throat
The bottom of the inside of a collar.

Throat Band
Found on farm harness. It is the strap which goes through the eyes at the bottom of the hames, to fasten them in position round the collar.

It is also known as a throat latch.

Throat Lash
The strap on a bridle which passes under the throat and prevents the bridle from being shaken or rubbed off the head. The throat lash should not be buckled too tightly. This causes unnecessary discomfort to the horse, by pressure on the windpipe, which will prevent him from flexing and carrying his head correctly. Too-loose a throat lash is dangerous as a bridle can be rubbed off on a pole head or shaft end.

Some bridles have the throat lash as a continuation of a part of the headpiece on the offside and only buckle to a headpiece point on the nearside. Others have a buckle at each end to buckle to headpiece points on both sides of the bridle. Some have a bearing rein swivel, sewn to each side, below the keepers under the buckles.

This strap is also referred to as a throat *latch*.

Throat Latch
Another name for throat band. *See* also Throat Lash.

Throat-latching

When a horse was inclined to pull, he was restrained by having his coupling rein passed through his partner's throat lash before it was buckled to the puller's bit.

Thrupp & Maberly

Coachbuilders from 1760. They took over the firm of Holland & Holland who were famous for their coaches. In 1925 Thrupp & Maberly joined Rootes Motors Ltd.

Thrupp, G. A.

A famous coachbuilder of the 19th century. Also the author of *The History of Coaches* and *The History of the Art of Coachbuilding*.

Tiger

The tiny groom, usually between fifteen and twenty-five years old, without which no well-appointed Cabriolet was complete. The tiger was always immaculately turned out in superbly cut livery, white breeches, highly polished top boots, shining silk top hat and a yellow-and-black waistcoat, striped *horizontally* (denoting that he was a member of the outside staff), which accounted for his nick-name. He travelled at the rear of the vehicle, helping to balance it, ready to attend to his master's requirements. The smaller the tiger, the more highly he was valued, as his tiny stature accentuated the grandness of the magnificent horse between the shafts. In spite of his size the tiger always stood proudly in absolute command of the massive animal which towered above him. The highlight of the day for a tiger was if the occasion arose for him to drive his master's horse, when seeing and reaching over the stiff apron at the front of the vehicle must have caused a certain degree of difficulty. This was, however, over-ridden by the pride of handling such a splended equipage.

Tilbury Gig

Invented and built in about 1820 by Tilbury of South Street, London. The stick-back, rounded seat had no boot and gave the erroneous impression that the vehicle was very light. It was, in fact, one of the heaviest two-wheeled pleasure carriages of the period. The Cabriolet was probably the heaviest. The excessive weight was due to the considerable amount of iron-work with which the Tilbury Gig was constructed. The shafts were iron-plated, as was the body, in order to give it the desired strength. It was hung on seven springs and for this reason was sometimes referred to as the Seven-Spring Gig. The mode of springing was known as Tilbury springs. It consisted of an elbow spring going from the underneath of each side of the front of the body to the shafts, two side-springs between the axle and the shafts and an elbow spring secured to each side of the seat. These were joined to the ends of a cross-spring which was secured by iron stays from a rear cross-bar.

The comfort of the ride given to travellers in a Tilbury Gig largely depended on the accuracy and adjustment of the springs. One which was not built with care would shake the passengers.

It was said that to drive in such a Tilbury Gig after a meal could be a most disagreeable experience.

By 1850 the Tilbury Gig had gone out of fashion in England.

Tilbury Springs
The mode of hanging which was used with a Tilbury Gig. It consisted of seven springs.

Tilbury Tug. *See* French Tilbury Tug.

Tilt
Some Cape Carts were fitted with a white canvas tilt which could be hung over rounded wooden supports so that the body of the vehicle was protected from the sun. There were sun blinds on each side which could be strapped out of the way if they were not required.

Time Bill
A time-table which was carried by the Mail Coach guard on which he had to record the exact times of arrival at each change. For this purpose he was issued, by the Post Office, with an official watch.

Any loss of time during a change had to be made up by faster driving over the next stage.

Tips
Wages of cabmen and coachmen were increased considerably by tips which they received from their passengers. The donation was not always voluntary. Coachmen on reaching the end of their stage would announce pointedly, 'Gentlemen, I leave you here'.

Tits
A flashy pair of horses was so described in the 19th century.

Token. *See* Mail Coach Halfpenny.

Tollgate
Also known as a turn-pike.

Tommy
The shaft horse, behind Gustavus, in the tandem which was driven at a trot to cover forty-five miles in under three hours by Mr Burke of Hereford. The match, for £100, was driven in 1839 over a five-mile stretch of road between Hampton and Sunbury with the distance being covered nine times. Tommy had previously been driven single to complete twenty miles in eighteen minutes over the hour. *See* Gustavus & Mr Burke.

Tonga
An Indian two-wheeled hooded vehicle to which a pair was put alongside a pole. Some were harnessed in Curricle fashion and others used the Cape Cart method while others had an outrigger alongside the shafts. In later years, Tongas were driven with a single horse and resembled a Ralli Car in appearance.

Tonga Draught
Used in India. Also known as Curricle draught. *See* Curricle Harness.

Tongue of Buckle
The central point which goes through the hole in the leather to hold the buckle in position. If the buckle is made of brass, it is best if the tongue is made of steel which is plated with brass. Solid brass may bend or break if it is subjected to any strain.

Tongue Pieces

Sometimes the centre framing piece on the top carriage of a four-wheeled vehicle is absent, and instead there are two more longitudinal pieces which are known as tongue pieces.

Tool

Another word for drive, e.g. 'The coachman tooled the team down the road.'

Top Band

Found on farm harness. It is the strap which goes through two of the uppermost dees on the hames to fasten them in position round the collar.

Top Bar

The uppermost slot into which the reins can be buckled on a curb bit. *See* Liverpool Bit.

Top Bed. *See* Transom.

Top Latch

Another name for top band.

Top Rein

The cord bearing rein which is used on hackneys when they are shown in waggons.

Tourist Omnibus

A Private Omnibus which was fitted with every conceivable convenience to enable passengers to enjoy a day at the races, or some other sporting occasion, with the maximum of comfort. The inside of the body had a dining table which could be set up between the seats and folded away when it was not required. Wine racks were stowed under one of the seats. There was also a washing-up bowl, which had a plug enabling water to be released, under the same seat. Plates, cutlery and ice were transported in fittings under the other seat. The boot under the driving seat was used for conveying the lunch basket and the horse's food. A rack in the inside of the roof carried passengers' hats and coats. On top of the roof was a folding seat and table as well as the roof seat at the front. Another table was erected on the foot-board for the convenience of those on the driving seat.

Tow

Used for stuffing cushions and carriage linings when a firmer filling than that given by horse hair was required.

Town Coach

Early town coaches of the 17th century were cumbersome vehicles hung on leather braces with a huge perch. They were gentlemen's carriages but when they became old and worn they were relegated to the ranks of the Hackney cabmen where they served in a state of filth and likely collapse.

By the end of the 18th century, Town Coaches were being greatly improved. William Felton offered an elegant coach for just under £189. The profusely decorated body was hung on whip springs from a perch undercarriage. The coachman drove from a Salisbury coach box which was covered with a hammer-cloth. The footmen travelled on a standing cushion between the hind standards.

The interior was luxuriously trimmed with swinging holders, quilting, Wilton carpeting and silk curtains.

The middle of the 19th century brought the design and production of the Town Coach to its climax. The beautifully finished four-seater body was hung on cee-springs from a perch undercarriage. The coachman drove a pair of magnificent upstanding horses from a box covered with a sumptuous hammer-cloth. Two liveried footmen stood on a cushion at the rear of the coach. The whole equipage was a perfect example of luxury and dignity.

The State Coach is a Town Coach which is turned out to perfection.

Trace Bearer. *See* Bearing Strap.

Trace Bolt
A quick-release system which was patented by Mr J. C. Waller. The trace was held in position in the splinter bar by a brass peg which went into a slot. The trace could be instantly freed by a spring being pulled which released the peg.

Trace Carrier. *See* Bearing Strap.

Trace Heel
The end of the trace which is nearest to the vehicle.

Trace Horse
The leader of a tandem is sometimes known by this name. Any horse which is added to the existing equipage in order to help to pull the load up a hill is called a trace horse. *See* Cock Horse.

Traces
It is by these that the draught is transmitted from the horse's collar to the vehicle. Traces are generally made of two layers of leather which are sewn with two or four rows of stitches, at ten to the inch, on each side. Traces for private driving are usually made with the point to buckle into the hame tug buckle where they can be adjusted for length. Some are sewn or clipped to the hame pull and have their adjustment at the vehicle end with a point and buckle. Best-quality traces are made with a third strip of leather running down the centre between the two outer layers. This shapes the trace to form a swell which is less likely to rub the horse's side than a flat trace.

A single trace for private driving is usually fastened to the trace hook or swingle tree by a crew hole. Traces which are used for pair or team work can have crew holes, cock eyes, French loops, running loops or quick-release ends.

Those which were used for commercial work often had chain ends for simple adjustment on the trace hooks and they were sewn to the hame ring.

The Army use wire traces which are made from leather-covered wire.

Trade Van
A flat-bottomed, four-wheeled, cart which was built for carrying a considerable load of light goods. The body has a panel at the bottom and wooden rails towards the top. It is surmounted by an iron rail to prevent the uppermost part of the load from slipping off. The single or pair is driven from a fairly high seat above the front axle and the wheels pass under the body to give a full lock. It is hung on two elliptic springs in front and two side-springs behind.

At the end of the 19th century, this type of trade van cost from £28, depending on the finish required. The brake was an additional extra which cost £2. 10 shillings.

Trandem
Three horses abreast harnessed with two poles.

Trandem Harness
The central horse is harnessed between two poles and the outside horses are harnessed on the outer sides of the poles. The long splinter bar has three pairs of roller bolts. Each horse wears a side of pair harness. The Whip holds two reins in his hand and each of these draught reins has two coupling reins. The centre horse is held purely by coupling reins and the outer horses are held on draught reins to the outer sides of their mouths and coupling reins to the inner sides.

Transom
A wood or iron transverse member used to secure the wheel plate, or fifth wheel, to the body of a four-wheeled vehicle.

Transom Plate
An iron strengthener for the transom.

Transverse Spring. *See* Double-Elbow Spring.

Trap
A slang term for any small horse-drawn vehicle. The name is believed to have originated when some seats could only be reached by means of passing under another movable seat in an enclosed vehicle so that the passenger was in fact imprisoned.

Trapper
Slang name for a trotting harness horse.

'Traveller's Guide'
A small book which was written by Mr Jasper Mottershead, as a guide for travellers. It described the roads from London to Edinburgh, Holyhead and Liverpool with details of the villages and points of interest. The scheduled times of arrival and departure of the Mail Coaches were listed.

Comments concerning inns were witheld owing to the continuous changes of keepers and staff. It is stated, however, that 'all Inns along the roads described are houses of plenty and comfort and that some even of profusion and magnificence'.

Rates of postage are also listed. The cost of sending a letter up to fifteen miles was 4 pence and between 230 and 300 miles cost a shilling. Other charges were proportionate.

The Traveller's Guide was printed by C. Hulbert, 'five doors from the County Hall', High Street, Shrewsbury.

Also known as a *Topographical Remembrancer*.

Travelling Carriage
One which was often specially built for conveying travellers in comparative

comfort for long distances. The body was designed to provide every possible convenience to passengers. Many were made with a bed which offered some chance of a night's sleep. The horses were frequently ridden postillion so that additional luggage boxes could be carried in place of the coachman's seat. Imperials and trunks were stowed over both axles. Vehicles such as the Britchka, the Dormeuse and the Fourgon were made purely for long excursions.

Many trips involved going across the Continent when post horses would be hired all the way.

Tray Body Buggy
An American four-wheeled vehicle which was so named because the body resembled a servant's tray. The boot was covered with leather and the back bed and hanging bars were ornately carved. The vehicle is said to have been perfected by George Watson of Philadelphia in 1840.

Tread
The name which is sometimes given to a single iron step on an iron stem which is bolted to the vehicle. Many country carts have such a step to enable passengers to reach the rear seats.

Tribus
A type of cab which was introduced in 1840 but did not find much favour. It carried three passengers who entered from a door at the back of the nearside. The cabman drove from a seat on the roof on the offside.

One variety of Tribus was drawn by a pair in Curricle harness and was known as the 'Curricle Tribus'.

Tricorne Hat
The traditional type of hat which is worn by coachmen driving State Coaches. *See* Livery.

Triga
A Grecian chariot with three horses harnessed abreast.

Trim
The upholstery of a carriage. *See* Trimmer.

Trimmer
The man who was responsible for upholstering the interior of carriages with such materials as morocco, silk and lace.

He also worked with stiff leather and had to be capable of making hoods, covering splash and dashboards and the areas of the shafts under the tug stops and breeching dees. Many other parts of the carriage accessories like the drag chain and tool budget were covered in leather. For this work a man needed to be an accurate cutter as well as a neat craftsman.

Those who specialized in leather work were known as budget trimmers. Their weekly wage, in the early 1800s, was between 3 and 4 guineas.

Triple Buckboard
A buckboard with three seats in a row. Although Single and Double Buckboards are quite common vehicles in America, the Triple Buckboard is rarely seen. One is on show in The Shelburne Museum, Vermont, U.S.A.

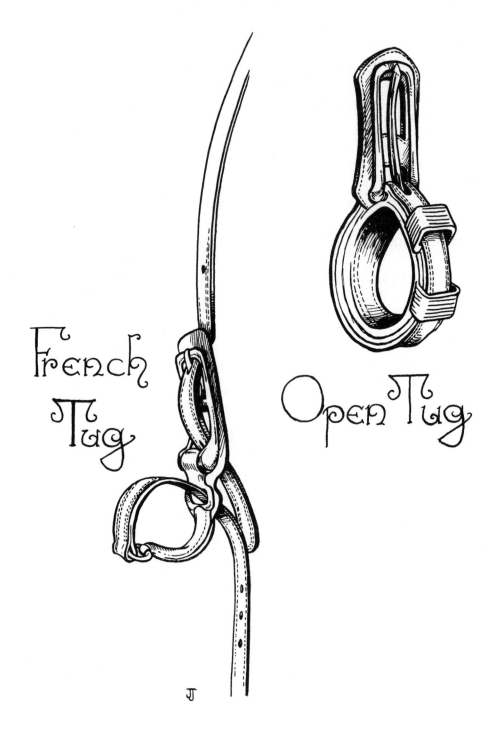

French
Tug

Open Tug

Troika

A Russian method of harnessing three horses, side by side. The centre horse is put to, between the shafts, under an arch called a 'douga' and works at a fast trot. The horses which are put on either side are known as outspanners. They are harnessed to outriggers, with swingle trees, and put to, outside the shafts. They are checked severely with outer side reins in such a way that their heads are pulled outwards away from the central horse. Bent in this manner, they are forced to work at a canter or gallop in order to keep up with the centre horse. Races are held in Moscow for such equipages. *See* Douga.

Trotter

Many of these animals owe their ancestry to the Norfolk Trotter. They are used for trotting races, on tracks, when they are driven in a minimum of light harness to a Sulky. Open bridles with overhead checks on to snaffle bits are frequently worn. Breast collars and light pads are usually employed.

A record was made in 1938 by 'Greyhound' who trotted one mile in one minute and fifty-five and a quarter seconds.

Truck

A general term applied in America for a vehicle which was used for commerical purposes such as a parcels delivery wagon, furniture wagon or milk wagon.

Tub Bodied Buggy

An early buggy which was used in America before 1850. The back and sides of the tub-shaped body were covered with embossed leather.

Tub-bottom Body

The description given to the rounded outline of the lower profile of the body of a vehicle such as a Sefton Landau.

Tub Cart

Also known as a Governess Cart.

Tug, Open

Part of the harness used on a single horse through which the shafts pass.

Two or three layers of leather are stitched together to form a strong oval-shaped band with a buckle at the top. This is buckled to the back band which goes through the top of the saddle. Keepers on the outside of the tug secure the back band as it goes down towards the belly band.

It is by the tugs that the vehicle is prevented from tipping up or down once the belly band is buckled. The seating should be carefully arranged so that when the vehicle is moving there is no weight on the horse's back. An unbalanced vehicle, which is shaft heavy, can put tremendous strain on to a horse. When the animal is trotting, the point of the tug buckle should 'float'.

Tug, Pair or Team

The part of the harness by which the traces are attached to the hames. The hame tug is fastened to the pull by a clip and rivets or to the hame ring by stitching. The tug is made up from two, three or four layers of leather depending on whether a safe is employed and whether a strip of leather is laid down the centre to form a swell. It terminates in the hame tug buckle to which the traces are attached.

The tug should fit the horse. One which is too long will cause the hame tug buckle to lie behind the pad when the horse is in draught. The point hanging from the pad should lie at the perpendicular when the hame tug is buckled in position.

Tug Stop

The metal fitting which is screwed to the outside of the shaft against which the tugs rest. If breeching is not used, this prevents the vehicle from running forwards on to the horse. The distance from the shaft tip to the tug stop varies according to the size of the animal. For a horse of 15 hands the stop is about 18 inches from the end of the shaft. The tug stop consists of a strip of metal which is rounded to fit the contour of the shaft and is secured by three or four screws. It has a knob which is about 1 inch long protruding outwards, or downwards, and it is against this that the tug rests. Designs vary considerably; some stops take a solid form and cannot be altered, others can be unscrewed and exchanged for a filler screw head with a short, threaded, body which is made to fit the hole from which the stop has been removed. There is usually a choice of three adjustments with this type, giving alternative fittings of about 2 inches in either direction. The filler screw heads have a screw slot so that they can be moved with a screw-driver. The stop has a hole drilled right through so that it can be undone with any long narrow piece of metal which is inserted to turn the stop in its socket. The stop is then removed without being damaged as would be the case if a pair of pliers was used. Some tug stops have a triangular strip going from the end of the stop towards the rear of the metal bar which attaches it to the shaft. This effectively prevents the reins from getting caught on the stop and is particularly useful when a horse is being taken out of a vehicle. The end of the reins, hanging from the saddle terret, can easily get caught on the tug stop and then the horse gets jabbed in the mouth when he is half-way out of the vehicle.

Tumbler Cart

A two-wheeled cart with a watertight body made of iron plates. It was built so that the body could be revolved on the axle enabling the load of sewage, or whatever liquid was carried, to be easily emptied. The large size conveyed 260 gallons.

Tuppy

A word used in the 1800s to tell horses to go on.

Turn

A slang term which was given to a well-maintained section of a turn-pike road.

Turn Cheek

A Buxton or similar bit which is made in a way that enables the cheekpiece to rotate inside the end of the mouthpiece where the latter is joined to the cheek. This allows the ring of the bit to be pulled slightly sideways by a coupling rein.

A bit with a turn cheek differs from one with a slide mouth, in that the mouthpiece cannot move up and down on the cheek.

Turner. *See* Axle Tree Maker.

Turnout

A general and accepted term to describe almost any horse-drawn equipage.

Turn-pike

A gate which was closed across the road barring the way. Road users had to rouse the turn-pike keeper and pay a toll which went towards the maintenance of that section of the road. The gate was then opened and the travellers continued on their journey.

Mail Coaches were exempt from paying tolls. The horn was sounded by the guard, as the Mail approached, and the keeper had the gate open so that the coach was not delayed.

Turn-pike Keeper

The man who was in charge of the turn-pike.

Turns

When driving a single or pair, an incline to the right can be achieved by turning the left wrist in such a way that the knuckles are away from the body and the palm is facing upwards. This applies tension to the right rein and looses the left rein. For a single-handed incline to the left, the hand is turned so that the knuckles come towards the body and the little finger goes away. This puts pressure on to the left rein and slackens the right rein. A stronger incline or turn to the right is made by placing the whole of the right hand, with the knuckles uppermost, over the right rein and applying the necessary amount of pressure. The hands must be kept close together. The right hand is brought very slightly to the left, NEVER to the right. The left hand goes to meet the right. On no account should a loop of slack rein hang between the hands. A turn to the left is made by placing the right hand with the knuckles uppermost, over the left rein just in front of the left hand. It must not cross the left hand but should be held level with, or slightly to the right of, the left hand.

A well-mannered and light-mouthed team can be inclined to the right with only the left hand on the reins by turning the hand so that the knuckles are upwards and at the same time holding the hand to the left of the body. This effectively tightens the offside reins and loosens the nearside reins. To incline to the left, the hand is carried to the right with the thumb near to the body. This tightens the nearside reins and slackens the offside and the team will react accordingly.

For both team and tandem an incline to the right can be made by placing the right hand, with the knuckles uppermost, over both offside reins with the third finger separating the reins. The right hand is held towards the left which is brought slightly forward. This results in a give in the nearside reins at the same time as increased tension on the offside reins.

An incline to the left can be achieved by the right hand being placed over the nearside reins, with the middle finger between the lead and wheel reins. The right hand lies in front of the left hand.

Sharper turns with a team or tandem are made by pointing, or looping, the reins. The advantage of pointing, is that once a loop is made, the right hand is left free to use the whip or assist the left hand through the turn. A sharp turn to the left is made by picking up the near lead rein with the right hand, about 6 inches in front of the left hand. A loop of rein is formed towards the body and secured under the left thumb. This effectively brings the leaders to the left. Simultaneously the wheelers must be prevented from cutting the corner by the off wheel rein being looped or held in opposition. As soon as the leaders have turned the corner, the loop is released by raising the thumb. The wheelers can then be allowed to follow round as the pressure on the off wheel rein is lessened. A turn to the right is made by looping the off lead rein and opposing the near wheel.

Sharp turns with a tandem have to be made with far more delicacy than with a team when the horses, working in pairs, balance each other.

Twenty-mule Team
This was used in America to draw the huge waggons containing loads of borax which sometimes weighed up to 36 tons. These long mule teams reached their peak in the 1880s.

The team was captained by a mule called a line mule who worked in the near lead. She was commanded by the 'skinner' who rode the near wheeler. He held a jerk line which ran the length of the team through rings on the nearside mules to the line mule. The signal to go to the right was a series of jerks, and a turn to the left was requested by a steady pull. A 4-foot pole, known as a jocky stick, was fixed between the near leader's hames and the off leader's bit to enable the commands from the skinner, to the line mule, to be transmitted to the off leader. Some skinners used the word 'haw' to go to the right and 'gee' for a left turn.

The five pairs of mules behind the leaders were known as the swing teams. Next came the eights, then the sixes and pointers. The wheelers came last, alongside the pole. All but the wheelers were put to stretchers which were hooked to a chain running the length of the team to the front of the waggon. The pointers had their stretchers fastened to either side of the point of the pole. When a corner had to be turned, the outside eights, sixes and pointers had to jump over the chain and pull almost at right angles to turn the load. Once the turn was completed, they stepped back over the chain.

Two-and-six and Two
The fine issued to cabmen of the late 19th century for such offences as loitering, parking on the wrong side of the road and drunken driving. It referred to 2 shillings and 6 pence plus 2 shillings costs, being the standard fine for a first offence.

Two Sets of Reins
These were sometimes put on to a young or difficult horse if trouble was anticipated. One pair would be buckled to plain or rough cheek. The second pair were put on to the bottom bar for use in the case of emergency.

Two Sweats. *See* Both Sides of the Road.

Tyre. *See* Clencher Tyre, also Wired-on Tyre.

U Bolt

A metal fitting with a thread at each end of the inverted 'U' which is used to attach the spring of a vehicle to the axle. It is usual to have a 'U' bolt passing over the spring on each side of the axle.

Umbrella Basket

A basket which is about 2 feet 3 inches deep and 10 inches in diameter with a flat side which lies against the body of the coach. It has a partition so that the horn can be carried, bell part uppermost, in one side and the umbrellas and sticks in the other side. The basket is attached by a strap to the roof seat iron on the near side at the back, and by another strap, lower down, to the handle on the coach.

Uncouple

The term which is used by farming people to describe taking horses out of their cart or implement.

It also refers to the unbuckling of the coupling reins with a pair or team.

Undercarriage

The under part of a vehicle including the springs, axles, iron-work and wooden timbers on which the body lies. This was originally known as the carriage of a vehicle.

Undress Livery

If servants were in attendance, in a carriage, on a country occasion when full livery would have been considered to be too dressy, they wore stable clothes. This was known, in the late 1800s and early 1900s as undress livery. Now, this refers to the black livery which is sometimes worn by The Queen's coachmen. *See* Livery.

Unicorn

A team made up from two wheelers and one leader. This is sometimes referred to as a spike team.

Also known by some authorities as a pick-axe team.

Union, The

An East Anglian Stage Coach.

Unpinned Ribbons

This refers to reins which are not buckled at the hand end.

Upper Bar

The uppermost slot to which the reins are attached on the branch of a bit such as a Liverpool.

Upper Benjamin

An overcoat, worn by coachmen. It was made of a heavy box cloth and was large enough to go over the already large greatcoat.

Upper Ground

The first part of the road on a coach journey in the nineteenth century.

Also known as the high ground.

Up to the Bit

Meaning that a horse is going freely forward. It is essential that leaders of a team should be up to their bits at all times.

Unicorn Harness

Valance
On the rumble seat of a Drag, when passengers are carried in place of grooms, a deep strip of patent leather, known as a valance, is buttoned to the front of the seat to prevent draughts. Many vehicles have a valance of heavy cloth or leather fixed to the front edge of the seat for the same reason. It adds greatly to the comfort of travelling.

Valencia
A type of striped material from which the groom's waistcoats were made.

Van
An American term for a caravan or any heavy wagon used for conveying goods.

Vanner
A general-purpose medium-weight horse which hauled delivery vans around streets from Monday to Saturday. Though large numbers of vanners were well built and compact animals who were capable of plenty of hard work, many possessed huge heads, short necks and heavy fronts which gave a misleading impression of strength. They lacked power in their quarters and hind legs and were frequently made to pull loads which were too heavy for their physical capabilities.

One compensation to being a van horse was that, for most, Sunday was a day of rest.

Many of London's vanners had their manes hogged and their tails either docked or the hair cut to just below the end of the dock.

Strong commercial harness, with the minimum amount of white metal furniture, was usually worn. Waterproof loin rugs, nosebags and webbing halters were frequently carried for use at lunch time.

Vehicle
A general and accepted term for almost any carriage.

The word originated from the Latin *vehiculum*, meaning a carriage.

Ventilated Front Boot
The front boot of a coach which has had holes kicked in it by the wheeler of a team.

Venture, The
One of two Road Coaches, the other was the 'Viking', which ran on the London and Brighton road between 1908 and 1914. They were put on by Mr Alfred G. Vanderbilt, from the U.S.A. who imported eighty standard-bred horses for the purpose.

The furniture on the harness of these coaches had bars formed as a 'V', embossed on them, which stood for 'Venture', 'Viking' and 'Vanderbilt'.

A memorial stone to Mr Vanderbilt exists on the road between Dorking and Horsham, near Capel.

Vestry Horse
A heavy and strong horse was needed for this work. *See* Dustcart Horse.

Viceman. *See* Axle Tree Maker.

Viceroy Waggon

A light and elegant wire-wheeled, pneumatic-tyred, waggon which is employed for showing hackneys. The single seat has a rounded back with turned spindles. It is supported by curving branches which go down towards the rear transverse side-spring. The floor and foot-board are placed between the front supports which go down to the transverse elliptic spring. A patent-leather dashboard is bolted to the foot-board. The arch under the seat permits the front wheels to turn until they contact the perch. The shafts curve down to join the front axle and are easily detachable so that either horse-size shafts, or those to fit a pony, may be used as required.

Victoria

There is uncertainty regarding the country of origin of this vehicle. Some authorities claim that it was of French design. Others maintain that it was the brainchild of an English coachbuilder, Mr J. C. Cooper, whose ideas were disregarded by conservative English clients but eventually found favour on the Continent. Some say that it originated as a vehicle called a Cab Phaeton which was built by a London coachbuilder, Mr David Davies in 1835, and used extensively on the Continent, as a Milord, and in England. After a few years, this carriage was employed in Paris as a Hackney vehicle where the Prince of Wales may have seen it. In 1845, a similar conveyance, a four-wheeled Cabriolet was built in Paris. In 1856 yet another carriage on the same lines, with a seat behind, for servants, and a hinged seat for a third passenger, was in use. The idea that the Victoria was developed for Queen Victoria, when she was a princess, from the George IV Phaeton to which a coachman's seat was added, is another theory. It appears quite likely that both French and English coachbuilders played equal parts in perfecting what was to become a highly fashionable carriage in the late 1800s. What is certain is that in 1869 the Prince of Wales, brought from Paris the vehicle which soon set a fashion. It became known as a Victoria Phaeton. The Princess quickly recognized the advantages of the carriage and, as soon as she had been seen to travel in the original or copied versions, people accepted that this was the 'correct' vehicle. It became popular as a lady's summer carriage for shopping, paying calls, etc, being comfortable, elegant and easily accessible. It was frequently used with a single horse, neatly and quietly appointed, with a coachman and possibly a footman in livery. The low curving body was entered by a step and was hung on elliptic or cee-springs. Curving wings followed the upper outline of the wheels to protect the passengers and steps from mud. The seat, which was at the rear and faced forward, accommodated two passengers and had a folding hood. A hinged seat, which when not in use could be folded up against the front boot, was often fitted to carry two children.

Coachbuilders responded to the demand for the new fashion and built Victorias in varying shapes and sizes. The word 'phaeton' was dropped as this suggested that the vehicle was owner driven and the Victoria was always driven by a coachman. Some were built with two seats so that four passengers could be carried, facing each other. These Double Victorias sometimes had small doors on either side. A version of this carriage was built by Messrs Thrupp & Maberly in 1885 and known as a Siamese Victoria.

Albert, Brougham and Canoe Victorias were built, with the latter two following the body shapes that their names suggest. They were used with animals ranging from a single horse or pair of ponies, to a pair of 16-hand horses for the large and high editions.

Victoria Gig
A cab-fronted gig. The hooded body is hung low on two side and one transverse spring, between the wheels, enabling easy access from the low step.

Victoria Hansom
A Hansom Cab which was built with a folding hood instead of a solid roof.

Victoria Phaeton. *See* George IV Phaeton.

Victoria Top
Also known as close top, folding head or folding hood.

Vidler, John
A coaehbuilder of Millbank, London, who was originally a partner in John Besant's establishment. The firm of Vidlers, continued to supply and service Mail Coaches until 1836.

Vienna Phaeton
A four-wheeled vehicle which is similar to a Victoria. The main differences are that it has higher wheels and the body is angular instead of curving.

'Viking', The
One of Mr Alfred Vanderbilt's two coaches which he brought to England. *See* The Venture.

Village Cart
A two-wheeled country cart. It was a descendant of the Dog Cart and built to a variety of designs for general practical purposes such as delivering the groceries or taking the family out for a Sunday drive.

Village Phaeton
A four-wheeled carriage which was built to seat six people. The rear of the vehicle resembled a two-wheeled Dog-Cart with back-to-back seats for four travellers. This was placed over the back axle between two elliptic springs. Facing the driver was another seat for two passengers which was placed just aft of the forecarriage. A high rein rail surmounted the back of this seat to carry the reins above and between the passengers' heads.

The price of a Village Phaeton by Hayes, in the last quarter of the 1800s, was from £35.

The vehicle could be fitted with a box, if the buyer wished, for additional seating.

Vis-a-Vis
A narrow four-wheeled closed carriage in which the two passengers sat facing each other.

The term Vis-à-Vis tends to be used generally for almost any carriage of questionable identity, providing that the passengers sit face-to-face. *See* Sociable.

Vis Landau
A four-seat carriage which was popular with members of the 'Whip Club' at the beginning of the 19th century.

'Vivid', The
This Road Coach was driven by Arthur Fownes, the owner, at the only meet for Road Coaches held by the Coaching Club. The meet took place in 1894 at Horse Guards Parade.

Volante
A Cuban two-wheeled hooded vehicle. The wheels are positioned at the end of the shafts, well behind the gig-shaped body which hangs on cee-springs.

Waggon
William B. Adams invented a Waggon made of sheet iron and hung on four wheels which were 5 feet high. It was designed to carry heavy loads such as wheat, flour or coal, and made with the body only 1 foot from the ground to facilitate loading and unloading. Earlier Waggons were said to be 4 feet from the floor which made the handling of heavy loads more difficult.

The Waggon could be drawn from either end and the load was discharged from the side. *See* also Broad-Wheeled Waggon.

Waggoner
A slang term used by coachmen of the nineteenth century in referring to a stone which was large enough to cause an accident if it was hit by a wheel.

Waggonette Brake
Also known as a Body Brake. This is a general purpose country vehicle which was found in most large establishments. It was built on the lines of a large Waggonette. The high box seat sometimes accommodated four people. On some large brakes there was a similar seat placed behind that of the driver which held another four passengers. Beyond these were two bench seats facing inwards for more people. There was plenty of room on the floor for luggage at the feet of the rear passengers. Very often these large brakes had an awning which could be erected for summer use. The body was sometimes built on a perch, sometimes without. Some were hung on four elliptic springs, others with a combination of elliptic and side springs. The Waggonette Brake was ideal when transport for a number of people or quantity or goods was required. It also found favour as an amateur four-in-hand vehicle for informal country outings such as coursing meetings or hunt race meetings, when the Drag would have been considered too dressy.

Wagon
A general term used in America to describe many varieties of four-wheeled vehicles.

Wagonette, Canopy Top
Some were built with a canopy, to protect passengers from excessive sun.

Wale
Part of a collar.

Waler
A breed of horse from New South Wales in Australia which was extensively imported into India for use by the Cavalry and for the driving of ceremonial carriages.

Wanklyn, Joan
A contemporary artist who is well known for her equine portraits.

Wap-John
Slang for a gentleman's coachman.

Ward's Terret
Designed by an English coachman, named Ward, for use on team leaders to prevent a lead coupling buckle from being pulled through the terret by a horse shying.

   The terret has a longitudinal bar across the centre with a narrow slit in the middle. The buckle and billet of the rein are passed through the lower half when the harness is put on and then the coupling rein is held sideways to enable it to go through the slit to the upper half of the terret where it lies. If a leader should shy violently away from his partner, the coupling buckle comes up against the divided terret but cannot be pulled through. *See* Runner.

Warner Wheels
They take their name from their inventor, a wheelwright from New Jersey, U.S.A., who made these wheels towards the end of the eighteen hundreds. The idea was soon adopted by British carriage makers. A cast iron band surrounds the hub at the point where the spoke ends enter. These are tapered to fit the mortices and then to enter the wooden hub. They were said to be self-tightening.

Washer
It is sometimes found that a wheel may be shaken backwards and forwards on its axle. This can be remedied by replacing the existing thin or worn washer, which is lying on the axle arm, with a new, thicker, one. A saddler can usually be persuaded to cut one from a piece of thick leather.

Watch
A pocket watch is frequently carried in a leather case which is clipped to the foot-board or dashboard of a private driving vehicle. A hole is cut in the front of the case to enable the dial to be seen at a glance.

Waterproof Quarter-cover. *See* Loin Cover.

Waterproofs. *See* Apron and India Rubber Loin Cover.

Watney, Sanders
President of the British Driving Society since its foundation in 1957, and of The Coaching Club from 1968 to 1975, and Patron of The Tandem Club since its formation in 1977.

Waybill

A type of printed form which was kept at the coach booking office. It was divided to show the seats which individual passengers would occupy on their journey.

The waybill was filled in, at the coach office, as seats were booked. It was handed to the guard before the coach departed so that he could show passengers to their correct seats. Short fares, which were picked up along the road, were entered on the waybill by the guard unless he and the coachman were practising 'shouldering', 'swallowing' or 'shadowing'.

Wedding Grey

Grey horses were not favoured by those who hired cabs but they were without equal for weddings and the jobmaster found constant demand for such animals. Tilling, who was one of London's largest jobmasters, averaged about six weddings a day. He kept forty grey horses, who did little else but wedding work.

Grey horses were also invariably used by the London Fire Brigade.

Weight of Vehicles

The average, small, two-wheeled Pony Cart weighs about 3 or 4 cwt., and a Gig is likely to go to about 7 cwt. A Park Phaeton weighs around 8 cwt., and a Hansom Cab up to half a ton. A four-in-hand Drag weighs about a ton.

In 1973, the F.E.I. Rules, which were laid down for Combined Driving Events, stated that the vehicle should weigh 1,320 lb. (600 kg), or more, for the Marathon phase. Extra weight could be made up as required with lead plating or sand bags.

Well Bottom

This alludes to the shape of the lower profile of the body of a vehicle. Many carriages, such as Sociables and Well-Bottom Gigs, were built with a square-shaped hollow to accommodate the traveller's legs and feet in comfort. This enabled the vehicle to remain low to the ground which afforded easier access and also made it less likely to overturn.

Well-bottom Gig

The body is hung low between elliptic springs on a cranked axle. The driver's and passenger's feet rest in a low box-shaped part of the body in front of and below, the axle.

Well Shape. *See* Well Bottom.

West-end Buckle

That which is rectangular with a square-shaped end. Those with rounded ends are known as round buckles.

Whale Bone

In the early 1800s this was bolted or screwed under lancewood shafts in order to strengthen them.

Wheeler

One of the pair which is nearest to the vehicle when a team is being driven.

Wheeler Bridle
This differs from a leader's bridle, in a team, in that leading eye rosettes or Roger rings are worn to carry the leaders' reins.

For an English four-in-hand team, these are worn on the outsides of the bridles. With a unicorn team they are worn on the insides.

American Western rigs have their rosettes or rings on the inner sides of the bridles as the reins go direct to the driver's hands instead of via the wheelers' pad terrets.

Wheeler Pad
The pad worn by a wheeler in a team differs from the leader's pad in that the former has an additional central terret through which the leader's rein passes.

Wheeler Ring. *See* Roger ring.

Wheeler Trace
The heel of a trace for a wheeler which is harnessed in a team, to a vehicle with a splinter bar and roller bolts, terminates in a French loop, a running loop, or a quick-release end.

If a vehicle with a splinter bar is used then wheel traces with dart holes are employed.

Wheel Hook. *See* Safety Chain.

Wheel Iron. *See* Splinter Bar Stay.

Wheel Iron or **Wheel Iron Stay**
A metal member of the bottom carriage of a four-wheeled vehicle running outside the futchells.

Wheel Plate. *See* Fifth Wheel.

Wheel Spanner
There are numerous shapes, types and sizes. They are usually double-ended, having a large six-sided ring spanner at one end for the removal of the hub cap and a smaller ring, box or set spanner at the other end to undo the axle nuts.

Wheelwright
The person who makes wheels and puts on the tyres.

In the early 1800s, the weekly wage taken home by this skilled craftsman was between £2 and £3 a week.

Names of active wheelwrights who are prepared to make wheels and carry out repairs to spokes, felloes, or whatever is necessary, may be obtained from The British Driving Society.

Wheelwrights Company, The
The Livery Company in the City of London.

Whiffle-Tree
Also known as Swingle Tree.

Whip, A

This should be carried at all times. It is with the whip that the necessary impulsion can be created and some faults corrected. Any attempt to drive without a whip is akin to riding side-saddle without a stick in the right hand.

The lash of a driving whip should be applied between the collar and the pad if kicking is to be avoided.

The stick of the whip is usually made from a supple wood, such as holly. The thong is bound to the stick in a goose-quill tube with black thread. A knot in the binding shows where the stick ends and the thong begins. At the end of the thong is a small lash. The stick usually has an 8-inch, leather-covered, hand part between the metal cap at the end and a metal ferule or collar.

Whips vary in length and type depending on the purpose for which they are made and the requirements of the individual. Dog-leg or rabbit-bitten sticks are preferred by some people whilst others find hickory or blackthorn to their liking.

The whip should be suitable for the turnout. If a small pony is being driven in a tiny vehicle by children, or a lady, then a whip with a 3 feet 6 inches long stick, measured from the butt cap to the knot, is quite adequate. The thong and lash is about 4 feet long. A larger stick would be inconvenient.

For a 15-hand horse, to a vehicle which is driven from a forward seat, a stick of about 4 foot 6 inches with a similarly sized thong and lash will be found comfortable to use.

A 14-hand pair, which is driven from a vehicle with a seat near the splinter bar, can be reached with a whip which has a 3 feet 9 inches long stick and a lash and thong of 6 feet. If the pair is driven from a low vehicle with a rear driving seat then a longer whip is needed.

A team whip has a stick of about 5 feet and a thong and lash of about 12 feet.

It is important, when buying a whip, to choose one which is well balanced. A heavy and badly balanced whip causes the wrist to ache. It also continually drops below the thumb muscle and gets in the way of the reins. A properly balanced whip lies unnoticed in the hand.

Whips should be kept hanging on a whip reel when they are not in use. One which is left standing in a corner will soon warp. The thong will adopt a disagreeable curve and the whip will be unpleasant to use and almost impossible to fold by anyone but the greatest experts.

Driving whips should never be cracked and never be used for lungeing or long reining. They are very delicate and the top of the stick, by the quill, is easily broken.

Thongs should not be chalked. They should be kept soft so that the whip is easy to apply and fold as desired.

Whip Bucket. *See* Whip Socket.

Whip Club

The Cambridge University Whip Club was founded in 1938 by Major General Viscount Monckton, Walter Scott and Denis Bennett under the Presidency of Sir Arthur Quiller-Couch, 'to encourage the art and sport of driving and to further the more general use of the horse'.

Members met on Sundays at various inn yards in the Cambridge area and drove to local village pubs which had adequate accommodation for the horses during lunch. On some occasions, visits were made to Newmarket Races. Club members dined annually at the Pitt Club.

Horses and ponies of every conceivable shape and size were hired or borrowed from livery stables, farmers and even dairies. Vehicles were either privately owned, hired from livery stables or borrowed from farmers.

There is no trace of the Club continuing much after the summer of 1940.

Whip, The
The person who drives a horse or horses. The name originates from the skill required to direct the whip on to the near leader of a team without disturbing the other three horses.

Whipple Tree
Another name for Swingle Tree.

Whip Reel
Made from a circular-shaped flat piece of wood with a slot chiselled from the outer edge of the circumference. The reel is secured to the wall by a central screw, about 7 feet from the ground.

The whip is hung by placing the thong, just above the quill, into the slot by which it is held firmly in position. This keeps the thong in the desired shepherd's-crook shape and prevents the stick from warping.

Whip Socket
The tubular holder for the whip. It is made of leather, wood or metal and is fastened to the vehicle by straps, or clips with screws or bolts. The positions for whip sockets are many and varied. They are always placed to the right of the driver. *See* Mounting.

Whip Spool. *See* Whip Reel.

Whip Spring
An early form of spring which was first used in about 1700. One end of the spring was attached to the platform of the undercarriage and from the other end the body of the carriage was hung by a strap or brace. Additional straps were fastened between the body and the springs to prevent excessive swaying which would have led to broken springs.

Whirlicote
An early horse-drawn conveyance which was used by the nobility on ceremonial occasions.

Whiskey
A light two-wheeled, Gig-like, vehicle of the late 18th century. The shafts were fixed to the underneath of the body which had caned sides and was hung on two horizontal springs.

It gained its name owing to the speed at which it whisked along.

Whitechapel Buggy
An American four-wheeled vehicle. The facing-forward, stick-sided seat, has a folding hood and there is a large open boot at the back. The buggy is hung on a

perch with side-bar springing. These bars run the length of the vehicle, outside the body, and are fixed to the ends of the two transverse semi-elliptic springs.

Whitechapel Cart
A general-purpose two-wheeled Dog Cart used for country pursuits which was originally employed by dealers. The high seat enables a tandem to be driven. The body is spacious and was useful for taking piglets or chickens, under a net, to market. It was equally popular as a shooting vehicle.

White Coach Office
One of Brighton's coach offices in Castle Square. It was run by a man called Snow who had all his coaches painted white.

White Hearse
Children were carried to their funerals in a white coffin in a white hearse which was draped with white curtains.

White Horse Cellar. *See* Hatchetts.

White, Sir Dymoke, Bart
President of The Coaching Club from 1956 to 1968.

Whitewash Act
A method applied by coachmen inexpert in the art of, but desiring to fold the thong of their team whip on the stick. The whip is held, point downwards, over the side of the coach and the stick and thong are stirred in a circle until the thong is wound around the stick.

Wilson Snaffle
A jointed or straight mouthpiece snaffle with a ring at each end of the mouthpiece and two floating rings on the mouthpiece. The headpiece of the bridle should be buckled to the floating rings. If mild action is required, the reins are buckled to both rings. If severe action is necessary, then the reins can be buckled to the mouthpiece rings only. *See* Bitting.

Window Shutters. *See* Stable shutters.

Windsor Greys
The misleading name which has been given to the grey carriage horses used in the Royal Mews. These grey horses, which are often seen in State carriages, were frequently kept at Windsor and were, at first, referred to as the greys from Windsor. Newspaper reports shortened this to the Windsor Greys which led to an erroneous belief that they were a breed instead of a type.

Windsor Wagon
An American Square Box Buggy which was hung on cross springs and side bars.

Wings
Also known as hounds. They are the two arms which act as strengtheners between the perch and the rear axle. They are joined to either side of the perch at one end and then they spread out, to form two sides of a triangle, to join the axle.

Round

Hatchet

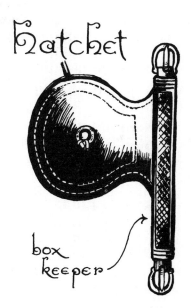

box
keeper

Shapes of Winkers

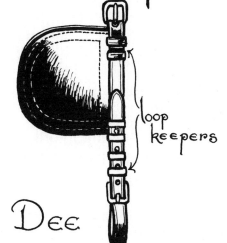

loop
keepers

Dee

Square

J

Winker Plate

Bridle winkers are made up by covering a shaped metal plate on both sides with plain or patent leather which is then stitched round the edge. The winker plate is necessary as it keeps the leather in a concave shape to avoid the eye being rubbed. Winkers which are made without plates are not satisfactory. They are too flat and the edges soon develop a curl. Winker plates are shaped to which ever basic form is required such as round, square, dee or hatchet and should conform to the line of the pad or saddle.

Winkers. *See* Blinkers.

Winker Stays

The small straps which go from the top of the winkers to the centre of the crown-piece. Here, they join together to a point which is received by a central buckle enabling the width of the winkers to be adjusted as required.

Wired-on Tyre

Some rubber tyres were secured in their square-shaped channels by one or two longitudinal wires which ran through the centre of the rubber. The ends of the wires were joined and the rubber was forced over the gap. The design was not entirely satisfactory as the wires tended to rust and break. The tyre was then abruptly released from its channel. Wired-on tyres were superseded by clencher tyres.

Wire Trace

Used by the Army.

It is a leather-covered galvanized steel wire rope which is joined to the collar and to other traces by means of shackles and quick release tugs. *See* Army Harness.

Wire Wheels

As used on a waggon for showing hackneys.

'Wonder', The

A famous London and Shrewsbury Stage Coach which was put on by Edward Sherman of the Bull and Mouth Inn, St. Martin's-le-Grand. Like all of Sherman's other Stage Coaches, the 'Wonder' was painted yellow and turned out to a high standard. The 'Wonder' completed the 154-mile journey each day in fifteen hours including stops for breakfast, lunch and dinner. In 1834 the fare was £1.

Wood

Many different types of wood were used by the coach builder. Ash, elm, deal, lancewood, mahogany and oak all played a part in the construction of carriages. *See* separate entries for details.

Woodcock Eye

The metal fitting at the end of the leader's trace.

More commonly known as a cock-eye.

Woosteree
A local name, used in New England, U.S.A., to describe a type of two-wheeled chaise with a Tilbury body.

Worsted
Bridle browbands of horses to Road Coaches were frequently covered with plaited worsted in a colour to match the coach.

Wrap Strap
Found on American fine harness replacing the belly band which is used with English light harness. The wrap strap lies over the girth, under the belly. It has a point strap at each end which is wrapped round the shafts, by the tugs, and fastened to a buckle sewn on to the strap in order to keep the shafts down.

Xerxes
The leader, who went in front of Arterxerxes in Surtee's fictitious tandem in 'Handley Cross'. He was a large brown horse with a rat tail and also acted as one of Mr John Jorrocks' hunters when he was not being driven.

Yard of Tin
Slang term for Coach Horn.
   Although the standard horns issued by the Post Office were 3 feet long and made of this metal – which accounts for the name – guards who prided themselves on their horn blowing usually carried instruments made of copper, brass, or even silver.

Yellow Bounder
Slang name for a post chaise. *See* Chariot.

Yellow Earl
A name which was given to Lord Lonsdale because his coach house was full of bright yellow carriages as this was his family colour.

Yew
A tree which is deadly poisonous to horses but useful for producing the sticks for driving whips owing to its elastic qualities.

Yoke. *See* Cape Cart Harness, Indian Cart Pole and Bugle.

Yoke Strap
These are sometimes used to prevent the two or three leaders of a team from pulling apart. The straps are buckled to the central dees of the breast collars. They are most commonly seen on Hungarian harness.

Yorkshire Bow
Another name for an Open Lot Wagon.

Yorkshire Coach Horse
As more elegant carriages were being built, so the demand for quality carriage horses increased. The Yorkshire Coach Horse was exactly the type of horse which was suitable to draw these fashionable vehicles. He originated in the East Riding of Yorkshire. Towards the end of the 18th century, thoroughbred stallions were being put to Cleveland Bay mares. The resulting cross produced strong, sound and upstanding bay and brown horses, of about 16 hands 2 inches, who were well suited to the work for which they had been bred.

Yorkshire Wagon
Also known as a Barrel Top Wagon.

Zebra
A team of zebras was regularly driven in and around London in the late 1890s by the Hon. Walter Rothschild. They were put to a miniature waggonette break and wore authentic team harness. Full collars were worn all round and breeching was added to the wheelers. Liverpool bits were used on the leaders and snaffles on the wheelers.

Zetland Phaeton
A vehicle which strongly resembles a four-wheeled Dog Cart. The two seats are placed back-to-back, high in the body, and have iron sides and independent lazy backs. The body has wooden rails at the top below the seats and has an arch under which the front wheels can turn. The side profile of the body is almost triangular when the driver and passengers are seated.

Zinc Collar Pad
A metal pad which can be fixed to the inside of the top of the collar. It is used when the horse has become sore at the top of his neck from excessive pressure and friction caused by working alongside a pole when breeching has not been employed. The pad keeps the collar off the injury and the medicinal qualities given off by the zinc act as a cure. *See* Collars.

Zinkeisen, Doris
A contemporary artist, now living in Badingham, Suffolk, who is famous for her pictures of driving subjects.

BIBLIOGRAPHY

English Pleasure Carriages. W. Bridges Adams, 1837

Tally-Ho. F. Field Whitehouse, 1878

Catalogue of Carriages. Hayes & Son

Harness. J. Philipson, 1882

Paris à Cheval. Crafty, 1883

Coaching Days and Coaching Ways. W. Outram-Tristram, 1893

The Horse World of London. W. J. Gordon, 1893

Equine Album.

Driving For Pleasure. F. C. Underhill, 1897

Album of Illustrations of Imperial and Royal State and Other Carriages. 1899

A Manual of Coaching, Fairman Rogers, 1900

Modern Horse Management. Maj. R. S. Timmis, D.S.O.

Early Carriages and Roads. Sir Walter Gilbey, Bart, 1903

Driving. The Duke of Beaufort and other Authorities, 1904

Driving. F. M. Ware, 1904

Hints on Driving. Capt. C. Morley Knight, R.A., 1905

Modern Carriages. Sir Walter Gilbey, Bart, 1905

The Wheelwright's Shop. G. Sturt, 1923

Romance of the Road. C. Aldin

Animal Management. The Veterinary Department of the War Office, 1933

Manual of Horsemastership, Equitation and Animal Transport. 1937

Horses of Britain. Lady Wentworth, 1944

The English Carriage. H. McCausland, 1948

Old Sporting. H. McCausland, 1948

Notes on The Correct Equipment of Park Drags and Road Coaches. 1951

Summerhays Encyclopaedia for Horsemen. R. S. Summerhays, 1952

A Century and a Half of Amateur Driving. Maj. A. B. Shone, 1955

Single and Pair Driving. Maj. Gen. G. H. A. White, C.B., C.M.G., D.S.O.

Catalogue of the Carriages at the Shelburne Museum, U.S.A. L. B. Carlisle, 1956

Catalogue of the Vehicles in the Carriage House at the Suffolk Museum, Stony Brook, Long Island, U.S.A.

Catalogue of Carriages, Hawthorn Mellody Museum, Libertyville, Illinois, U.S.A.

Kings of the Highway. J. Tilling, 1957

The Horse in the Furrow. G. E. Evans, 1960

Mailcoachmen of the Late Eighteenth Century. E. Vale, 1960

The Elegant Carriage. M. Watney, 1961

Felton's Carriages. 1962

B.D.S. Journals. 1962–74

Carriage Journals. The Carriage Association of America Incorporated, 1963–74

The Official Pictorial Guide. The Royal Mews, Buckingham Palace, London, 1964

Horses of the World. D. Machin Goodall, 1965

Coaching Days of England. H. Burgess, 1966

The Carriage Gazette. 1967

Carriages. J. Damase, 1968

On The Box Seat. T. Ryder, 1969

American Horse Drawn Vehicles. J. D. Rittenhouse

The Science Museum Illustrated Catalogue of Carriages. 1970

The History of the Coaching Club 1871–1971. R. A. Brown, o.b.e., 1971

Discovering Harness and Saddlery. Maj. G. Tylden, 1971

Salute the Carthorse. P. A. Wright, 1971

A Guide to the Transport Museum, Hull. J. Bartlett, m.a., f.s.a., f.m.a., 1971

Heavy Horse Handbook. I. Weatherley, 1972

The English Gypsy Caravan. C. H. Ward Jackson and D. E. Harvey, 1973

The Heavy Horse. T. Keegan, 1973

100 *Horsedrawn Carriages.* R. A. Brown, o.b.e., 1973

Ralli Car

Norfolk Cart

Whiskey

Tandem Club Cart

Gig

Two-Wheeled Dog Cart

Market Cart

Battlesden Car